IN THE NAME OF

ALLAH

THE ALL-COMPASSIONATE, ALL-MERCIFUL

THE MESSENGERS AND THE MESSAGES

- Title: THE MESSENGERS AND THE MESSAGES
- Author: 'Umar S. al-Ashqar
- Arabic Edition 1 (1990)
- Translated from Arabic edition 6 (1995)
- English Edition 1 (1999)
- Current retranslated English Edition 3 (2005)
- Translator: Nasiruddin al-Khattab
- Editor: Huda Khattab
- Layout: IIPH, Riyadh, Saudi Arabia
- Cover Designer: Haroon Vicente Pascual, Arlington, U.S.A.

ISLAMIC CREED SERIES 4

THE MESSENGERS AND THE MESSAGES

In the Light of the Qur'an and Sunnah

'Umar S. al-Ashqar

Translated by:
Nasiruddin al-Khattab

INTERNATIONAL ISLAMIC PUBLISHING HOUSE

King Fahd National Library Cataloging-in-Publication Data

Al-Ashqar, Umar S.

The messengers and the messages in the light of the Qur'an and Sunnah. / Umar S. al-Ashqar ; translated by Nasiruddin al-Khattab - 3rd ed.,- Riyadh , 2005

...p ; 22 cm ,- **(Islamic creed series ; 4)**

1- Messengers of Allah (Islamic creed) I-Nasiruddin al-Khattab (trans.) II-Title III-Series

242 dc 1471/23

Legal Deposit no. **1471/23**
ISBN Hard Cover : **9960-672-88-3**
ISBN Soft Cover : **9960-672-94-8**

International Islamic Publishing House (IIPH)
P.O.Box 55195 Riyadh 11534, Saudi Arabia
Tel: 966 1 4650818 - 4647213 - Fax: 4633489
E-Mail: iiph@iiph.com.sa . www.iiph.com.sa

Please take part in this noble work by conveying your comments to ***IIPH*** *through e-mail, fax or postal-mail address.*

CONTENTS

CHAPTER SIX

THE INFALLIBILITY OF THE PROPHETS

PART TWO

THE DIVINELY-REVEALED MESSAGES

PUBLISHER'S NOTE

All praise and thanks are due to The Cherisher and The Sustainer, Lord of the Universe - Allah. May His blessings and peace be on the last of the prophets and messengers, Muhammad, his family, Companions and all those who follow in his footsteps till the end of time.

The institution of Messengership and Prophethood is one of the three fundamentals of the Islamic creed - *Tawheed* (Monotheism), *Risaalah* (messengership) and *Ma'ad* (Hereafter) - second only to the belief in one and only God - Allah. Dr. 'Umar S. al-Ashqar has dealt at length with this institution drawing evidence from the noble Qur'an, the Sunnah, and the writings of the highly reputed authorities and nobles of the ummah. The Arabic original has proven to be very popular and has gone through several editions. This is the new English translation of the latest Arabic edition of the book, by brother Nasiruddin al-Khattab, the translator of all his Creed series.

It is with great pleasure that we present this authorized English version of the book to our readers. By the grace of Allah, its translation to a number of other languages is also underway. May Allah bless the efforts of the author and all involved in its publication with acceptance, and make it a source of guidance for those who seek enlightenment.

Muhammad ibn 'Abdul-Muḥsin Al-Tuwaijri
General Manager
International Islamic Publishing House, IIPH
Riyadh, Saudi Arabia

TRANSLATOR'S FOREWORD

We live in a world of need, a world of greed. It is a world of imbalance, where twenty percent of the world's population enjoy eighty percent of the world's resources and the rest live in abject poverty. Those who live in poverty suffer from disease, starvation and illiteracy, while those who live with plenty are also suffering - from high crime rates, alcoholism, addictions and a wide range of mental and psychological problems. Oppression, injustice and wars are widespread, and the enviroment is in crisis. Everyone from the US president to the man in the street is thinking only of their instant needs, what they can get for themselves now, with no thought for the consequences of future generations.

All of this points to a lack of guidance, a lack of knowledge of the greater picture, a lack of awareness that this life is not the only life, that in the Hereafter we will have to account for our actions. It also tells us that the word of the *Shayṭaan* (Satan) is the word which is prevailing in this world today, as the strives to fulfill his oath to lead mankind to destruction in this world and to doom in the Hereafter.

This is an ancient conflict, one which stems from the day when Adam was created, when *Iblees* (Devil) refused to prostrate to him as commanded by Allah. Since then, the *Shayṭaan* (Satan) has been launching his attacks against mankind. But from that time, Allah has been sending His message to mankind, reminding them of the purpose for which they were created, namely, to worship Him alone. This message of *Tawḥeed* (Islamic Monotheism), accompanied by laws which regulate human life on the individual, social and political levels, is the message brought by all the Prophets and Messengers, down through the ages, to all the nations. Human stubbornness and forgetfulness, combined with the wiles of the *Shayṭaan*, meant that mankind kept wandering away from the path of *Tawheed*, so Allah sent a series of Messengers to bring them back to the purpose for which they had been created.

﴿إِنَّآ أَرْسَلْنَٰكَ بِٱلْحَقِّ بَشِيرًا وَنَذِيرًا ۚ وَإِن مِّنْ أُمَّةٍ إِلَّا خَلَا فِيهَا نَذِيرٌ ﴿٢٤﴾﴾

﴿Verily! We have sent you with the truth, a barear of glad tidings, and a warner. And there never was a nation but a warner had passed among them.﴾ *(Qur'an 35: 24)*

﴿رُّسُلًا مُّبَشِّرِينَ وَمُنذِرِينَ لِئَلَّا يَكُونَ لِلنَّاسِ عَلَى ٱللَّهِ حُجَّةٌۢ بَعْدَ ٱلرُّسُلِ ۚ وَكَانَ ٱللَّهُ عَزِيزًا حَكِيمًا ﴿١٦٥﴾﴾

﴿Messengers as bearers of good news as well as warning in order that mankind should have no plea against Allah after the Messengers. And Allah is Ever All-Powerful, All-Wise.﴾ *(Qur'an 4: 165)*

The messages of the earlier Prophets and Messengers were entrusted to their priests and rabbis, to be preserved and conveyed to subsequent generations by them. But they failed to fulfill that trust, concealing, distorting or omitting parts of the message until the word of truth was lost. Finally, Allah sent His last Messenger (ﷺ) (Blessings and Peace be upon him) with the ultimate message addressed to all of mankind, the message of Islam, and He Himself guaranteed to preserve it until the Day of Resurrection.

In this book, Dr. Al-Ashqar presents a thorough study of the Messengers and their Message. Based primarily on the texts of the Qur'an and *Aḥaadeeth*, he also presents quotations from the Bible and other scriptures to demonstrate that the Message is one and that the final Message, that which was brought by our Prophet Muhammad (ﷺ) is the culmination of the call of all the Messengers, and only perfect message in existance, the only path to Paradise, that will abide until the Day Resurrection.

Translations of the meanings of Qur'anic verses have been taken from the "Interpretation of the meanings of the Noble Qur'an" by Dr. Muhammad Muḥsin Khan and Dr. Muhammad Taqi-ud-Deen al Hilali. Translations of Biblical quotations have been taken from the "Holy Bible New International Version" (NIV), one of the most prominent Bible translations in use in the English-speaking world.

May Allah reward the author for his scholarship and for his efforts in coveying that knowledge to the Muslims. May He guide us all and help us to follow in the footsteps of the Messengers, who called mankind to worship Him alone and showed us the way to Paradise.

Naṣiruddin al-Khaṭṭab

INTRODUCTION

﴿ ٱلْحَمْدُ لِلَّهِ ٱلَّذِىٓ أَنزَلَ عَلَىٰ عَبْدِهِ ٱلْكِتَـٰبَ وَلَمْ يَجْعَل لَّهُۥ عِوَجَا ۜ ﴿١﴾ قَيِّمًا لِّيُنذِرَ بَأْسًا شَدِيدًا مِّن لَّدُنْهُ وَيُبَشِّرَ ٱلْمُؤْمِنِينَ ٱلَّذِينَ يَعْمَلُونَ ٱلصَّـٰلِحَـٰتِ أَنَّ لَهُمْ أَجْرًا حَسَنًا ﴿٢﴾ مَّـٰكِثِينَ فِيهِ أَبَدًا ﴿٣﴾ ﴾

﴾All the praises and thanks be to Allah, Who has sent down to His slave [Muhammad] the Book [the Qur'an], and has not placed therein any crookedness. [He has made it] straight to give warning [to the disbelievers] of a severe punishment from Him, and to give glad tidings to the believers [in the Oneness of Allah Islamic Monotheism], who do righteous deeds, that they shall have a fair reward [i.e. Paradise]. They shall abide therein for ever.﴿ *(Qur'an 18: 1-3)*

Praise be to Allah (ﷻ) "the Exalted," Who has sent down to us a Book in which there is news of what happened before our time, and of what will happen after we are gone, a Book which judges between us, which is serious and is not a jest. Any tyrant who rejects it, Allah will destroy him, and whoever seeks guidance from anything else, Allah will send him astray. It is the strong rope of Allah, the wise Reminder, the Straight Path. It is that by virtue of which none will be misguided by his whims and desires. It cannot be confused with other speech, and its wonders will never cease. The scholars will never have their fill of it. Whoever speaks according to it speaks the truth, whoever acts in accordance with it will be rewarded, whoever judges according to it establishes justice, and whoever calls people to it is guided to the straight path.[1]

---

[1] Tirmidhi in his *Sunan*. Its isnad is *ḍa'eef* but its meaning is good. We have not quoted it in the text as it is a hadith attributed to the Messenger (ﷺ).

And I send blessing and peace upon His slave and Messenger Muhammad (ﷺ), "Whom Allah sent with guidance and the true religion just before the onset of the Hour, bringing glad tidings and a warning, calling people to Allah by His leave as a lamp spreading light. Prophethood came to an end with him, and through him Allah guided those who were astray and taught those who were ignorant. Through his prophethood, blind eyes, deaf ears and sealed hearts were opened. Through his prophethood, the earth was filled with light after it had been filled with darkness. Through him, Allah brought together hearts that had been alienated from one another, put right the nation that had gone astray and showed the clear way. Allah opened his heart for him, removed from him his burden and raised high his fame. He subjected those who opposed him to humiliation. He sent him after a lengthy gap between messengers, when the Books had been lost, when words had been distorted, when laws had been altered, when every nation resorted to darkness relying on their own views, when they had formed wrong ideas about Allah and they judged between people on the basis of their corrupt opinions, whims and desires. So Allah guided people through him and showed them the right way. Through him, Allah brought people forth from darkness into light, He made their blind eyes see and He guided them away from misguidance. He made him the criterion that distinguishes between Paradise and Hell, between the righteous and the evil. Guidance and success lie in following him and misguidance and doom lie in disobeying and opposing him. People are tested concerning him in their graves, for they are questioned about him in the grave."[2]

And I send blessings upon his pure family and his righteous Companions, the purest of hearts among the ummah, the best in

---

[2] These good words come from the great scholar *Shaykh al-Islam* Ibn Taymiyah (may Allah have mercy on him), see *Lawaami' al-Anwaar al-Bahiyah*, 2/262.

knowledge and the least pretentious; and upon those who follow their path, seeking the light of Islam, who adhere to the guidance of the Qur'an and follow the Final Messenger.

This is the fourth book in the series, "*'Aqeedah* (Islamic Creed) in the light of the Qur'an and Sunnah." Like the previous volumes, it explains *'aqeedah* in the light of the original sources, far removed from dry sophistication and philosophical terminology.

The topics of the Messengers and the Messages are interconnected, so I thought that they should both be presented in one volume. Because of the interconnection between them, Part One of this book, which discusses the Messengers, is somewhat lengthy and Part Two, which discusses their messages, is shorter. That is only because discussion of the Messengers inevitably involves discussion of their messages.

Part One consists of eight chapters. In Chapter One I defined *Nabi* (Prophet) and *Rasool* (Messenger), and explained the difference between them; the obligation of believing in the Prophets and Messengers; the *kufr* (disbelief) of one who claims to believe in Allah but disbelieves in the Messengers or makes any distinction between Messengers. I also discussed the number of Messengers and the names of Messengers and Prophets that have been mentioned in the Qur'an and Sunnah.

In Chapter Two I discussed how much we need the Messengers and their Messages, and how man cannot rely on his reason alone and do without the revelation and laws of Allah.

In Chapter Three I explained in detail the tasks and mission of the Messengers.

In Chapter Four I discussed the way in which Allah teaches His Prophets and Messengers, that is *waḥy* (revelation); I explained the various forms of Revelation and the attributes of the angel who brought the Revelation to the Messenger.

In Chapter Five I described the attributes of the Messengers, and explained that the Prophets were human, and the implications of this humanity. I also indicated that the Prophets attained human perfection. At the end of this chapter I listed the unique characteristics that set the Messengers apart from the rest of mankind.

In Chapter Six I discussed in some detail the infallibility of the Messengers, and explained the matters in which they are infallible and the matters in which they are not infallible. I mentioned the views of some of the various sects and arguments of their points of view, and in what sense they are wrong.

In Chapter Seven I talked at length about the signs of Prophethood. I mentioned the signs of the previous Messengers and discussed in more detail the signs of our Prophet Muhammad (ﷺ). I described how the Prophets foretold the coming of our Messenger Muhammad (ﷺ), and quoted a few examples. I explained that among the signs of the truth of the Messengers are how they live and the essence of their call. Looking at these two matters inevitably guide to the truth, for those who have been given insight and the desire for guidance. The fifth sign that I mentioned is the support given by Allah to His Messengers and Prophets.

Chapter Eight deals with the virtues of the Prophets and how some of them are superior to others. The Prophets are the best of creation, but they also differ in status amongst themselves. Some people went astray when they favoured people other than the Prophets over the Prophets, thus going against the consensus of the Muslims. Here I have explained what was wrong with their views.

Part Two deals with the Divine Messages. This part consists of two chapters.

The first chapter deals with the belief in the Messages; here I stated that it is obligatory to believe in all the Messages, and explained what form that belief should take.

In the second chapter, I compared the divine messages, by discussing the following points:

1) The source of these Messages and the purpose behind their revelation.

2) The fact that some were sent to specific people and some were universal.

3) Whether they were protected against distortion and alteration.

4) Points on which these messages are unanimous and points on which they differ.

5) The length of time during which each Message is applicable, whether it is long or short, and the time when they were revealed.

At the end of this chapter I explained the status of the final Message in relation to the previous messages.

Finally, I ask Allah (ﷻ) to bless us, our time and our deeds, to make our actions sincerely for His sake, and to protect us from mistakes in our words and deeds. May He benefit His slaves by this book, for He is the All-Hearing and Ever-Near Who answers prayers. May Allah bless His slave and Messenger, and all his family and Companions, and grant them peace.

Dr. 'Umar Sulaymaan al-Ashqar

PART ONE

THE MESSENGERS AND PROPHETS

CHAPTER ONE
DEFINITIONS

DEFINITION OF A *NABI* (PROPHET)[1]

In Arabic, the word *Nabi* (Prophet) is derived from the word *naba'*, which means news. Allah (ﷻ), says:

﴿ عَمَّ يَتَسَآءَلُونَ ① عَنِ ٱلنَّبَإِ ٱلْعَظِيمِ ② ﴾

﴾What are they asking [one another] about? About the great news [*An-Nabaa' al-'Aẓeem*] [i.e. Islamic Monotheism, the Qur'an, which Prophet Muhammad brought and the Day of Resurrection].﴿ *(Qur'an 78: 1-2)*

The Prophet is called *Nabi* in Arabic because he is told, i.e., Allah tells him and reveals to him:

﴿ ... قَالَتْ مَنْ أَنۢبَأَكَ هَٰذَا قَالَ نَبَّأَنِىَ ٱلْعَلِيمُ ٱلْخَبِيرُ ③ ﴾

﴾...She said: 'Who told you this [*man anba'aka haadha*]?' He said: 'The All-Knower, the All-Aware [Allah] has told me.'﴿ *(Qur'an 66: 3)*

He tells what Allah (ﷻ) commands him and reveals to him:

﴿ ۞ نَبِّئْ عِبَادِىٓ أَنِّىٓ أَنَا ٱلْغَفُورُ ٱلرَّحِيمُ ㊾ ﴾

﴾Declare [*nabbi'*] [O' Muhammad] unto My slaves, that truly, I am the Oft-Forgiving, the Most-Merciful.﴿ *(Qur'an 15: 49)*

﴿ وَنَبِّئْهُمْ عَن ضَيْفِ إِبْرَٰهِيمَ ㊿ ﴾

[1] *Lisaan al-'Arab*, 3/561, 573; *Baṣaa'ir Dhawiy at-Tamyeez*, 5/14; *Lawaami' al-Anwaar al-Bahiyah*, 1/49, 2/265.

﴾And tell them [*wa nabbi'hum*] about the guests [the angels] of Ibraheem [Abraham].﴿ *(Qur'an 15: 51)*

It is said that the word *nubuwwah* (Prophethood) is derived from the word *nabwah*, which means a raised portion of land. The Arabs used the word *nabi* to refer to landmarks which could be used for navigation. This semantic denotation befits the word *nabi*, because a Prophet is the one who has a high status in this world and in the Hereafter, and the Prophets are the most noble of creation, the signposts by whom people are guided and reformed in this world and in the Hereafter.

DEFINITION OF A *RASOOL* (MESSENGER)[2]

In Arabic, *irsaal* means directing. If you send a person on a mission then he is your *rasool* (messenger). Allah (ﷻ) says, describing what the queen of Saba' (Sheba) said:

﴿ وَإِنِّي مُرْسِلَةٌ إِلَيْهِم بِهَدِيَّةٍ فَنَاظِرَةٌۢ بِمَ يَرْجِعُ ٱلْمُرْسَلُونَ ﴿٣٥﴾ ﴾

﴾But verily, I am going to send him a present, and see with what [answer] the messengers [*al-mursaloon*] return.﴿ *(Qur'an 27: 35)*

The word *rasool* may also refer to the person who follows the news of the one whom he sent, based on the Arabic saying, *jaa'at al-ibl rasalan* meaning, the camels came one after another.

So the Messengers are called *rusul* (sing. *rasool*) because they receive direction from Allah (ﷻ):

﴿ ثُمَّ أَرْسَلْنَا رُسُلَنَا تَتْرَا ... ﴿٤٤﴾ ﴾

[2] *Lisaan al-'Arab*, 2/1166-1167; *Al-Miṣbaaḥ al-Muneer*, Pp. 226.

﴿Then We sent Our Messengers [*arsalnaa rusulanaa*] in succession...﴾ *(Qur'an 23: 44)*

So they are sent with specific messages and are enjoined to convey it and follow it.

The difference between a Messenger and a Prophet

The view of those who say that there is no difference between a Messenger and a Prophet is not correct. The falseness of this view is indicated by the reports which mention the number of Prophets and Messengers. The Messenger (ﷺ) mentioned that the number of Prophets was 124,000, and the number of Messengers was three hundred and in teens.[3] This difference is also indicated by the conjunction *wa* (translated here as "or") used in the Qur'an to connect Prophets to Messengers, in the *aayah* (verse):

﴿ وَمَآ أَرْسَلْنَا مِن قَبْلِكَ مِن رَّسُولٍ وَلَا نَبِيٍّ إِلَّآ إِذَا تَمَنَّىٰٓ أَلْقَى ٱلشَّيْطَٰنُ فِىٓ أُمْنِيَّتِهِۦ ... ﴿٥٢﴾ ﴾

﴿Never did We send a Messenger or a Prophet before you but when he did recite the Revelation or narrated or spoke, *Shayṭaan* [Satan] threw [some falsehood] in it...﴾ *(Qur'an 22: 52)*

Allah, the All-Glorious, All-High, describes some of His Messengers as being both Prophets and Messengers, which indicates that being a Messenger is something additional to being a Prophet, as when He says concerning Moosa (Moses) (عليه السلام) (may Allah's peace be upon him):

﴿ وَٱذْكُرْ فِى ٱلْكِتَٰبِ مُوسَىٰٓ ۚ إِنَّهُۥ كَانَ مُخْلَصًا وَكَانَ رَسُولًا نَّبِيًّا ﴿٥١﴾ ﴾

---

[3] A *ṣaḥeeḥ* hadith narrated by Aḥmad in his *Musnad.*

﴾And mention in the Book [this Qur'an] Moosa [Moses]. Verily, he was chosen and he was a Messenger [and] a Prophet.﴿ *(Qur'an 19: 51)*

The commonly-held view among the scholars is that a Messenger is more general than a Prophet. The Messenger is the one to whom laws (shari'ah) are revealed and he is commanded to convey them, whereas a Prophet is the one who receives revelation but he is not commanded to convey it. On this basis, every Messenger is a Prophet, but every Prophet is not a Messenger.[4]

What they mentioned is unlikely to be correct for several reasons:

1) Allah (ﷻ) stated that He sent the Prophets as He sent the Messengers: ﴾Never did We send a Messenger or a Prophet before you...﴿ *(Qur'an 22: 52)*

The word "send" implies that the Prophet must also convey the message.

2) Not conveying the Message means concealing the Revelation of Allah. Allah did not send down His revelation to be buried in the heart of one person, and to be died when that person dies.

3) The Messenger (ﷺ) said,

> "The nations were shown to me, and I saw a Prophet who had a group of people with him, a Prophet with one or two people with him, and a Prophet who had no one with him..."[5]

This indicates that the Prophets are commanded to convey the Message, and that they vary in the extent to which people responded to them.

---

[4] *Sharḥ al-'Aqeedah aṭ-Ṭaḥaawiyah*, 167; *Lawaami' al-Anwaar al-Bahiyah*, 1/49.

[5] Bukhari, Muslim, Tirmidhi and Nasaa'i.

The favoured definition is that, “A Messenger is the one who receives the revelation of a new law (shari‘ah), and a Prophet is the one who is sent to confirm the law of the one who came before him.”[6]

The Children of Israel were led by the Prophets. Every time a Prophet died, another Prophet would come, as is stated in the hadith.[7] The Prophets of the Children of Israel were all sent to confirm the Law of Moosa (Moses), the *Tawraat* (Torah), and they were commanded to convey the Revelation of Allah to their people:

﴿ أَلَمْ تَرَ إِلَى ٱلْمَلَإِ مِنۢ بَنِىٓ إِسْرَٰٓءِيلَ مِنۢ بَعْدِ مُوسَىٰٓ إِذْ قَالُوا۟ لِنَبِىٍّ لَّهُمُ
ٱبْعَثْ لَنَا مَلِكًا نُّقَٰتِلْ فِى سَبِيلِ ٱللَّهِ ۖ قَالَ هَلْ عَسَيْتُمْ إِن
كُتِبَ عَلَيْكُمُ ٱلْقِتَالُ أَلَّا تُقَٰتِلُوا۟ ... ﴿٢٤٦﴾ ﴾

﴾Have you not thought about the group of the Children of Israel after [the time of] Moosa [Moses]? When they said to a Prophet of theirs, ‘Appoint for us a king and we will fight in Allah’s Way.’ He said, ‘Would you then refrain from fighting, if fighting was prescribed for you?’...﴿ *(Qur’an 2: 246)*

As is clear from the *aayah* (verse), a Prophet is the one who receives revelation concerning something that is obligatory upon his people; this can only mean that he is obliged to convey the message.

This conclusion is drawn from studying the case of Dawood (David), Sulaymaan (Solomon), Zakariya (Zachariya) and Yahyaa (John), who are all Prophets. They were leaders of the Children of Israel, who judged among them and conveyed the truth to them. And Allah knows best.

---

[6] *Tafseer al-Aaloosi*, 17/157.

[7] Bukhari in his *Ṣaḥeeḥ*. See *Fatḥ al-Baari*, 6/495.

Belief in the Prophets and Messengers is one of the basic principles of faith

Belief in the Messengers is one of the basic principles of faith. Allah (ﷻ) says:

﴿ قُلْ ءَامَنَّا بِٱللَّهِ وَمَآ أُنزِلَ عَلَيْنَا وَمَآ أُنزِلَ عَلَىٰٓ إِبْرَٰهِيمَ وَإِسْمَٰعِيلَ وَإِسْحَٰقَ وَيَعْقُوبَ وَٱلْأَسْبَاطِ وَمَآ أُوتِىَ مُوسَىٰ وَعِيسَىٰ وَٱلنَّبِيُّونَ مِن رَّبِّهِمْ لَا نُفَرِّقُ بَيْنَ أَحَدٍ مِّنْهُمْ وَنَحْنُ لَهُۥ مُسْلِمُونَ ﴿٨٤﴾ ﴾

﴿Say [O' Muhammad]: We believe in Allah and in what has been sent down to us, and what was sent down to Ibraaheem [Abraham], Ismaa'eel [Ishmael], Isḥaaq [Isaac], Ya'qoob [Jacob] and *Al-Asbaaṭ* [the offspring of the twelve sons of Ya'qoob (Jacob)] and what was given to Moosa [Moses], 'Eesa [Jesus] and the Prophets from their Lord. We make no distinction between one another among them and to Him [Allah] we have submitted [in Islam].﴾ *(Qur'an 3: 84)*

Whoever does not believe in the Messengers has gone astray and is a loser:

﴿ ... وَمَن يَكْفُرْ بِٱللَّهِ وَمَلَٰٓئِكَتِهِۦ وَكُتُبِهِۦ وَرُسُلِهِۦ وَٱلْيَوْمِ ٱلْءَاخِرِ فَقَدْ ضَلَّ ضَلَٰلًۢا بَعِيدًا ﴿١٣٦﴾ ﴾

﴿...And whosoever disbelieves in Allah, His Angels, His Books, His Messengers, and the Last Day, then indeed he has strayed far away.﴾ *(Qur'an 4: 136)*

The connection between belief in Allah and belief in the Messengers and their message

Those who claim to believe in Allah but disbelieve in the Messengers and Books do not estimate Allah with the estimation due to Him:

﴿وَمَا قَدَرُواْ ٱللَّهَ حَقَّ قَدْرِهِۦٓ إِذْ قَالُواْ مَآ أَنزَلَ ٱللَّهُ عَلَىٰ بَشَرٍ مِّن شَيْءٍ... ﴿٩١﴾﴾

﴿They [the Jews, Quraysh pagans, idolaters] did not estimate Allah with an estimation due to Him when they said: 'Nothing did Allah send down to any human being [by Revelation]'...﴾ *(Qur'an 6: 91)*

Those who estimate Allah (ﷻ) with the estimation due to Him know His attributes of knowledge, wisdom and mercy, and they inevitably know for certain that He sent the Messengers and revealed the Books, because this is what is implied by His attributes, for He did not create this universe in vain:

﴿أَيَحْسَبُ ٱلْإِنسَٰنُ أَن يُتْرَكَ سُدًى ﴿٣٦﴾﴾

﴿Does man think that he will be left neglected [without being punished or rewarded for the obligatory duties enjoined by his Lord Allah on him]?﴾*(Qur'an 75: 36)*

Whoever disbelieves in the Messengers whilst claiming to believe in Allah is a *kaafir* in the sight of Allah, and his belief will not avail him anything. Allah (ﷻ) says:

﴿إِنَّ ٱلَّذِينَ يَكْفُرُونَ بِٱللَّهِ وَرُسُلِهِۦ وَيُرِيدُونَ أَن يُفَرِّقُواْ بَيْنَ ٱللَّهِ وَرُسُلِهِۦ وَيَقُولُونَ نُؤْمِنُ بِبَعْضٍ وَنَكْفُرُ بِبَعْضٍ وَيُرِيدُونَ أَن يَتَّخِذُواْ بَيْنَ ذَٰلِكَ سَبِيلًا ﴿١٥٠﴾ أُوْلَٰٓئِكَ هُمُ ٱلْكَٰفِرُونَ حَقًّا ... ﴿١٥١﴾﴾

﴿Verily, those who disbelieve in Allah and His Messengers and wish to make distinction between Allah and His Messengers [by believing in Allah and disbelieving in His Messengers] saying, 'We believe in some but reject others,' and wish to adopt a way in between. They are in truth disbelievers...﴾

(Qur'an 4: 150-151)

The *aayah* states that the one who claims to believe in Allah but disbelieves in the Messengers is a *kaafir*: ﴿...And wish to make distinction between Allah and His Messengers...﴾. Qurṭubi said concerning this *aayah*: "Allah states that making a distinction between Allah and His Messengers is *kufr* (disbelief). This is *kufr* because Allah has enjoined upon people to worship Him in the way which He prescribed via His Messengers. If they deny the Messengers, then they deny their teachings, thus they fail to achieve the true servitude to Allah which is enjoined upon them; this is like denying the Creator, and denying the Creator is *kufr* because that implies achieving no true servitude to Him. The same applies to making a distinction between Allah and His Messengers."[8]

The Prophets and Messengers form a large group

The wisdom of Allah dictated that He would send a warner to each of the nations before this ummah; He did not send any Messenger to the whole of mankind apart from Muhammad (ﷺ). His justice dictated that He would not punish anyone until after proof had been established against them:

﴿... وَمَا كُنَّا مُعَذِّبِينَ حَتَّىٰ نَبْعَثَ رَسُولًا ﴿١٥﴾﴾

﴿...And We never punish until We have sent a Messenger [to give warning].﴾ *(Qur'an 17: 15)*

Hence the number of Messengers and Prophets who have come throughout human history is immense. Allah (ﷻ) says:

﴿... وَإِن مِّنْ أُمَّةٍ إِلَّا خَلَا فِيهَا نَذِيرٌ ﴿٢٤﴾﴾

﴿...And there never was a nation but a warner had passed among them.﴾ *(Qur'an 35: 24)*

---

8 *Tafseer al-Qurṭubi*, 6/5.

The Messenger of Allah (ﷺ) told us of a number of Prophets and Messengers. It is narrated that Abu Dharr stated: "I said, 'O' Messenger of Allah, how many Messengers were there?' He said, 'Three hundred and umpteen, a large number.'" According to the report of Abu Umaamah, Abu Dharr stated: "I said, 'O' Messenger of Allah, what is the complete number of Prophets?' He said,

> '124,000, among whom the Messengers were three hundred and fifteen, a large number.'"

- This is narrated by Aḥmad in his *Musnad*.[9]

Among the Prophets and Messengers there are those whose stories Allah has not told us

This huge number of Prophets and Messengers tells us that those whose names we know are very few, and that there are very many whose names we do not know. The Qur'an states this clearly in more than one place. Allah (ﷻ) says:

﴿ وَرُسُلًا قَدْ قَصَصْنَٰهُمْ عَلَيْكَ مِن قَبْلُ وَرُسُلًا لَّمْ نَقْصُصْهُمْ عَلَيْكَ ... ﴿١٦٤﴾ ﴾

﴾And Messengers We have mentioned to you before, and Messengers We have not mentioned to you...﴿ *(Qur'an 4: 164)*

﴿ وَلَقَدْ أَرْسَلْنَا رُسُلًا مِّن قَبْلِكَ مِنْهُم مَّن قَصَصْنَا عَلَيْكَ وَمِنْهُم مَّن لَّمْ نَقْصُصْ عَلَيْكَ ... ﴿٧٨﴾ ﴾

﴾And, indeed We have sent Messengers before you [O' Muhammad], of some of them We have related to you

---

[9] *Mishkaat al-Maṣaabeeḥ*, 3/122. The editor of *Al-Mishkaat*, *Shaykh* Naaṣiruddeen al-Albaani, said, its isnad is *ṣaḥeeḥ*.

their story. And of some We have not related to you their story...﴿ *(Qur'an 40: 78)*

It is not permissible for us to disbelieve in those whose names have been told to us by Allah in the Qur'an or by His Messenger (ﷺ); at the same time we believe that Allah has other Messengers and Prophets of whom we know nothing.

The Prophets and Messengers who are mentioned in the Qur'an

Allah (ﷻ) mentions twenty-five Prophets and Messengers in His Book. In various places He mentions Adam, Hood, Ṣaaliḥ, Shu'ayb, Ismaa'eel (Ishmael), Idrees (Enoch), Dhu'l-Kifl and Muhammad (may Allah's peace be upon them all).

Allah (ﷻ) says:

﴿ إِنَّ ٱللَّهَ ٱصْطَفَىٰٓ ءَادَمَ ... ﴿٣٣﴾ ﴾

﴾Allah chose Adam...﴿ *(Qur'an 3: 33)*

﴿ وَإِلَىٰ عَادٍ أَخَاهُمْ هُودًا ... ﴿٥٠﴾ ﴾

﴾And to the 'Aad [people We sent] their brother Hood...﴿ *(Qur'an 11: 50)*

﴿ وَإِلَىٰ ثَمُودَ أَخَاهُمْ صَٰلِحًا ... ﴿٦١﴾ ﴾

﴾And to Thamood [people We sent] their brother Ṣaaliḥ [Saleh]...﴿ *(Qur'an 11: 61)*

﴿ وَإِلَىٰ مَدْيَنَ أَخَاهُمْ شُعَيْبًا ... ﴿٨٤﴾ ﴾

﴾And to the Madyan [Midian] people [We sent] their brother Shu'ayb...﴿ *(Qur'an 11: 84)*

﴿ وَإِسْمَٰعِيلَ وَإِدْرِيسَ وَذَا ٱلْكِفْلِ كُلٌّ مِّنَ ٱلصَّٰبِرِينَ ﴿٨٥﴾ ﴾

﴿And [remember] Ismaa'eel [Ishmael], Idrees and *Dhu'l-Kifl* [Isaiah]: all were from among *Aṣ-Ṣaabiroon* [the patient].﴾ *(Qur'an 21: 85)*

﴿ مُّحَمَّدٌ رَّسُولُ ٱللَّهِ ... ﴿٢٩﴾ ﴾

﴿Muhammad is the Messenger of Allah...﴾ *(Qur'an 48: 29)*

Allah (سبحانه وتعالى) mentions eighteen of them in one place - in *Soorah al-An'aam*:

﴿ وَتِلْكَ حُجَّتُنَآ ءَاتَيْنَٰهَآ إِبْرَٰهِيمَ عَلَىٰ قَوْمِهِۦ ۚ نَرْفَعُ دَرَجَٰتٍ مَّن نَّشَآءُ ۗ إِنَّ
رَبَّكَ حَكِيمٌ عَلِيمٌ ﴿٨٣﴾ وَوَهَبْنَا لَهُۥٓ إِسْحَٰقَ وَيَعْقُوبَ ۚ كُلًّا هَدَيْنَا ۚ
وَنُوحًا هَدَيْنَا مِن قَبْلُ ۖ وَمِن ذُرِّيَّتِهِۦ دَاوُۥدَ وَسُلَيْمَٰنَ وَأَيُّوبَ وَيُوسُفَ
وَمُوسَىٰ وَهَٰرُونَ ۚ وَكَذَٰلِكَ نَجْزِى ٱلْمُحْسِنِينَ ﴿٨٤﴾ وَزَكَرِيَّا وَيَحْيَىٰ وَعِيسَىٰ
وَإِلْيَاسَ ۖ كُلٌّ مِّنَ ٱلصَّٰلِحِينَ ﴿٨٥﴾ وَإِسْمَٰعِيلَ وَٱلْيَسَعَ وَيُونُسَ وَلُوطًا ۚ
وَكُلًّا فَضَّلْنَا عَلَى ٱلْعَٰلَمِينَ ﴿٨٦﴾ ﴾

﴿And that was Our Proof which We gave Ibraaheem [Abraham] against his people. We raise whom We will in degrees. Certainly your Lord is All-Wise, All-Knowing. And We bestowed upon him Isḥaaq [Isaac] and Ya'qoob [Jacob], each of them We guided, and before him, We guided Nooḥ [Noah], and among his progeny Dawood [David], Sulaymaan [Solomon], Ayyoob [Job], Yoosuf [Joseph], Moosa [Moses], and Haaroon [Aaron]. Thus do We reward *Al-Muḥsinoon* [the good-doers]. And Zakariyya [Zachariah], and Yaḥyaa [John] and 'Eesa [Jesus] and Ilyaas [Elias], each one of them was of the righteous. And Ismaa'eel [Ishmael] and Al-Yasaa' [Elisha], and Yoonus [Jonah] and Looṭ [Lot], and each one of them We preferred above the *'Aalameen* [mankind and jinn (of their times)].﴾ *(Qur'an 6: 83-86)*

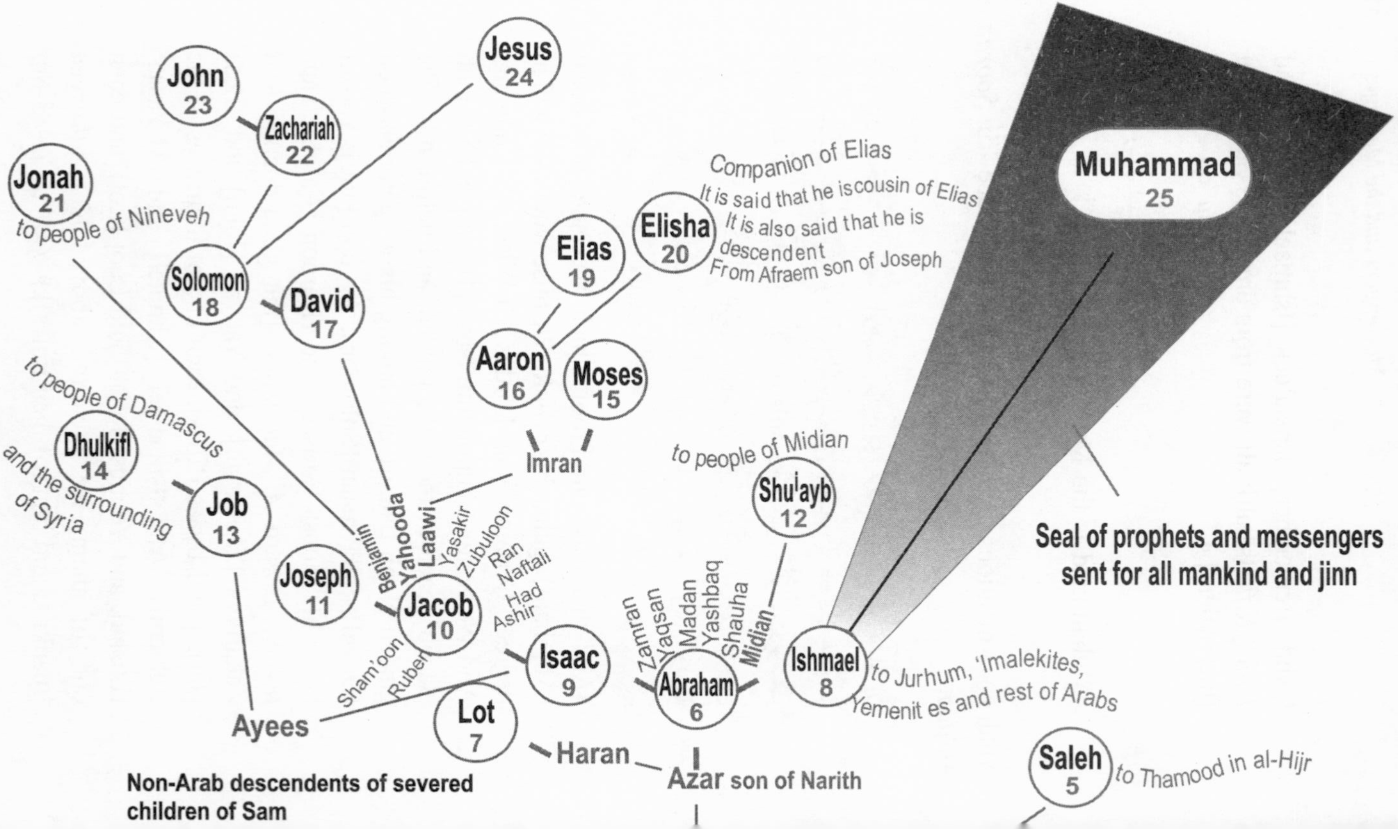
Muhammad
25
Seal of prophets and messengers
sent for all mankind and jinn
Jesus
24
John
23
Zachariah
22
Jonah
21
to people of Nineveh
Solomon
18
David
17
Elisha
20
Companion of Elias
It is said that he iscousin of Elias
It is also said that he is
descendent
From Afraem son of Joseph
Elias
19
Aaron
16
Moses
15
Imran
to people of Damascus
Dhulkifl
14
and the surrounding
of Syria
Job
13
Joseph
11
Benjamin
Yahooda
Laawi
Yasakir
Zubuloon
Ran
Naftali
Had
Ashir
Jacob
10
Sham'oon
Ruben
to people of Midian
Shu'ayb
12
Isaac
9
Zamran
Yaqsan
Madan
Yashbaq
Shauha
Midian
Abraham
6
Ishmael
8
to Jurhum, 'Imalekites,
Yemenit es and rest of Arabs
Ayees
Lot
7
Haran
Azar son of Narith
Non-Arab descendents of severed
children of Sam
Saleh
5
to Thamood in al-Hijr

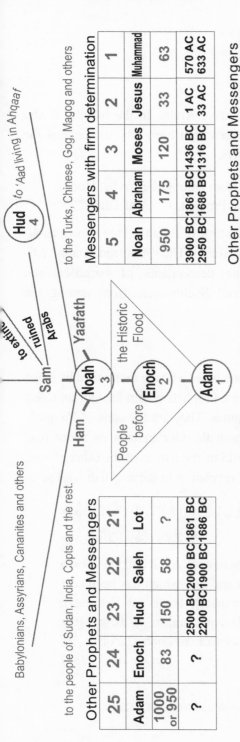

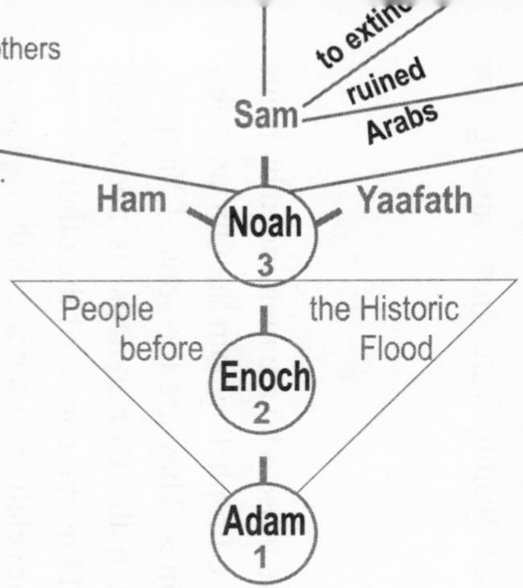

Other Prophets and Messengers

25	24	23	22	21
Adam	Enoch	Hud	Saleh	Lot
1000 or 950	83	150	58	?
?	?	2500 BC 2200 BC	2000 BC 1900 BC	1861 BC 1686 BC

Messengers with firm determination

5	4	3	2	1
Noah	Abraham	Moses	Jesus	Muhammad
950	175	120	33	63
3900 BC 2950 BC	1861 BC 1686 BC	1436 BC 1316 BC	1 AC 33 AC	570 AC 633 AC

Other Prophets and Messengers

20	19	18	17	16	15	14	13	12	11	10	9	8	7	6
Ishmael	Isaac	Jacob	Joseph	Shu'ayb	Job	Dhulkifl	Aaron	David	Solomon	Elias	Elisha	Jonah	Zachariah	John
143 or 130	180 or 187	147	110	?	92	75	122	70	52	?	?	?	130	30
1781 BC 1638 BC	1761 BC 1581 BC	1700 BC 1653 BC	1610 BC 1500 BC	1600 BC 1500 BC			1439 BC 1317 BC	1042 BC 972 BC	985 BC 933 BC	Approx. 900 BC	Approx. 900 BC	Approx. 800 BC	100 BC 30 AC	1 AC 30 AC

Leads from father to son —

Leads from forefather ——

Circles the name of a messenger

Genealogical Tree of the Prophets and Messengers

Referred to in the Noble Qur'an

Four from among the Arabs

Among these twenty-five, four were Arabs. In the hadith of Abu Dharr (رضي الله عنه) (may Allah be pleased with him) which mentions the Prophets and Messengers, it says,

> "Among them were four from among the Arabs: Hood, Ṣaaliḥ, Shu'ayb and your Prophet, O' Abu Dharr."[10]

The Arabs who existed before the time of Ismaa'eel are known as *Al-'Arab al-'Aaribah* (the original Arabs). The "Arabized Arabs" (*Al-'Arab al-Musta'ribah*) are the descendents of Ismaa'eel ibn Ibraaheem al-Khaleel. Hood and Ṣaaliḥ were from among the original Arabs.

The sons of Ya'qoob

The Prophets mentioned above are those who are mentioned by name in the Qur'an. There are also some Prophets whom the Qur'an refers to, but we do not know their names. They are the sons of Ya'qoob. They were twelve men, of whom the Qur'an tells us about one, namely Yoosuf; Allah has not told us the names of the other eleven, but He has told us that He sent revelation to them. Allah (سبحانه وتعالى) says:

> ﴿ قُولُوٓاْ ءَامَنَّا بِٱللَّهِ وَمَآ أُنزِلَ إِلَيۡنَا وَمَآ أُنزِلَ إِلَىٰٓ إِبۡرَٰهِـۧمَ وَإِسۡمَٰعِيلَ وَإِسۡحَٰقَ وَيَعۡقُوبَ وَٱلۡأَسۡبَاطِ ... ﴿١٣٦﴾ ﴾
>
> ﴿Say [O' Muslims]: 'We believe in Allah and that which has been sent down to us and that which has been sent down to Ibraaheem [Abraham], Ismaa'eel [Ishmael], Isḥaaq [Isaac], Ya'qoob [Jacob], and to *Al-Asbaaṭ* [the offspring of the twelve sons of Ya'qoob (Jacob)]...'﴾
>
> *(Qur'an 2: 136)*

---

[10] Ibn Ḥibbaan in his *Ṣaḥeeḥ*; *Al-Bidaayah wan-Nihaayah*, 1/120.

﴿ أَمْ تَقُولُونَ إِنَّ إِبْرَاهِيمَ وَإِسْمَاعِيلَ وَإِسْحَاقَ وَيَعْقُوبَ وَالْأَسْبَاطَ كَانُوا هُودًا أَوْ نَصَارَىٰ ... ﴿١٤٠﴾

﴿Or say you that Ibraaheem [Abraham], Ismaa'eel [Ishmael], Isḥaaq [Isaac], Ya'qoob [Jacob] and *Al-Asbaaṭ* [the offspring of the twelve sons of Ya'qoob (Jacob)] were Jews or Christians?...﴾ *(Qur'an 2: 140)*

Prophets whom we know of from the Sunnah

There are also Prophets whom we know of from the Sunnah, although their names are not mentioned in the Qur'an. They are:

Sheeth

Ibn Katheer said: "He was a Prophet according to the *marfoo'* hadith narrated by Ibn Ḥibbaan in his *Ṣaḥeeḥ* from Abu Dharr, which says that fifty pages were revealed to him."[11]

Yoosha' ibn Noon (Joshua the son of Nun)

Abu Hurayrah narrated that the Messenger of Allah (ﷺ) said:

> "One of the Prophets set out on a military campaign, and he said to his people, 'No man should follow me who is on the verge of consummating marriage or who has raised a building but has not yet put a roof on it, or who has bought sheep or other livestock and is waiting for them to give birth.' He attacked a feddan of the village at the time of *'Aṣr*, then he said to the sun, 'You are subject to the divine command and I am subject to the divine command; O' Allah, do not let it set on me for a while.'"[12]

---

[11] *Al-Bidaayah wan-Nihaayah*, 1/99.

[12] Aḥmad and Muslim. See *Al-Bidaayah wan-Nihaayah*, 1/323.

The evidence that this Prophet was Yoosha' is the fact that the Prophet (ﷺ) said:

> "The sun was prevented from setting on Yoosha' when he marched to *Bayt al-Maqdis* (Jerusalem)."[13]

Righteous people who may or may not have been Prophets

Dhu'l-Qarnayn

Allah (ﷻ) mentions the story of Dhu'l-Qarnayn at the end of *Soorah al-Kahf* (the 18th chapter of the Qur'an). One of the things that He tells us is that He spoke to Dhu'l-Qarnayn:

﴿... قُلْنَا يَـٰذَا ٱلْقَرْنَيْنِ إِمَّآ أَن تُعَذِّبَ وَإِمَّآ أَن تَتَّخِذَ فِيهِمْ حُسْنًا ﴿٨٦﴾﴾

> ﴿...We [Allah] said [by inspiration]: 'O' Dhu'l-Qarnayn! Either you punish them, or treat them with kindness'﴾
> *(Qur'an 18: 86)*

Were these words spoken through a Prophet who was with him, or was he himself a Prophet? Al-Fakhr ar-Raazi was sure that he was a Prophet.[14] Ibn Ḥajar said: "This is narrated from 'Abdullah ibn 'Amr, and this is the apparent meaning of the Qur'anic verses."[15] Those who denied that he was a Prophet include 'Ali ibn Abi Ṭaalib (رضي الله عنه).[16]

Tubba'

Tubba' is also mentioned in the Qur'an. Allah (ﷻ) says:

---

[13] Ibn Katheer said in *Al-Bidaayah wan-Nihaayah* (1/323): this has been narrated only by Aḥmad with this isnad. It meets the conditions of Bukhari.

[14] *Fatḥ al-Baari*, 6/382.

[15] Ibid.

[16] This report is narrated by Al-Ḥaakim from 'Ali (رضي الله عنه). He said, its isnad is *ṣaḥeeḥ*. See *Fatḥ al-Baari*, 6/382.

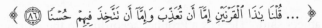

﴿أَهُمْ خَيْرٌ أَمْ قَوْمُ تُبَّعٍ وَالَّذِينَ مِن قَبْلِهِمْ أَهْلَكْنَاهُمْ إِنَّهُمْ كَانُوا مُجْرِمِينَ ﴿٣٧﴾﴾

﴿Are they better or the people of Tubba‘ and those before them? We destroyed them because they were indeed *Mujrimoon* [disbelievers, polytheists, sinners, criminals].﴾ *(Qur'an 44: 37)*

﴿كَذَّبَتْ قَبْلَهُمْ قَوْمُ نُوحٍ وَأَصْحَابُ الرَّسِّ وَثَمُودُ ﴿١٢﴾ وَعَادٌ وَفِرْعَوْنُ وَإِخْوَانُ
لُوطٍ ﴿١٣﴾ وَأَصْحَابُ الْأَيْكَةِ وَقَوْمُ تُبَّعٍ كُلٌّ كَذَّبَ الرُّسُلَ فَحَقَّ وَعِيدِ ﴿١٤﴾﴾

﴿Denied before them [i.e. these pagans of Makkah] the people of Nooḥ [Noah], and the Dwellers of Rass, and Thamood, and ‘Aad, and Fir‘aun [Pharaoh], and the brethren of Looṭ [Lot], and the Dwellers of the Wood, and the people of Tubba‘. Everyone of them denied [their] Messengers, so My Threat took effect.﴾ *(Qur'an 50: 12-14)*

Was Tubba‘ a Prophet whom Allah sent to his people, then they disbelieved in him and were destroyed because of that? Allah knows best.

It is better not to make any definite statement concerning Dhu'l-Qarnayn and Tubba‘

It is better to refrain from stating that these two men were Prophets, because it is narrated in a *ṣaḥeeḥ* hadith that the Messenger (ﷺ) said:

> "I do not know whether Tubba‘ was a Prophet or not, and I do not know whether Dhu'l-Qarnayn was a Prophet or not."[17]

If the Messenger (ﷺ) did not know, then how can we know?

---

[17] Al-Ḥaakim and Al-Bayhaqi. See *Ṣaḥeeḥ al-Jaami‘ aṣ-Ṣagheer*, 5/121.

Al-Khiḍr

Al-Khiḍr was a righteous slave of Allah to whom Moosa (Moses) (عليه السلام) (may Allah's peace be upon him) travelled in order to seek knowledge from him. Allah has told us their story in *Soorah al-Kahf.*

The story indicates that he was a Prophet for several reasons:[18]

1) Allah (تعالى) says:

﴿ فَوَجَدَا عَبْدًا مِّنْ عِبَادِنَآ ءَاتَيْنَٰهُ رَحْمَةً مِّنْ عِندِنَا وَعَلَّمْنَٰهُ مِن لَّدُنَّا عِلْمًا ﴿٦٥﴾ ﴾

﴾Then they found one of Our slaves, on whom We had bestowed mercy from Us, and whom We had taught knowledge from Us.﴿ *(Qur'an 18: 65)*

The apparent meaning is that this mercy was the mercy of Prophethood, and this knowledge was that which was revealed to him.

2) Moosa (Moses) (عليه السلام) said to him:

﴿ ... هَلْ أَتَّبِعُكَ عَلَىٰٓ أَن تُعَلِّمَنِ مِمَّا عُلِّمْتَ رُشْدًا ﴿٦٦﴾ قَالَ إِنَّكَ لَن تَسْتَطِيعَ مَعِىَ صَبْرًا ﴿٦٧﴾ وَكَيْفَ تَصْبِرُ عَلَىٰ مَا لَمْ تُحِطْ بِهِۦ خُبْرًا ﴿٦٨﴾ قَالَ سَتَجِدُنِىٓ إِن شَآءَ ٱللَّهُ صَابِرًا وَلَآ أَعْصِى لَكَ أَمْرًا ﴿٦٩﴾ قَالَ فَإِنِ ٱتَّبَعْتَنِى فَلَا تَسْـَٔلْنِى عَن شَىْءٍ حَتَّىٰٓ أُحْدِثَ لَكَ مِنْهُ ذِكْرًا ﴿٧٠﴾ ﴾

﴾...'May I follow you so that you teach me something of that knowledge [guidance and true path] which you have been taught [by Allah]?' He [Khiḍr] said: 'Verily, you will not be able to have patience with me! And how can

---

[18] These reasons were mentioned by Ibn Katheer in *Al-Bidaayah wan-Nihaayah*, 1/ 326.

> you have patience about a thing which you know not?' Moosa [Moses] said: 'If Allah wills, you will find me patient, and I will not disobey you in aught.' He [Khiḍr] said: 'Then, if you follow me, ask me not about anything till I myself mention of it to you.'} *(Qur'an 18: 66-70)*

If he was not a Prophet, he would not have been infallible, and Moosa (Moses) - who was a great Prophet and a noble Messenger, and who must himself have been infallible - would not have been so keen to seek knowledge from a mere *wali* (friend of Allah) who was not infallible. Because he was determined to go to him and search for him, even if that took a long time - and it is said that it took eighty years - and then when he met him he humbled himself before him and showed respect towards him, and followed him in a manner which indicated that he was keen to learn from him. This indicates that he was a Prophet like him, who received revelation just as he did, and that he had been given divine knowledge and secrets of Prophethood that Allah had not given to Moosa (Moses) with whom He spoke, the Prophet of the Children of Israel.

3) Al-Khiḍr killed that boy, but that was only because of revelation that he received from the All-Knowing Sovereign. This is independent proof of his Prophethood, and clear proof of his infallibility,[19] because a *wali* is not permitted to kill people simply

---

[19] Some groups among this ummah have gone astray by violating the sacred limits of Allah and committing sins, and when they are denounced for that evil, they say that the hidden reality of the matter is different from what you see, and they quote the story of Al-Khiḍr as evidence for that, how he damaged the ship and killed the boy. This is serious misguidance which opens the door to evil which can never be closed thereafter. Stating that Al-Khiḍr was a Prophet closes this door. Moreover, no one among this ummah has the right to go against the shari'ah of Islam; what is *ḥalaal* is that which is permitted by Allah and what is *ḥaraam* is that which is forbidden by Allah. Whoever wants to go against shari'ah will be punished appropriately for doing so, no matter what he claims.

because of some thought that occurs to him, for his thoughts are not necessarily infallible, and it is possible for a *wali* to commit sins, according to consensus. When Al-Khiḍr killed that boy who had not yet reached the age of puberty, knowing that if he reached maturity he would become a *kaafir* and would force his parents to become *kaafir* too because of their intense love for him which would make them follow him. So killing him served a great purpose which outweighed any benefits which may have resulted from letting him live, in order to protect his parents from falling into *kufr* and suffering the consequent punishment. This is a sign that he was a Prophet and that he was supported by Allah with infallibility.

4) When Al-Khiḍr explained to Moosa (Moses) what his deeds meant, he said after that:

﴿... رَحۡمَةً مِّن رَّبِّكَۚ وَمَا فَعَلۡتُهُۥ عَنۡ أَمۡرِيۚ ... ﴿٨٢﴾﴾

﴾...As a Mercy from your Lord. And I did them not of my own accord...﴿ *(Qur'an 18: 82)*

- meaning, I did not do them on my own initiative, rather I was commanded to do so by revelation.[20]

---

[20] A large number of scholars are of the view that Al-Khiḍr is still alive and did not die, and many reports have been narrated concerning that. The suggestion that he is alive has opened the door to many myths and lies. Many people claim that they have met Al-Khiḍr, that he gave them advice and commanded them to do things. They narrated many strange stories concerning such things, reports which a sound mind would reject.

Some of the greatest scholars of hadith, such as Bukhari, Ibn Diḥyah, Ibn Katheer and Ibn Ḥajar al-'Asqallaani have sought to prove that these reports are *ḍa'eef* (weak). The strongest evidence to refute those who say that Al-Khiḍr is alive is the fact that there is no *ṣaḥeeḥ* hadith to support this notion. If he were alive, it would have been obligatory for him to come to the Messenger (ﷺ), to follow him and support him. Allah made a covenant with the Prophets from before that they would believe in Muhammad and support him if he came during their time: =

Disbelieving in one Messenger is like disbelieving in all the Messengers

Disbelieving in one of the Messengers is like disbelieving in all of the Messengers. Allah (ﷻ) says:

﴿ كَذَّبَتْ قَوْمُ نُوحٍ الْمُرْسَلِينَ ﴿١٠٥﴾ ﴾

﴿The people of Nooḥ [Noah] belied the Messengers.﴾ *(Qur'an 26: 105)*

﴿ كَذَّبَتْ عَادٌ الْمُرْسَلِينَ ﴿١٢٣﴾ ﴾

﴿'Aad [people] belied the Messengers﴾ *(Qur'an 26: 123)*

﴿ كَذَّبَتْ ثَمُودُ الْمُرْسَلِينَ ﴿١٤١﴾ ﴾

= ﴿And [remember] when Allah took the Covenant of the Prophets, saying: 'Take whatever I gave you from the Book and *Ḥikmah* [understanding of the Laws of Allah], and afterwards there will come to you a Messenger [Muhammad] confirming what is with you; you must, then, believe in him and help him.' Allah said: 'Do you agree [to it] and will you take up My Covenant [which I conclude with you]?' They said: 'We agree.' He said: 'Then bear witness; and I am with you among the witnesses [for this]'﴾ *(Qur'an 3: 81)*

The Messenger (ﷺ), said that if Moosa (Moses) had been alive, he would have had no choice but to follow him. Ibraaheem al-Ḥarbi asked Aḥmad ibn Ḥanbal about the idea of Al-Khiḍr and Ilyaas still being alive, and whether they could still be seen and whether stories could be narrated from them. Aḥmad said, I think that all of these stories are coming from the *Shayṭaan* (Satan). (*Majmoo' al-Fataawa Shaykh al-Islam*, 4/337). Bukhari was asked about Al-Khiḍr and Ilyaas, are they among the living? He said, "How could that be so when the Prophet (ﷺ) said, 'In one hundred year's time there will be no one left who is on the face of the earth now.'" (*Majmoo' al-Fataawa Shaykh al-Islam*, 4/337)

A number of prominent scholars went to a great length to quote evidence which disproves these myths, such as Ibn Katheer in *Al-Bidaayah wan-Nihaayah*, 1/326; *Shaykh* Muhammad al-Ameen ash-Shanqeeṭi in *Aḍwaa' al-Bayaan*, 4/184. Ibn Ḥajar al-'Asqallaani wrote an essay concerning that, entitled *Az-Zahr an-Naḍr fi Naba' al-Khiḍr*; this is published in *Majmoo'ah ar-Rasaa'il al-Muneeriyah*, 2/195.

﴿Thamood [people] belied the Messenger.﴾

(Qur'an 26: 141)

﴿ كَذَّبَتْ قَوْمُ لُوطٍ ٱلْمُرْسَلِينَ ﴿١٦٠﴾ ﴾

﴿The people of Looṭ [Lot] - [who dwelt in the towns of Sodom in Palestine] belied the Messengers.﴾

(Qur'an 26: 160)

It is known that every nation disbelieved in its Messenger, but disbelief in one Messenger is counted as disbelief in all the Messengers. That is because the Messengers are bearers of one Message; they call to one religion; the One Who sends them is the same. They are as one, with the earlier ones foretelling the coming of the later ones, and the later ones confirming the message of the earlier ones.

Therefore, to believe in some of the Messengers and not in others constitutes disbelief in all of them. Allah (ﷻ) has described the one who does this as being a *kaafir*:

﴿ إِنَّ ٱلَّذِينَ يَكْفُرُونَ بِٱللَّهِ وَرُسُلِهِۦ وَيُرِيدُونَ أَن يُفَرِّقُوا۟ بَيْنَ ٱللَّهِ وَرُسُلِهِۦ وَيَقُولُونَ نُؤْمِنُ بِبَعْضٍ وَنَكْفُرُ بِبَعْضٍ وَيُرِيدُونَ أَن يَتَّخِذُوا۟ بَيْنَ ذَٰلِكَ سَبِيلًا ﴿١٥٠﴾ أُو۟لَٰٓئِكَ هُمُ ٱلْكَٰفِرُونَ حَقًّا ... ﴿١٥١﴾ ﴾

﴿Verily, those who disbelieve in Allah and His Messengers and wish to make distinction between Allah and His Messengers [by believing in Allah and disbelieving in His Messengers] saying, 'We believe in some but reject others,' and wish to adopt a way in between. They are in truth disbelievers...﴾

(Qur'an 4: 150-151)

Allah (ﷻ) has commanded us not to make any distinction between the Messengers, and to believe in them all:

﴿ قُولُوٓاْ ءَامَنَّا بِٱللَّهِ وَمَآ أُنزِلَ إِلَيۡنَا وَمَآ أُنزِلَ إِلَىٰٓ إِبۡرَٰهِـۧمَ وَإِسۡمَٰعِيلَ وَإِسۡحَٰقَ وَيَعۡقُوبَ وَٱلۡأَسۡبَاطِ وَمَآ أُوتِيَ مُوسَىٰ وَعِيسَىٰ وَمَآ أُوتِيَ ٱلنَّبِيُّونَ مِن رَّبِّهِمۡ لَا نُفَرِّقُ بَيۡنَ أَحَدٖ مِّنۡهُمۡ وَنَحۡنُ لَهُۥ مُسۡلِمُونَ ﴿١٣٦﴾ ﴾

﴾Say [O' Muslims]: 'We believe in Allah and that which has been sent down to us and that which has been sent down to Ibraaheem [Abraham], Ismaa'eel [Ishmael], Isḥaaq [Isaac], Ya'qoob [Jacob], and to *Al-Asbaaṭ* [the offspring of the twelve sons of Ya'qoob (Jacob)], and that which has been given to Moosa [Moses] and 'Eesa [Jesus], and that which has been given to the Prophets from their Lord. We make no distinction between any of them, and to Him we have submitted [in Islam].'﴿ *(Qur'an 2: 136)*

Whoever follows this path is rightly-guided:

﴿ فَإِنۡ ءَامَنُواْ بِمِثۡلِ مَآ ءَامَنتُم بِهِۦ فَقَدِ ٱهۡتَدَواْۖ ... ﴿١٣٧﴾ ﴾

﴾So if they believe in the like of that which you believe then they are rightly guided...﴿ *(Qur'an 2: 137)*

But the one who goes against that has gone astray and is misguided:

﴿ ... وَّإِن تَوَلَّوۡاْ فَإِنَّمَا هُمۡ فِي شِقَاقٖۖ فَسَيَكۡفِيكَهُمُ ٱللَّهُۚ وَهُوَ ٱلسَّمِيعُ ٱلۡعَلِيمُ ﴿١٣٧﴾ ﴾

﴾...But if they turn away, then they are only in opposition. So Allah will suffice for you against them. And He is the All-Hearer, the All-Knower.﴿ *(Qur'an 2: 137)*

Allah praised the Messenger of this ummah and the believers who follow him for their belief and for not making any distinction between the Messengers. He (سبحانه وتعالى) said:

﴿ءَامَنَ ٱلرَّسُولُ بِمَآ أُنزِلَ إِلَيْهِ مِن رَّبِّهِۦ وَٱلْمُؤْمِنُونَۚ كُلٌّ ءَامَنَ بِٱللَّهِ
وَمَلَٰٓئِكَتِهِۦ وَكُتُبِهِۦ وَرُسُلِهِۦ لَا نُفَرِّقُ بَيْنَ أَحَدٍ مِّن رُّسُلِهِۦۚ ... ﴿٢٨٥﴾﴾

﴾The Messenger [Muhammad] believes in what has been sent down to him from his Lord, and [so do] the believers. Each one believes in Allah, His Angels, His Books, and His Messengers. [They say], 'We make no distinction between one another of His Messengers,'...﴿ *(Qur'an 2: 285)*

Allah (سبحانه وتعالى) promises a great reward to those who do not make any distinction between His Messengers:

﴿وَٱلَّذِينَ ءَامَنُوا۟ بِٱللَّهِ وَرُسُلِهِۦ وَلَمْ يُفَرِّقُوا۟ بَيْنَ أَحَدٍ مِّنْهُمْ أُو۟لَٰٓئِكَ سَوْفَ
يُؤْتِيهِمْ أُجُورَهُمْۗ وَكَانَ ٱللَّهُ غَفُورًا رَّحِيمًا ﴿١٥٢﴾﴾

﴾And those who believe in Allah and His Messengers and make no distinction between any of them [Messengers], We shall give them their rewards; and Allah is Ever Oft-Forgiving, Most Merciful.﴿ *(Qur'an 4: 152)*

Allah (سبحانه وتعالى) condemned the People of the Book for believing in some of the Messengers and disbelieving in others:

﴿وَإِذَا قِيلَ لَهُمْ ءَامِنُوا۟ بِمَآ أَنزَلَ ٱللَّهُ قَالُوا۟ نُؤْمِنُ بِمَآ أُنزِلَ عَلَيْنَا
وَيَكْفُرُونَ بِمَا وَرَآءَهُۥ وَهُوَ ٱلْحَقُّ مُصَدِّقًا لِّمَا مَعَهُمْۗ ... ﴿٩١﴾﴾

﴾And when it is said to them [the Jews], 'Believe in what Allah has sent down,' they say, 'We believe in what was sent down to us.' And they disbelieve in that which came after it, while it is the truth confirming what is with them...﴿ *(Qur'an 2: 91)*

The Jews do not believe in 'Eesa (Jesus) (عليه السلام) or in Muhammad (ﷺ), and the Christians do not believe in Muhammad (ﷺ).

No-one can be said to be a Prophet without evidence

The scholars of *tafseer* and biography have mentioned the names of many Prophets, transmitted from the Children of Israel, or based on views whose soundness cannot be proven. If these reports contradict anything that is proven to us from the Book of Allah or the Sunnah of His Messenger (ﷺ), we have to reject it, such as the view of those who say that the three messengers who were sent to the people of the town mentioned in *Soorah Ya-Seen* (the 36th chapter of the Qur'an) were from among the followers of 'Eesa (Jesus), or that Jarjees and Khaalid ibn Sinaan were Prophets who came after 'Eesa.[21]

We reject all of that, because it is proven in the *ṣaḥeeḥ* hadith that there is no Prophet between 'Eesa ibn Maryam and our Messenger (ﷺ).[22] The messengers mentioned in *Soorah Ya-Seen* were either Messengers sent before 'Eesa, which is more likely to be correct, or - as some of the *mufassireen* (exegetes) say - they were messengers sent by 'Eesa (Jesus), which is unlikely, because Allah says that He is the One Who sent them, and the word *rusul* (Messengers) in general is used in the usual sense. The report which says that Khaalid ibn Sinaan was an Arab Prophet whose people rejected him is a (claimed) hadith which is not *ṣaḥeeḥ*, and it contradicts a *ṣaḥeeḥ* hadith in which the Messenger (ﷺ) said that the number of Prophets from among the Arabs was four.[23]

With regard to the reports transmitted from the Children of Israel, which name some of the Prophets for whom there is no evidence in the Qur'an and Sunnah, we neither reject them nor believe in them, because they may be true or they may be false.

---

[21] *Fatḥ al-Baari*, 6/489.

[22] A *ṣaḥeeḥ* hadith narrated by Bukhari and others. See *Fatḥ al-Baari*, 4/477.

[23] Ibn Ḥibbaan in his *Ṣaḥeeḥ*.

No-one can be said to be a Prophet without evidence

The scholars of *tafseer* and biography have mentioned the names of many Prophets, transmitted from the Children of Israel, or based on views whose soundness cannot be proven. If these reports contradict anything that is proven to us from the Book of Allah or the Sunnah of His Messenger (ﷺ), we have to reject it, such as the view of those who say that the three messengers who were sent to the people of the town mentioned in *Soorah Ya-Seen* (the 36th chapter of the Qur'an) were from among the followers of 'Eesa (Jesus), or that Jirjees and Khaalid ibn Sinaan were Prophets who came after 'Eesa.

We reject all of that because it is proven in the *saheeh* Sunnah that there is no Prophet between 'Eesa ibn Maryam and our Messenger (ﷺ). The messengers mentioned in *Soorah Ya-Seen* were either Messengers sent before 'Eesa, which is more likely to be correct, as some of the *mufassireen* (exegetes) say, or they were messengers sent by 'Eesa (Jesus), which is unlikely, because Allah says that He is the One Who sent them, and the word *rusul* (Messengers) in general is used in the usual sense. The report which says that Khaalid ibn Sinaan was an Arab Prophet whose people rejected him is a (defined) hadith which is not *saheeh*, and it contradicts a *saheeh* hadith in which the Messenger (ﷺ) said that the number of Prophets from among the Arabs was four.

With regard to the reports transmitted from the Children of Israel which name some of the Prophets for whom there is no evidence in the Qur'an and Sunnah, we neither reject them nor believe in them, because they may be true or they may be false.

Fath al-Baari, 6/489.

A *saheeh* hadith narrated by Bukhaari and others. See *Fath al-Baari*, 6/...

Ibn Hibbaan in his *Saheeh*.

CHAPTER TWO
THE NEED OF MANKIND FOR THE MESSENGERS AND THEIR MESSAGES

INTRODUCTION

If people in the past used to argue with the Messengers, reject their teachings and turn away from them, mankind today in the twentieth century - when they have reached the pinnacle of material advancement, penetrated the depths of the oceans, gone far into space, split the atom and discovered many of the natural forces which exist in this universe - are even more in conflict with the Messengers, more emphatically rejecting their teachings and turning away from them even more. Mankind's attitude today towards the Messengers and their teachings is like that of wild donkeys when they see a lion; they flee from it without paying heed to anything else.

Allah (ﷻ) says:

﴿ فَمَا لَهُمْ عَنِ ٱلتَّذْكِرَةِ مُعْرِضِينَ ۝٤٩ كَأَنَّهُمْ حُمُرٌ مُّسْتَنفِرَةٌ ۝٥٠ فَرَّتْ مِن قَسْوَرَةٍ ۝٥١ ﴾

﴿Then what is wrong with them [i.e. the polytheists, the disbelievers] that they turn away from [receiving] admonition? As if they were [frightened] wild donkeys. Fleeing from a hunter, or a lion, or a beast of prey.﴾ *(Qur'an 74: 49-51)*

Mankind today - more than before - refuses to submit to the Messengers and their teachings because they are too proud of their knowledge and are too arrogant to follow men who lived centuries before them:

﴿ ذَٰلِكَ بِأَنَّهُۥ كَانَت تَّأۡتِيهِمۡ رُسُلُهُم بِٱلۡبَيِّنَٰتِ فَقَالُوٓاْ أَبَشَرٞ يَهۡدُونَنَا فَكَفَرُواْ وَتَوَلَّواْۚ وَّٱسۡتَغۡنَى ٱللَّهُۚ وَٱللَّهُ غَنِيٌّ حَمِيدٞ ﴾

﴿That was because there came to them their Messengers with clear proofs [signs], but they said: 'Shall mere men guide us?' So they disbelieved and turned away [from the truth]. But Allah was not in need [of them]. And Allah is Rich [Free of all needs], Worthy of all praise.﴾ *(Qur'an 64: 6)*

Today the *Shayṭaan* (Satan) whispers into human minds, calling them to rebel against Allah and against the shari'ah of Allah and to reject the teachings of the Messengers, on the grounds that the shari'ah of Allah places restrictions on their minds and is an obstacle against progress, that it causes civilization and progress to stagnate. The nations nowadays have set up systems, laws and legislation based on rejection of the teachings of the Messengers. Some nations even made atheism the basis of their constitutions - known as secularism. Many governments which control the affairs of the Muslims are following such a path. They may include a clause in the constitution just to please the common people, saying that the state religion is Islam, but then this clause is cancelled out by the preceding and following clauses and by the laws which govern the people.

Is it right to say that mankind has now reached a level where they no longer have any need for the Messengers and their teachings? Is mankind now able to guide itself without any reference to the teachings of the Messengers?

To answer that, we need to look no further than the state of those nations which we call advanced and civilized, such as America, Britain, France, Russia and China, to see the extent of the misery which prevails in those countries. We do not deny that they have reached a high level of material advancement, but with regard to the matters which the Messengers and their teachings came to reform, they have gone far astray. No one can deny that distress, psychological pain and complexes are nowadays the hallmark of the civilized world. Man in the civilized world of today has lost his humanity, he has lost himself. Hence the youths are rebelling. They are rebelling against values, morals, customs and laws. They have started to reject the life they are living in and to follow everyone who makes noise in the east or the west, any philosopher or dervish who waves a banner at them, any way which they think will bring them happiness. The western world has turned into a world whose structure is being undermined by crime, which is led by deviation and a sense of loss. The pillars of the major nations have been shaken by scandals, and what is still hidden is worse than what is known. Those who are known as civilized peoples nowadays are destroying themselves with their own hands. Their civilization is killing them. Their civilization is producing poisons which spread amongst them, killing people, dividing societies. Those who are known as civilized peoples are like a huge bird that wants to fly high in the sky, but it has only one wing.

We need the Messengers and their teachings in order to reform our hearts, enlighten our souls and guide our minds...

We need the Messengers in order to give direction to our lives, to connect us to life and to the Creator of life.

We need the Messengers so that we do not go astray or deviate and fall into the fetid swamp.

A valuable comment from Ibn al-Qayyim

Ibn al-Qayyim said, explaining how people need the Messengers and their teachings: "Hence we know that above all else, people need to know about the Messenger and the message he brought, to believe what he told us and to obey what he enjoined upon us, because there is no way to attain happiness and success, either in this world or in the Hereafter, except at the hands of the Messengers. There is no way to know about good and evil in detail except through them. No one can attain the pleasure of Allah at all except through following their teachings. Good words, deeds and attitudes can only be attained through their guidance and the teachings they brought. They are the standard example: attitudes, manners and actions are to be measured against their words and attitudes. Following them makes the people of misguidance stand out. So our need for them is greater than the body's need for the soul, or the need of the eye for light, or the soul's need for its life. Whatever need or necessity you may think of, a person's need for the Messengers is many times greater. What do you think of the importance of a Prophet who, if his guidance goes away from you even for an instant, your heart will be corrupted, and you will be like a fish taken out of the water and placed in the frying pan? This is the state of man when he deviates from the way of the Messenger. Indeed he is much worse off, but no one realizes this except one in whose heart there is life, for the dead person does not feel the pain of a wound. Because a person's happiness in this world and in the Hereafter is connected to the guidance of the Prophet (ﷺ), then each person who is sincere with himself and who wants to attain salvation and happiness has to know enough about his (the Prophet's) teachings, biography and way to ensure that he is not one of those who are ignorant of him so that he be included among his followers and his party. People vary with regard to this: some follow a little, some follow a lot and some are deprived completely. Bounty is in the hand of Allah; He gives to whomsoever He wills, and Allah is the Owner of great bounty."[1]

---

[1] *Zaad al-Ma'ad*, 1/15.

Ibn Taymiyah explains the need for the Messengers and the Message

Among those who explained this matter was *Shaykh al-Islam* Ibn Taymiyah (may Allah have mercy on him), who said:

"The Message is essential for mankind; they cannot do without it. They need it above all other things. The message is the soul, light and life of the world. How could there be any prosperity or guidance for the world without its soul, life and light? This world is cursed with darkness, unless the sun of the message shines upon it. If the sun of the message does not shine in a person's heart and fill it with life, then he too is in darkness and he is dead. Allah (ﷻ) says:

﴿ أَوَمَن كَانَ مَيْتًا فَأَحْيَيْنَٰهُ وَجَعَلْنَا لَهُۥ نُورًا يَمْشِى بِهِۦ فِى ٱلنَّاسِ كَمَن مَّثَلُهُۥ فِى ٱلظُّلُمَٰتِ لَيْسَ بِخَارِجٍ مِّنْهَا ... (١٢٢) ﴾

﴿Is he who was dead [without Faith by ignorance and disbelief] and We gave him life [by knowledge and Faith] and set for him a light [of Belief] whereby he can walk amongst men - like him who is in the darkness [of disbelief, polytheism and hypocrisy] from which he can never come out?...﴾ *(Qur'an 6: 122)*

This is the description of the believer who was dead in the darkness of ignorance, then Allah revived him with the spirit of the Message and the light of faith, gave him light by which to walk among people. But the *kaafir* is dead at heart, walking in darkness."

And he explained: "Allah called His Message *rooḥ* (soul), and if the *rooḥ* is absent then there is no life. Allah (ﷻ) says:

﴿ وَكَذَٰلِكَ أَوْحَيْنَآ إِلَيْكَ رُوحًا مِّنْ أَمْرِنَا ۚ مَا كُنتَ تَدْرِى مَا ٱلْكِتَٰبُ وَلَا ٱلْإِيمَٰنُ وَلَٰكِن جَعَلْنَٰهُ نُورًا نَّهْدِى بِهِۦ مَن نَّشَآءُ مِنْ عِبَادِنَا ۚ ... (٥٢) ﴾

﴾And thus We have sent to you [O' Muhammad] *Rooḥ* [a revelation, and a mercy] of Our Command. You knew not what is the Book, nor what is Faith? But We have made it [this Qur'an] a light wherewith We guide whosoever of Our slaves We will...﴿ *(Qur'an 42: 52)*

Here He mentions two elements, *rooḥ* and light. *Rooḥ* means life, and light means light."

And he explains: "Allah gives an allegory of the revelation which He sent down, likening it to life and light in the heart, to the water which He sends down from the sky to revive the earth, and to fire which produces light. This is as He (ﷻ) says:

﴿ أَنزَلَ مِنَ ٱلسَّمَآءِ مَآءً فَسَالَتْ أَوْدِيَةٌۢ بِقَدَرِهَا فَٱحْتَمَلَ ٱلسَّيْلُ زَبَدًا رَّابِيًا ۚ وَمِمَّا يُوقِدُونَ عَلَيْهِ فِى ٱلنَّارِ ٱبْتِغَآءَ حِلْيَةٍ أَوْ مَتَٰعٍ زَبَدٌ مِّثْلُهُۥ ۚ كَذَٰلِكَ يَضْرِبُ ٱللَّهُ ٱلْحَقَّ وَٱلْبَٰطِلَ ۚ فَأَمَّا ٱلزَّبَدُ فَيَذْهَبُ جُفَآءً ۖ وَأَمَّا مَا يَنفَعُ ٱلنَّاسَ فَيَمْكُثُ فِى ٱلْأَرْضِ ۚ كَذَٰلِكَ يَضْرِبُ ٱللَّهُ ٱلْأَمْثَالَ ﴿١٧﴾ ﴾

﴾He sends down water [rain] from the sky, and the valleys flow according to their measure, but the flood bears away the foam that mounts up to the surface - and [also] from that [ore] which they heat in the fire in order to make ornaments or utensils, rises a foam like unto it, thus does Allah [by parables] show forth truth and falsehood. Then, as for the foam it passes away as scum upon the banks, while that which is for the good of mankind remains in the earth. Thus Allah sets forth parables [for the truth and falsehood, i.e. Belief and disbelief].﴿ *(Qur'an 13: 17)*."

Shaykh al-Islam Ibn Taymiyah says, commenting on this *aayah* (verse): "Knowledge is likened to the rain that comes down from the sky, because it brings life to the heart just as the water sustains life and revives bodies. Hearts are likened to valleys because they are the places where knowledge resides, just as the valleys are the places where water resides. The heart may contain a great amount of knowledge just as a valley may contain a great amount of water; or the heart may contain a little knowledge just as a valley may contain a little water. Allah tells us that foam or scum rises to the surface of the water and is carried away, and that which benefits people stays in the land and settles there. Similarly the heart is mixed with doubts and desires, then they are thrown away, and faith and the Qur'an remain there, which benefits the person and others too. Allah (ﷻ) says: ﴿...And [also] from that [ore] which they heat in the fire in order to make ornaments or utensils, rises a foam like unto it, thus does Allah [by parables] show forth truth and falsehood...﴾ *(Qur'an 13: 17)*

This is another allegory, related to fire. The first referred to life and the second to light. He explains that something similar to these two examples is mentioned elsewhere: "These are the two examples mentioned in *Soorah al-Baqarah* (the 2nd chapter of the Qur'an), where Allah (ﷻ) says:

﴿ مَثَلُهُمْ كَمَثَلِ ٱلَّذِى ٱسْتَوْقَدَ نَارًا فَلَمَّآ أَضَآءَتْ مَا حَوْلَهُۥ ذَهَبَ ٱللَّهُ
بِنُورِهِمْ وَتَرَكَهُمْ فِى ظُلُمَٰتٍ لَّا يُبْصِرُونَ ﴿١٧﴾ صُمٌّۢ بُكْمٌ عُمْىٌ فَهُمْ لَا
يَرْجِعُونَ ﴿١٨﴾ أَوْ كَصَيِّبٍ مِّنَ ٱلسَّمَآءِ فِيهِ ظُلُمَٰتٌ وَرَعْدٌ وَبَرْقٌ يَجْعَلُونَ
أَصَٰبِعَهُمْ فِىٓ ءَاذَانِهِم مِّنَ ٱلصَّوَٰعِقِ حَذَرَ ٱلْمَوْتِ ۚ وَٱللَّهُ مُحِيطٌۢ بِٱلْكَٰفِرِينَ ﴿١٩﴾ ﴾

﴿Their likeness is as the likeness of one who kindled a fire; then, when it lighted all around him, Allah took away their light and left them in darkness. [So] they could not see. They are deaf, dumb, and blind, so they return not [to the Right Path]. Or like a rainstorm from the sky, wherein is darkness, thunder, and lightning. They thrust their fingers in their ears to keep out the stunning thunderclap for fear of death. But Allah ever encompasses the disbelievers [i.e. Allah will gather them all together].﴾ *(Qur'an 2: 17-19).*"

After explaining how the believer is described, the *Shaykh* said: "And as for the *kaafir* (disbeliever), he is in darkness, *kufr* and *shirk*, and is not alive. If he is alive, then his is a bestial life. He has no sublime spiritual life which is brought about by faith and which brings a person happiness and success in this world and in the Hereafter. Allah has made His Messengers mediators between Him and His slaves, to tell what will benefit them and what will harm them, and to complete their knowledge of what is good for them in this world and in the Hereafter. He sent them all to call people to Allah and to show them the way to Him, and to tell them what will happen to them in the Hereafter."

Then he explained these basic principles which are referred to here:

"The first principle is affirming the divine attributes, *Tawḥeed* (oneness of deity) and the divine decree, referring to the Days of Allah when He will recompense His friends and His enemies. These are the stories which Allah tells to His slaves and the parables which He sets forth to them.

The second principle is giving details of the laws, commands, prohibitions and permissions, explaining what Allah likes and what He hates. The third principle is belief in the Last Day, Paradise and Hell, and reward and punishment."

He then explains that,

"These three principles are the focal point of creation and commandment, and happiness and success depend on them. There is no way of knowing them except through the Messengers, for reason alone cannot guide a person to their details or knowledge of their realities, even though the mind may realize the necessity of these principles in general, just as a sick person may realize that he needs medicine and someone who can treat him, but he does not know the details of his sickness or how it is to be treated."[2]

Comparison between the need of the body for knowledge of medicine and the need of the body and soul for knowledge of the Messengers

In his book *Miftaaḥ Daar as-Sa'aadah* (Key to the Abode of Bliss), Ibn al-Qayyim made a comparison in which he stated that people's need for shari'ah is greater than their need for knowledge of medicine, even though people's need for the latter is so essential for the well-being of their bodies. Their need for the message is greater than their need for any other kind of knowledge. He said: "People's need for shari'ah is essential, greater than their need for anything else. The need for shari'ah cannot be compared to the need for medicine. Do you not see that most people live without doctors, and that doctors can only be found in the big cities? All the Bedouin and all the people living in remote villages, most of the children of Adam, have no need for doctors. They are physically better off and of a stronger constitution than those who go to doctors, and their life expectancy is the same. Allah has given the sons of Adam the instinct to consume that which will benefit them and to avoid that which will harm them. Each people has been given customs and traditions which tell them how to deal with the diseases that may attack them, so that many of the principles of medicine are based on people's customs, traditions and experience.

But shari'ah is based on the definition of knowing what pleases Allah or angers Him, in matters where people have been given a choice. It is based on pure Revelation. The need for that is greater than the need for breathing, let alone the need for food and drink (because such

[2] The previous quotes on this topic are taken from *Majmoo' al-Fataawa Shaykh al-Islam*, 9/93-96.

needs are not on the same level as the need for shari'ah), because the worst that can happen when one is deprived of air, food and drink is the death of the body and the separation of the soul from it. But the worst that can happen when one is deprived of shari'ah is the total corruption of the heart and soul, and eternal doom. There is a vast difference between this and the death of the body. People do not need anything more than they need to know what the Messenger (ﷺ) brought and to follow it and call others to it, to persevere in doing so, and to strive against those who deviate from it until they return to it. People cannot be sound without that at all. There is no way to attain happiness and the greater victory except by going through that."[3]

Is it possible for reason to do without Revelation?

People nowadays claim that they are able to do without the Messengers and their Message by means of the reason that Allah (ﷻ) has bestowed upon them. Hence we see them promulgating laws, dictating what is permitted and what is forbidden, planning and directing that as they wish, basing all of that on their reason, what they think is right or wrong, and what they approve of or disapprove of. They have their predecessors who said the same things - namely the Brahmins, a sect among the Magians (Zoroastrians) - who claimed that sending the Messengers was a folly which did not befit the Most Wise, because reason had no need for the Messengers, because if what the Messengers brought suited their reason, they would do it, even if that was not dictated by revelation, and if it went against their reason, then if they needed it, they would do it, otherwise they would not.[4]

In the heat of debate and argument, the Muslim should not hasten to deny the ability of reason to recognize what is good or evil. "Allah

---

[3] *Miftaaḥ Daar as-Sa'aadah*, 2/2.

[4] *Lawaami' al-Anwaar al-Bahiyah*, 2/256.

has given His slaves the instinct to differentiate between good and evil. He has instilled this ability in their reason, the ability to distinguish between the two, just as He has given them the instinct to differentiate between what is beneficial and what is harmful, what suits them and what does not. He has given them the faculties to understand all that and to differentiate between these kinds of things.

The first instinct (which gives people the ability to differentiate between good and evil) is the quality of man that sets him apart from other animals. The second instinct (which enables man to differentiate between what is beneficial and what is harmful) is something which is shared by all kinds of animals."[5]

We should note the following:

1) There are some matters which are in man's best interests, but man cannot come to know them on the basis of reason alone, because they do not fall within the capabilities of his reason. "How can reason know Allah and His names and attributes? How can reason know the details of His laws and His religion which He has prescribed for His slaves? How can reason know the details of what He loves and is pleased with, what angers Him and what He dislikes? How can reason know the details of His reward and punishments, what He has prepared for His friends and what He has prepared for His enemies, the extent and degrees of those rewards and punishments? How can reason know the matters of the unseen which Allah does not tell to any of His creation except the Messengers whom He chose... and other matters which the Messengers brought and conveyed from Allah, which reason has no way of knowing?"[6]

2) When reason recognizes that something is good or bad, it understands that in general terms. It cannot understand it in details as

---

[5] *Miftaaḥ Daar as-Sa'aadah*, 2/116.

[6] *Miftaaḥ Daar as-Sa'aadah*, Pp. 117.

brought by shari'ah. Even if it does understand some details, it is limited to a few details; that is not a comprehensive understanding. "Reason can recognize the beauty of justice, but as to whether a specific action is just or unjust, this may be beyond the comprehension of reason in every single deed and action."[7]

3) Reason may become confused about some deeds, for a deed may include some good things and some bad things, and reason will not know whether its harm outweighs its benefit or vice versa. So reason would not be able to be decisive concerning that. Then shari'ah comes and explains it, and enjoins things where the benefits outweigh the harms, and forbids things where the harms outweigh the benefits. Similarly, in cases where an action may be beneficial to one person but harmful to another, and reason cannot reach a conclusion concerning that, shari'ah comes and explains the matter, so it instructs the one for whom it is beneficial to do it, and forbids the one for whom it is harmful. Similarly in cases where a matter appears outwardly to be harmful, but inwardly it is very beneficial, but reason could not reach that conclusion - shari'ah comes and explains the hidden benefits and tells us what outweighs what."[8]

Concerning this, Ibn Taymiyah said: "The Prophets brought that which could not be known by reason alone; they did not bring anything irrational (that could be rejected on the basis of reason). They told us of things which could not possibly be known by reason alone, but which do not go against reason."[9]

4) Whatever conclusions are reached by reason, even if they are correct, are no more than assumptions, which could be undermined by opposite opinions and the views of heretics.

---

[7] *Miftaaḥ Daar as-Sa'aadah*, 2/117.

[8] Ibid.

[9] *Majmoo' al-Fataawa Shaykh al-Islam*, 2/312.

Even if those conclusions survive that, if they are not based on revelation then they are mere speculation in which truth may be confused with falsehood.

The falseness of the Brahmins' view

There is no need to prove that the Brahmins are wrong when they say that reason has no need for revelation. All that we need to do is to point out the conclusion to which their reason, which they claim has no need for revelation, led them. This is what one of their leaders[10] in the twentieth century boasted: "When I see a cow, I do not see an animal, because I worship the cow and I will argue for cow-worship before the entire world." His reasoning led him to prefer his cow-mother to the mother who gave birth to him: "My cow-mother is better than my real mother in several ways. For our real mothers breastfeed us for one or two years, and expect lifelong service from us in return for that, but our cow-mothers give us milk all the time, and they do not ask for anything in return for that apart from ordinary food..." This cow-worshipper continued to compare between his cow-mother and his real mother, producing evidence to demonstrate the superiority of his cow-mother to his real mother, until he said, "Millions of Indians turn to the cow in worship and veneration, and I count myself as one of these millions."

A while ago I read in Al-'Arabi magazine, published from Kuwait, about a luxurious temple, covered with white marble, to which gifts and offerings are sent from throughout India. It only remains for you to know that the gods to whom these offerings are sent and to whom vows are made in this luxurious temple are... rats.

---

[10] This was the leader of India, Gandhi. See what he said in *Muqaaranat al-Adyaan*, 4/32 (*Naẓaraat fin-Nubuwwah*, Pp. 27).

These are some of the foolish notions to which they have been led by their reason, which they claim has no need for revelation.

Limits of reason's role

Those who want to do away with revelation do a great disservice to reason and waste the energies of reason in fields for which it is not suited. "Reason has its own specialized field; if it works outside that field, then it will go wrong and will become extremely confused. If it works outside its own field, it will stumble and will not be able to go far. If it is expected to do more than it is able to, this will result in failure and exhaustion.

The physical world and the realm of nature is the vast field of reason, where it may enjoy complete freedom in exploring its hidden treasures and in discovering the connections between cause and effect; it may explore and invent, and examine in depth the beneficial sciences in all spheres of life and make the wheel of human progress move forward.

But if it is given a task that lies outside its field, I mean beyond the field of nature, then after lengthy, exhausting study and examination it does not come back with a full answer or with anything that may solve the problem, rather it comes back with foolish ideas and weird notions."[11]

The position of reason in relation to revelation

Many people claim that revelation cancels out reason and extinguishes its light, causing it to become ineffective and lazy. This is a false claim, with no share of soundness. Divine revelation directs reason to examine and ponder the universe, it urges man to populate this earth and develop it. In the area of revealed knowledge the

---

[11] *Naẓaraat fin-Nubuwwah*, Pp. 17.

function of reason is to examine the revelation so as to be certain that it can indeed be attributed to Allah; once it is clear that it is sound, then one has to understand what the Revelation is saying to him, and use the reason which Allah bestowed upon him to understand and ponder the revelation, then strive one's utmost to apply it.

The relation of the revelation to reason is like that of the sun or light to the eye. If revelation is kept away from reason, man will not benefit from his reason, just as a person cannot benefit from his eyes if he lives in darkness, but when the sun sends its light, he is able to benefit from his eyes. So for those who are possessed of reason, when revelation shines on their minds and hearts, they see and are guided.

﴿... فَإِنَّهَا لَا تَعْمَى ٱلْأَبْصَٰرُ وَلَٰكِن تَعْمَى ٱلْقُلُوبُ ٱلَّتِى فِى ٱلصُّدُورِ ﴿٤٦﴾﴾

﴾...Verily, it is not the eyes that grow blind, but it is the hearts which are in the breasts that grow blind.﴿

(Qur'an 22: 46)

CHAPTER THREE
THE TASKS AND MISSIONS OF THE MESSENGERS

The Qur'an and Sunnah explain to us the mission and tasks of the Messengers, as we shall see below.

1 - CONVEYING THE MESSAGE CLEARLY

The Messengers are Allah's ambassadors to His slaves, the bearers of His revelation. Their primary mission is to convey this trust to the slaves of Allah. To quote the Qur'an:

﴿ ۞ يَـٰٓأَيُّهَا ٱلرَّسُولُ بَلِّغْ مَآ أُنزِلَ إِلَيْكَ مِن رَّبِّكَ ۖ وَإِن لَّمْ تَفْعَلْ فَمَا بَلَّغْتَ رِسَالَتَهُۥ ... ﴿٦٧﴾ ﴾

﴾O' Messenger [Muhammad]! Proclaim [the Message] which has been sent down to you from your Lord. And if you do not, then you have not conveyed His Message...﴿ *(Qur'an 5: 67)*

Conveying the Message needs a lot of courage but no fear from people when the message goes against their beliefs, telling them to do things which they find unacceptable and forbidding them to do things which they like and are used to:

﴿ ٱلَّذِينَ يُبَلِّغُونَ رِسَـٰلَـٰتِ ٱللَّهِ وَيَخْشَوْنَهُۥ وَلَا يَخْشَوْنَ أَحَدًا إِلَّا ٱللَّهَ ... ﴿٣٩﴾ ﴾

﴾Those who convey the Message of Allah and fear Him, and fear none save Allah...﴿ *(Qur'an 33: 39)*

Conveying the message may mean reciting the texts which Allah has revealed, without adding anything or taking anything away:

﴿ ... اَتْلُ مَآ أُوحِىَ إِلَيْكَ مِنَ ٱلْكِتَبِ ﴾ (٤٥)

﴿Recite [O' Muhammad] what has been revealed to you
of the Book [the Qur'an]...﴾   *(Qur'an 29: 45)*

﴿ ... كَمَآ أَرْسَلْنَا فِيكُمْ رَسُولًا مِّنكُمْ يَتْلُواْ عَلَيْكُمْ ءَايَٰتِنَا ... ﴾ (١٥١)

﴿Similarly [to complete My Blessings on you], We have
sent among you a Messenger [Muhammad] of your own,
reciting to you Our Verses [the Qur'an]...﴾
(Qur'an 2: 151)

If what is revealed is not a text that can be recited, then conveying the
message means explaining the commands and prohibitions, ideas and
knowledge which are revealed by Allah, without altering or changing
anything.

Conveying the message also means that the Messenger explains the
revelation which Allah (ﷻ) has sent down to His slaves, because he
is more able than anyone else to explain its meanings and objectives,
and he knows better than others what Allah meant by His revelation.
Concerning this Allah said to His Messenger (ﷺ):

﴿ ... وَأَنزَلْنَآ إِلَيْكَ ٱلذِّكْرَ لِتُبَيِّنَ لِلنَّاسِ مَا نُزِّلَ إِلَيْهِمْ وَلَعَلَّهُمْ
يَتَفَكَّرُونَ ﴾ (٤٤)

﴿...And We have also sent down unto you [O'
Muhammad] the *Dhikr* [reminder and the advice (i.e. the
Qur'an)], that you may explain clearly to men what is
sent down to them, and that they may give thought.﴾
(Qur'an 16: 44)

The Messenger's explanation of the divine revelation may take the
form of words. The Messenger (ﷺ) explained many matters which
his Companions found hard to understand, as when he explained the
meaning of the word *zulm* in the *aayah* (verse),

﴿ ٱلَّذِينَ ءَامَنُوا۟ وَلَمْ يَلْبِسُوٓا۟ إِيمَـٰنَهُم بِظُلْمٍ أُو۟لَـٰٓئِكَ لَهُمُ ٱلْأَمْنُ وَهُم مُّهْتَدُونَ ﴿٨٢﴾ ﴾

﴾It is those who believe [in the Oneness of Allah and worship none but Him Alone] and confuse not their Belief with *Ẓulm* [wrong, i.e. by worshipping others besides Allah], for them [only] there is security and they are the guided.﴿ *(Qur'an 6: 82)*

The Messenger (ﷺ) explained that what was meant here was *shirk*, not a person wronging himself by sinning.

The Messenger (ﷺ) also explained the *aayaat* (verses) which speak of Prayer, Zakah, Ḥajj etc. in words.

Just as the explanation may take the form of words, it may also take the form of actions. The actions of the Messenger (ﷺ) - in prayer, charity, Ḥajj and other things - explained the words of the Qur'anic texts.

If people turn away from the call of the Messengers and ignore it, the Messengers are not able to do more than convey the message:

﴿ ... وَإِن تَوَلَّوْا۟ فَإِنَّمَا عَلَيْكَ ٱلْبَلَـٰغُ ... ﴿٢٠﴾ ﴾

﴾...But if they turn away, your duty is only to convey the Message...﴿ *(Qur'an 3: 20)*

2 - CALLING PEOPLE TO ALLAH

The role of the Messengers is not limited only to explaining the truth and conveying the message. They also have to invite people to follow their call and respond to it, to apply it to themselves in belief, word and deed. In this regard they all set out from the same starting point. They all tell the people, you are the slaves of Allah, and Allah is your Lord and God. Allah has sent us to teach you how to worship Him, because we are the Messengers of Allah, sent by Him, so you have to obey us and follow us.

﴿ وَلَقَدْ بَعَثْنَا فِى كُلِّ أُمَّةٍ رَّسُولًا أَنِ ٱعْبُدُوا۟ ٱللَّهَ وَٱجْتَنِبُوا۟ ٱلطَّٰغُوتَ ... ﴿٣٦﴾ ﴾

﴿And verily, We have sent among every Ummah [community, nation] a Messenger [proclaiming]: 'Worship Allah [Alone], and avoid [or keep away from] *Ṭaaghoot* [all false deities, i.e. do not worship *Ṭaaghoot* besides Allah]'...﴾ *(Qur'an 16: 36)*

﴿ وَمَآ أَرْسَلْنَا مِن قَبْلِكَ مِن رَّسُولٍ إِلَّا نُوحِىٓ إِلَيْهِ أَنَّهُۥ لَآ إِلَٰهَ إِلَّآ أَنَا۠ فَٱعْبُدُونِ ﴿٢٥﴾ ﴾

﴿And We did not send any Messenger before you [O' Muhammad] but We revealed to him [saying]: '*Laa ilaaha illa Ana* [none has the right to be worshipped but I (Allah)], so worship Me [Alone and none else].'﴾ *(Qur'an 21: 25)*

Every Messenger said to his people:

﴿ فَٱتَّقُوا۟ ٱللَّهَ وَأَطِيعُونِ ﴿١٠٨﴾ ﴾

﴿So fear Allah, keep your duty to Him, and obey me.﴾ *(Qur'an 26: 108, 110, 126, 131, 144, 150, 163, 179)*

The Messengers strove their utmost to call people to Allah. It is sufficient for you to read *Soorah Nooḥ* (the 71st chapter of the Qur'an) in order to understand the efforts which he made for nine hundred and fifty years, calling them night and day, in secret and openly, using all methods of encouraging and warning, promises and threats, trying to open their hearts to see the signs that exist in the universe, but they turned away:

﴿ قَالَ نُوحٌ رَّبِّ إِنَّهُمْ عَصَوْنِي وَٱتَّبَعُوا۟ مَن لَّمْ يَزِدْهُ مَالُهُۥ وَوَلَدُهُۥٓ إِلَّا خَسَارًا ﴿٢١﴾ ﴾

﴿Nooḥ [Noah] said: 'My Lord! They have disobeyed me, and followed one whose wealth and children give him no increase but loss.'﴾ *(Qur'an 71: 21)*

Examples which make the Messengers' role clear

The angels coined likenesses for the Messenger (ﷺ) which explain his role and his task. According to a hadith:

> "I saw in a dream that Jibreel (Gabriel) was standing at my head and Mikaa'eel was standing at my feet. One of them said to the other, 'Coin a likeness for him.' He said, 'Listen and understand. The likeness of you and your ummah is like that of a king who has a house, in which he builds a room, where he places a table filled with food. He sends a Messenger to invite the people to share his food. Some of them respond to the messenger and others do not. Allah is the King, the house is Islam, the room is Paradise, you, O' Muhammad, are the Messenger. Whoever responds to you enters Islam, and whoever enters Islam will enter Paradise, and whoever enters Paradise will eat of whatever is there.'"

- This has been narrated by Bukhari and Tirmidhi.[1]

3 - BRINGING GLAD TIDINGS AND WARNINGS

The call of the Messengers to Allah is always accompanied by glad tidings and warnings, because there is a very strong connection between the call to Allah and glad tidings and warnings. Therefore

[1] *Ṣaḥeeḥ al-Jaami'*, 2/319.

the Qur'an limits the mission of the Messengers to these two things in some verses:

﴿ وَمَا نُرْسِلُ ٱلْمُرْسَلِينَ إِلَّا مُبَشِّرِينَ وَمُنذِرِينَ ... ﴿٥٦﴾ ﴾

﴾And We send not the Messengers except as givers of glad tidings and warners...﴿ *(Qur'an 18: 56)*

The Messenger (ﷺ) coined a similar likeness for himself, when he said:

"My likeness and that of the message with which Allah has sent me is that of a man who comes to some people and says, 'O' people, I have seen the army with my own eyes, and I am a clear warner, so save yourselves!' So some of his people obey him and flee by night, they move at their own pace and are saved; and some of them disbelieve him, so they stay where they are, and the next morning the army comes upon them and destroys them. This is the likeness of the one who obeys me and follows the message I have brought, and the likeness of the one who disobeys me and disbelieves in the message of truth that I have brought." (Bukhari and Muslim)[2]

The glad tidings and warnings which the Messengers bring apply both to this world and the Hereafter. In this world they bring glad tidings to the obedient of a good life:

﴿ مَنْ عَمِلَ صَٰلِحًا مِّن ذَكَرٍ أَوْ أُنثَىٰ وَهُوَ مُؤْمِنٌ فَلَنُحْيِيَنَّهُۥ حَيَوٰةً طَيِّبَةً ... ﴿٩٧﴾ ﴾

﴾Whoever works righteousness - whether male or female - while he [or she] is a true believer [of Islamic

[2] *Ṣaḥeeḥ al-Jaami'*, 5/205.

Monotheism] verily, to him We will give a good life [in this world with respect, contentment and lawful provision]...﴾ *(Qur'an 16: 97)*

﴿ ... فَمَنِ ٱتَّبَعَ هُدَاىَ فَلَا يَضِلُّ وَلَا يَشْقَىٰ ﴿١٢٣﴾ ﴾

﴿...Then whoever follows My Guidance he shall neither go astray, nor shall be distressed.﴾ *(Qur'an 20: 123)*

And they promise them glory, power and security:

﴿ وَعَدَ ٱللَّهُ ٱلَّذِينَ ءَامَنُوا۟ مِنكُمْ وَعَمِلُوا۟ ٱلصَّـٰلِحَـٰتِ لَيَسْتَخْلِفَنَّهُمْ فِى ٱلْأَرْضِ كَمَا ٱسْتَخْلَفَ ٱلَّذِينَ مِن قَبْلِهِمْ وَلَيُمَكِّنَنَّ لَهُمْ دِينَهُمُ ٱلَّذِى ٱرْتَضَىٰ لَهُمْ وَلَيُبَدِّلَنَّهُم مِّنۢ بَعْدِ خَوْفِهِمْ أَمْنًا ۚ يَعْبُدُونَنِى لَا يُشْرِكُونَ بِى شَيْـًٔا ۚ ... ﴿٥٥﴾ ﴾

﴿Allah has promised those among you who believe and do righteous good deeds, that He will certainly grant them succession to [the present rulers] in the land, as He granted it to those before them, and that He will grant them the authority to practise their religion which He has chosen for them [i.e. Islam]. And He will surely, give them in exchange a safe security after their fear [provided] they [believers] worship Me and do not associate anything [in worship] with Me...﴾

(Qur'an 24: 55)

They seek to scare the sinners with loss in this world:

﴿ وَمَنْ أَعْرَضَ عَن ذِكْرِى فَإِنَّ لَهُۥ مَعِيشَةً ضَنكًا ... ﴿١٢٤﴾ ﴾

﴿But whosoever turns away from My Reminder [i.e. neither believes in this Qur'an nor act on its teachings] verily, for him is a life of hardship...﴾

(Qur'an 20: 124)

And they warn them of punishment and doom in this world:

﴿ فَإِنْ أَعْرَضُوا فَقُلْ أَنذَرْتُكُمْ صَٰعِقَةً مِّثْلَ صَٰعِقَةِ عَادٍ وَثَمُودَ ﴿١٣﴾ ﴾

﴾But if they turn away, then say [O' Muhammad]: 'I have warned you of a *Ṣaa'iqah* [a destructive awful cry, torment, hit, thunderbolt] like the *Ṣaa'iqah* which overtook 'Aad and Thamood [people].﴿ *(Qur'an 41: 13)*

And they give glad tidings to the obedient of Paradise and its blessings in the Hereafter:

﴿ ... وَمَن يُطِعِ ٱللَّهَ وَرَسُولَهُۥ يُدْخِلْهُ جَنَّٰتٍ تَجْرِى مِن تَحْتِهَا ٱلْأَنْهَٰرُ خَٰلِدِينَ فِيهَا ۚ وَذَٰلِكَ ٱلْفَوْزُ ٱلْعَظِيمُ ﴿١٣﴾ ﴾

﴾...Whosoever obeys Allah and His Messenger [Muhammad] will be admitted to Gardens under which rivers flow [in Paradise], to abide therein, and that will be the great success.﴿ *(Qur'an 4: 13)*

They scare the evildoers and sinners with warnings of Allah's punishment in the Hereafter:

﴿ وَمَن يَعْصِ ٱللَّهَ وَرَسُولَهُۥ وَيَتَعَدَّ حُدُودَهُۥ يُدْخِلْهُ نَارًا خَٰلِدًا فِيهَا وَلَهُۥ عَذَابٌ مُّهِينٌ ﴿١٤﴾ ﴾

﴾And whosoever disobeys Allah and His Messenger [Muhammad], and transgresses His limits, He will cast him into the Fire, to abide therein; and he shall have a disgraceful torment.﴿ *(Qur'an 4: 14)*

Whoever studies the calls of the Messengers will find that their call is characterized by glad tidings and warnings. It seems that glad tidings and warnings, as they were brought by the Messengers, are the key to the human soul. The human soul has a natural desire to seek good for its own sake, and to ward off evil from itself. When the Messengers explain to people the great good which they could attain through faith and righteous deeds, then human souls strive to attain that, and when they explain the great harm that befalls man as a result of *kufr* (disbelief) and misguidance, then people try to keep away from such things. The joy and blessings of Allah, of which the Messengers gave glad tidings, is a joy that is immense and wondrous. Listen to what Allah says, describing the blessed state of the believers in the Paradise of delight:

﴿عَلَىٰ سُرُرٖ مَّوۡضُونَةٖ ١٥ مُّتَّكِـِٔينَ عَلَيۡهَا مُتَقَٰبِلِينَ ١٦ يَطُوفُ عَلَيۡهِمۡ وِلۡدَٰنٞ
مُّخَلَّدُونَ ١٧ بِأَكۡوَابٖ وَأَبَارِيقَ وَكَأۡسٖ مِّن مَّعِينٖ ١٨ لَّا يُصَدَّعُونَ عَنۡهَا وَلَا يُنزِفُونَ
١٩ وَفَٰكِهَةٖ مِّمَّا يَتَخَيَّرُونَ ٢٠ وَلَحۡمِ طَيۡرٖ مِّمَّا يَشۡتَهُونَ ٢١ وَحُورٌ عِينٞ
٢٢ كَأَمۡثَٰلِ ٱللُّؤۡلُوِ ٱلۡمَكۡنُونِ ٢٣ جَزَآءَۢ بِمَا كَانُواْ يَعۡمَلُونَ ٢٤ لَا يَسۡمَعُونَ
فِيهَا لَغۡوٗا وَلَا تَأۡثِيمًا ٢٥ إِلَّا قِيلٗا سَلَٰمٗا سَلَٰمٗا ٢٦ وَأَصۡحَٰبُ ٱلۡيَمِينِ مَآ أَصۡحَٰبُ
ٱلۡيَمِينِ ٢٧ فِي سِدۡرٖ مَّخۡضُودٖ ٢٨ وَطَلۡحٖ مَّنضُودٖ ٢٩ وَظِلّٖ مَّمۡدُودٖ ٣٠
وَمَآءٖ مَّسۡكُوبٖ ٣١ وَفَٰكِهَةٖ كَثِيرَةٖ ٣٢ لَّا مَقۡطُوعَةٖ وَلَا مَمۡنُوعَةٖ ٣٣
وَفُرُشٖ مَّرۡفُوعَةٍ ٣٤ إِنَّآ أَنشَأۡنَٰهُنَّ إِنشَآءٗ ٣٥ فَجَعَلۡنَٰهُنَّ أَبۡكَارًا ٣٦ عُرُبًا أَتۡرَابٗا
٣٧ لِّأَصۡحَٰبِ ٱلۡيَمِينِ ٣٨﴾

﴾[They will be] on thrones woven with gold and precious stones. Reclining thereon, face to face. Immortal boys will go around them [serving], with cups, and jugs, and a glass of flowing wine, wherefrom they will get neither any aching of the head nor any intoxication. And with fruit that they may choose. And with the flesh of fowls that they desire. And [there will be] Ḥoor [fair females] with wide lovely eyes [as wives for *Al-Muttaqoon* - the pious]. Like unto preserved pearls. A reward for what they used to do. No *Laghw* [dirty, false, evil vain talk] will they hear therein, nor any sinful speech [like backbiting]. But only the saying of: *Salaam! Salaam!* [greetings with peace]! And those on the Right Hand - how [fortunate] will be those on the Right Hand? [They will be] among thornless lote trees, and among *Ṭalḥ* [banana trees] with fruits piled one above another, and in shade long-extended, and by water flowing constantly, and fruit in plenty, whose supply is not cut off [by change of season] nor are they out of reach. and on couches or thrones, raised high. Verily, We have created them [maidens] of special creation. And made them virgins. Loving [their husbands only], [and] of equal age. For those on the Right Hand.﴿

(Qur'an 56: 15-38)

Look at the punishment of the *kuffaar* (disbelievers) in the abode of doom:

﴿ وَأَصْحَٰبُ ٱلشِّمَالِ مَآ أَصْحَٰبُ ٱلشِّمَالِ ﴿٤١﴾ فِى سَمُومٍ وَحَمِيمٍ ﴿٤٢﴾ وَظِلٍّ مِّن يَحْمُومٍ ﴿٤٣﴾ لَّا بَارِدٍ وَلَا كَرِيمٍ ﴿٤٤﴾ إِنَّهُمْ كَانُوا۟ قَبْلَ ذَٰلِكَ مُتْرَفِينَ ﴿٤٥﴾ ﴾

﴾And those on the left hand - how [unfortunate] will be those on the Left Hand? In fierce hot wind and boiling water, and shadow of black smoke, [that shadow] neither cool, nor [even] pleasant, verily, before that, they indulged in luxury.﴿ *(Qur'an 56: 41-45)*

﴿ ثُمَّ إِنَّكُمْ أَيُّهَا ٱلضَّآلُّونَ ٱلْمُكَذِّبُونَ ﴿٥١﴾ لَءَاكِلُونَ مِن شَجَرٍ مِّن زَقُّومٍ ﴿٥٢﴾ فَمَالِـُٔونَ مِنْهَا ٱلْبُطُونَ ﴿٥٣﴾ فَشَٰرِبُونَ عَلَيْهِ مِنَ ٱلْحَمِيمِ ﴿٥٤﴾ فَشَٰرِبُونَ شُرْبَ ٱلْهِيمِ ﴿٥٥﴾ هَٰذَا نُزُلُهُمْ يَوْمَ ٱلدِّينِ ﴿٥٦﴾ ﴾

﴾Then moreover, verily, - you the erring-ones, the deniers [of Resurrection]! You verily, will eat of the trees of *Zaqqoom*. Then you will fill your bellies therewith, and drink boiling water on top of it. And you will drink

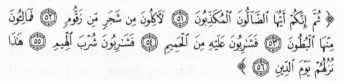

[that] like thirsty camels! That will be their entertainment on the Day of Recompense!﴿ *(Qur'an 56: 51-56)*

It is sufficient for you to study the book *At-Targheeb wat-Tarheeb* by Al-Ḥaafiẓ al-Mundhiri, and read from it to your brothers and those whom you are calling to Allah, then see what effect this has on yourself and on the hearts of the listeners.

Some of those who do not understand the call of Islam criticize the callers for their use of warnings and glad tidings. They say, "So and so is a preacher," and they condemn them for not being philosophical about the things to which they are calling people. They want the callers to refrain from preaching and scaring and encouraging people. They need to look at themselves and examine their own position in the light of the Qur'anic texts and the *aḥaadeeth* of the Messenger (ﷺ) which describe the methods of *da'wah* and explain the mission of the noble Messengers.

4 - REFORMING AND PURIFYING PEOPLE'S SOULS

Allah (ﷻ) is Most Merciful to His slaves. Part of that mercy is His reviving their souls through His revelation and illuminating them with His light:

﴿ وَكَذَٰلِكَ أَوْحَيْنَآ إِلَيْكَ رُوحًا مِّنْ أَمْرِنَاۚ مَا كُنتَ تَدْرِى مَا ٱلْكِتَٰبُ وَلَا ٱلْإِيمَٰنُ وَلَٰكِن جَعَلْنَٰهُ نُورًا نَّهْدِى بِهِۦ مَن نَّشَآءُ مِنْ عِبَادِنَاۚ ... ﴿٥٢﴾ ﴾

﴾And thus We have sent to you [O' Muhammad] *Rooḥ* [a revelation, and a mercy] of Our Command. You knew not what is the Book, nor what is Faith? But We have made it [this Qur'an] a light wherewith We guide whosoever of Our slaves We will...﴿ *(Qur'an 42: 52)*

Through this divine revelation, Allah brings people forth from darkness into Light, from the darkness of *kufr* (disbelief), *shirk* (polytheism) and ignorance into the light of Islam and truth.

﴿ ٱللَّهُ وَلِيُّ ٱلَّذِينَ ءَامَنُوا۟ يُخْرِجُهُم مِّنَ ٱلظُّلُمَـٰتِ إِلَى ٱلنُّورِ ... ﴿٢٥٧﴾ ﴾

﴾Allah is the *Wali* [Protector or Guardian] of those who believe. He brings them out from darkness into light...﴿ *(Qur'an 2: 257)*

Allah sent His Messengers with His guidance to bring forth the people from darkness into light. Allah (ﷻ) says:

﴿ وَلَقَدْ أَرْسَلْنَا مُوسَىٰ بِـَٔايَـٰتِنَآ أَنْ أَخْرِجْ قَوْمَكَ مِنَ ٱلظُّلُمَـٰتِ إِلَى ٱلنُّورِ ... ﴿٥﴾ ﴾

﴾And indeed We sent Moosa [Moses] with Our *Aayaat* [signs, proofs, and evidences] [saying]: 'Bring out your people from darkness into light'...﴿ *(Qur'an 14: 5)*

Without this light, hearts become blind. To quote the Qur'an:

﴿ ... فَإِنَّهَا لَا تَعْمَى ٱلْأَبْصَـٰرُ وَلَـٰكِن تَعْمَى ٱلْقُلُوبُ ٱلَّتِى فِى ٱلصُّدُورِ ﴿٤٦﴾ ﴾

﴾...Verily, it is not the eyes that grow blind, but it is the hearts which are in the breasts that grow blind.﴿ *(Qur'an 22: 46)*

Their blindness means their going astray from the truth, their forsaking that which will benefit them and their turning to that which will harm them.

﴿ وَيَعْبُدُونَ مِن دُونِ ٱللَّهِ مَا لَا يَنفَعُهُمْ وَلَا يَضُرُّهُمْ ... ﴿٥٥﴾ ﴾

﴾And they [disbelievers, polytheists] worship besides Allah, that which can neither profit them nor harm them...﴿ *(Qur'an 25: 55)*

The Messengers' bringing forth people from darkness to light can only be achieved by teaching them the guidance of their Lord, and purifying their souls by teaching them about their Lord and His names and attributes, and teaching them about His angels, His Books and His Messengers, and teaching them about what will benefit them and what will harm them, and showing them the path which will lead to His love, and teaching them how to worship Him. Allah (ﷻ) says:

﴿ هُوَ ٱلَّذِى بَعَثَ فِى ٱلْأُمِّيِّـۧنَ رَسُولًا مِّنْهُمْ يَتْلُوا۟ عَلَيْهِمْ ءَايَـٰتِهِۦ وَيُزَكِّيهِمْ وَيُعَلِّمُهُمُ ٱلْكِتَـٰبَ وَٱلْحِكْمَةَ وَإِن كَانُوا۟ مِن قَبْلُ لَفِى ضَلَـٰلٍ مُّبِينٍ ﴿٢﴾ ﴾

﴾He it is Who sent among the unlettered ones a Messenger [Muhammad] from among themselves, reciting to them His Verses, purifying them [from the filth of disbelief and polytheism], and teaching them the Book [this Qur'an, Islamic laws and Islamic jurisprudence] and *Al-Ḥikmah* [*As-Sunnah*: legal ways, orders, acts of worship of Prophet Muhammad]. And verily, they had been before in manifests error.﴿

(Qur'an 62: 2)

﴿ رَبَّنَا وَٱبْعَثْ فِيهِمْ رَسُولًا مِّنْهُمْ يَتْلُوا۟ عَلَيْهِمْ ءَايَـٰتِكَ ... ﴿١٢٩﴾ ﴾

﴾Our Lord! Send amongst them a Messenger of their own [and indeed Allah answered their invocation by sending Muhammad], who shall recite unto them Your Verses...﴿ *(Qur'an 2: 129)*

5 - CORRECTING DEVIANT IDEAS AND SPURIOUS BELIEFS

In the beginning, people were of sound nature, worshipping Allah Alone and not associating anyone with Him. But when they split up and became different from one another, Allah sent the Messengers to bring people back to the right path and to rescue them from misguidance:

﴿ كَانَ ٱلنَّاسُ أُمَّةً وَٰحِدَةً فَبَعَثَ ٱللَّهُ ٱلنَّبِيِّـۧنَ مُبَشِّرِينَ وَمُنذِرِينَ ... ﴿٢١٣﴾ ﴾

﴾Mankind were one community and Allah sent Prophets with glad tidings and warnings...﴿ *(Qur'an 2: 213)*

- i.e., mankind was one community, united in *Tawḥeed*, faith and worship of Allah, then they differed, and Allah sent the Prophets to bring glad tidings and warnings.

Each Messenger called his people to the straight path; he explained it to them and called them to follow it. This is something which all the Messengers had in common. And every Messenger corrected the deviation that was occuring in his time and in his land. There is no limit to deviation from the straight path, for it takes many forms. Each Messenger strove to correct the deviation that existed at his time. Prophet Nooḥ (Noah) denounced his people for worshipping idols, as did Prophet Ibraaheem (Abraham); Prophet Hood denounced his people for their arrogance and tyranny in the land; Prophet Ṣaaleḥ denounced them for their corruption in the land and for their following the corrupt; Prophet Looṭ (Lot) fought against the sin of sodomy which was widespread amongst his people; Prophet Shu'ayb fought against his people's practice of cheating in weights and measures, and so on. All of these sins and others which the nations committed go beyond the limits of the straight path and are a deviation from it. The Messengers explained this path and fought against deviation from it in any way.

6 - ESTABLISHING PROOF

There is no one to whom leaving no excuse is dearer than to Allah. Allah sent the Messengers and revealed the Books so that people would have no excuse on the Day of Resurrection:

﴿ رُّسُلًا مُّبَشِّرِينَ وَمُنذِرِينَ لِئَلَّا يَكُونَ لِلنَّاسِ عَلَى ٱللَّهِ حُجَّةٌ بَعْدَ ٱلرُّسُلِ ... ﴿١٦٥﴾ ﴾

﴾Messengers as bearers of good news as well as of warning in order that mankind should have no plea against Allah after the [coming of] Messengers...﴿
(Qur'an 4: 165)

If Allah did not send the Messengers, then the people would come on the Day of Resurrection disputing with Allah and saying: "How can You punish us and send us to Hell when You did not send to us anyone who could tell us what You wanted of us?" As Allah (ﷻ) says:

﴿ وَلَوْ أَنَّآ أَهْلَكْنَٰهُم بِعَذَابٍ مِّن قَبْلِهِۦ لَقَالُوا۟ رَبَّنَا لَوْلَآ أَرْسَلْتَ إِلَيْنَا رَسُولًا فَنَتَّبِعَ ءَايَٰتِكَ مِن قَبْلِ أَن نَّذِلَّ وَنَخْزَىٰ ﴿١٣٤﴾ ﴾

﴾And if We had destroyed them with a torment before this [i.e. Messenger Muhammad and the Qur'an], they would surely, have said: 'Our Lord! If only You had sent us a Messenger, we should certainly have followed Your *Aayaat* [proofs, evidences, verses, lessons, signs, revelations, etc.], before we were humiliated and disgraced'﴿
(Qur'an 20: 134)

- i.e., if Allah had destroyed them with a punishment because of their *kufr* before He had sent a Messenger to them, they would have said: "Why did You not send us a Messenger so that we could have known what You wanted of us and we could have followed Your signs and followed the path You wanted."

On the Day of Resurrection, when Allah gathers together the first and the last, Allah will bring to each nation its Messenger so that he may testify against them that he conveyed the Message of his Lord, and establish proof against them. The Qur'an tells us:

﴿ فَكَيْفَ إِذَا جِئْنَا مِن كُلِّ أُمَّةٍ بِشَهِيدٍ وَجِئْنَا بِكَ عَلَىٰ هَٰٓؤُلَآءِ
شَهِيدًا ﴿٤١﴾ يَوْمَئِذٍ يَوَدُّ ٱلَّذِينَ كَفَرُوا۟ وَعَصَوُا۟ ٱلرَّسُولَ لَوْ تُسَوَّىٰ بِهِمُ
ٱلْأَرْضُ وَلَا يَكْتُمُونَ ٱللَّهَ حَدِيثًا ﴿٤٢﴾ ﴾

﴾How [will it be] then, when We bring from each nation a witness and We bring you [O' Muhammad] as a witness against these people? On that day those who disbelieved and disobeyed the Messenger [Muhammad] will wish that they were buried in the earth, but they will never be able to hide a single fact from Allah.﴿

(Qur'an 4: 41-42)

﴿ وَيَوْمَ نَبْعَثُ فِى كُلِّ أُمَّةٍ شَهِيدًا عَلَيْهِم مِّنْ أَنفُسِهِمْ ۖ وَجِئْنَا بِكَ
شَهِيدًا عَلَىٰ هَٰٓؤُلَآءِ ... ﴿٨٩﴾ ﴾

﴾And [remember] the Day when We shall raise up from every nation a witness against them from amongst themselves. And We shall bring you [O' Muhammad] as a witness against these...﴿ *(Qur'an 16: 89)*

Hence those who refused to follow the Messengers and turned away from their guidance will not be able to do anything but admit their wrongdoing when punishment befell them in this world:

﴿ وَكَمْ قَصَمْنَا مِن قَرْيَةٍ كَانَتْ ظَالِمَةً وَأَنشَأْنَا بَعْدَهَا قَوْمًا ءَاخَرِينَ
﴿١١﴾ فَلَمَّآ أَحَسُّوا۟ بَأْسَنَآ إِذَا هُم مِّنْهَا يَرْكُضُونَ ﴿١٢﴾ لَا تَرْكُضُوا۟ وَٱرْجِعُوٓا۟ إِلَىٰ
مَآ أُتْرِفْتُمْ فِيهِ وَمَسَٰكِنِكُمْ لَعَلَّكُمْ تُسْـَٔلُونَ ﴿١٣﴾ قَالُوا۟ يَٰوَيْلَنَآ إِنَّا كُنَّا ظَٰلِمِينَ
﴿١٤﴾ فَمَا زَالَت تِّلْكَ دَعْوَىٰهُمْ حَتَّىٰ جَعَلْنَٰهُمْ حَصِيدًا خَٰمِدِينَ ﴿١٥﴾ ﴾

﴾How many a town [community] given to wrongdoing, have We destroyed, and raised up after them another people! Then, when they perceived [saw] Our Torment [coming], behold, they [tried to] flee from it. Flee not, but return to that wherein you lived a luxurious life, and to your homes, in order that you may be questioned. They cried: 'Woe to us! Certainly we have been *Ẓaalimoon* [polytheists, wrongdoers and disbelievers in the Oneness of Allah].' And that cry of theirs ceased not, till We made them as a field that is reaped, extinct [dead].﴾ *(Qur'an 21: 11-15)*

On the Day of Resurrection, when they are driven to that terrible fate, before they are thrown into Hell, they will be asked about their sins and they will confess:

﴿ تَكَادُ تَمَيَّزُ مِنَ ٱلْغَيْظِ ۖ كُلَّمَآ أُلْقِىَ فِيهَا فَوْجٌ سَأَلَهُمْ خَزَنَتُهَآ أَلَمْ يَأْتِكُمْ نَذِيرٌ ﴿٨﴾ قَالُوا۟ بَلَىٰ قَدْ جَآءَنَا نَذِيرٌ فَكَذَّبْنَا وَقُلْنَا مَا نَزَّلَ ٱللَّهُ مِن شَىْءٍ إِنْ أَنتُمْ إِلَّا فِى ضَلَٰلٍ كَبِيرٍ ﴿٩﴾ وَقَالُوا۟ لَوْ كُنَّا نَسْمَعُ أَوْ نَعْقِلُ مَا كُنَّا فِىٓ أَصْحَٰبِ ٱلسَّعِيرِ ﴿١٠﴾ فَٱعْتَرَفُوا۟ بِذَنۢبِهِمْ فَسُحْقًا لِّأَصْحَٰبِ ٱلسَّعِيرِ ﴿١١﴾ ﴾

﴾It almost bursts up with fury. Every time a group is cast therein, its keeper will ask: 'Did no warner come to you?' They will say: 'Yes, indeed a warner did come to us, but we belied him and said: 'Allah never sent down anything [of Revelation]; you are only in great error.'' And they will say: 'Had we but listened or used our intelligence, we would not have been among the dwellers of the blazing Fire!' Then they will confess their sin. So, away with the dwellers of the blazing Fire!﴾ *(Qur'an 67: 8-11)*

When they start to scream in Hell, after the torment surrounds them on all sides and they cry and yell, the keeper of Hell will say to them:

﴿ ... أَوَلَمْ تَكُ تَأْتِيكُمْ رُسُلُكُم بِٱلْبَيِّنَٰتِ ۖ قَالُوا۟ بَلَىٰ ۚ قَالُوا۟ فَٱدْعُوا۟ ۗ وَمَا دُعَٰٓؤُا۟ ٱلْكَٰفِرِينَ إِلَّا فِى ضَلَٰلٍ ﴿٥٠﴾ ﴾

﴾...'Did there not come to you, your Messengers with

[clear] evidences [and signs]?' They will say: 'Yes.' They will reply: 'Then call [as you like]! And the invocation of the disbelievers is nothing but in vain [as it will not be answered by Allah]!'》 *(Qur'an 40: 50)*

7 - DIRECTING THE AFFAIRS OF THE UMMAH

Those who respond to the Messengers form a *jamaa'ah* (community) and ummah (nation). They need one who will direct their affairs. The Messengers play this role during their lifetimes, and they judge among the people according to the rulings of Allah:

﴿ ... فَٱحۡكُم بَيۡنَهُم بِمَآ أَنزَلَ ٱللَّهُ ... ﴿٤٨﴾ ﴾

《...So judge among them by what Allah has revealed...》 *(Qur'an 5: 48)*

The Lord of Glory called to Prophet Dawood, saying:

﴿ يَـٰدَاوُۥدُ إِنَّا جَعَلۡنَـٰكَ خَلِيفَةً فِى ٱلۡأَرۡضِ فَٱحۡكُم بَيۡنَ ٱلنَّاسِ بِٱلۡحَقِّ ... ﴿٢٦﴾ ﴾

《O' Dawood [David]! Verily, We have placed you as a successor [and vicegerent] on the earth; so judge you between men in truth [and justice]...》 *(Qur'an 38: 26)*

The Prophets of the Children of Israel used to direct their affairs according to the *Tawraat* (Torah). According to the hadith,

"The affairs of the Children of Israel were directed by the Prophets. Whenever a Prophet died, another Prophet would succeed him."

- This has been narrated by Bukhari, Muslim, Aḥmad and Ibn Maajah.[3]

---

[3] *Ṣaḥeeḥ al-Jaami' aṣ-Ṣagheer*, 4/190.

And Allah (ﷻ) says concerning the *Tawraat* (Torah):

﴿... يَحْكُمُ بِهَا ٱلنَّبِيُّونَ ٱلَّذِينَ أَسْلَمُوا۟ لِلَّذِينَ هَادُوا۟ ... ﴿٤٤﴾﴾

﴾...By which the Prophets, who submitted themselves to Allah's Will, judged for the Jews...﴿ *(Qur'an 5: 44)*

The Messengers judged between the people, and they led the ummah in peace and in war, taking care of judicial matters and taking care of the people's interests. In all of that they acted in obedience to Allah, so obeying them in all that constituted obedience to Allah:

﴿مَّن يُطِعِ ٱلرَّسُولَ فَقَدْ أَطَاعَ ٱللَّهَ ... ﴿٨٠﴾﴾

﴾He who obeys the Messenger [Muhammad], has indeed obeyed Allah...﴿ *(Qur'an 4: 80)*

No one can attain the pleasure and love of Allah without obeying the Messenger:

﴿قُلْ إِن كُنتُمْ تُحِبُّونَ ٱللَّهَ فَٱتَّبِعُونِى يُحْبِبْكُمُ ٱللَّهُ ... ﴿٣١﴾﴾

﴾Say [O' Muhammad to mankind]: 'If you [really] love Allah, then follow me [i.e. accept Islamic Monotheism, follow the Qur'an and the Sunnah], Allah will love you...'﴿ *(Qur'an 3: 31)*

Hence the slogan of the Muslims which they always declare is "hearing and obeying":

﴿إِنَّمَا كَانَ قَوْلَ ٱلْمُؤْمِنِينَ إِذَا دُعُوٓا۟ إِلَى ٱللَّهِ وَرَسُولِهِۦ لِيَحْكُمَ بَيْنَهُمْ أَن يَقُولُوا۟ سَمِعْنَا وَأَطَعْنَا ... ﴿٥١﴾﴾

﴾The only saying of the faithful believers, when they are called to Allah [His Words, the Qur'an] and His Messenger, to judge between them, is that they say: 'We hear and we obey.'...﴿ *(Qur'an 24: 51)*

And Allah (ﷻ) says concerning the *Tawrât* (Torah):

﴿يحكم بها النبيون الذين أسلموا للذين هادوا ...﴾

﴿...by which the Prophets, who submitted themselves to Allah's Will, judged for the Jews...﴾ *(Qur'an 5: 44)*

The Messengers judged between the people, and they led the *ummah* in peace and in war, taking care of judicial matters and taking care of the people's interests. In all of that they acted in obedience to Allah, so obeying them in all that constituted obedience to Allah:

﴿من يطع الرسول فقد أطاع الله ...﴾

﴿He who obeys the Messenger [Muhammad], has indeed obeyed Allah...﴾ *(Qur'an 4: 80)*

No one can attain the pleasure and love of Allah without obeying the Messenger:

﴿قل إن كنتم تحبون الله فاتبعوني يحببكم الله ...﴾

﴿Say [O' Muhammad to mankind]: 'If you [really] love Allah, then follow me [i.e. accept Islamic Monotheism, follow the Qur'an and the Sunnah], Allah will love you...'﴾ *(Qur'an 3: 31)*

Hence the slogan of the Muslims which they always declare is "hearing and obeying":

﴿إنما كان قول المؤمنين إذا دعوا إلى الله ورسوله ليحكم بينهم أن يقولوا سمعنا وأطعنا ...﴾

﴿The only saying of the faithful believers, when they are called to Allah [His Words, the Qur'an] and His Messenger, to judge between them, is that they say: 'We hear and we obey'...﴾ *(Qur'an 24: 51)*

CHAPTER FOUR
REVELATION - *AL-WAHY*

Prophethood is a divine gift[1]

Prophethood is a divine gift which cannot be attained merely by longing and hoping, or by striving and trying. The philosophers lied when they claimed that Prophethood could be attained simply by striving, doing all kinds of acts of worship, taking on the most difficult acts of worship, and persisting in disciplining oneself and purifying one's thoughts.

Allah (ﷻ) has stated in more than one *aayah* (verse) that Prophethood is a divine blessing. Allah says:

﴿ أُوْلَٰٓئِكَ ٱلَّذِينَ أَنْعَمَ ٱللَّهُ عَلَيْهِم مِّنَ ٱلنَّبِيِّـۧنَ مِن ذُرِّيَّةِ ءَادَمَ وَمِمَّنْ حَمَلْنَا مَعَ نُوحٍ وَمِن ذُرِّيَّةِ إِبْرَٰهِيمَ وَإِسْرَٰٓءِيلَ وَمِمَّنْ هَدَيْنَا وَٱجْتَبَيْنَآ ... ﴿٥٨﴾ ﴾

﴿Those were they unto whom Allah bestowed His Grace from among the Prophets, of the offspring of Adam, and of those whom We carried [in the ship] with Nooh [Noah], and of the offspring of Ibraaheem [Abraham] and Israel, and from among those whom We guided and chose...﴾ *(Qur'an 19: 58)*

Allah tells us what Prophet Ya'qoob said to his son Yoosuf:

﴿ وَكَذَٰلِكَ يَجْتَبِيكَ رَبُّكَ ... ﴿٦﴾ ﴾

---

[1] The *Mu'tazilah* believed that the sending of the Messengers and the revelation of the Books was obligatory upon Allah. The truth is that this is a favour bestowed by Allah upon His slaves, and a mercy to them. Saying that He had to, may be acceptable, if we say that He made it obligatory upon Himself. See *Lawaami' al-Anwaar al-Bahiyah*, 2/256, 258.

﴾Thus will your Lord choose you...﴿ *(Qur'an 12: 6)*

And Allah said to Moosa (Moses) (ﷺ):

﴾... يَـٰمُوسَىٰٓ إِنِّى ٱصْطَفَيْتُكَ عَلَى ٱلنَّاسِ بِرِسَـٰلَـٰتِى وَبِكَلَـٰمِى ... ﴿١٤٤﴾﴿

﴾...O' Moosa [Moses] I have chosen you above men by My Messages, and by My speaking [to you]...﴿ *(Qur'an 7: 144)*

Umayyah ibn Abi aṣ-Ṣalṭ hoped that he would be the Prophet of this ummah, and he composed a lot of poetry addressed to Allah, praying to Him, but he did not achieve what he wanted. Allah indeed spoke the truth when He (ﷻ) said:

﴾...ٱللَّهُ أَعْلَمُ حَيْثُ يَجْعَلُ رِسَالَتَهُۥ ... ﴿١٢٤﴾﴿

﴾...Allah knows best with whom to place His Message...﴿ *(Qur'an 6: 124)*

Hence when it was suggested that one of the two great men of Makkah and Aṭ-Ṭaa'if, 'Urwah ibn Mas'ood al-Thaqafi or Al-Waleed ibn al-Mugheerah, be chosen for the role of Prophet or Messenger, Allah denounced that suggestion and stated that this was objectionable. For He is the Mighty God Who provides their provision and divide it among them in this world, so how can it be permissible for them to interfere in deciding who deserves to receive the mercy of Prophethood or Messengership?

﴾وَقَالُوا۟ لَوْلَا نُزِّلَ هَـٰذَا ٱلْقُرْءَانُ عَلَىٰ رَجُلٍ مِّنَ ٱلْقَرْيَتَيْنِ عَظِيمٍ ﴿٣١﴾ أَهُمْ يَقْسِمُونَ رَحْمَتَ رَبِّكَ ۚ نَحْنُ قَسَمْنَا بَيْنَهُم مَّعِيشَتَهُمْ فِى ٱلْحَيَوٰةِ ٱلدُّنْيَا ... ﴿٣٢﴾﴿

﴾And they say: 'Why is not this Qur'an sent down to some great man of the two towns [Makkah and Ṭaa'if]?' Is it they who would portion out the Mercy of your

Lord? It is We Who portion out between them their livelihood in this world...﴿ *(Qur'an 43: 31-32)*

In this chapter we will discuss the way in which those whom Allah chose became Prophets.

The way in which Allah communicated with His Prophets and Messengers

Allah calls this way *waḥy* (revelation). Allah (ﷻ) says:

﴿ إِنَّآ أَوْحَيْنَآ إِلَيْكَ كَمَآ أَوْحَيْنَآ إِلَىٰ نُوحٍ وَٱلنَّبِيِّـۧنَ مِنۢ بَعْدِهِۦ ۚ وَأَوْحَيْنَآ إِلَىٰٓ إِبْرَٰهِيمَ وَإِسْمَـٰعِيلَ وَإِسْحَـٰقَ وَيَعْقُوبَ وَٱلْأَسْبَاطِ وَعِيسَىٰ وَأَيُّوبَ وَيُونُسَ وَهَـٰرُونَ وَسُلَيْمَـٰنَ ۚ وَءَاتَيْنَا دَاوُۥدَ زَبُورًا ﴿١٦٣﴾ ﴾

﴾Verily, We have sent the Revelation to you [O' Muhammad] as We sent the Revelation to Nooḥ [Noah] and the Prophets after him; We [also] sent the Revelation to Ibraaheem [Abraham], Ismaa'eel [Ishmael], Isḥaaq [Isaac], Ya'qoob [Jacob], and *Al-Asbaaṭ* [the offspring of the twelve sons of Ya'qoob (Jacob)], 'Eesa [Jesus], Ayyoob [Job], Yoonus [Jonah], Haaroon [Aaron], and Sulaymaan [Solomon]; and to Dawood [David] We gave the *Zaboor* [Psalms].﴿ *(Qur'an 4: 163)*

'Waḥy' (revelation) means a rapid, secret communication, no matter how it was done.[2] It may take the form of inspiration, as was the revelation of Allah to the Disciples:

﴿ وَإِذْ أَوْحَيْتُ إِلَى ٱلْحَوَارِيِّـۧنَ أَنْ ءَامِنُوا۟ بِى وَبِرَسُولِى ... ﴿١١١﴾ ﴾

﴾And when I [Allah] inspired [*awḥaytu*] *Al-Ḥawaariyoon* [the disciples of 'Eesa (Jesus)] to believe in Me and My Messenger...﴿ *(Qur'an 5: 111)*

---

[2] *Fatḥ al-Baari*, 1/9; *Al-Miṣbaaḥ al-Muneer*, 651, 652.

- and as was the revelation to the mother of Moosa:

﴿ وَأَوْحَيْنَآ إِلَىٰٓ أُمِّ مُوسَىٰٓ أَنْ أَرْضِعِيهِ ... ﴿٧﴾ ﴾

﴿And We inspired [*awḥaynaa*] the mother of Moosa [Moses] [telling]: 'Suckle him [Moosa (Moses)]...'﴾ *(Qur'an 28: 7)*

It may also mean communicating via signs or gestures. The Qur'an calls the gestures of Zakariyya (Zacharya) to his people a revelation (*waḥy*):

﴿ فَخَرَجَ عَلَىٰ قَوْمِهِۦ مِنَ ٱلْمِحْرَابِ فَأَوْحَىٰٓ إِلَيْهِمْ أَن سَبِّحُوا۟ بُكْرَةً وَعَشِيًّا ﴿١١﴾ ﴾

﴿Then he came out to his people from *Al-Miḥraab* [a praying place or a private room] and he told them by signs [*awḥaa ilayhim*] to glorify Allah's Praises in the morning and in the afternoon.﴾ *(Qur'an 19: 11)*

But on most occasions in the Qur'an where the word *waḥy* is used, it refers to when Allah tells those whom He has chosen from among His slaves everything that He wants them to know of various kinds of guidance and knowledge, in a secret manner, not the manner that is usual among mankind.

Different forms of Allah's Revelation to His Messengers

Allah (ﷻ) says, describing these different forms:

﴿ ۞ وَمَا كَانَ لِبَشَرٍ أَن يُكَلِّمَهُ ٱللَّهُ إِلَّا وَحْيًا أَوْ مِن وَرَآئِ حِجَابٍ أَوْ يُرْسِلَ رَسُولًا فَيُوحِىَ بِإِذْنِهِۦ مَا يَشَآءُ ۚ إِنَّهُۥ عَلِىٌّ حَكِيمٌ ﴿٥١﴾ ﴾

﴿It is not given to any human being that Allah should speak to him unless [it be] by Revelation, or from behind a veil, or [that] He sends a Messenger to reveal what He wills by His Leave. Verily, He is Most High, Most Wise.﴿ *(Qur'an 42: 51)*

There are three such forms:

The first form: Where revelation is cast into the heart of the Prophet to whom revelation is sent, so that the Prophet has no doubt that what has been cast into his heart is from Allah. It is narrated in *Ṣaḥeeḥ ibn Ḥibbaan* that the Messenger of Allah (ﷺ) said:

> "The Holy Spirit (i.e., Jibreel/Gabriel) inspired into my heart that no soul will die until its provision and lifespan have been completed, so fear Allah and do not strive too hard in seeking provision."[3]

Ibn al-Jawzi was of the view that the phrase *illa waḥiyan* "unless (it be) by Revelation" meant inspiration in a dream.[4]

The dreams of the Prophets

The way in which Ibn al-Jawzi interprets the first form (as referring to dreams) is undoubtedly a part of revelation, for the dreams of the Prophets are true. Hence the Close Friend of the Most Merciful, Ibraaheem (Abraham) (عليه السلام), hastened to sacrifice his son when he saw in a dream that he should do so. These dreams are counted as a divine command. Allah (تعالى) says concerning Ibraaheem and his son Ismaa'eel:

﴿ فَلَمَّا بَلَغَ مَعَهُ ٱلسَّعْىَ قَالَ يَـٰبُنَىَّ إِنِّىٓ أَرَىٰ فِى ٱلْمَنَامِ أَنِّىٓ أَذْبَحُكَ فَٱنظُرْ
مَاذَا تَرَىٰ ۚ قَالَ يَـٰٓأَبَتِ ٱفْعَلْ مَا تُؤْمَرُ ۖ سَتَجِدُنِىٓ إِن شَآءَ ٱللَّهُ مِنَ ٱلصَّـٰبِرِينَ

---

[3] *Tafseer Ibn Katheer*, 6/215, commentary on the chapter *Ash-Shoora* 42: 51.

[4] *Zaad al-Maseer*, 7/297.

﴿ ١٠٢ فَلَمَّآ أَسْلَمَا وَتَلَّهُۥ لِلْجَبِينِ ١٠٣ وَنَـٰدَيْنَـٰهُ أَن يَـٰٓإِبْرَٰهِيمُ ١٠٤ قَدْ صَدَّقْتَ
ٱلرُّءْيَآ ۚ إِنَّا كَذَٰلِكَ نَجْزِى ٱلْمُحْسِنِينَ ١٠٥ ﴾

﴿And, when he [his son] was old enough to walk with him, he said: 'O' my son! I have seen in a dream that I am slaughtering you [offering you in sacrifice to Allah]. So look what you think!' He said: 'O' my father! Do that which you are commanded, In sha' Allah [if Allah wills], you shall find me of *As-Ṣaabiroon* [the patient].' Then, when they had both submitted themselves [to the Will of Allah], and he had laid him prostrate on his forehead [or on the side of his forehead for slaughtering]; We called out to him: 'O' Ibraaheem! You have fulfilled the dream!' Verily, thus do We reward the *Muḥsinoon* [good-doers].﴾ *(Qur'an 37: 102-105)*

According to a hadith narrated by Bukhari and Muslim from 'Aa'ishah (may Allah be pleased with her):

"The first instance of Revelation that happened to the Messenger of Allah (ﷺ) came in the form of good dreams which he saw in his sleep; he did not see any dream but it came true like the breaking of day."[5]

The second form: When Allah speaks to His Messengers from behind a veil. This is how Allah spoke to Moosa (Moses) (عليه السلام). Allah (سبحانه وتعالى) mentions that in more than one place in His Book.

﴿ وَلَمَّا جَآءَ مُوسَىٰ لِمِيقَـٰتِنَا وَكَلَّمَهُۥ رَبُّهُۥ ... ١٤٣ ﴾

﴿And when Moosa [Moses] came at the time and place appointed by Us, and his Lord [Allah] spoke to him...﴾ *(Qur'an 7: 143)*

---

[5] *Jaami' al-Uṣool*, 12/37.

﴿ فَلَمَّآ أَتَىٰهَا نُودِيَ يَـٰمُوسَىٰٓ ﴿١١﴾ إِنِّيٓ أَنَا۠ رَبُّكَ فَٱخۡلَعۡ نَعۡلَيۡكَ إِنَّكَ بِٱلۡوَادِ ٱلۡمُقَدَّسِ طُوٗى ﴿١٢﴾ وَأَنَا ٱخۡتَرۡتُكَ فَٱسۡتَمِعۡ لِمَا يُوحَىٰٓ ﴿١٣﴾ إِنَّنِيٓ أَنَا ٱللَّهُ لَآ إِلَـٰهَ إِلَّآ أَنَا۠ فَٱعۡبُدۡنِي وَأَقِمِ ٱلصَّلَوٰةَ لِذِكۡرِيٓ ﴿١٤﴾ ﴾

﴾And when he came to it [the fire], he was called by name: 'O' Moosa [Moses]! Verily, I am your Lord! So take off your shoes; you are in the sacred valley, Ṭuwa. And I have chosen you. So listen to that which will be revealed [to you]. Verily, I am Allah! *Laa ilaaha illa Ana* [none has the right to be worshipped but I], so worship Me, and perform *Aṣ-Ṣalaah* [*Iqaamat-aṣ-Ṣalaah*] for My remembrance.'﴿ *(Qur'an 20: 11-14)*

Among those to whom Allah (ﷻ) spoke was Adam (ﷺ):

﴿ قَالَ يَـٰٓـَٔادَمُ أَنۢبِئۡهُم بِأَسۡمَآئِهِمۡ ... ﴿٣٣﴾ ﴾

﴾He said: 'O' Adam! Inform them of their names'...﴿ *(Qur'an 2: 33)*

And Allah spoke to His slave and Messenger Muhammad (ﷺ) when he was taken up to heaven.

The third form: Revelation to the Messenger via the angel. This is what Allah (ﷻ) meant in the *aayah* (verse):

﴿ ... أَوۡ يُرۡسِلَ رَسُولٗا فَيُوحِيَ بِإِذۡنِهِۦ مَا يَشَآءُ ... ﴿٥١﴾ ﴾

﴾...Or [that] He sends a Messenger to reveal what He wills by His Leave...﴿ *(Qur'an 42: 51)*

This Messenger is Jibreel (Gabriel), or it may be another angel, but that is in very few cases.[6]

---

[6] *'Aalam al-Malaa'ikah* (The World of the Noble Angels) by Al-Ashqar, Pp. 40.

How the angel came to the Messenger

By studying the texts on this matter, we find that the angel may come in three ways[7]:

1) The Messenger sees him in the form in which Allah created him. This happened only twice to our Messenger (ﷺ).

2) The revelation comes to him (with a sound like) the ringing of a bell, then it goes away, and the Messenger understands what had been said.

3) The angel appears to him and speaks with him and addresses him, and he understands what the angel says to him. This was the easiest way for the Messenger (ﷺ) to bear. This happened to our Prophet when Jibreel (Gabriel) came to him for the first time in the cave of Ḥiraa'.

Portents of Revelation

Before he saw the angel, the Messenger (ﷺ) used to see a light and hear a voice, but he did not see the angel who was causing the light, or see the one who was addressing him. Muslim narrated in his *Ṣaḥeeḥ* that Ibn 'Abbaas said: "The Messenger of Allah (ﷺ) stayed in Makkah for fifteen years, hearing the voice and seeing the light for seven years, but without seeing anything, and eight years during which revelation came to him. And he stayed in Madeenah for ten years."[8]

---

[7] *'Aalam al-Malaa'ikah* (The World of the Noble Angels) by Al-Ashqar, Pp. 40.

[8] Nawawi's commentary on Muslim, 15/104. What Ibn 'Abbaas mentioned is different to what is known of the period during which he was receiving revelation in Makkah. What is known is that he received revelation from the age of forty and he migrated at the age of fifty-three, so the period involved was thirteen years.

An-Nawawi said: "He (ﷺ) used to hear the voice and see the light." Al-Qaaḍi said: "i.e., the voice calling from the angels, and he saw the light, i.e., the light of the angels, and the light of the signs of Allah, until he saw the angel with his own eyes, and the angel conveyed to him verbally the revelation of Allah."[9]

The effect of the angel on the Messenger

Among the claims which those who disbelieve in the Messengers make is that what happened to the Messenger (ﷺ) was some kind of epilepsy, or that the devils made some kind of contact with him. This is a lie, for these are two entirely different matters. The one who suffers an epileptic fit turns yellow, becomes light and loses his balance, as also happens to the one who is afflicted by the *Shayṭaan* (Satan); the *Shayṭaan* may speak through his mouth and address the people present, and when he recovers from his loss of consciousness the person is unaware and does not remember anything that the *Shayṭaan* (Satan) said on his lips to the people present. But in the case of the Messenger (ﷺ), when the angel contacted him, caused his body to increase in size and his face was filled with light. Moreover the people sitting with him did not hear anything that was said, rather they heard a sound like the buzzing of bees around his head.[10] Afterwards the Messenger would stand up and he would be aware of everything that the angel had told him, and he was the one who would tell his Companions what had been revealed to him.

'Aa'ishah (may Allah be pleased with her and with her father) told us that, "The Messenger (ﷺ) would receive revelation on an intensely cold day, and by the time it departed from him, his forehead would be dripping with sweat."[11]

---

[9] Nawawi's commentary on Muslim, 15/104.

[10] Tirmidhi, see *Jaami' al-Uṣool*, 12/41.

[11] Bukhari: *Kitaab Badu'al-Waḥy* (see *Fatḥ al-Baari*, 1/18).

And she told us that his camel - if he received revelation whilst riding on it - would almost sink to its knees because of his weight.[12] One of the *Ṣaḥaabah* (Companions of the Prophet) mentioned that his thigh was beneath the thigh of the Prophet (ﷺ) when revelation came to him. At the moment when revelation was coming to him, the thigh of the Prophet (ﷺ) almost crushed the thigh of the *Ṣaḥaabi* (the Companion).[13]

Ya'laa ibn Umayyah told us that he witnessed an occasion when revelation came to the Messenger (ﷺ); before that he had wished that he could witness that (situation and) condition. He said: "I came in and he was red in the face. He stayed like that for a while, then (this condition) departed from him."[14]

---

[12] This has been referred to by Al-Bayhaqi in *Ad-Dalaa'il*, quoting from 'Aa'ishah. See *Fatḥ al-Baari*, 1/21.

[13] Bukhari: *Ṣalaah*, 12; *Jihaad*, 31; Nasaa'i: *Jihaad*, 4; Aḥmad: 5/184.

[14] The hadith of Ya'laa is narrated by Bukhari and others. Bukhari: *Kitaab Faḍaa'il al-Qur'an. Fatḥ al-Baari*, 9/9.

CHAPTER FIVE
THE ATTRIBUTES OF THE MESSENGERS

Being human

The wisdom of the All-Knowing, All-Wise dictated that the Messengers whom He sent to mankind should be human themselves.

﴿ قُلْ إِنَّمَآ أَنَا۠ بَشَرٌ مِّثْلُكُمْ ... ﴿١١٠﴾ ﴾

﴿Say [O' Muhammad]: 'I am only a man like you...'﴾
(Qur'an 18: 110)

Man is qualified to convey the message

Those who object and think that it is very unlikely that Allah would choose some humans to convey the Message do not give man his due. Man is qualified to undertake the ultimate trust, the trust of Allah which the heavens and the earth and the mountains could not bear.

﴿ إِنَّا عَرَضْنَا ٱلْأَمَانَةَ عَلَى ٱلسَّمَٰوَٰتِ وَٱلْأَرْضِ وَٱلْجِبَالِ فَأَبَيْنَ أَن يَحْمِلْنَهَا وَأَشْفَقْنَ مِنْهَا وَحَمَلَهَا ٱلْإِنسَٰنُ إِنَّهُۥ كَانَ ظَلُومًا جَهُولًا ﴿٧٢﴾ ﴾

﴿Truly, We did offer *Al-Amaanah* [the trust or moral responsibility or honesty and all the duties which Allah has ordained] to the heavens and the earth, and the mountains, but they declined to bear it and were afraid of it [i.e. afraid of Allah's Torment]. But man bore it. Verily, he was unjust [to himself] and ignorant [of its results].﴾
(Qur'an 33: 72)

Those who find it strange that Allah would choose human Messengers look only at the outward appearance of man; they view him only as a body which eats, drinks and sleeps, which walks on the earth to fulfil its own needs.

﴿وَقَالُوا۟ مَالِ هَٰذَا ٱلرَّسُولِ يَأْكُلُ ٱلطَّعَامَ وَيَمْشِى فِى ٱلْأَسْوَاقِ... ⑦﴾

﴾And they say: 'Why does this Messenger [Muhammad] eat food, and walk about in the markets [as we]...?'﴿ *(Qur'an 25: 7)*

They do not look at the essence of man, the soul which was breathed into him by Allah (ﷻ):

﴿فَإِذَا سَوَّيْتُهُۥ وَنَفَخْتُ فِيهِ مِن رُّوحِى فَقَعُوا۟ لَهُۥ سَٰجِدِينَ ٢٩﴾

﴾So, when I have fashioned him completely and breathed into him [Adam] the soul which I created for him, then fall [you] down prostrating yourselves unto him.﴿ *(Qur'an 15: 29)*

It is this soul which distinguishes man and makes him human and gives him the role of *khaleefah* (vicegerent) on earth. Allah equipped him to be able to have contact with Him by means of that sublime soul which distinguishes him, so it is no wonder that Allah would choose one of this race, one who had the potential to receive revelation, so that He could reveal to him that by means of which he could guide his brothers to the right path whenever they lost their way, and give them help whenever they needed help.[1]

﴿قَالَتْ لَهُمْ رُسُلُهُمْ إِن نَّحْنُ إِلَّا بَشَرٌ مِّثْلُكُمْ وَلَٰكِنَّ ٱللَّهَ يَمُنُّ عَلَىٰ مَن يَشَآءُ مِنْ عِبَادِهِۦ... ١١﴾

﴾Their Messengers said to them: 'We are no more than human beings like you, but Allah bestows His Grace to whom He wills of His slaves...'﴿ *(Qur'an 14: 11)*

---

[1] *Fi Ẓilaal al-Qur'an*, 19/2552.

Again the Messengers are prepared (and trained) in a special way to fulfil the role of being Prophets and Messengers, and they are chosen by Allah:

﴿ وَٱصْطَنَعْتُكَ لِنَفْسِى ﴿٤١﴾ ﴾

﴾And I have chosen you for Myself.﴿ *(Qur'an 20: 41)*

Think of how this applies in the case of our Prophet Muhammad (ﷺ), how Allah took such care of him despite the fact that he was an orphan and poor. Allah (ﷻ) says:

﴿ أَلَمْ يَجِدْكَ يَتِيمًا فَـَٔاوَىٰ ﴿٦﴾ وَوَجَدَكَ ضَآلًّا فَهَدَىٰ ﴿٧﴾ وَوَجَدَكَ عَآئِلًا فَأَغْنَىٰ ﴿٨﴾ ﴾

﴾Did He not find you [O' Muhammad] an orphan and gave you a refuge? And He found you unaware [of the Qur'an, its legal laws and Prophethood] and guided you? And He found you poor and made you rich [self-sufficient with self-contentment]?﴿ *(Qur'an 93: 6-8)*

He cleansed him and purified him, took away from him the evil of the *Shayṭaan* (Satan) and removed the share of the *Shayṭaan* from him, from the time when he was very young. It is narrated from Anas (رضي الله عنه) that Jibreel (Gabriel) (عليه السلام) came to the Messenger of Allah (ﷺ) when he was playing with some other boys. He wrestled him to the ground then he opened his heart and removed a clot from his heart. He said, this is the share of the Satan from you, then he washed it with Zamzam water in a basin of gold. Then the heart was joined together and restored to its place. The boys came running to his mother,[2] meaning his wet-nurse, saying, "Muhammad has been killed!" They rushed towards him and found that he had lost his colour. Anas said,

---

[2] This was his "foster-mother" Ḥaleemah as-Sa'diyyah.

"I used to see the mark of those stitches on his chest." This is narrated by Muslim.[3]

Something similar happened when Jibreel (Gabriel) came to prepare him (ﷺ) for the great journey on which he was taken up to the highest heavens. In the hadith of the *Israa'* (Night Journey) it says:

> "The roof of my house was opened when I was in Makkah, and Jibreel came down and opened my chest, then he washed it with Zamzam water, then he brought a basin filled with wisdom and faith, and poured it into my chest, then he closed it again." (Bukhari and Muslim)[4]

Why were the Messengers not angels?

Many of the enemies of the Messengers objected to the fact that human Messengers were sent. This was one of the greatest stumbling blocks that prevented people from believing:

﴿ وَمَا مَنَعَ ٱلنَّاسَ أَن يُؤْمِنُوٓا۟ إِذْ جَآءَهُمُ ٱلْهُدَىٰٓ إِلَّآ أَن قَالُوٓا۟ أَبَعَثَ ٱللَّهُ بَشَرًا رَّسُولًا ﴿٩٤﴾ ﴾

> ﴿And nothing prevented men from believing when the guidance came to them, except that they said: 'Has Allah sent a man as [His] Messenger?'﴾ *(Qur'an 17: 94)*

They thought that following beliefs and laws brought by the Messengers was something abhorrent because they were human and they looked upon this as a great loss.

﴿ وَلَئِنْ أَطَعْتُم بَشَرًا مِّثْلَكُمْ إِنَّكُمْ إِذًا لَّخَـٰسِرُونَ ﴿٣٤﴾ ﴾

---

[3] *Mishkaat al-Maṣaabeeḥ*, 3/152.

[4] *Ṣaḥeeḥ al-Jaami' aṣ-Ṣagheer*, 4/81.

﴿If you were to obey a human being like yourselves, then verily, you indeed would be losers.﴾ *(Qur'an 23: 34)*

﴿ فَقَالُوٓاْ أَبَشَرًا مِّنَّا وَٰحِدًا نَّتَّبِعُهُۥٓ إِنَّآ إِذًا لَّفِى ضَلَٰلٍ وَسُعُرٍ ﴿٢٤﴾ ﴾

﴿And they said: 'A man, alone among us - shall we follow him? Truly, then we should be in error and distress [or madness]!'﴾ *(Qur'an 54: 24)*

The enemies of the Messengers suggested that the Messengers who were sent to them should be angels whom they could see, or at least that an angelic Messenger should be sent alongside the human Messenger:

﴿ ۞ وَقَالَ ٱلَّذِينَ لَا يَرْجُونَ لِقَآءَنَا لَوْلَآ أُنزِلَ عَلَيْنَا ٱلْمَلَٰٓئِكَةُ أَوْ نَرَىٰ رَبَّنَا ... ﴿٢١﴾ ﴾

﴿And those who expect not a Meeting with Us [i.e. those who deny the Day of Resurrection and the life of the Hereafter] said: 'Why are not the angels sent down to us, or why do we not see our Lord?'...﴾ *(Qur'an 25: 21)*

﴿ وَقَالُواْ مَالِ هَٰذَا ٱلرَّسُولِ يَأْكُلُ ٱلطَّعَامَ وَيَمْشِى فِى ٱلْأَسْوَاقِ لَوْلَآ أُنزِلَ إِلَيْهِ مَلَكٌ فَيَكُونَ مَعَهُۥ نَذِيرًا ﴿٧﴾ ﴾

﴿And they say: 'Why does this Messenger [Muhammad] eat food, and walk about in the markets [as we]. Why is not an angel sent down to him to be a warner with him?'﴾ *(Qur'an 25: 7)*

When we study the Qur'anic texts, we can refute this specious argument from several angles:

1) Allah chose them as humans and not angels because that is a greater test. According to a hadith *qudsi* narrated by Muslim,

"I have only sent you in order to test you and to test others by you."[5]

2) This is an honour to those whom Allah has favoured. For Allah chose some of His slaves to be Messengers as a sign of honour and grace. In the words of the Qur'an:

﴿ أُوْلَـٰٓئِكَ ٱلَّذِينَ أَنْعَمَ ٱللَّهُ عَلَيْهِم مِّنَ ٱلنَّبِيِّـۧنَ مِن ذُرِّيَّةِ ءَادَمَ وَمِمَّنْ حَمَلْنَا مَعَ نُوحٍ وَمِن ذُرِّيَّةِ إِبْرَٰهِيمَ وَإِسْرَٰٓءِيلَ وَمِمَّنْ هَدَيْنَا وَٱجْتَبَيْنَآ ... ﴿٥٨﴾ ﴾

﴿Those were they unto whom Allah bestowed His Grace from among the Prophets, of the offspring of Adam, and of those whom We carried [in the ship] with Nooḥ [Noah], and of the offspring of Ibraaheem [Abraham] and Israel, and from among those whom We guided and chose...﴾ *(Qur'an 19: 58)*

3) Humans are more able to lead and direct, and they are more suited to be leaders and examples. Sayyid Quṭb says concerning this: "There is a reason why the Message is sent to mankind through a man, for a man feels what they feel, he experiences the same things, feels the same pains, understands their inclinations and longings, and knows their needs and burdens. So he feels compassion for their weaknesses and shortcomings, and he hopes that they will become stronger and overcome their failings. He leads them step-by-step, understanding their motives, emotions and responses, because at the end of the day he is one of them. He leads them on the path that leads to Allah, guided by the revelation of Allah, helped by Him to overcome the obstacles that may lie in their way.

For their part, they find that they are able to trust his ability, because he is a human being like them, who is trying to raise them step by step. He lives among them, demonstrating the characteristics, deeds

[5] *Mukhtaṣar Ṣaḥeeḥ Muslim* by Al-Mundhiri, Pp. 283.

and responsibilities which he tells them that Allah has enjoined upon them and which He wants from them. Thus his personality becomes a living example of the belief which he is conveying to them; his life, movements and actions become an open book for them, which they transmit line by line and put into practice idea by idea. They see it fulfilled as he is among them, and this inspires them to imitate it, because it is embodied in a human being."[6]

4) It is difficult to see the angels. When the *kuffaar* (disbelievers) suggested seeing the angels, and that the Messengers sent to them should be angels, they did not understand the nature of the angels or the difficulties that this would present to them.

Having contact with the angels and seeing them is no simple matter. Even though the Messenger (ﷺ) was the best of mankind and was given a great deal of physical and mental strength, when he saw Jibreel (Gabriel) (عليه السلام) in his true form, he was filled with great terror and fled to his home trembling. It was physically hard on him when the revelation came to him, hence Allah, the Almighty, All-Powerful, said, refuting them:

﴿ يَوْمَ يَرَوْنَ ٱلْمَلَـٰٓئِكَةَ لَا بُشْرَىٰ يَوْمَئِذٍ لِّلْمُجْرِمِينَ ... ﴿٢٢﴾ ﴾

﴿On the Day they will see the angels no glad tidings will there be for the *Mujrimoon* [criminals, disbelievers, polytheists, sinners] that day...﴾ *(Qur'an 25: 22)*

That is because the disbelievers only see the angels at the time of death or when punishment comes down, so if they were to see the angels that would be the day of their doom.

So sending human Messengers was necessary, so that they would be able to speak with them and understand what they said. If Allah had

[6] *Fi Ẓilaal al-Qur'an*, 19/2553.

sent angels to them as Messengers none of that would have been possible. The Qur'an stated:

﴿ وَمَا مَنَعَ ٱلنَّاسَ أَن يُؤْمِنُوٓاْ إِذْ جَآءَهُمُ ٱلْهُدَىٰٓ إِلَّآ أَن قَالُوٓاْ أَبَعَثَ ٱللَّهُ بَشَرًا رَّسُولًا ﴿٩٤﴾ قُل لَّوْ كَانَ فِى ٱلْأَرْضِ مَلَٰٓئِكَةٌ يَمْشُونَ مُطْمَئِنِّينَ لَنَزَّلْنَا عَلَيْهِم مِّنَ ٱلسَّمَآءِ مَلَكًا رَّسُولًا ﴿٩٥﴾ ﴾

﴾And nothing prevented men from believing when the guidance came to them, except that they said: 'Has Allah sent a man as [His] Messenger?' Say: 'If there were on the earth, angels walking about in peace and security, We should certainly have sent down for them from the heaven an angel as a Messenger.'﴿ *(Qur'an 17: 94-95)*

If the inhabitants of the earth had been angels, then Allah (ﷻ) would have sent one of their own kind to them as a Messenger. But because those who live on the earth are human beings, the mercy and wisdom of Allah (ﷻ) dictate that their Messenger should be one of their own kind.

﴿ لَقَدْ مَنَّ ٱللَّهُ عَلَى ٱلْمُؤْمِنِينَ إِذْ بَعَثَ فِيهِمْ رَسُولًا مِّنْ أَنفُسِهِمْ ... ﴿١٦٤﴾ ﴾

﴾Indeed, Allah conferred a great favour on the believers when He sent among them a Messenger [Muhammad] from among themselves...﴿ *(Qur'an 3: 164)*

Humans cannot see angels and learn from them easily. This means that even if Allah wanted to send an angel as a Messenger to mankind, He would have to make him a man. Allah (ﷻ) says:

﴿ وَلَوْ جَعَلْنَٰهُ مَلَكًا لَّجَعَلْنَٰهُ رَجُلًا وَلَلَبَسْنَا عَلَيْهِم مَّا يَلْبِسُونَ ﴿٩﴾ ﴾

﴾And had We appointed him an angel, We indeed would have made him a man, and We would have certainly

> confused them in which they are already confused [i.e. the Message of Prophet Muhammad].﴿ *(Qur'an 6: 9)*

So Allah tells us that, "If He had sent an angelic Messenger, he would have come in the form of a man, so that they would have been able to speak with him and learn from him, but if that had been the case they would have become confused."[7]

They would have become confused because of his appearing as a man; they would not have been able to be sure that he was an angel, and if this is the case then what point would there be in sending Messengers from among the angels in this way? Sending angelic Messengers in this way would not serve the required purpose, because an angel would not be able to feel the emotions that humans feel, even if he looked like them.

Implications of the humanity of the Prophets and Messengers

The fact that they were human implies that they had the same attributes as all other human beings. That includes the fact that they had physical bodies which needed food and drink as all other humans do, and that they excreted as humans do, because that is one of the inevitable results of eating and drinking. Allah (ﷻ) says:

> ﴿ وَمَآ أَرْسَلْنَا قَبْلَكَ إِلَّا رِجَالًا نُّوحِىٓ إِلَيْهِمْ فَسْـَٔلُوٓا۟ أَهْلَ ٱلذِّكْرِ إِن كُنتُمْ لَا تَعْلَمُونَ ۝٧ وَمَا جَعَلْنَٰهُمْ جَسَدًا لَّا يَأْكُلُونَ ٱلطَّعَامَ وَمَا كَانُوا۟ خَٰلِدِينَ ۝٨ ﴾

> ﴾And We sent not before you [O' Muhammad] but men to whom We revealed. So ask the people of the Reminder [Scriptures - the *Tawraat* (Torah), the *Injeel* (Gospel)] if you do not know. And We did not create

---

[7] *Tafseer Ibn Katheer*, 3/9.

them [the Messengers, with] bodies that ate not food, nor were they immortals.﴿ *(Qur'an 21: 7-8)*

They were born just as other humans are born. They had fathers and mothers, uncles and aunts. They got married and had children:

﴿ وَلَقَدْ أَرْسَلْنَا رُسُلًا مِّن قَبْلِكَ وَجَعَلْنَا لَهُمْ أَزْوَاجًا وَذُرِّيَّةً ... ﴿٣٨﴾ ﴾

﴾And indeed We sent Messengers before you [O' Muhammad], and made for them wives and offspring...﴿ *(Qur'an 13: 38)*

They had the same experiences as other human beings. They slept and got up, they enjoyed good health and suffered from sickness, the same thing that comes to all human beings came to them, namely death. Among the things that Ibraaheem (Abraham) (ﷺ), the Close Friend of the Most Merciful, said to his Lord was:

﴿ وَالَّذِي هُوَ يُطْعِمُنِي وَيَسْقِينِ ﴿٧٩﴾ وَإِذَا مَرِضْتُ فَهُوَ يَشْفِينِ ﴿٨٠﴾ وَالَّذِي يُمِيتُنِي ثُمَّ يُحْيِينِ ﴿٨١﴾ ﴾

﴾And it is He Who feeds me and gives me to drink. And when I am ill, it is He Who cures me. And Who will cause me to die, and then will bring me to life [again].﴿ *(Qur'an 26: 79-81)*

And Allah said to His slave and Messenger Muhammad (ﷺ):

﴿ إِنَّكَ مَيِّتٌ وَإِنَّهُم مَّيِّتُونَ ﴿٣٠﴾ ﴾

﴾Verily, you [O' Muhammad] will die, and verily, they [too] will die.﴿ *(Qur'an 39: 30)*

And He said, explaining that this is His way with all the Messengers.

﴿ وَمَا مُحَمَّدٌ إِلَّا رَسُولٌ قَدْ خَلَتْ مِن قَبْلِهِ الرُّسُلُ ۚ أَفَإِين مَّاتَ أَوْ قُتِلَ انقَلَبْتُمْ عَلَىٰ أَعْقَابِكُمْ ۚ ... ﴿١٤٤﴾ ﴾

﴾Muhammad is no more than a Messenger, and indeed [many] Messengers have passed away before him. If he dies or is killed, will you then turn back on your heels [as disbelievers]?...﴿ *(Qur' an 3: 144)*

And it has been narrated in a description of the Messenger (ﷺ):

"He was a human being like any other; he would mend his garment, milk his sheep and serve himself."[8]

It is narrated that the Messenger (ﷺ) said to Umm Sulaym:

"O' Umm Sulaym, do you not know that I asked my Lord and said, 'I am a human being: sometimes I feel happy like human beings do, and sometimes I feel angry like human beings do. If I invoke Allah against anyone among my ummah who does not deserve that, may that be a means of purification for him and a means of his drawing closer to Allah on the Day of Resurrection.'"[9]

The Prophets were exposed to trials

The humanity of the Prophets implies that they would be exposed to trials and tribulations, like all other human beings. Human beings may be imprisoned as Prophet Yoosuf (ﷺ) was. To quote the Qur'an:

﴿ قَالَ رَبِّ ٱلسِّجْنُ أَحَبُّ إِلَيَّ مِمَّا يَدْعُونَنِيٓ إِلَيْهِ ... ﴿٣٣﴾ ﴾

﴾He said: 'O' my Lord! Prison is dearer to me than that to which they invite me'...﴿ *(Qur'an 12: 33)*

Allah (ﷻ) mentions that he:

---

[8] Aḥmad in his *Musnad*; Bukhari: *Al-Adab al-Mufrad*. The isnad of Aḥmad is *ṣaḥeeḥ* according to the conditions of Muslim. See *Silsilat al-Aḥaadeeth aṣ-Ṣaḥeeḥah*, hadith no. 671.

[9] Muslim, See *Silsilat al-Aḥaadeeth aṣ-Ṣaḥeeḥah*, hadith no. 84.

﴿ ... فَلَبِثَ فِى ٱلسِّجْنِ بِضْعَ سِنِينَ ﴿٤٢﴾ ﴾

﴾...stayed in prison a few [more] years.﴿ *(Qur'an 12: 42)*

Their people may harm them and make them bleed, as they did to the Messenger (ﷺ) at the battle of Uḥud when they harmed him and made him bleed, and they broke his eyetooth. They may expel them from their homes, as Ibraaheem (Abraham) migrated from Iraq to Syria, and as our Prophet Muhammad (ﷺ) migrated from Makkah to Madeenah. The opponents may kill them too.

Allah (ﷻ) says:

﴿ ... أَفَكُلَّمَا جَآءَكُمْ رَسُولٌۢ بِمَا لَا تَهْوَىٰٓ أَنفُسُكُمُ ٱسْتَكْبَرْتُمْ فَفَرِيقًا كَذَّبْتُمْ وَفَرِيقًا تَقْتُلُونَ ﴿٨٧﴾ ﴾

﴾...Is it that whenever there came to you a Messenger with what you yourselves desired not, you grew arrogant? Some you disbelieved and some you killed.﴿ *(Qur'an 2: 87)*

They may fall sick, as Allah tested His Prophet Ayyoob (Job), and he bore it with patience. It is narrated that the Messenger (ﷺ) said:

"The Prophet of Allah Ayyoob continued to suffer that trial for eighteen years, and everyone near and far spurned him except for two men among his brothers..."[10]

Among the things he suffered was the loss of his family and wealth, and he had many children and much wealth.

The Qur'an tells:

---

[10] Abu Ya'laa in his *Musnad*; Abu Na'eem in *Al-Ḥilyah*; waḍ-Ḍiyaa' in *Al-Mukhtaarah*; Ibn Ḥibbaan in his *Ṣaḥeeḥ*. See *Silsilat al-Aḥaadeeth aṣ-Ṣaḥeeḥah*, hadith no. 17.

﴿ ۞ وَأَيُّوبَ إِذْ نَادَىٰ رَبَّهُۥٓ أَنِّى مَسَّنِىَ ٱلضُّرُّ وَأَنتَ أَرْحَمُ ٱلرَّٰحِمِينَ ﴿٨٣﴾ فَٱسْتَجَبْنَا لَهُۥ فَكَشَفْنَا مَا بِهِۦ مِن ضُرٍّ ۖ وَءَاتَيْنَٰهُ أَهْلَهُۥ وَمِثْلَهُم مَّعَهُمْ رَحْمَةً مِّنْ عِندِنَا وَذِكْرَىٰ لِلْعَٰبِدِينَ ﴿٨٤﴾ ﴾

﴾And [remember] Ayyoob [Job], when he cried to his Lord: 'Verily, distress has seized me, and You are the Most Merciful of all those who show mercy.' So We answered his call, and We removed the distress that was on him, and We restored his family to him [that he had lost] and the like thereof along with them as a mercy from Ourselves and a Reminder for all those who worship Us.﴿ *(Qur'an 21: 83-84)*

The Prophets did not merely suffer tribulation; they were the most sorely tested of mankind. It is narrated from Aṣ-Ṣa'b ibn Sa'd that his father said: I said to the Messenger of Allah (ﷺ) "Which of the people are most sorely tested?" He said,

> "The Prophets, then the next best and the next best. A man will be tested according to his level of religious commitment. If his religious commitment is strong then he will be tested more severely; if there is some weakness in his religious commitment then he will be tested according to his level of religious commitment. The trial will persist until it leaves him walking on the face of the earth with no sin on him."[11]

Abu Sa'eed al-Khudri visited the Messenger (ﷺ) when he was not feeling well. He laid his hand on the Messenger (ﷺ) and found that he could feel his fever through the blanket. He said, "O' Messenger of Allah, how hard it is for you!" He said,

[11] Tirmidhi, he said it is a *ṣaḥeeḥ ḥasan* hadith; also Ibn Maajah and others. *Silsilat al-Aḥaadeeth aṣ-Ṣaḥeeḥah*, hadith no. 143.

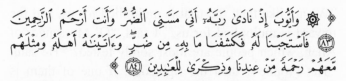

"We are like that; the trial is multiplied for us, and the reward is multiplied for us." I said, "O' Messenger of Allah, which people are most sorely tested?" He said, "The Prophets, then the righteous. If one of them is tested with poverty, until he has nothing left but the cloak he is wearing, he would rejoice over that trial as one of you rejoices over a time of ease."[12]

The Prophets engage in human work

One of the implications of their being human is that they did the same kinds of work as other humans do. For example, the Messenger (ﷺ) was engaged in trade, before his Mission began. The Prophets also tended sheep. Jaabir ibn 'Abdullah (رضي الله عنه) said: "We were with the Messenger of Allah (ﷺ) picking the fruits of the araak tree.

The Messenger of Allah (ﷺ) said,

'You should take the black ones, for they are the best.' They said, 'Did you ever tend sheep?' He said, 'Was there ever any Prophet who did not tend sheep?'"

- This is narrated by Bukhari in his *Saheeh*.[13] Among the Prophets who the Qur'an says tended sheep is Moosa (Moses) (عليه السلام). He worked as a shepherd for a number of years, and the righteous slave said to him:

---

[12] Ibn Maajah, Ibn Sa'd, Al-Ḥaakim, who said it is *ṣaheeh* according to the conditions of Muslim, and Adh-Dhahabi agreed with him. *Shaykh* Naaṣir said, it is as they said. See *Silsilat al-Aḥaadeeth aṣ-Ṣaheehah*, hadith no. 144.

If this is how the Prophets are, then the righteous should learn from that and should not think badly of Allah when a trial befalls them. Those who make accusations against the righteous because they suffer trials should give up such deviant notions.

[13] *Fatḥ al-Baari*, 6/438.

﴿قَالَ إِنِّيٓ أُرِيدُ أَنۡ أُنكِحَكَ إِحۡدَى ٱبۡنَتَيَّ هَٰتَيۡنِ عَلَىٰٓ أَن تَأۡجُرَنِي ثَمَٰنِيَ
حِجَجٖۖ فَإِنۡ أَتۡمَمۡتَ عَشۡرٗا فَمِنۡ عِندِكَۖ وَمَآ أُرِيدُ أَنۡ أَشُقَّ عَلَيۡكَۚ
سَتَجِدُنِيٓ إِن شَآءَ ٱللَّهُ مِنَ ٱلصَّٰلِحِينَ ﴿٢٧﴾ قَالَ ذَٰلِكَ بَيۡنِي وَبَيۡنَكَۖ
أَيَّمَا ٱلۡأَجَلَيۡنِ قَضَيۡتُ فَلَا عُدۡوَٰنَ عَلَيَّۖ وَٱللَّهُ عَلَىٰ مَا نَقُولُ وَكِيلٞ ﴿٢٨﴾﴾

﴿'I intend to wed one of these two daughters of mine to you, on condition that you serve me for eight years; but if you complete ten years, it will be [a favour] from you. But I intend not to place you under a difficulty. If Allah wills, you will find me one of the righteous.' He [Moosa (Moses)] said: 'That [is settled] between me and you: whichever of the two terms I fulfil, there will be no injustice to me, and Allah is Surety over what we say.'﴾

(Qur'an 28: 27-28)

Ibn Ḥajar said: "What the Imams - the leading pious scholars - said is that the reason behind the Prophets tending sheep was that they would learn to be humble, their hearts would become accustomed to solitude, and, they would be moving on thereby from taking care of sheep to taking care of nations."[14]

Among the Prophets who were engaged in human work was Prophet Dawood (David) (عليه السلام). He was a blacksmith who made chain mail (shields). Allah (سبحانه وتعالى) says:

﴿وَعَلَّمۡنَٰهُ صَنۡعَةَ لَبُوسٖ لَّكُمۡ لِتُحۡصِنَكُم مِّنۢ بَأۡسِكُمۡۖ فَهَلۡ أَنتُمۡ
شَٰكِرُونَ ﴿٨٠﴾﴾

﴿And We taught him the making of metal coats of mail [for battles], to protect you in your fighting. Are you then grateful?﴾ *Qur'an 21: 80)*

[14] *Fatḥ al-Baari*, 6/439.

He was a blacksmith, but at the same time he was a king, and he used to eat from what his hands earned.

And the Prophet of Allah Zakariyya (Zachariya) (ﷺ) used to work as a carpenter.[15]

They do not have any divine or angelic qualities

The fact that they are human implies that they are not divine, and they do not have any of the qualities of divinity at all. Hence the Messengers declared that they had no power and no strength of their own, and they sought the protection of Allah, the One, and they did not lay claim to any of the attributes of Allah. Allah (ﷻ) says, explaining that 'Eesa (Jesus) (ﷺ) had nothing to do with the things that were attributed to him:

﴿ وَإِذْ قَالَ ٱللَّهُ يَٰعِيسَى ٱبْنَ مَرْيَمَ ءَأَنتَ قُلْتَ لِلنَّاسِ ٱتَّخِذُونِى وَأُمِّىَ إِلَٰهَيْنِ مِن دُونِ ٱللَّهِ ۖ قَالَ سُبْحَٰنَكَ مَا يَكُونُ لِىٓ أَنْ أَقُولَ مَا لَيْسَ لِى بِحَقٍّ ۚ إِن كُنتُ قُلْتُهُۥ فَقَدْ عَلِمْتَهُۥ ۚ تَعْلَمُ مَا فِى نَفْسِى وَلَآ أَعْلَمُ مَا فِى نَفْسِكَ ۚ إِنَّكَ أَنتَ عَلَّٰمُ ٱلْغُيُوبِ ﴿١١٦﴾ مَا قُلْتُ لَهُمْ إِلَّا مَآ أَمَرْتَنِى بِهِۦٓ أَنِ ٱعْبُدُوا۟ ٱللَّهَ رَبِّى وَرَبَّكُمْ ۚ وَكُنتُ عَلَيْهِمْ شَهِيدًا مَّا دُمْتُ فِيهِمْ ۖ فَلَمَّا تَوَفَّيْتَنِى كُنتَ أَنتَ ٱلرَّقِيبَ عَلَيْهِمْ ۚ وَأَنتَ عَلَىٰ كُلِّ شَىْءٍ شَهِيدٌ ﴿١١٧﴾ ﴾

﴾And [remember] when Allah will say [on the Day of Resurrection]: 'O' 'Eesa [Jesus], son of Maryam [Mary]! Did you say unto men: 'Worship me and my mother as two gods besides Allah?' He will say: 'Glory be to You! It was not for me to say what I had no right [to say]. Had I said such a thing, You would surely have known it. You know what is in my inner-self though I do

[15] This is proven in a *ṣaḥeeḥ* hadith narrated by Muslim in his *Ṣaḥeeḥ*. See *Mishkaat al-Maṣaabeeḥ*, 3/117.

not know what is in Yours; truly, You, only You, are the All-Knower of all that is hidden [and unseen]. Never did I say to them aught except what You [Allah] did command me to say: 'Worship Allah, my Lord and your Lord.' And I was a witness over them while I dwelt amongst them, but when You took me up, You were the Watcher over them; and You are a Witness to all things.'》 *(Qur'an 5: 116-117)*

This is what 'Eesa (Jesus) will say in the place of standing on the Day of the greatest Gathering. These are true words which will deny those foolish lies which the Christians attributed to the slave and Messenger of Allah 'Eesa. Some of them said that the Messiaḥ, son of Maryam, was God incarnated in the womb of Maryam.

﴿لَقَدْ كَفَرَ ٱلَّذِينَ قَالُوٓا۟ إِنَّ ٱللَّهَ هُوَ ٱلْمَسِيحُ ٱبْنُ مَرْيَمَ... ﴿٧٢﴾﴾

《Surely, they have disbelieved who say: 'Allah is the Messiaḥ ['Eesa (Jesus)], son of Maryam [Mary].'...》 *(Qur'an 5: 72)*

Another group says that God is the third of the three.

﴿لَّقَدْ كَفَرَ ٱلَّذِينَ قَالُوٓا۟ إِنَّ ٱللَّهَ ثَالِثُ ثَلَٰثَةٍ ... ﴿٧٣﴾﴾

《Surely, disbelievers are those who said: 'Allah is the third of the three [in a Trinity].'...》 *(Qur'an 5: 73)*

A third group says that he is the son of God, exalted be Allah far above all that they say.

﴿وَقَالُوا۟ ٱتَّخَذَ ٱلرَّحْمَٰنُ وَلَدًا ﴿٨٨﴾ لَّقَدْ جِئْتُمْ شَيْـًٔا إِدًّا ﴿٨٩﴾﴾

《And they say: 'The Most Gracious [Allah] has begotten a son [or offspring or children] [as the Jews say: 'Uzayr [Ezra] is the son of Allah, and the Christians say that He has begotten a son ['Eesa (Jesus)], and the pagan Arabs say that He has begotten daughters [angels and others].' Indeed you have brought forth [said] a terrible evil thing.﴿ *(Qur'an 19: 88-89)*

The Christians exaggerated greatly concerning 'Eesa (Jesus), thereby insulting and offending Allah greatly. They claimed that "The Lord of the worlds came down from the Throne of His Might and was incarnated in the womb of a female, where he stayed for a while amongst the blood of the womb and the darkness of the bowels, under layers of flesh and fat, then he emerged as a nursing infant, growing little by little, crying, eating, drinking and urinating, playing with other children. Then he was sent to school with the children of the Jews, where he learned the things that people should learn, and his foreskin was cut off when he was circumcised. Then the Jews started to expel him from place to place, then they arrested him and subjected him to various kinds of humiliation and disgrace, and they placed on his head the awful crown of thorns, and they made him ride on a donkey that had no reins or bridle. Then they drove him to the wood of the cross, slapping him and spitting on his face, surrounding him from front and from behind, on his right and on his left. Then they set up that cross which makes the hearts and bodies tremble, then they tied his hands and feet with ropes, then they nailed them with those nails which break the bones, and tear the flesh, and he asked for help and said 'Have mercy on me,' but not one person among them showed him any mercy. All this, when he was the controller of the upper and lower realms, of whom everyone in the heavens and on earth asked every day. Then he died and was buried in the earth beneath a huge rock of granite, then he rose from the grave and ascended to his throne and dominion after he has been what he had been."[16]

---

[16] *Hidaayah al-Ḥiyaari* (see *Al-Jaami' al-Fareed*, Pp. 479).

What insult can be greater than this which is attributed to the Creator, may He be exalted! What misguidance can be greater than this misguidance?

Human perfection

Undoubtedly human beings vary greatly in their appearance and attitude and in the gifts they have been given. Some are ugly, some are beautiful and some are in between. Some are blind, some are one-eyed and some see with both eyes. Those who have sight vary in how beautiful their eyes are and in how strong their vision is. Some of them are deaf, some have complete hearing, and some are in between. Some have no chivalry at all; others are chivalrous and have a noble purpose.

Undoubtedly the Prophets and Messengers represent the highest form of human perfection. That is because Allah (ﷻ) selected them and chose them for Himself, so He (ﷻ) inevitably chose those who were the most pure in heart and attitude, the most excellent in disposition.

﴿ ... ٱللَّهُ أَعۡلَمُ حَيۡثُ يَجۡعَلُ رِسَالَتَهُۥ ... ﴿١٢٤﴾ ﴾

﴾...Allah knows best with whom to place His Message...﴿ *(Qur'an 6: 124)*

Physical perfection

Allah (ﷻ) warns us against annoying the Messenger (ﷺ) as the Children of Israel annoyed Prophet Moosa (Moses):

﴿ يَٰٓأَيُّهَا ٱلَّذِينَ ءَامَنُواْ لَا تَكُونُواْ كَٱلَّذِينَ ءَاذَوۡاْ مُوسَىٰ فَبَرَّأَهُ ٱللَّهُ مِمَّا قَالُواْۚ وَكَانَ عِندَ ٱللَّهِ وَجِيهٗا ﴿٦٩﴾ ﴾

﴾O' you who believe! Be not like those who annoyed Moosa [Moses], but Allah cleared him of that which

> they alleged, and he was honourable before Allah.﴿
> *(Qur'an 33: 69)*

Our Messenger (ﷺ) explained that the way in which the Children of Israel annoyed Moosa was by accusing him of having some physical defect in his body. Bukhari[17] narrated that Abu Hurayrah (رضي الله عنه) stated: the Messenger of Allah ﷺ said:

> "Moosa (Moses) was a very shy and modest man, who never showed any part of his skin out of shyness. Those among the Children of Israel who annoyed him did so by saying 'He is only so modest because of some defect in his body[18] - either leprosy or a scrotal hernia or some other defect.' Allah wanted to demonstrate that Moosa was free from what they were attributing to him. He went out alone one day, put his garment on a rock and bathed. When he had finished, he went to pick up his garment, but the rock rolled away with his garment. Moosa picked up his stick (and ran) naked, and his entire body was exposed, and it was the best that Allah had created. Thus Allah cleared him of what they had accused him of. Then the rock stood still, and Moosa (Moses) took his garment and put it on, then he beat the rock with his stick. By Allah, the rock still bears the marks of that beating, three or four or five (marks). This is what Allah says: ﴾O' you who believe! Be not like those who annoyed Moosa [Moses], but Allah cleared him of that which they alleged, and he was honourable before Allah.﴿ *(Qur'an 33: 69)*."

---

[17] *Fatḥ al-Baari*, 6/437.

[18] This indicates that bathing naked was permissible according to the laws of the Children of Israel.

Ibn Ḥajar al-'Asqallaani said, commenting on this hadith: This shows that the Prophets, in both their physical appearance and attitude, were the most perfect, and that whoever accused a Prophet of having any physical defect thus annoyed him and the one who does that may be a *kaafir* (non-believer).[19]

Their outward appearances differed

The fact that the Messengers were the most physically perfect of people does not mean that they all looked the same. The kind of perfection which is admired varies, and that is a sign of the perfect power of the One Creator.

The Messenger (ﷺ) described some of the Prophets and Messengers to us. Muslim narrated that he (ﷺ) said:

> "On the night when I was taken on the *Israa'* (Night Journey), I saw Moosa, who was a kind of man who looked as if he were one of the men of (the tribe of) Shanu'ah."[20]

And he (ﷺ) said concerning 'Eesa (Jesus):

> "There was no Prophet between him and me. He will come down, and when you see him you will recognize him. He is a man of an average height, with a ruddy white complexion. He will come down wearing two garments lightly dyed with saffron, as if his head is dripping, even if it will not be wet."[21]

And the *Ṣaḥaabah* (Companions) described our Messenger (ﷺ) to us. They said that, "He was the best of people, of average height but

---

[19] *Fatḥ al-Baari*, 6/438.

[20] *Fatḥ al-Baari*, 6/428. Shanu'ah is a tribe in Yemen.

[21] Abu Dawood and *Aḥmad*. See *Ṣaḥeeḥ al-Jaami'*, 5/90.

more tall than short, broad shouldered, with smooth cheeks, intensely black hair, eyes that looked as if they were ringed with kohl, long eyelashes; when he stepped he stepped with the whole of his foot, and when he put on his cloak it was as smooth as silver."[22]

Perfect manners and attitude

The Prophets attained a high level in this regard and deserved to be praised by the Lord of Creation. Allah praised His Close Friend Ibraaheem (Abraham) (ﷺ), as He (ﷻ) said:

﴿ إِنَّ إِبْرَٰهِيمَ لَحَلِيمٌ أَوَّٰهٌ مُّنِيبٌ ﴿٧٥﴾ ﴾

﴿Verily, Ibraaheem [Abraham] was, without doubt, forbearing, used to invoke Allah with humility, and was repentant [to Allah all the time, again and again].﴾

(Qur'an 11: 75)

The daughter of the righteous slave said, describing Moosa (Moses):

﴿ ... يَٰٓأَبَتِ ٱسْتَـْٔجِرْهُ ۖ إِنَّ خَيْرَ مَنِ ٱسْتَـْٔجَرْتَ ٱلْقَوِىُّ ٱلْأَمِينُ ﴿٢٦﴾ ﴾

﴿...O' my father! Hire him! Verily, the best of men for you to hire is the strong, the trustworthy.﴾

(Qur'an 28: 26)

Allah praised Ismaa'eel (ﷺ) for being true to his promise:

﴿ وَٱذْكُرْ فِى ٱلْكِتَٰبِ إِسْمَٰعِيلَ ۚ إِنَّهُۥ كَانَ صَادِقَ ٱلْوَعْدِ وَكَانَ رَسُولًا نَّبِيًّا ﴿٥٤﴾ ﴾

﴿And mention in the Book [the Qur'an] Ismaa'eel [Ishmael]. Verily, he was true to what he promised, and he was a Messenger, [and] a Prophet.﴾

(Qur'an 19: 54)

---

[22] Bayhaqi. See *Ṣaḥeeḥ al-Jaami'*, 4/199.

And Allah praised the character of our Prophet Muhammad (ﷺ):

﴿وَإِنَّكَ لَعَلَىٰ خُلُقٍ عَظِيمٍ ﴿٤﴾﴾

﴿And verily, you [O' Muhammad] are on an exalted [standard of] character.﴾ *(Qur'an 68: 4)*

Allah described the character of our Prophet (ﷺ) as being exalted, and He affirmed this in three ways: by swearing by the letter noon, by the pen and by what the angels write in the Records of men; by introducing this sentence with the particle *'inna'* (translated here as "verily"); and by inserting the particle *lam* (L) (for emphasis) in the predicate of this sentence.

One aspect of the noble character of the Prophet (ﷺ) for which Allah praised him is the mercy and kindness which He (ﷻ) created in him:

﴿لَقَدْ جَآءَكُمْ رَسُولٌ مِّنْ أَنفُسِكُمْ عَزِيزٌ عَلَيْهِ مَا عَنِتُّمْ حَرِيصٌ عَلَيْكُم بِٱلْمُؤْمِنِينَ رَءُوفٌ رَّحِيمٌ ﴿١٢٨﴾﴾

﴿Verily, there has come unto you a Messenger [Muhammad] from amongst yourselves. It grieves him that you should receive any injury or difficulty. He [Muhammad] is anxious over you; for the believers [he is] full of pity, kind, and merciful.﴾ *(Qur'an 9: 128)*

These characteristics had a great impact in guiding and teaching people. Muslim narrated that Safwaan ibn Umayyah said: "The Messenger of Allah (ﷺ) gave me what he gave me, although he was the most hated of Allah's creation to me. But he kept on giving to me until he became one of the most beloved of people to me."

Muslim narrated that a man asked the Messenger (ﷺ) and he gave him a flock of sheep that was grazing between two mountains. The man came to his people and told them, "I've become a Muslim, for Muhammad gives so much as if he does not fear poverty."

If the Messengers did not have these perfect characteristics which Allah bestowed upon them, people would not have followed them. That is because people do not willingly follow one who has many shortcomings and few virtues.

The best of people in lineage

The Messengers are of noble descent. All the Messengers after Nooḥ (Noah) were from among his descendents, and all the Messengers after Ibraaheem (Abraham) were from the line of Ibraaheem. Allah (ﷻ) says:

﴿ وَلَقَدْ أَرْسَلْنَا نُوحًا وَإِبْرَٰهِيمَ وَجَعَلْنَا فِى ذُرِّيَّتِهِمَا ٱلنُّبُوَّةَ وَٱلْكِتَـٰبَ ... ﴿٢٦﴾ ﴾

> ﴾And indeed, We sent Nooḥ [Noah] and Ibraaheem [Abraham], and placed in their offspring Prophethood and Scripture...﴿ *(Qur'an 57: 26)*

Hence Allah chose as His Messengers those who were the best among their peoples in terms of lineage. According to a hadith narrated by Bukhari, the Messenger (ﷺ) said:

> "I have been sent (as a Messenger) in the best of all the generations of Adam's offspring since their creation."[23]

In *Musnad Aḥmad* and *Sunan at-Tirmidhi* it is narrated that the Messenger (ﷺ) said:

> " I am Muhammad ibn 'Abdullah ibn 'Abdul-Muṭṭalib. Allah created mankind and made me one of the best of them, then He made them into two groups and put me in the best group, then He made them into tribes and put me in the best tribe, then He made them into families and put

[23] *Fatḥ al-Baari*, 6/566.

> me in the best family. So I am the best of you in terms of family, and the best of you as an individual."[24]

In *Ṣaḥeeḥ Muslim* and *Sunan an-Nasaa'i*, it says:

> "Allah chose Kinaanah from among the children of Ismaa'eel; from among Kinaanah He chose Quraysh, and from among Quraysh He chose Bani Haashim."

The Prophets were free men, far removed from slavery

Among the attributes of perfection is the fact that the Prophets were not slaves. As-Safaareeni says concerning this: "Slavery is a kind of shortcoming that does not befit the position of Prophethood. A Prophet called people night and day, and it is not easy for a slave to do such a thing. Slavery is also a kind of shortcoming that puts people off and makes them reluctant to follow such a person or to take him as a leader and example. It may be the consequence of *kufr* (disbelief), and the Prophets are far above such a thing."[25]

Talents and abilities

The Prophets were given brilliant minds, great intelligence, eloquent tongues, strong intuition, and other talents and abilities which were essential to the conveying of the Message and the teaching and directing of those who followed it.

---

[24] Aḥmad and Tirmidhi. *Ṣaḥeeḥ al-Jaami'*, 2/22.

[25] *Lawaami' al-Anwaar al-Bahiyah*, Pp. 2/265.

The objection may be raised that the Messenger of Allah Yoosuf (ﷺ) was sold by those who rescued him from the well, and thus he became a slave. The response to this is that in this case slavery was a kind of trial for him, and that he was a free man to whom this wrong was done, but this slavery did not last for long, and Allah granted him power and authority after that.

The Messenger (ﷺ) memorized all that was taught to him and never forgot a single word:

﴿ سَنُقۡرِئُكَ فَلَا تَنسَىٰٓ ﴿٦﴾ ﴾

﴾We shall make you to recite [the Qur'an], so you [O' Muhammad] shall not forget [it].﴿ *(Qur'an 87: 6)*

They used to explain the religion of Allah to those who were opposed to it, and the Prophets used to prove that their enemies were wrong. In this field, Ibraaheem (Abraham) (عليه السلام) defeated his opponent:

﴿ ... فَبُهِتَ ٱلَّذِي كَفَرَۗ وَٱللَّهُ لَا يَهۡدِي ٱلۡقَوۡمَ ٱلظَّٰلِمِينَ ﴿٢٥٨﴾ ﴾

﴾...So the disbeliever was utterly defeated. And Allah guides not the people, who are *Zaalimoon* [wrongdoers].﴿ *(Qur'an 2: 258)*

And Allah (ﷻ) said, commenting on the debate of Ibraaheem with his people:

﴿ وَتِلۡكَ حُجَّتُنَآ ءَاتَيۡنَٰهَآ إِبۡرَٰهِيمَ عَلَىٰ قَوۡمِهِۦۚ نَرۡفَعُ دَرَجَٰتٖ مَّن نَّشَآءُۗ ... ﴿٨٣﴾ ﴾

﴾And that was Our Proof which We gave Ibraaheem [Abraham] against his people. We raise whom We will in degrees...﴿ *(Qur'an 6: 83)*

The Prophet Moosa (Moses) (may peace be upon him) used to debate with Pharaoh until he defeated him, then Pharaoh resorted to threats and the use of force:

﴿ قَالَ فِرۡعَوۡنُ وَمَا رَبُّ ٱلۡعَٰلَمِينَ ﴿٢٣﴾ قَالَ رَبُّ ٱلسَّمَٰوَٰتِ وَٱلۡأَرۡضِ وَمَا بَيۡنَهُمَآۖ إِن كُنتُم مُّوقِنِينَ ﴿٢٤﴾ قَالَ لِمَنۡ حَوۡلَهُۥٓ أَلَا تَسۡتَمِعُونَ ﴿٢٥﴾ قَالَ رَبُّكُمۡ وَرَبُّ ءَابَآئِكُمُ ٱلۡأَوَّلِينَ ﴿٢٦﴾ قَالَ إِنَّ رَسُولَكُمُ ٱلَّذِيٓ أُرۡسِلَ إِلَيۡكُمۡ لَمَجۡنُونٞ

﴿ قَالَ رَبُّ ٱلْمَشْرِقِ وَٱلْمَغْرِبِ وَمَا بَيْنَهُمَآ ۖ إِن كُنتُمْ تَعْقِلُونَ ﴿٢٨﴾ قَالَ لَئِنِ ٱتَّخَذْتَ إِلَٰهًا غَيْرِى لَأَجْعَلَنَّكَ مِنَ ٱلْمَسْجُونِينَ ﴿٢٩﴾ ﴾

﴿Fir'awn [Pharaoh] said: 'And what is the Lord of the *'Aalameen* [mankind, jinn and all that exists]?' Moosa [Moses] said: 'The Lord of the heavens and the earth, and all that is between them, if you seek to be convinced with certainty.' Fir'awn [Pharaoh] said to those around: 'Do you not hear [what he says]?' Moosa [Moses] said: 'Your Lord and the Lord of your ancient fathers!' [Fir'awn (Pharaoh)] said: 'Verily, your Messenger who has been sent to you is a madman!' [Moosa (Moses)] said: 'Lord of the east and the west, and all that is between them, if you did but understand!' [Fir'awn (Pharaoh)] said: 'If you choose an *ilaah* [god] other than me, I will certainly put you among the prisoners.'﴾

(Qur'an 26: 23-29)

Achieving true enslavement to Allah

We have discussed the perfection by means of which Allah made His Messengers loved by people, in their outward appearance and in their inward characteristics, and the gifts and talents which they were given. But there is another kind of perfection which Allah helped His Messengers and Prophets to attain, the achievement of true enslavement to Allah (*'uboodiyah*) in themselves.

The more a person attains a state of true enslavement to Allah, the closer he gets to attaining human perfection. The further away he is from attaining true enslavement to Allah, the more he falls and goes astray.

The Messengers won the race in this respect. Their lives were a series of efforts to attain this true enslavement to Allah. And the Seal of the

Messengers, the leader of the Prophets, was praised by his Lord for achieving the noblest degree of true enslavement to Allah, which is described in relation to revelation (*waḥy*):

﴿ فَأَوْحَىٰٓ إِلَىٰ عَبْدِهِۦ مَآ أَوْحَىٰ ﴿١٠﴾ ﴾

﴾So [Allah] revealed to His slave [Muhammad through Jibreel (Gabriel)] whatever He revealed.﴿

(Qur'an 53: 10)

And in relation to the sending down of the Book:

﴿ تَبَارَكَ ٱلَّذِى نَزَّلَ ٱلْفُرْقَانَ عَلَىٰ عَبْدِهِۦ لِيَكُونَ لِلْعَـٰلَمِينَ نَذِيرًا ﴿١﴾ ﴾

﴾Blessed be He Who sent down the criterion [of right and wrong, i.e. this Qur'an] to His slave [Muhammad] that he may be a warner to the *'Aalameen* [mankind and jinn].﴿ *(Qur'an 25: 1)*

And in relation to *du'aa'* (supplication):

﴿ وَأَنَّهُۥ لَمَّا قَامَ عَبْدُ ٱللَّهِ يَدْعُوهُ ... ﴿١٩﴾ ﴾

﴾And when the slave of Allah [Muhammad] stood up invoking Him [his Lord Allah] in prayer...﴿

(Qur'an 72: 19)

And in relation to the *Israa'* (Night Journey):

﴿ سُبْحَـٰنَ ٱلَّذِىٓ أَسْرَىٰ بِعَبْدِهِۦ لَيْلًا مِّنَ ٱلْمَسْجِدِ ٱلْحَرَامِ إِلَى ٱلْمَسْجِدِ ٱلْأَقْصَا ٱلَّذِى بَـٰرَكْنَا حَوْلَهُۥ ... ﴿١﴾ ﴾

﴾Glorified [and Exalted] be He [Allah] [above all that (evil) they associate with Him] Who took His slave [Muhammad] for a journey by night from *Al-Masjid al-Ḥaraam* [at Makkah] to *Al-Masjid al-Aqsa* [in Jerusalem], the neighbourhood whereof We have blessed...﴿ *(Qur'an 17: 1)*

Because of this perfect enslavement to Allah, he (ﷺ) deserves to be given precedence over all of mankind in this world and in the Hereafter. Hence as recorded by Bukhari and Muslim, the Messiah (عليه السلام) will tell the people, when they ask him to intercede, after asking all the Messengers who came before him, "Go to Muhammad, the slave whose past and future sins were all forgiven by Allah."[26]

A description of this perfect enslavement to Allah was narrated to us by our mother 'Aa'ishah (may Allah be pleased with her and with her father), who said: "I said, 'O' Messenger of Allah, may Allah cause me to be sacrificed for you, eat as you are reclining, for that will be easier for you.' He (ﷺ) bowed his head until his forehead almost touched the ground and said,

'I would rather eat as a slave eats and sit as a slave sits.'"

- This is narrated by Al-Baghawi in *Sharḥ as-Sunnah*, by Ibn Sa'd and by Imam Aḥmad in *Az-Zuhd*.[27]

Masculinity

Another aspect of the perfection that Allah granted is that He (سبحانه وتعالى) chose all the Messengers whom He sent from among men. Allah did not send any Messenger from among women. This exclusivity is indicated by the *aayah* (verse):

﴿ وَمَآ أَرْسَلْنَا قَبْلَكَ إِلَّا رِجَالًا نُّوحِىٓ إِلَيْهِمْ ... ۝٧ ﴾

﴿And We sent not before you [O' Muhammad] but men to whom We revealed...﴾ *(Qur'an 21: 7)*

---

[26] *Sharḥ al-'Aqeedah aṭ-Ṭaḥaawiyah*, Pp. 157.

[27] *Ṣaḥeeḥ al-Jaami' aṣ-Ṣagheer*, 1/122.

The reason why the Messengers were men

The Messengers were men and not women for reasons which were dictated by the nature of their task. For example:

1) The role of Messenger requires a great many tasks to be performed: addressing men and women, meeting people in secret and openly, moving throughout the land, confronting liars and establishing proof against them and debating with them, preparing and leading armies, and going through the sufferings of war. All of that is suitable for men but not for women.

2) The role of Messenger demands that the Messengers should be in charge of those who follow him, so he issues commands and prohibitions to his followers, and he rules and judges among them. If a woman were entrusted with such tasks, she would not be able to do them properly, and there would be people who would refuse to follow and obey her.

3) Masculinity is more perfect, as we have explained above. Hence Allah (ﷻ) has given the role of responsibility to men over women:

﴿ ٱلرِّجَالُ قَوَّٰمُونَ عَلَى ٱلنِّسَآءِ ... ﴿٣٤﴾ ﴾

﴾Men are the protectors and maintainers of women...﴿
(Qur'an 4: 34)

And the Messenger (ﷺ) said that women are lacking in reason and religious commitment.

4) Women have to cope with things that prevent them from doing many tasks, such as menstruation, pregnancy, childbirth and *nifaas* [postnatal bleeding (bleeding following childbirth)], which is accompanied by psychological stresses and pains, in addition to the care that is required by the child. All of that prevents her from being able to fulfil the role of Messenger and carrying out its duties.

Prophethood of women

Some of the scholars[28] - including Abu al-Ḥasan al-Ash‘ari, Qurṭubi and Ibn Ḥazam - said that Allah (ﷻ) blessed some women with Prophethood.

Those who say that some women were Prophets are agreed on the Prophethood of Maryam. Some of them also attribute Prophethood to other women, namely Ḥawwaa’, Saarah, the mother of Moosa, Haajar and Aasiyah.

When these people were shown the *aayah* (verse) which says that men can be Messengers but not women, they said, we do not dispute that; the position of Messenger is for men, but the position of Prophet is not included in the Qur’anic text, and the objections to women being Messengers do not apply in the case of Prophethood, because Prophethood may be limited only to the person who is a Prophet, with no need to convey it to others.

Their evidence

The proof quoted by these people is that the Qur’an says that Allah sent revelation/inspiration to some women. For example, He sent revelation/inspiration to the mother of Moosa:

﴿ وَأَوْحَيْنَآ إِلَىٰٓ أُمِّ مُوسَىٰٓ أَنْ أَرْضِعِيهِ ۖ فَإِذَا خِفْتِ عَلَيْهِ فَأَلْقِيهِ فِى ٱلْيَمِّ وَلَا تَخَافِى وَلَا تَحْزَنِىٓ ۖ إِنَّا رَآدُّوهُ إِلَيْكِ وَجَاعِلُوهُ مِنَ ٱلْمُرْسَلِينَ ﴿٧﴾ ﴾

﴿And We inspired the mother of Moosa [Moses] [telling]: ‘Suckle him [Moosa (Moses)], but when you fear for him, then cast him into the river and fear not,

[28] The Jews claimed that Maryam, the sister of Moosa (Moses) and Haaroon (Aaron), was a Prophetess (*Lawaami‘ al-Anwaar al-Bahiyah*, 2/266).

> nor grieve. Verily, We shall bring him back to you, and shall make him one of [Our] Messengers.'﴿ *(Qur'an 28: 7)*

And Allah, the Almighty, All-Powerful, sent Jibreel to Maryam (Mary), and he spoke to her:

﴿... فَأَرْسَلْنَا إِلَيْهَا رُوحَنَا فَتَمَثَّلَ لَهَا بَشَرًا سَوِيًّا ﴿١٧﴾ قَالَتْ إِنِّي أَعُوذُ
بِالرَّحْمَٰنِ مِنكَ إِن كُنتَ تَقِيًّا ﴿١٨﴾ قَالَ إِنَّمَا أَنَا رَسُولُ رَبِّكِ لِأَهَبَ لَكِ
غُلَامًا زَكِيًّا ﴿١٩﴾﴾

> ﴾...Then We sent to her Our *Rooḥ* [angel Jibreel (Gabriel)], and he appeared before her in the form of a man in all respects. She said: 'Verily, I seek refuge with the Most Gracious [Allah] from you, if you do fear Allah.' [The angel] said: 'I am only a messenger from your Lord, [to announce] to you the gift of a righteous son.'﴿ *(Qur'an 19: 17-19)*

And the angels addressed her, saying:

﴿... يَٰمَرْيَمُ إِنَّ ٱللَّهَ ٱصْطَفَىٰكِ وَطَهَّرَكِ وَٱصْطَفَىٰكِ عَلَىٰ نِسَآءِ ٱلْعَٰلَمِينَ
﴿٤٢﴾ يَٰمَرْيَمُ ٱقْنُتِى لِرَبِّكِ وَٱسْجُدِى وَٱرْكَعِى مَعَ ٱلرَّٰكِعِينَ ﴿٤٣﴾﴾

> ﴾...'O' Maryam [Mary]! Verily, Allah has chosen you, purified you [from polytheism and disbelief], and chosen you above the women of the *'Aalameen* [mankind and jinn] [of her lifetime]. O' Maryam! Submit yourself with obedience to your Lord [Allah, by worshipping none but Him Alone] and prostrate yourself, and bow down along with *Ar-Raaki'oon* [those who bow down].'﴿ *Qur'an 3: 42,43)*

Abu al-Ḥasan al-Ash'ari suggested that everyone to whom the angel came from Allah with a ruling, command, prohibition or news was a

Prophet.[29] Such things happened to the mother of Moosa and Maryam, and to others. According to the text of the Qur'an it also happened to Ḥawwaa', Saarah, Haajar and Aasiyah.

They also quote as evidence the fact that Allah chose Maryam (Mary) above the women of mankind and the jinn: ﴿...And chosen you above the women of the *'Aalameen* [mankind and jinn] [of her lifetime]...﴾ *(Qur'an 3: 42).*

And the Prophet (ﷺ) said:

> "Many men attained perfection, but no women attained perfection except Aasiyah the wife of Pharaoh and Maryam the daughter of 'Imraan."[30]

They said: those who attain the state of perfection are the Prophets.

Refutation of their view

What they say cannot be taken as proof of the Prophethood of women. Their view may be refuted from several angles:

1) We do not accept their view that a Prophet is not commanded to convey the message, to teach and mix with people. Our view is that there is no difference between a Prophet and a Messenger in this regard; the difference is that a Prophet is sent with the laws of the Messenger who came before him.

If this is the case, then the reasons why a woman Messenger cannot be sent apply also to the sending of a woman Prophet. There are many reasons which make woman incapable of playing the role of a Prophet.

---

[29] *Fatḥ al-Baari*, 6/447.

[30] A hadith whose authenticity is agreed upon by Bukhari and Muslim. See *Mishkaat al-Maṣaabeeḥ*, 3/118.

2) The revelation sent by Allah to these women, the mother of Moosa and Aasiyah, happened in the form of dreams. We know that dreams may form a part of revelation, and that this may happen to people other than the Prophets.

3) We do not accept their view that everyone who is addressed by the angels is a Prophet. In the hadith it says that Allah sent an angel to a man who was visiting one of his brothers in faith in another town. He asked him why he was visiting him, and when he said that he loved him for the sake of Allah, he (the angel) told him that Allah had sent him to tell him that He loved him. And the story of the bald man, the leper and the blind man is well known. And Jibreel (Gabriel) came to teach the *Ṣaḥaabah* (the Companions of the Prophet Muhammad) about their religion by questioning the Prophet (ﷺ), and the *Ṣaḥaabah* witnessed and heard that.[31]

4) The Prophet (ﷺ) refrained from stating whether or not Dhu'l-Qurnayn was a Prophet, even though the Qur'an says that Allah sent inspiration to him:

﴿ ... قُلْنَا يَٰذَا ٱلْقَرْنَيْنِ إِمَّآ أَن تُعَذِّبَ وَإِمَّآ أَن تَتَّخِذَ فِيهِمْ حُسْنًا ﴿٨٦﴾ ﴾

﴿...We [Allah] said [by inspiration]: 'O' Dhu'l-Qarnayn! Either you punish them, or treat them with kindness.'﴾

(Qur'an 18: 86)

5) They cannot quote as evidence the texts which say that Allah chose Maryam, for Allah clearly states that He has chosen people other than the Prophets:

﴿ ثُمَّ أَوْرَثْنَا ٱلْكِتَٰبَ ٱلَّذِينَ ٱصْطَفَيْنَا مِنْ عِبَادِنَا ۖ فَمِنْهُمْ ظَالِمٌ لِّنَفْسِهِۦ وَمِنْهُم مُّقْتَصِدٌ وَمِنْهُمْ سَابِقٌۢ بِٱلْخَيْرَٰتِ بِإِذْنِ ٱللَّهِ ۚ ... ﴿٣٢﴾ ﴾

---

[31] Concerning these and similar stories, see the second book in this series, *'Aalam al-Malaa'ikah al-Abraar* (The World of the Noble Angels).

﴾Then We gave the Book [the Qur'an] as inheritance to such of Our slaves whom We chose [the followers of Muhammad]. Then of them are some who wrong their ownselves, and of them are some who follow a middle course, and of them are some who are, by Allah's Leave, foremost in good deeds...﴿ *(Qur'an 35: 32)*

He chose the family of Ibraaheem (Abraham) and the family of 'Imraan over mankind and the jinn, and among their families are undoubtedly people who are not Prophets:

﴿ ۞ إِنَّ ٱللَّهَ ٱصۡطَفَىٰٓ ءَادَمَ وَنُوحٗا وَءَالَ إِبۡرَٰهِيمَ وَءَالَ عِمۡرَٰنَ عَلَى ٱلۡعَٰلَمِينَ ٣٣ ﴾

﴾Allah chose Adam, Nooḥ [Noah], the family of Ibraaheem [Abraham] and the family of 'Imraan above the *'Aalameen* [mankind and jinn] [of their times].﴿ *(Qur'an 3: 33)*

6) The word perfection mentioned in the hadith, which they use as evidence, does not necessarily imply Prophethood, because it may be applied to the perfection or completion of anything and reaching the highest level in some respect. What is meant is women who attained perfection in all the virtues that apply to women; hence perfection here is not the perfection of the Prophets.

7) In some *aḥaadeeth* it is clearly stated that Khadeejah (may Allah be pleased with her) was one of the perfect women.[32] This clearly shows that perfection here is not the perfection of Prophethood.

8) In some *aḥaadeeth* it is clearly stated that Faaṭimah will be the leader of the women of the people of Paradise, apart from Maryam

[32] This hadith is narrated by Ibn Mardawayh. See *Al-Bidaayah wan-Nihaayah*, 2/61.

the daughter of 'Imraan.[33] This rules out the Prophethood of women other than Maryam, such as the mother of Moosa and Aasiyah, because Faaṭimah was definitely not a Prophet. This hadith clearly states that she is superior to other women, and if the mother of Moosa and Aasiyah were Prophets they would be superior to Faaṭimah.

9) Maryam is described as being a *ṣiddeeqah* (the truthful) in the context of praising her and describing her virtues. Allah (ﷻ) says:

﴿ مَّا ٱلْمَسِيحُ ٱبْنُ مَرْيَمَ إِلَّا رَسُولٌ قَدْ خَلَتْ مِن قَبْلِهِ ٱلرُّسُلُ وَأُمُّهُۥ صِدِّيقَةٌ ۖ كَانَا يَأْكُلَانِ ٱلطَّعَامَ ... ﴿٧٥﴾ ﴾

﴿The Messiah ['Eesa (Jesus)], son of Maryam [Mary], was no more than a Messenger; many were the Messengers that passed away before him. His mother [Maryam (Mary)] was a *Ṣiddeeqah* [i.e. she believed in the Words of Allah and His Books]. They both used to eat food [as any other human being, while Allah does not eat]...﴾ *(Qur'an 5: 75)*

If there were any higher description, it would have been mentioned, but there is no mention in the Qur'an or in the *ṣaḥeeḥ* hadith of the Prophet that any women were Prophets.

Al-Qaaḍi 'Iyaaḍ narrated from a group of scholars that Maryam was not a Prophet. An-Nawawi said in *Al-Adhkaar* that Imam al-Ḥaramayn narrated that there was consensus on the point that Maryam was not a Prophet.[34] In *Sharḥ al-Muhadhdhab* it is attributed to a group of scholars, and Al-Ḥasan al-Baṣri was quoted as saying that there are no Prophets among women or the jinn.[35]

---

[33] This is narrated by Aḥmad, and its isnad is *jayyid*. *Fatḥ al-Baari*, 6/477.

[34] We cannot say that there is consensus after knowing that some of the scholars differed concerning this matter. But there may have been consensus before this difference of opinion arose.

[35] *Fatḥ al-Baari*, 6/471, 473.

Matters which are unique to the Prophets and not shared by other humans

1 - *Waḥy* (Revelation)

Allah has bestowed revelation upon them to the exclusion of other human beings. Allah (ﷻ) says:

﴿ قُلْ إِنَّمَآ أَنَا۠ بَشَرٌ مِّثْلُكُمْ يُوحَىٰٓ إِلَىَّ أَنَّمَآ إِلَٰهُكُمْ إِلَٰهٌ وَٰحِدٌ ... ﴿١١٠﴾ ﴾

﴾Say [O' Muhammad]: 'I am only a man like you. It has been revealed to me that your *Ilah* [God] is One *Ilah* [God i.e. Allah].'...﴿ *(Qur'an 18: 110)*

This revelation implies a number of things which distinguish them from other people. For example, Allah spoke to some of them and they were contacted by some of the angels; Allah taught them some matters of the unseen, past and future; and Allah showed them something of the world of the unseen.

An example of that is the *Israa'* (Night Journey) of the Messenger (ﷺ) to *Bayt al-Maqdis* (Jerusalem) and his ascent into the higher heavens, where he saw the angels and Prophets, and was shown Paradise and Hell. He was also shown those who are being punished in their graves and heard their torment. In the hadith it says:

> "Were it not for the fear that you would not bury [your dead], I would have prayed to Allah to make you hear the torment of the grave."[36]

2 - Infallibility (*'Aṣmah*)

This will be discussed in a separate section.

---

[36] Aḥmad, Muslim, Abu Dawood and Nasaa'i; *Ṣaḥeeḥ al-Jaami' aṣ-Ṣagheer*, 5/75.

3 - The Prophets' eyes sleep but their hearts do not

One of the distinct characteristics that Allah has given to them is that their eyes sleep but their hearts do not. It is narrated by Bukhari from Anas (ﷺ) in the hadith of the *Israa'*:

> "The Prophet's eyes sleep, but his heart does not. Such are the Prophets: their eyes sleep but their hearts do not."[37]

Even if this was the wording of Anas, it could not be based on mere personal opinion, as Ibn Ḥajar says.[38] This is narrated from the words of the Prophet (ﷺ), and it was reported in a *ṣaḥeeḥ* hadith that he said:

> "We Prophets, our eyes sleep but our hearts do not."

And the Prophet ﷺ said describing himself,

> "My eyes sleep but my heart does not."[39]

4 - The Prophets were given the choice at the time of death

Another of the unique characteristics of the Prophets is that they are given the choice between this world and the Hereafter. The mother of the believers 'Aa'ishah (may Allah be pleased with her) narrated: I heard the Messenger of Allah (ﷺ) say:

> "There is no Prophet who fell sick but he was given the choice between this world and the Hereafter."[40] During his final illness his voice became very hoarse, and I

---

[37] *Fatḥ al-Baari*, 6/579.

[38] Ibid.

[39] Narrated by Ibn Sa'd and Ibn Ḥibbaan. See *Ṣaḥeeḥ al-Jaami' aṣ-Ṣagheer*, 3/55.

[40] Bukhari and Muslim, See *Silsilat al-Aḥaadeeth aṣ-Ṣaḥeeḥah*, 2/316.

heard him say, ﴾...In the company of those on whom Allah has bestowed His Grace, of the Prophets, the *Ṣiddiqoon* [those followers of the Prophets who were first and foremost to believe in them], the martyrs, and the righteous...﴿ *(Qur'an 4: 69)*, and I knew that he had been given the choice."[41]

We have quoted elsewhere the hadith which says that the Angel of Death gave Moosa (Moses) the choice, and Moosa struck the Angel of Death and put out his eye.[42]

5 - A Prophet is only buried where he dies

Other matters which Allah has decreed only for the Prophets are matters which have to do with what happens after they die:

A Prophet is buried nowhere but in the place where he died. According to a hadith,

"No Prophet was ever buried except where he died."[43]

Hence the *Ṣaḥaabah* - may Allah be pleased with them - buried the Messenger (ﷺ) in the room of 'Aa'ishah where he had died.

6 - The earth does not consume their bodies

One of the ways in which Allah honours His Prophets and Messengers is that the earth does not consume their bodies. No matter how long a time passes, their bodies remain preserved from decay. According to a hadith:

---

[41] *Ṣaḥeeḥ al-Bukhari bi Sharḥihi Fatḥ al-Baari*, 8/255.

[42] See our book *'Aalam al-Malaa'ikah* (The World of the Noble Angels).

[43] Imam Aḥmad in his *Musnad* with a *ṣaḥeeḥ* isnad. See *Ṣaḥeeḥ al-Jaami' aṣ-Ṣagheer*, 5/46.

> "Allah has forbidden the earth to consume the bodies of the Prophets."

The historians mentioned the story of strange events and wonders. Ibn Katheer narrated in *Al-Bidaayah wan-Nihaayah* [44] that Yoonus ibn Bakeer said:

"When we conquered Tastar, we found among the property of the house of Al-Harmazaan a bed on which there was a dead man, at whose head was a book. We took that book and brought it to 'Umar, and he called Ka'b to look at it and had him translate it into Arabic. (He said) I was the first man among the Arabs to read it, and I read it as I read the Qur'an.

I asked Abu al-'Aaliyah, 'What was in it?' He said, 'Your biographies and affairs, what you will say, and what will happen after that.'

I questioned, 'What did you do with that man?' He said, 'We dug thirteen scattered graves for him in one day, and when night came we buried him and leveled all the graves, so that the people would not know where he was buried and would not exhume him.'[45]

I asked further, 'What benefit did they hope for from him?' He said, 'If the sky withheld (its rain), they would carry him out on his bed, then ask for rain.'

---

[44] *Al-Bidaayah wan-Nihaayah*, 2/40.

[45] This is indicative of the level of understanding that the Muslims had at that time, because honouring the dead means burying them, whether he is a Prophet or not. They dug many graves so that the people would not know where he was buried, and so that they would not be able to exhume his body, for that would have been an act of disrespect towards that noble Prophet. Moreover, they might have taken his grave as a shrine, and built a mosque over it or directed prayers towards it or sought blessings from it, as many of those who have gone astray from the Straight Path do in many Muslim countries.

I asked, 'Who do you think this man was?' He said, 'A man called Daniel.'

I questioned, 'How long do you think he had been dead?' He said, he died three hundred years ago.'

I querried, 'Had anything changed in his body?' He said, 'No, apart from some hairs on the nape of his neck. For the flesh of the Prophets is not consumed by the earth, or by wild animals.'''

Ibn Katheer said: This is a *ṣaḥeeḥ* isnad going back to Abu al-'Aaliyah.

It seems that this was one of the Prophets of the Children of Israel, and the *Ṣaḥaabah* thought that it was Daniel, because Daniel had been seized by the king of Persia, and he remained imprisoned by him. But it seems that the estimation of those who found him was not correct, for Daniel lived eight hundred years before Islam. If their estimation was correct, then this man was not a Prophet, because there was no Prophet between 'Eesa and our Messenger Muhammad (Peace and blessings be upon them both). In that case he would have been a righteous slave but not a Prophet. It is more likely that he was a Prophet, because those whose bodies are preserved are the Prophets, not others. It is also likely that the book which was found by his head was the Book of a Prophet, because of the matters of the unseen included in that book which imply that it could not have been anything but a divine Revelation. What makes us think it more likely that he was from among the Children of Israel is two things:

1) The *Ṣaḥaabah* thought that he was Daniel, and they knew this from other evidence that was not mentioned in this report.

2) The book which was found by his head appears to have been written in Hebrew, because the one who translated it was Ubayy ibn Ka'b, who had been a Jew before he became a Muslim.

7 - They are alive in their graves

It is narrated in a *ṣaḥeeḥ* (authentic) hadith that the Prophet (ﷺ) said:

> "The Prophets are alive in their grave, praying."[46]

It is also narrated that the Messenger (ﷺ) said:

> "I passed by Moosa (Moses) on the night of the *Israa'* (Night Journey) at *Al-Katheeb al-Aḥmar* and he was standing praying in his grave."[47]

Muslim narrated from Abu Hurayrah (رضي الله عنه) in the story of the *Israa'* that the Prophet (ﷺ) said:

> "I saw myself among a group of the Prophets, and Moosa (Moses) was standing praying... and 'Eesa ibn Maryam (Jesus) was standing praying, and Ibraaheem (Abraham) was standing praying."[48]

---

[46] Narrated by the *jamaa'ah* from Anas. See *Ṣaḥeeḥ al-Jaami'*, 2/414.

[47] Muslim: *Kitaab al-Faḍaa'il*, hadith no. 1641; See *Sharḥ an-Nawawi 'ala al-Muslim*, 15/133.

[48] *Fatḥ al-Baari*, 6/487.

CHAPTER SIX
THE INFALLIBILITY OF THE PROPHETS

Are the Messengers infallible and protected from error and sin, and is their infallibility general and comprehensive? This is what we will try to explain here.

Infallibility in bearing and conveying the message

The ummah is unanimous that the Messengers are infallible in their bearing of the Message.[1] They do not forget anything of that which Allah has revealed except for things that have been abrogated. Allah guaranteed His Messenger (ﷺ) that He would make him to recite the Qur'an so that he would not forget anything of that which had been revealed to him, apart from that which Allah willed he should forget:

﴿ سَنُقْرِئُكَ فَلَا تَنسَىٰٓ ۝٦ إِلَّا مَا شَآءَ ٱللَّهُ ... ۝٧ ﴾

﴿We shall make you to recite [the Qur'an], so you [O' Muhammad] shall not forget [it], except what Allah may will...﴾ *(Qur'an 87: 6-7)*

And He guaranteed that He would collect it in the heart of His Prophet (ﷺ):

﴿ لَا تُحَرِّكْ بِهِۦ لِسَانَكَ لِتَعْجَلَ بِهِۦٓ ۝١٦ إِنَّ عَلَيْنَا جَمْعَهُۥ وَقُرْءَانَهُۥ ۝١٧ فَإِذَا قَرَأْنَٰهُ فَٱتَّبِعْ قُرْءَانَهُۥ ۝١٨ ﴾

﴿Move not your tongue concerning [the Qur'an, O' Muhammad] to make haste therewith. It is for Us to

[1] More than one scholar narrated that there was consensus on their infallibility in this regard. See *Majmoo' al-Fataawa*, 10/291; *Lawaami' al-Anwaar al-Bahiyah*, 2/304.

> collect it and to give you [O' Muhammad] the ability to recite it [the Qur'an]. And when We have recited it to you [O' Muhammad through Jibreel (Gabriel)], then follow its [the Qur'an's] recitation.﴿ *(Qur'an 75: 16-18)*

And they are infallible in their conveying of the Message. The Messengers did not conceal anything of that which Allah revealed to them, because to do so would be an act of betrayal and it is impossible for the Messengers to do such a thing. Allah (ﷻ) says:

﴿ يَٰٓأَيُّهَا ٱلرَّسُولُ بَلِّغْ مَآ أُنزِلَ إِلَيْكَ مِن رَّبِّكَ ۖ وَإِن لَّمْ تَفْعَلْ فَمَا بَلَّغْتَ رِسَالَتَهُۥ ... ﴿٦٧﴾ ﴾

> ﴾O' Messenger [Muhammad]! Proclaim [the Message] which has been sent down to you from your Lord. And if you do not, then you have not conveyed His Message...﴿ *(Qur'an 5: 67)*

If there had been any act of concealment or changing of that which Allah had revealed, then the punishment of Allah would have befallen the one who concealed or changed anything. In the words of the Qur'an:

﴿ وَلَوْ تَقَوَّلَ عَلَيْنَا بَعْضَ ٱلْأَقَاوِيلِ ﴿٤٤﴾ لَأَخَذْنَا مِنْهُ بِٱلْيَمِينِ ﴿٤٥﴾ ثُمَّ لَقَطَعْنَا مِنْهُ ٱلْوَتِينَ ﴿٤٦﴾ ﴾

> ﴾And if he [Muhammad] had forged a false saying concerning Us [Allah], We surely would have seized him by his right hand [or with power and might], and then We certainly would have cut off his life artery [aorta].﴿ *(Qur'an 69: 44-46)*

Infallibility includes their not forgetting anything that Allah had revealed to them, thus no part of the Revelation can be lost. Their not forgetting anything when conveying the Message is also included in the *aayah* (verse): ﴿We shall make you to recite [the Qur'an], so you [O' Muhammad] shall not forget [it].﴾ *(Qur'an 87: 6)*

Another indication of his infallibility in conveying the message is the *aayah* (verse):

﴿ وَمَا يَنطِقُ عَنِ ٱلْهَوَىٰٓ ۝٣ إِنْ هُوَ إِلَّا وَحْىٌ يُوحَىٰ ۝٤ ﴾

﴿Nor does he speak of [his own] desire. It is only a Revelation revealed.﴾ *(Qur'an 53: 3-4)*

Matters which do not contradict infallibility

Natural human emotions do not contradict infallibility. The Prophet Ibraaheem (Abraham) (ﷺ) conceived a fear of his guests when he saw that they did not stretch forth their hands towards the food that he offered them. He did not know that they were angels who had appeared in human form:

﴿ فَلَمَّا رَءَآ أَيْدِيَهُمْ لَا تَصِلُ إِلَيْهِ نَكِرَهُمْ وَأَوْجَسَ مِنْهُمْ خِيفَةً قَالُوا۟ لَا تَخَفْ إِنَّآ أُرْسِلْنَآ إِلَىٰ قَوْمِ لُوطٍ ۝٧٠ ﴾

﴿But when he saw their hands went not towards it [the meal], he mistrusted them, and conceived a fear of them. They said: 'Fear not, we have been sent against the people of Looṭ [Lot].'﴾ *(Qur'an 11: 70)*

Prophet Moosa (Moses) (ﷺ) promised Al-Khiḍr that he would be patient when he accompanied him, and that he would not ask about anything that the righteous slave did until he himself told him. But he could not control himself when he saw the strange things that he did, and he asked questions, then he raised objections, then he made suggestions.[2] On each occasion the righteous slave reminded him

[2] The first time was due to forgetfulness, but the second and third time were deliberate.

and said:

﴿ ... أَلَمْ أَقُل لَّكَ إِنَّكَ لَن تَسْتَطِيعَ مَعِىَ صَبْرًا ﴿٧٥﴾ ﴾

﴾...Did I not tell you that you can have no patience with me?﴿ *(Qur'an 18: 75)*

When he explained to him the reasons for his actions, he said to him:

﴿ ... ذَٰلِكَ تَأْوِيلُ مَا لَمْ تَسْطِع عَّلَيْهِ صَبْرًا ﴿٨٢﴾ ﴾

﴾...That is the interpretation of those [things] over which you could not hold patience.﴿ *(Qur'an 18: 82)*

Prophet Moosa became very angry, and he grabbed his brother's head and dragged him towards him, and threw down the tablets on which the guidance was written, when he came back to his people after meeting his Lord, and found them worshipping the calf:

﴿ وَلَمَّا رَجَعَ مُوسَىٰٓ إِلَىٰ قَوْمِهِۦ غَضْبَٰنَ أَسِفًا قَالَ بِئْسَمَا خَلَفْتُمُونِى مِنۢ بَعْدِىٓ أَعَجِلْتُمْ أَمْرَ رَبِّكُمْ وَأَلْقَى ٱلْأَلْوَاحَ وَأَخَذَ بِرَأْسِ أَخِيهِ يَجُرُّهُۥٓ إِلَيْهِ قَالَ ٱبْنَ أُمَّ إِنَّ ٱلْقَوْمَ ٱسْتَضْعَفُونِى وَكَادُوا۟ يَقْتُلُونَنِى فَلَا تُشْمِتْ بِىَ ٱلْأَعْدَآءَ وَلَا تَجْعَلْنِى مَعَ ٱلْقَوْمِ ٱلظَّٰلِمِينَ ﴿١٥٠﴾ ﴾

﴾And when Moosa [Moses] returned to his people, angry and grieved, he said: 'What an evil thing is that which you have done [i.e. worshipping the calf] during my absence. Did you hasten and go ahead as regards the matter of your Lord [you left His worship]?' And he threw down the Tablets and seized his brother by [the hair of] his head and dragged him towards him. Haaroon [Aaron] said: 'O' son of my mother! Indeed the people judged me weak and were about to kill me, so make not the enemies rejoice over me, nor put me amongst the people who are *Ẓaalimoon* [wrongdoers].'﴿

(Qur'an 7: 150)

According to a hadith:

> "Being told of something is not like seeing it for oneself. For Allah told Moosa (Moses) what his people had done with the calf, and he did not throw down the Tablets, but when he saw with his own eyes what they had done, he threw down the Tablets and they broke."[3]

Adam's forgetfulness and denial

Another example is the forgetfulness and denial of Adam (ﷺ). Tirmidhi narrated from Abu Hurayrah (ﷺ) that the Messenger of Allah (ﷺ) said:

> "When Allah created Adam, He wiped his back, and there fell from his back every soul which He would create from his (Adam's) offspring until the Day of Resurrection. He put a flash of light between the eyes of each one, then he showed them to Adam, who said, 'O' Lord, who are these?' He said, 'These are your offspring.' Then he saw a man among them and he liked that which was between his eyes. He said, 'O' Lord, who is this?' He said, 'This is a man from the last of the nations among your descendents. He is called Dawood (David).' He said, 'O' Lord, how long will he live?' He said, 'Sixty years.' He said, 'O' Lord, give him forty more years from my lifespan.' When Adam's life was over and the Angel of Death came to him, he said,

[3] Aḥmad: *Musnad;* Ṭabaraani: *Al-Awsaṭ*, with a *ṣaḥeeḥ* isnad. See *Ṣaḥeeḥ al-Jaami' aṣ-Ṣagheer*, 5/87.

'Don't I have forty years of my life left?' He said, 'Did you not give them to your son Dawood?' Adam denied, and his descendents denied; Adam forgot and his descendents forgot; Adam erred and his descendents erred.'"[4]

A Prophet burned the city of the ants

Another example is what happened in the case of one of the Prophets who became angry when an ant bit him. He gave orders that the city of the ants should be burned. But Allah rebuked him for that. According to the hadith narrated by Abu Hurayrah (ﷺ) from the Prophet (ﷺ):

> "One of the Prophets stopped to rest beneath a tree, and an ant bit him. He gave orders that his luggage be removed from beneath the tree, then he gave orders that the house (of the ants) should be burned with fire. Then Allah revealed to him (saying), 'Would it not have been sufficient (to punish) a single ant (the one that bit you)?'"

- This is recorded by Bukhari, Abu Dawood and Nasaa'i.[5]

Our Prophet prayed *ẓuhr* as two *rak'ahs* out of forgetfulness

Our Prophet (ﷺ) also forgot things that had nothing to do with conveying the Message or with matters of shari'ah. For example as narrated by Ibn Seereen from Abu Hurayrah (ﷺ) that,

> "The Messenger of Allah (ﷺ) led us in praying one of

---

[4] Tirmidhi said, this is a *ṣaḥeeḥ ḥasan* hadith. Al-Ḥaakim: *Mustadrak*; he said (it is) *ṣaḥeeḥ* according to the conditions of Muslim. *Al-Bidaayah wan-Nihaayah*, 1/87.

[5] *Ṣaḥeeḥ al-Jaami'*, 5/28.

the afternoon[6] prayers, and he prayed two *rak'ahs* (units), then he said the *tasleem* (i.e., ended by saying *Asslamu 'alaykum*). Then he got up and went to a piece of wood that was lying in the mosque, and leaned against it as if he were angry. He placed his right hand over his left and interlaced his fingers, then he put his right cheek on the back of his left hand. Those who were in a hurry exited through the doors of the mosque, saying that the prayer had been shortened. Among the people were Abu Bakr and 'Umar, but they hesitated to speak to him. Amongst them was also a man known as Dhu'l-Yadayn, who said, 'O' Messenger of Allah, did you forget or has the prayer been shortened?' He said, 'I did not forget, neither has the prayer been shortened.' [The Prophet (ﷺ)] said, 'Is what Dhu'l-Yadayn said true?' They said, 'Yes.' So he stood up and prayed what he had missed, then he said the *tasleem*, then he said *'Allahu Akbar'* and prostrated as he had prostrated the first time, or longer. Then he raised his head, then said *takbeer* again, then prostrated as he had prostrated before, or longer. Then he raised his head and said *'Allahu Akbar'*."

(The subnarrator) said: "I think that they asked him (Ibn Seereen) whether the Prophet (ﷺ) said *tasleem* at the end. He said, I heard that 'Imraan ibn Ḥuṣayn said, then he said *tasleem*." Agreed upon by Bukhari and Muslim, but the version narrated by Muslim does not say that he put one hand on top of the other or that he interlaced his fingers.

---

[6] Az-Zahri said: *Al-'Ishaa* (translated here as 'afternoon') in Arabic refers to the time between the zenith of the sun and its setting. What is referred to here may be *Ẓuhr* or *'Aṣr*. (*Nayl al-Awṭaar*, 3/115) One of the reports states that it was definitely *Ẓuhr.*

According to another report:

> "Whilst I was performing *Ẓuhr* with the Prophet (ﷺ), he said *tasleem* after two *rak'ahs*. Then a man from Bani Sulaym stood up and said, 'O' Messenger of Allah, has the prayer been shortened or did you forget?'"

- This version is narrated by Aḥmad and Muslim.

This indicates that this event happened in his presence and after he became a Muslim.

According to a report whose authenticity is agreed upon by Bukhari and Muslim, the Prophet (ﷺ) said:

> "I did not forget and it has not been shortened." He said, "No, rather you forgot."

This indicates that Dhu'l-Yadayn spoke after he knew that it had not been abrogated.[7]

The Messenger (ﷺ) clearly stated that he was subject to forgetfulness just like all other human beings. According to a hadith narrated by Ibn Mas'ood, the Prophet (ﷺ) said,

> "I am only human. I forget as you forget, and if I forget then remind me."[8]

He said this after forgetting something in one of the prayers.

The hadith which says, "I forget or I am made to forget so that I may establish the Sunnah," cannot be used to contradict the hadith quoted

---

[7] The various versions of the hadith that we have quoted here are taken from *Muntaqi al-Akhbaar lil Majd* by Ibn Taymiyah. See its commentary *Nayl al-Awṭaar*, 3/114.

[8] This has been narrated by the *jamaa'ah* except for Tirmidhi; *Nayl al-Awṭaar*, 3/125.

above, because this hadith - as Ibn Ḥajar said - has no basis; it is one of the statements of Maalik for which no isnad going back to the Prophet (ﷺ) can be found even after intensive research.[9]

They may err when trying to judge between people

The Prophets and Messengers strove to pass judgement concerning matters which they were faced with, and they judged according to what they saw, for they had no knowledge of the unseen, and they might make mistakes when trying to reach the right conclusion. An example of that is the fact that the Prophet of Allah Dawood (David) (عليه السلام) failed to pass the correct judgement, whilst Allah helped his son Sulaymaan (Solomon) (عليه السلام) (to reach the right conclusion) concerning the same matter.

Bukhari narrated from Abu Hurayrah (رضي الله عنه) that he heard the Prophet (ﷺ) say:

> "There were two women who each had a child. The wolf came and took away the child of one of them, and she said to her companion, 'It took away your child,' and the other woman said, 'No, it took away your child.' So they referred to Dawood (David) for judgement, and he judged in favour of the older woman. Then they went to Sulaymaan ibn Dawood and told him about the matter. He said, 'Bring me a knife, and I will cut (the child) in half and share him between them.' The younger woman said, 'Do not do that, may Allah have mercy on you! He is her son.' Then he passed judgement in favour of the younger woman."[10]

---

[9] *Nayl al-Awṭaar*, 3/117.

[10] Bukhari: *Kitaab Aḥaadeeth al-Anbiyaa', Baab Qawlihi ta'aala, "Wa wahabna li Dawood Sulaymaan."* See *Fatḥ al-Baari*, 6/458.

The Messenger (ﷺ) explained and commented on this story. Umm Salamah (may Allah be pleased with her) the wife of the Prophet (ﷺ) narrated that, "The Prophet (ﷺ) heard a dispute at the door (*Ḥujrah*) of his apartment, so he went out to them and said,

> 'I am only human. Disputes are referred to me, but some of you may be more eloquent in arguing their case than others, so I think that he is telling the truth and I judge in his favour because of that. If I judge in a person's favour at the expense of a Muslim's rights, that is a piece of the Fire for him, so let him take it or leave it.'"[11]

Those who deny these emotions of the Prophets and Messengers go against the texts

The *Shi'ah* who follow the twelve Imams (*ithna' 'ashari*)[12] said that infallibility means that the Prophets could never be forgetful, make mistakes or feel fear or any other human emotion. We have quoted the texts from the Qur'an and Sunnah which indicate the opposite. These are texts which are not open to any other interpretation. So you must follow the Qur'an and Sunnah in which alone there is guidance.

Infallibility from sin

The evil actions which the Jews attributed to the Prophets and Messengers[13]

The Jews attribute evil actions to the Prophets and Messengers, such as:

---

[11] Bukhari: *Kitaab al-Maẓaalim, Baab Ithm man khaasama fil-baaṭil*. See *Fatḥ al-Baari*, 5/107.

[12] *'Aqaa'id al-Imaamiyah* by Muhammad Riḍa al-Muẓaffar, Pp. 79.

[13] The texts mentioned here are taken from the book *Muhammad Nabi al-Islam*, Pp. 145.

1) They say that the Prophet of Allah Haaroon (Aaron) made a calf and worshipped it along with the Children of Israel. (Exodus 32:1ff).

The Qur'an explained how misguided they were when it told us that the one who made the calf which seemed mooing was As-Saamiri, and that Haaroon had denounced them in the strongest terms.

2) They say that Prophet Ibraaheem (Abraham), the Close Friend of the Most Merciful, offered his wife Saarah to Pharaoh in order to gain favour because of her. (Genesis 12:14ff)

They told lies about the Close Friend of the Most Merciful. The Messenger (ﷺ) told us the story about Prophet Ibraaheem when he went to Egypt: the king of Egypt was a tyrant, and whenever he saw a beautiful woman who was married, he would kill the husband and take her for himself. When Ibraaheem was asked about her, he said that she was his sister, meaning his sister in Islam. The Messenger (ﷺ) told us that Allah protected Saarah when she went to the tyrant, and he did not harm her in any way.

3) They say that Prophet Looṭ (Lot) (عليه السلام) drank wine until he was intoxicated, then he committed incest with his two daughters, one after the other. (Genesis 19:30ff). Allah forbid that the Prophet Looṭ should do such a thing. He is the one who promoted virtue all his life and fought against perversion. But the Jewish hatred extends to the most perfect of human beings. May the curse of Allah be upon the evildoers.

4) They say that Prophet Ya'qoob (Jacob) (عليه السلام) stole flocks (of sheep) from his father-in-law, and took his family away without his (father-in-law's) knowledge. (Genesis 31:17ff)

5) They say that Reuben committed adultery with the wife of his father Ya'qoob, and that Prophet Ya'qoob (عليه السلام) knew of this evil deed but said nothing. (Genesis 35:22)

6) They say that Prophet Dawood (David) (ﷺ) committed adultery with the wife of one of the commanders of his army, then he plotted to kill the man. The man was killed, then Dawood took the wife and added her to his wives, and she bore him Sulaymaan. (II Samuel 11:1ff)

7) They say that at the end of his life, Prophet Sulaymaan (Solomon) turned apostate and worshipped idols and built temples for them. (I Kings 11:5ff)

These are some of the evil actions and major sins which this nation, subject to Divine wrath (i.e., the Jews) attributed to the pure Prophets of Allah, who are far removed from what they attribute to them. But these are sick souls who attribute evil actions to those whom Allah has chosen from among His creation so as to make it easier for them to justify their own sins and shortcomings when they are denounced for their sins or when anybody objects to them.

The Christians attribute evil actions to the Prophets

The Christians are no better than the Jews in this regard. They also attributed evil actions to the Prophets and Messengers, by affirming the distorted and altered Bible which exists nowadays, and contains things we have mentioned above, in addition to the things mentioned in the distorted Gospels (New Testament), including the following:

1) In the Gospel of Matthew it says that Jesus descended from Solomon the son of David, and that their grandfather was Perez who descended from the illegitimate offspring of Judah (Yehudah) the son of Jacob. (Matthew 1:3, 6)

2) In the Gospel of John 2:4, it says that Jesus rebuked his mother in the midst of a group of people. Compare this to the description of him given in the Qur'an - ﴾And dutiful to my mother﴿ *(Qur'an 19: 32)*?

3) They say that Jesus testified that all the Prophets who had come to the Children of Israel were thieves and robbers. (John 10:8)

These are just a few of the many examples with which those distorted Gospels are filled where things are attributed to the Prophets and Messengers of which they are innocent.[14] The Prophets and Messengers are the most innocent, pure and virtuous of people. By Allah, these people have gone astray in what they attribute to the righteous and pure Prophets of Allah.

The view of the Muslim ummah on the infallibility of the Prophets and their being protected from committing sin

The Muslim ummah is agreed that the kind of sins which the Jews and Christians attribute to the Prophets of Allah, such as adultery, theft, betrayal, and making and worshipping idols, are not sins that any of the Prophets or Messengers could ever commit under any circumstances, and that they are infallible and protected from that.

Infallibility and being protected against committing minor sins

Most of the scholars of Islam said that the Prophets were not infallible against minor sins. Ibn Taymiyah said: "The view that the Prophets were infallible against major sins but not minor sins is the view of most of the scholars of Islam, and of all different groups. It is even the view of most of *ahl al-kalaam* (Islamic philosophers - scholarstics), as was stated by Abu al-Ḥasan al-Aamidi that this is the view of most of the Ash'aris. This is also the view of most of the scholars of *tafseer* and hadith, and the *fuqahaa'*. Indeed, it is not narrated that any of the *salaf*, Imams, *Ṣaḥaabah*, *Taabi'een* or

[14] For more examples, see the book *Muhammad Nabi al-Islam*, Pp. 146.

succeeding generations said anything that went against this view..."[15]

Evidence

The majority of scholars quoted evidence for their views:

1) Adam's sin of eating from the tree from which Allah had forbidden him to eat:

﴿ وَإِذْ قُلْنَا لِلْمَلَٰٓئِكَةِ ٱسْجُدُوا۟ لِءَادَمَ فَسَجَدُوٓا۟ إِلَّآ إِبْلِيسَ أَبَىٰ ﴿١١٦﴾
فَقُلْنَا يَٰٓـَٔادَمُ إِنَّ هَٰذَا عَدُوٌّ لَّكَ وَلِزَوْجِكَ فَلَا يُخْرِجَنَّكُمَا مِنَ ٱلْجَنَّةِ فَتَشْقَىٰٓ
﴿١١٧﴾ إِنَّ لَكَ أَلَّا تَجُوعَ فِيهَا وَلَا تَعْرَىٰ ﴿١١٨﴾ وَأَنَّكَ لَا تَظْمَؤُا۟ فِيهَا وَلَا
تَضْحَىٰ ﴿١١٩﴾ فَوَسْوَسَ إِلَيْهِ ٱلشَّيْطَٰنُ قَالَ يَٰٓـَٔادَمُ هَلْ أَدُلُّكَ عَلَىٰ شَجَرَةِ
ٱلْخُلْدِ وَمُلْكٍ لَّا يَبْلَىٰ ﴿١٢٠﴾ فَأَكَلَا مِنْهَا فَبَدَتْ لَهُمَا سَوْءَٰتُهُمَا وَطَفِقَا
يَخْصِفَانِ عَلَيْهِمَا مِن وَرَقِ ٱلْجَنَّةِ ۚ وَعَصَىٰٓ ءَادَمُ رَبَّهُۥ فَغَوَىٰ ﴿١٢١﴾ ﴾

﴿And [remember] when We said to the angels: 'Prostrate yourselves to Adam.' They prostrated themselves [all] except *Iblees* [Satan]; he refused. Then We said: 'O' Adam! Verily, this is an enemy to you and to your wife. So let him not get you both out of Paradise, so that you will be distressed. Verily, you have [a promise from Us] that you will never be hungry therein nor naked. And you [will] suffer not from thirst therein nor from the sun's heat.' Then *Shayṭaan* [Satan] whispered to him, saying: 'O' Adam! Shall I lead you to the Tree of Eternity and to a kingdom that will never waste away?' Then they both ate of the tree, and so their private parts became manifest to them, and they began to cover themselves with the leaves of the Paradise for their

[15] *Majmoo' al-Fataawa Shaykh al-Islam*, 4/319.

covering. Thus did Adam disobey his Lord, so he went astray.﴿ *(Qur'an 20: 116-121)*

This *aayah* (verse) is very clear and unambiguous. It clearly states that Adam disobeyed his Lord.

2) Prophet Nooḥ (Noah) prayed to his Lord for his *kaafir* (disbelieving) son:

﴿ وَنَادَىٰ نُوحٌ رَّبَّهُۥ فَقَالَ رَبِّ إِنَّ ٱبْنِى مِنْ أَهْلِى وَإِنَّ وَعْدَكَ ٱلْحَقُّ وَأَنتَ أَحْكَمُ ٱلْحَٰكِمِينَ ﴿٤٥﴾ ﴾

﴾And Nooḥ [Noah] called upon his Lord and said, 'O' my Lord! Verily, my son is of my family! And certainly, Your Promise is true, and You are the Most Just of the judges.'﴿ *(Qur'an 11: 45)*

But his Lord rebuked him for saying that, and told him that he (his son) was not part of his family, and that this action of his was not a righteous deed:

﴿ قَالَ يَٰنُوحُ إِنَّهُۥ لَيْسَ مِنْ أَهْلِكَ ۖ إِنَّهُۥ عَمَلٌ غَيْرُ صَٰلِحٍ ۖ فَلَا تَسْـَٔلْنِ مَا لَيْسَ لَكَ بِهِۦ عِلْمٌ ۖ إِنِّىٓ أَعِظُكَ أَن تَكُونَ مِنَ ٱلْجَٰهِلِينَ ﴿٤٦﴾ ﴾

﴾He said: 'O' Nooḥ [Noah]! Surely, he is not of your family; verily, his work is unrighteous, so ask not of Me that of which you have no knowledge! I admonish you, lest you should be one of the ignorant.'﴿ *(Qur'an 11: 46)*

So Prophet Nooḥ asked his Lord for forgiveness for his sin; he repented and turned to Him:

﴿ قَالَ رَبِّ إِنِّىٓ أَعُوذُ بِكَ أَنْ أَسْـَٔلَكَ مَا لَيْسَ لِى بِهِۦ عِلْمٌ ۖ وَإِلَّا تَغْفِرْ لِى وَتَرْحَمْنِىٓ أَكُن مِّنَ ٱلْخَٰسِرِينَ ﴿٤٧﴾ ﴾

﴿Nooḥ [Noah] said: 'O' my Lord! I seek refuge with You from asking You that of which I have no knowledge. And unless You forgive me and have mercy on me, I would indeed be one of the losers.'﴾ *(Qur'an 11: 47)*

The *aayah* (verse) clearly shows that what he did was a sin, for which he needed to be forgiven.

3) Prophet Moosa (Moses) wanted to help the one who was from among his people, so he struck and killed his Egyptian opponent (then repented):

﴿... قَالَ هَٰذَا مِنْ عَمَلِ ٱلشَّيْطَٰنِ ۖ إِنَّهُۥ عَدُوٌّ مُّضِلٌّ مُّبِينٌ ﴿١٥﴾ قَالَ رَبِّ إِنِّى ظَلَمْتُ نَفْسِى فَٱغْفِرْ لِى فَغَفَرَ لَهُۥٓ ۚ إِنَّهُۥ هُوَ ٱلْغَفُورُ ٱلرَّحِيمُ ﴿١٦﴾﴾

﴿...He said: 'This is of *Shayṭaan's* [Satan's] doing, verily, he is a plain misleading enemy.' He said: 'My Lord! Verily, I have wronged myself, so forgive me.' Then He forgave him. Verily, He is the Oft-Forgiving, the Most Merciful.﴾ *(Qur'an 28: 15-16)*

Prophet Moosa admitted that he had wronged himself; he asked Allah (ﷻ) to forgive him, and Allah says that He forgave him.

4) Prophet Dawood (David) (عليه السلام) hastened to pass judgement before he had heard what the second party had to say. But he hastened to repent and Allah forgave him his sin:

﴿... فَٱسْتَغْفَرَ رَبَّهُۥ وَخَرَّ رَاكِعًا وَأَنَابَ ۩ ﴿٢٤﴾ فَغَفَرْنَا لَهُۥ ذَٰلِكَ ... ﴿٢٥﴾﴾

﴿...And he sought forgiveness of his Lord, and he fell down prostrate and turned [to Allah] in repentance. So We forgave him that...﴾ *(Qur'an 38: 24-25)*

5) Our Prophet Muhammad (ﷺ) was rebuked by his Lord for some things:

﴿ يَٰٓأَيُّهَا ٱلنَّبِىُّ لِمَ تُحَرِّمُ مَآ أَحَلَّ ٱللَّهُ لَكَ ۖ تَبْتَغِى مَرْضَاتَ أَزْوَٰجِكَ ۚ وَٱللَّهُ غَفُورٌ رَّحِيمٌ ۝١ ﴾

﴾O' Prophet! Why do you forbid [for yourself] that which Allah has allowed to you, seeking to please your wives? And Allah is Oft-Forgiving, Most Merciful.﴿ *(Qur'an 66: 1)*

This *aayah* was revealed because the Prophet (ﷺ) forbade himself honey, or he forbade himself to Maariyah al-Qibṭiyyah.

His Lord rebuked him because he frowned at the blind man Ibn Umm Maktoom, and was too busy to speak to him because he was preoccupied with trying to call the tyrants of the *kuffaar* (disbelievers) to Allah. So he turned away from the blind man who was keen to please his Lord, who in the view of Allah was the one to whom the Messenger (ﷺ) should have paid attention.

﴿ عَبَسَ وَتَوَلَّىٰٓ ۝١ أَن جَآءَهُ ٱلْأَعْمَىٰ ۝٢ وَمَا يُدْرِيكَ لَعَلَّهُۥ يَزَّكَّىٰٓ ۝٣ أَوْ يَذَّكَّرُ فَتَنفَعَهُ ٱلذِّكْرَىٰٓ ۝٤ ﴾

﴾[The Prophet] frowned and turned away. Because there came to him the blind man [i.e. 'Abdullah ibn Umm Maktoom, who came to the Prophet while he was preaching to one or some of the Quraysh chiefs]. And how can you know that he might become pure [from sins]? Or he might receive admonition, and the admonition might profit him?﴿ *(Qur'an 80: 1-4)*

The Messenger (ﷺ) accepted a ransom from some of the prisoners captured at Badr. Then Allah (ﷻ) revealed the words:

﴿ لَّوْلَا كِتَٰبٌ مِّنَ ٱللَّهِ سَبَقَ لَمَسَّكُمْ فِيمَآ أَخَذْتُمْ عَذَابٌ عَظِيمٌ ۝٦٨ ﴾

﴾Were it not a previous ordainment from Allah, a severe

torment would have touched you for what you took.﴾
(Qur'an 8: 68)

These few examples will suffice. The Qur'an also describes how Prophet Yoonus got angry with his people, and left them, without permission from his Lord; and what the children of Ya'qoob did to their brother Yoosuf when they threw him into the well, then Allah sent revelation to them and made them Prophets.

Those who say that the Prophets are infallible and protected against committing minor sins

Some researchers think it is unacceptable to attribute to the Prophets the minor sins[16] which the texts of the Qur'an and Sunnah state that they committed. They think that this is a terrible thing to say and claim that saying that they committed such actions is a slander against the Messengers and Prophets. Then they contrive to interpret the texts, and their interpretation goes so far as to distort the verses of the Qur'an, as Ibn Taymiyah said.[17] It would have been better for them to interpret the texts according to their true meaning, and to respect the texts of the Qur'an and Sunnah, and to derive their belief concerning this matter and all other matters from the Qur'an and the *aḥaadeeth* of the Messenger. This is how we should judge all matters, and this is what we are commanded to do. With regard to this misinterpretation and distortion after the Qur'an clearly states that they (the Prophets) did such things (committed minor sins), this is judging according to one's own whims and desires, and we seek refuge with Allah from that.

---

[16] The *Ithna' 'Ashari Shi'ah* are unanimous in their view that the Prophets and Imams did not commit minor sins. See *'Aqaa'id al-Imamiyah* by Muhammad Riḍa, Pp. 80, 95; *'Aqaa'id al-Imamiyah al-Ithna 'Ashariyah* by Ibraheem al-Moosawi al-Zanjaani, Pp. 157.

[17] *Majmoo' al-Fataawa*, 10/313.

These misinterpretations are widespread among modern writers. They are corrupt misinterpretations, akin to the misinterpretations of the *Baaṭiniyah* and *Jahamiyah*, as Ibn Taymiyah said.[18]

Two specious arguments[19]

Those who said that the Prophets could not commit minor sins mentioned two specious arguments:

1) That Allah (ﷻ) has commanded us to follow the Messengers and take them as examples:

﴿لَّقَدۡ كَانَ لَكُمۡ فِي رَسُولِ ٱللَّهِ أُسۡوَةٌ حَسَنَةٌ ... ٢١﴾

﴾Indeed in the Messenger of Allah [Muhammad] you have a good example to follow...﴿ *(Qur'an 33: 21)*

This applies to every Messenger, so the command to follow the Messenger implies that his beliefs, actions and words are all inevitably acts of obedience, because if it were possible for a Messenger to commit an act of disobedience towards Allah, this would contradict his being an example to be followed, because it would imply that this sin committed by the Messenger must be reconciled with the command to follow him. We are commanded to follow the example of the Messenger (ﷺ) but if what he does is a sin, then we are not allowed to follow him in that case; this is a contradiction for it is impossible for Allah to command His slave to do a thing when He has forbidden it.

What they say would be correct, if the sin of the Messenger remained hidden and was not clear, so that we would become confused about

---

[18] Ibid.

[19] Among those who discussed these two specious arguments at length and refuted them was *Shaykh al-Islam* Ibn Taymiyah. See *Majmoo' al-Fataawa*, 10/293-313, 15/150.

obedience and sin. But Allah drew the attention of His Messengers and Prophets to the sins that they committed, and helped them to repent without any delay, so the argument presented by these people becomes baseless. Rather, the example that we should follow in this case is haste in repenting when one falls into sin, and not delaying that, following the example of the noble Messengers and Prophets who hastened to repent and did not put it off.

2) They imagine that sin contradicts the idea of perfection, and that it is a shortcoming even if one repents. This is not correct, for repentance wipes out sin and it does not contradict perfection. The one who has sinned is not to be blamed after he has repented; rather in many cases a person is better after he repents from sin than he was before he committed the sin. That is because of the regret and fear of Allah in his heart, and because he strives to repent and make *du'aa'*, and because he does righteous deeds, hoping that they will wipe out the evil deeds. One of the *salaf* said: "After he repented, Dawood (David) (ﷺ) was better than he had been before he sinned." Another said: "If repentance were not the most beloved thing to Him, He would not have tested the noblest of creation with sin."

It is proven in the books of *Saheeh* that Allah feels more joy at the repentance of His slave than a man who lost his camel in the wilderness, on which was his food and drink, then he fell asleep then when he awoke he found his camel standing by his head and said, "O' Allah, You are my slave and I am Your Lord!" making this mistake because of his intense joy. In the Qur'an it says:

﴿... إِنَّ ٱللَّهَ يُحِبُّ ٱلتَّوَّٰبِينَ وَيُحِبُّ ٱلْمُتَطَهِّرِينَ ﴿٢٢٢﴾﴾

﴿...Truly, Allah loves those who turn unto Him in repentance and loves those who purify themselves.﴾

(Qur'an 2: 222)

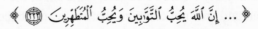

And Allah (ﷻ) says, describing the reward of those who repent:

﴿ إِلَّا مَن تَابَ وَءَامَنَ وَعَمِلَ عَمَلًا صَٰلِحًا فَأُوْلَٰٓئِكَ يُبَدِّلُ ٱللَّهُ سَيِّـَٔاتِهِمْ حَسَنَٰتٍ ... ﴿٧٠﴾ ﴾

﴾Except those who repent and believe [in Islamic Monotheism], and do righteous deeds; for those, Allah will change their sins into good deeds...﴿

(Qur'an 25: 70)

On the Day of Resurrection, Allah will place His screen over His slave, then He will remind him of his minor sins, until the slave will think that he is doomed. Then Allah will say to him: "I have replaced them with good deeds for you." At that point the slave will ask Him to show him his major sins which he was scared of being shown. No doubt he will be better off after his bad deeds have been changed into good deeds than he would have been if he had never committed those sins and if this transformation of bad deeds into good had never taken place.

It is known that no Prophet committed a sin but he hastened to repent and seek forgiveness. This is indicated by the fact that the Qur'an never mentions the sins of the Prophets but that is accompanied by repentance and seeking forgiveness. Adam and his wife sinned then hastened to repent, saying:

﴿ ... رَبَّنَا ظَلَمْنَآ أَنفُسَنَا وَإِن لَّمْ تَغْفِرْ لَنَا وَتَرْحَمْنَا لَنَكُونَنَّ مِنَ ٱلْخَٰسِرِينَ ﴿٢٣﴾ ﴾

﴾...'Our Lord! We have wronged ourselves. If You forgive us not, and bestow not upon us Your Mercy, we shall certainly be of the losers.'﴿ *(Qur'an 7: 23)*

When the blow of Prophet Moosa killed the Egyptian, he hastened to seek forgiveness and mercy, saying,

﴿... رَبِّ إِنِّي ظَلَمْتُ نَفْسِي فَٱغْفِرْ لِي ... ﴿١٦﴾﴾

﴾...My Lord! Verily, I have wronged myself, so forgive me...﴿ *(Qur'an 28: 16)*

The moment Prophet Dawood (David) realized his mistake, he prostrated and sought forgiveness from his Lord:

﴿... فَٱسْتَغْفَرَ رَبَّهُۥ وَخَرَّ رَاكِعًا وَأَنَابَ ۩ ﴿٢٤﴾﴾

﴾...And he sought forgiveness of his Lord, and he fell down prostrate and turned [to Allah] in repentance.﴿ *(Qur'an 38: 24)*

The Prophets were not left to persist in sin, neither did they delay repentance. Allah protected them from that, and after they repented they became more perfect than they had been before.

Thus these two specious arguments are laid to rest, and they cannot be used in the arena of argument or debate. The clear evidence is sufficient to guide us to that which is more correct.

Infallibility is a sign of humanity

The Prophets and Messengers were human beings, to whom Allah gave infallibility in their bearing and conveying the Message. So they did not forget or omit anything. Hence the Revelation which Allah sent down reached those to whom He sent it complete and whole, as Allah willed it. This infallibility was a factor in all their affairs. Some of them committed minor errors because they were human, but the mercy of Allah saved them, Allah drew their attention to their mistakes and enabled them to repent and turn to Him.

Shaykh Muṣṭafa al-Maraaghi, the *Shaykh* of Al-Azhar University, said: "The Revelations did not offer infallibility to the Prophets in every action that they did. They were vulnerable to making mistakes, but they were distinguished from the rest of humanity by the fact that Allah did not let them persist in sin after it appeared, and He (ﷻ) warned them for that on occasion."[20]

Honouring and respecting the Prophets

It is not permissible to use these minor sins which the Prophets committed as a means of slandering them or disparaging them. These are minor issues, restricted in number, for which Allah has forgiven them and of which He has purified them. The Muslim has to learn a lesson for himself from this. For if the noble Messengers whom Allah chose could be upbraided and warned by Allah (ﷻ) for such matters, then we must be very cautious and feel afraid because of our sins and wrongdoing. We have to follow the examples of the Messengers and Prophets in hastening to repent and turn to Allah, always turning to Him and seeking His forgiveness.

Infallibility of people other than Prophets

Ahl as-Sunnah wal-Jamaa'ah do not attribute infallibility to anyone other than the Prophets and Messengers, not even the best of this ummah after its Prophet, Muhammad (ﷺ), namely the *Ṣaḥaabah* - the Companions - (may Allah be pleased with them). Even Abu Bakr and 'Umar were not infallible. The first Rightly-Guided *Khaleefah*, (Caliph) Abu Bakr aṣ-Ṣiddeeq (رضي الله عنه) said, in the first *khuṭbah* (speech) that he gave after he became *khaleefah* (Caliph), "O' people, I have been appointed over you but I am not the best amongst you. If I do well then support me, and if I err, then correct me." When a woman disputed with 'Umar ibn al-Khaṭṭaab (رضي الله عنه) and produced evidence, he said, "The woman is right and 'Umar is wrong."

---

[20] *Ḥayaat Muhammad* by Haykal. See the Introduction to this book by *Shaykh al-Maraaghi*, Pp. 11.

The "infallibility" of Al-Mu'izz al-Faaṭimi

The followers of Al-Mu'izz Ma'd ibn Tameem, whom some people called *Al-Mu'izz li Deenillah al-Faaṭimi*, claimed that he and his descendents were infallible and incapable of committing sin.

This is a false claim by means of which they wanted to misguide the people by giving this tyrant the status of a Prophet, so that what he said would become a religion to be followed. But this person whom they called Al-Mu'izz, and those who were called Faaṭimis or Faṭimids were not descended from Faaṭimah (may Allah be pleased with her), rather they descended from 'Ubaydullah al-Qaddaaḥ. They attributed this infallibility to their Imams and the like, even though, as Abu Ḥaamid al-Ghazaali said in the book which he wrote to refute them, "Their *madhhab* (way) was outwardly Raafiḍi, but inwardly it was pure *kufr*."[21]

The infallibility of the Imams (religious and temporal leaders)

The *Shi'ah* claim that their twelve Imams are infallible and incapable of sinning. The infallibility which they attribute to them is the same as that they attribute to the Prophets. One of the prominent contemporary *Shi'ah* scholar says, explaining their concept of the infallibility of their Imams: "The Imams cannot be thought of as being forgetful or negligent. We believe that they are aware of everything that is in the interests of the Muslims."[22] Ibraheem al-Moosawi az-Zanjaani quotes *Aṣ-Ṣadooq* as saying, "Our belief concerning the Prophets, Messengers, Imams and angels is that they are infallible and pure, free from every impurity (*danas*). They do not commit any sin, whether minor or major. They do not disobey Allah in what He commands them to do, and they do as they are

[21] *Majmoo' al-Fataawa Shaykh al-Islam*, 4/320.

[22] *Al-Ḥukoomah al-Islaamiyah* by Al-Khomeini, Pp. 91.

commanded."[23] They regard as *kaafir* those who do not say that the Imams are infallible. Immediately following the words quoted above, he said: "Whoever denies that they are infallible in any way has described them as ignorant, and whoever describes them as ignorant is a *kaafir*."[24]

Then he said: "Our belief concerning them is that they are infallible and they have the attributes of perfection and knowledge of all their affairs from beginning to end, they cannot be described in any way as falling short or as disobeying Allah."[25]

Al-Majlisi said: "Our Imami (*Shi'ah*) companions are unanimous in their belief that the Prophets and Imams are infallible and incapable of sin, whether minor or major sins, whether they are done deliberately or by mistake or because of forgetfulness, before being appointed as Prophets or Imams and afterwards, from the moment of birth until they meet Allah. No one differed concerning that except Aṣ-Ṣadooq Muhammad ibn Baabawayh and his *shaykh* Ibn al-Waleed. They said that it is possible that Allah may cause them to forget, but not the type of forgetfulness caused by the *Shayṭaan* (Satan). But this had to do with matters other than conveying and explaining the rulings."[26]

In their view, the infallibility of the Imams is a primary matter of belief, hence they denounce as *kaafir* those who disagree with them with regard to that. This leads to many other matters, such as: they regard the words which are attributed to their Imams as *shar'i* evidence at par with the Qur'an and Sunnah. Hence in their view,

---

[23] *'Aqaa'id al-Imaamiyah al-Ithnaa' 'Ashariyah*, Pp. 157.

[24] Ibid.

[25] Ibid.

[26] *Biḥaar al-Anwaar* by Mawlaa Muhammad Baaqir al-Majlisi, 25/350-351. See *Al-Imaamah* by As-Saaloos, Pp. 21.

legislation of shari'ah did not come to an end with the death of the Messenger (ﷺ), rather it continued until the occultation of their twelfth Imam, and they even believe that it is possible for messages to be received from their Hidden Imam via his deputy.

They also believe that their Imams are more entitled to the position of *khaleefah* (Caliph) than others, so they are more entitled to that than Abu Bakr, 'Umar, 'Uthmaan, or any others among the *Ṣaḥaabah* (may Allah be pleased with them all).

The secret of infallibility[27]

The Prophets and Messengers are made infallible by means of *waḥy*:

﴿ وَمَا يَنطِقُ عَنِ ٱلْهَوَىٰٓ ۝٣ إِنْ هُوَ إِلَّا وَحْىٌ يُوحَىٰ ۝٤ ﴾

﴾Nor does he speak of [his own] desire. It is only a Revelation revealed.﴿ *(Qur'an 53: 3-4)*

So what is the secret of the Imams' infallibility? The scholars of the Imami *Shi'ah* say that Allah gave the Imams spirits (*arwaaḥ*) by which He guides them. Al-Kulayni, in his book *Uṣool al-Kaafi*, gave this subject the titles "*Baab fihi dhikr al-Arwaaḥ allati fil-Aa'immah* (Chapter in which mention is made of the spirits that reside in the Imams)" (1/271-272) and "*wa Baab ar-Rooḥ allati yusaddid Allah bihaa al-Aa'immah* (Chapter on the spirit by which Allah guides the Imams)" (1/273-274). The chapters contain six reports, including one from Abu 'Abdullah, saying that the *rooḥ* mentioned in the *aayah*:

﴿ وَكَذَٰلِكَ أَوْحَيْنَآ إِلَيْكَ رُوحًا مِّنْ أَمْرِنَا ... ۝٥٢ ﴾

﴾And thus We have sent to you [O' Muhammad] *Rooḥ* [a

[27] The quotations given here are taken from *Al-Imaamah 'inda al-Jumhoor wal-Firaq al-Mukhtalifah*, by Dr. 'Ali Aḥmad as-Saaloos, Pp. 20.

revelation, and a mercy] of Our Command...﴿
(Qur'an 42: 52)

- is a creature that is greater than Jibreel and Mikaa'eel, who was with the Messenger of Allah (ﷺ) to inform and guide him, and was with the Imams after him.

In the first chapter, he quotes Al-Imam aṣ-Ṣaadiq as saying that *Rooḥ al-Qudus* (the Holy Spirit, i.e., Jibreel) came only to the Prophets, and when the Prophet died, *Rooḥ al-Qudus* moved to be with the Imams; *Rooḥ al-Qudus* does not sleep and is never negligent or heedless or arrogant, and the Imam can see by means of him.[28] In the footnotes, this "seeing" is explained as meaning that he can see things far away in other parts of the world, and what is in the clouds in the sky, and in general whatever is beneath the Throne and what is under the ground.

In *Biḥaar al-Anwaar* by Mawlaa Muhammad Baaqir al-Majlisi (25/ 47-99), in *Baab al-Arwaaḥ allati fihim* (Chapter on the spirits which reside in them i.e., the Imams), he says that they are supported by *Rooḥ al-Qudus*. Ibn Baabawayh al-Qummi said in *Risaalah li'ṣ-Ṣadooq fil-I'tiqaadaat* (Pp. 108-109): "... Our belief concerning the *ṣaḥeeḥ* reports concerning the Imams is that they are in accordance with the Book of Allah and there is no contradiction in their meanings, because they are taken via revelation from Allah." This Al-Qummi, who is also the author of the book *Faqeeh man la yahḍuruhu faqeeh*, one of the four books of hadith which the Ja'faris follow, says: "The scholars of the *Shi'ah* think that if the Prophet did not appoint a successor, then he has fallen short as a Prophet and Messenger, and has neglected his ummah."[29]

---

[28] *'Aqaa'id al-Imaamiyah al-Ithnaa' 'Ashariyah* by Ibraheem al-Moosawi al-Zanjaani, Pp. 161.

[29] op. cit., Pp. 171.

One of the things that show their claims about the Imams to be false is the fact that the infallible one is to be followed without any evidence, and it is permissible to go against the one who is not infallible; and that going against him may be obligatory if we know that he has gone against a (divine) text. But Allah has commanded us to obey Him and to obey the Messenger; in the case of anyone other than the Messenger, we are to obey them if they command us to obey the Messenger; if there is any dispute, the matter is to be referred to the Book of Allah and the Sunnah of His Messenger:

﴿ يَٰٓأَيُّهَا ٱلَّذِينَ ءَامَنُوٓاْ أَطِيعُواْ ٱللَّهَ وَأَطِيعُواْ ٱلرَّسُولَ وَأُوْلِي ٱلۡأَمۡرِ مِنكُمۡۖ فَإِن تَنَٰزَعۡتُمۡ فِي شَيۡءٖ فَرُدُّوهُ إِلَى ٱللَّهِ وَٱلرَّسُولِ إِن كُنتُمۡ تُؤۡمِنُونَ بِٱللَّهِ وَٱلۡيَوۡمِ ٱلۡأٓخِرِۚ ذَٰلِكَ خَيۡرٞ وَأَحۡسَنُ تَأۡوِيلًا ٥٩ ﴾

﴿O' you who believe! Obey Allah and obey the Messenger [Muhammad], and those of you [Muslims] who are in authority. [And] if you differ in anything amongst yourselves, refer it to Allah and His Messenger, if you believe in Allah and in the Last Day. That is better and more suitable for final determination.﴾

(Qur'an 4: 59)

If the Imams were infallible, the command would be to refer to Allah and to the Messenger and the Imams. The fact that we are not commanded to refer to them in cases of dispute shows that they are not infallible.

The Caliph 'Ali (رضي الله عنه) and his two sons and others disagreed with one another concerning matters of knowledge and *fatwas* (religious rulings), just as all scholars disagreed with one another. If they had been infallible, then it would have been impossible for one infallible person to dispute with another. With regard to the matter of fighting, Al-Ḥasan differed with his father, and he disliked a lot of what his father did. In the end Caliph 'Ali agreed with Al-Ḥasan and it became clear to him that he had done something other what he did, that would have been better. He issued *fatwas* and later issued other *fatwas* indicating a change of mind, but one who is infallible would not issue *fatwas* that contradict one another, unless one abrogated another. Al-Ḥasan advised his brother Al-Ḥusayn not to obey the people of Iraq, and not to pursue this matter; if he had been infallible it would not have been permissible for Al-Ḥusayn to go against him.[30]

[30] *Majmoo' al-Fataawa*, 35/120, 125, 126.

CHAPTER SEVEN
SIGNS OF PROPHETHOOD

INTRODUCTION

The Prophets whom Allah sent to His slaves told the people: we have been sent by Allah, and you have to believe what we tell you, and obey us by doing what we command you to do and by abstaining from what we forbid you to do. Allah tells us in *Soorah ash-Shu'araa'* the 26th chapter of the Qur'an that the Prophet Nooḥ (Noah) addressed his people, saying:

﴿... أَلَا تَتَّقُونَ ﴿١٠٦﴾ إِنِّي لَكُمْ رَسُولٌ أَمِينٌ ﴿١٠٧﴾ فَاتَّقُوا اللَّهَ وَأَطِيعُونِ ﴿١٠٨﴾﴾

﴾...Will you not fear Allah and obey Him? I am a trustworthy Messenger to you. So fear Allah, keep your duty to Him, and obey me.﴿ *(Qur'an 26: 106-108)*

The same words were spoken by the Messengers of Allah Hood, Ṣaaliḥ, Looṭ (Lot) and Shu'ayb to their peoples. Indeed, this is what every Messenger said to his people when he called them (to Allah). As this is the case, then Allah has to establish clear signs, evidence and proof to confirm that the claim of the Messengers to be the Messengers of Allah is true, in order that proof may be established against the people, so that no one will have any excuse for not believing in them and obeying them.

﴿لَقَدْ أَرْسَلْنَا رُسُلَنَا بِالْبَيِّنَاتِ ... ﴿٢٥﴾﴾

﴾Indeed We have sent Our Messengers with clear proofs...﴿ *(Qur'an 57: 25)*

- i.e., with evidence and clear signs which will demonstrate that they are telling the truth.

DIFFERENT KINDS OF SIGNS

The kinds of signs which proved the veracity of each Messenger are many and varied. Some of those who listed the signs of Prophethood of our Prophet Muhammad counted nearly one thousand signs. These signs may be divided into different groups, each containing similar signs. We have divided the signs into five groups:

1) Signs and miracles which Allah caused in order to show that His Messengers were true.
2) Foretelling by earlier Prophets of the coming of later Prophets.
3) Lifestyle and conduct of the Prophets.
4) The content of the Messengers' call.
5) Allah's help and support.

We will look at each of these five in more detail.

1 - SIGNS AND MIRACLES

The word *aayah* (translated here as a 'sign') in Arabic means a sign which indicates something. What is meant here is something extraordinary which Allah (ﷻ) causes to happen at the hands of His Messengers and Prophets, something the like of which human beings are unable to reproduce, such as turning a stick into a snake which moves quickly. These extraordinary signs which cannot be denied or rejected indicate that they are telling the truth in conveying the message they bring.

Definition of signs and miracles

Scholars tend to call these signs *mu'jizaat* (miracles). *Mu'jizah*, in Arabic, is a noun derived from the word *al-'ajz*, which refers to the inability to do something, take a decision or control the affairs of something.[1]

---

[1] *Baṣaa'ir Dhawiy at-Tamyeez*, 1/65.

Al-Fakhr ar-Raazi defined a miracle as, customarily meaning, something extraordinary, accompanied by a challenge which no one is able to meet.[2]

Ibn Ḥamdaan al-Ḥanbali defined it as words or actions that are extraordinary, if that is accompanied by the claim to be a Messenger and he does it in the context of challenging, and no one is able to meet that challenge or do anything like it or anything that even comes close to it.[3]

Based on the above, the following cannot be counted as miracles (*mu'jizaat*):

1) The feats which Allah gave to the Prophets but which did not occur in the context of a challenge, such as making water appear from between the fingers of the Messenger (ﷺ), his increasing a small amount of food, the *tasbeeḥ* (saying *Subḥaanallah*) of the pebbles in his hand, the trees coming to him, the weeping of the palm stump, etc.

2) The feats which Allah gave to people other than the Prophets, which the scholars of later generations called *karaamah*. Those who differentiate between *mu'jizah* and *karaamah* were the later scholars. But the word *mu'jizah* in Arabic and in the usage of the earlier scholars such as Imam Aḥmad includes all of that.[4]

We have given them the name *aayah* (sign) as is mentioned in the Qur'an. This is a comprehensive word which includes everything that Allah gave to His Prophets to show that they were true, whether or not it was intended as a challenge.

---

[2] *Lawaami' al-Anwaar al-Bahiyah*, 2/289-290.

[3] Ibid.

[4] *Majmoo' al-Fataawa Shaykh al-Islam*, 11/311; *Lawaami' al-Anwaar al-Bahiyah*, 2/290.

Kinds of signs

If we examine the signs and miracles which Allah gave to His Messengers and Prophets, we will find that they are related to three things: knowledge, power and independence of means.[5]

Telling of unseen matters of the past and things which are yet to come, such as when the Prophet 'Eesa (Jesus) told his people what they were eating and what they were storing in their houses, and when our Messenger (ﷺ) told of the previous nations, and he told of the tribulations and signs of the Hour which were to come in the future, all of that has to do with **knowledge**.

Changing a stick into a snake, healing the leper and the blind, raising the dead, splitting the moon and the like, all have to do with **power**.

Allah's protecting the Messenger (ﷺ) from the people, guarding him against those who wanted to do him harm, and enabling him to fast continually without affecting his energy, all has to do with **independence of means**.

These three matters - knowledge, power and independence of means - to which the signs and miracles were related, are limited and only Allah has the power to do all things. Hence Allah (ﷻ) commanded His Messenger to disassociate himself from any such claim:

﴿ قُل لَّآ أَقُولُ لَكُمْ عِندِى خَزَآئِنُ ٱللَّهِ وَلَآ أَعْلَمُ ٱلْغَيْبَ وَلَآ أَقُولُ لَكُمْ إِنِّى مَلَكٌ إِنْ أَتَّبِعُ إِلَّا مَا يُوحَىٰٓ إِلَىَّ ... ﴿٥٠﴾ ﴾

﴾Say [O' Muhammad]: 'I don't tell you that with me are the treasures of Allah, nor [that] I know the Unseen; nor I tell you that I am an angel. I but follow what is revealed to me...'﴿ *(Qur'an 6: 50)*

---

[5] *Majmoo' al-Fataawa Shaykh al-Islam*, 11/312-313.

The Messenger (ﷺ) disassociated himself from any claim to have knowledge of the unseen, or to posses the treasures of the earth, or to be an angel who had no need for food, drink or wealth. The Messengers may possess some of these attributes in a limited sense which makes them different from the majority of people in that regard, so they learn that which Allah taught them, they may be able to do things that Allah enables them to do, and they may possess independence of means by the support of Allah.

Examples of the signs of the Messengers

1) The sign of Allah's Prophet Ṣaaliḥ (عليه السلام)

The Prophet Ṣaaliḥ called his people to worship Allah the One, the Unique:

﴿ وَلَقَدْ أَرْسَلْنَآ إِلَىٰ ثَمُودَ أَخَاهُمْ صَـٰلِحًا أَنِ ٱعْبُدُوا۟ ٱللَّهَ ... ﴿٤٥﴾ ﴾

﴿And indeed We sent to Thamood their brother Ṣaaliḥ [Saleh], saying: 'Worship Allah [Alone and none else]...'﴾ *(Qur'an 27: 45)*

But they disbelieved in him and demanded of him a sign to prove that he was telling the truth:

﴿ قَالُوٓا۟ إِنَّمَآ أَنتَ مِنَ ٱلْمُسَحَّرِينَ ﴿١٥٣﴾ مَآ أَنتَ إِلَّا بَشَرٌ مِّثْلُنَا فَأْتِ بِـَٔايَةٍ إِن كُنتَ مِنَ ٱلصَّـٰدِقِينَ ﴿١٥٤﴾ ﴾

﴿They said: 'You are only of those bewitched! You are but a human being like us. Then bring us a sign if you are of the truthful.'﴾ *(Qur'an 26: 153-154)*

Ibn Katheer said: "The *mufassireen* (Exegetes) stated that Thamood gathered together one day in their meeting-place, and the Messenger of Allah Ṣaaliḥ came to them and called them to Allah. He reminded them, warned them, preached to them and exhorted them. They said to him, 'If you can bring forth to us from this rock' - and they pointed to a rock there - a she-camel, with such-and-such features' - and they demanded features which are rarely found in camels, including the demand that it should be ten months pregnant. Their Prophet Ṣaaliḥ said to them, 'If I respond to your demand in the manner that you want, will you believe in what I have brought to you and in the message with which I have been sent?' They said, 'Yes.' So he made them promise, then he went to his prayer-place and prayed for as long as Allah willed he should pray, Then he petitioned his Lord, asking Him to respond to their request. Allah commanded that rock to split, revealing a huge she-camel which was ten months pregnant, just as they had asked for. When they saw it with their own eyes, they saw a great miracle, a dazzling sign and definitive proof. Many of them believed, but most of them persisted in their *kufr*.[6] Allah stated that He responded to their demand for a sign:

﴿ قَالَ هَٰذِهِۦ نَاقَةٌ لَّهَا شِرْبٌ وَلَكُمْ شِرْبُ يَوْمٍ مَّعْلُومٍ ﴿١٥٥﴾ ﴾

﴾He said: 'Here is a she-camel: it has a right to drink [water], and you have a right to drink [water] [each] on a day, known.﴿ *(Qur'an 26: 155)*

﴿ ... قَدْ جَآءَتْكُم بَيِّنَةٌ مِّن رَّبِّكُمْ ۖ هَٰذِهِۦ نَاقَةُ ٱللَّهِ لَكُمْ ءَايَةً ۖ فَذَرُوهَا تَأْكُلْ فِىٓ أَرْضِ ٱللَّهِ ۖ وَلَا تَمَسُّوهَا بِسُوٓءٍ ... ﴿٧٣﴾ ﴾

﴾...Indeed there has come to you a clear sign [the miracle of the coming out of a huge she-camel from the midst of a rock] from your Lord. This she-camel of Allah is a sign unto you; so you leave her to graze in Allah's earth, and touch her not with harm...﴿ *(Qur'an 7: 73)*

---

[6] *Al-Bidaayah wan-Nihaayah*, 1/134.

And Allah (ﷻ) stated that this was a clear sign with no ambiguity, hence He described it as being "clear":

﴿ ... وَءَاتَيْنَا ثَمُودَ ٱلنَّاقَةَ مُبْصِرَةً ... ﴿٥٩﴾ ﴾

﴾...And We sent the she-camel to Thamood as a clear sign...﴿ *(Qur'an 17: 59)*"

2) The miracle of the Prophet Ibraaheem (Abraham) (ﷺ)

The Prophet Ibraaheem (Abraham) smashed the idols of his people which they used to worship, and they built the fire and threw him in. But Allah (ﷻ) commanded the fire not to harm him:

﴿ قَالُوا۟ حَرِّقُوهُ وَٱنصُرُوٓا۟ ءَالِهَتَكُمْ إِن كُنتُمْ فَـٰعِلِينَ ﴿٦٨﴾ قُلْنَا يَـٰنَارُ كُونِى بَرْدًا وَسَلَـٰمًا عَلَىٰٓ إِبْرَٰهِيمَ ﴿٦٩﴾ وَأَرَادُوا۟ بِهِۦ كَيْدًا فَجَعَلْنَـٰهُمُ ٱلْأَخْسَرِينَ ﴿٧٠﴾ ﴾

﴾They said: 'Burn him and help your *aalihah* [gods], if you will be doing.' We [Allah] said: 'O' fire! Be you coolness and safety for Ibraaheem [Abraham]!' And they wanted to harm him, but We made them the worst losers.﴿ *(Qur'an 21: 68-70)*

Another of the signs which happened at the hands of Prophet Ibraaheem was the raising of the dead. Allah (ﷻ) tells us the story of that:

﴿ وَإِذْ قَالَ إِبْرَٰهِـۧمُ رَبِّ أَرِنِى كَيْفَ تُحْىِ ٱلْمَوْتَىٰ ۖ قَالَ أَوَلَمْ تُؤْمِن ۖ قَالَ بَلَىٰ وَلَـٰكِن لِّيَطْمَئِنَّ قَلْبِى ۖ قَالَ فَخُذْ أَرْبَعَةً مِّنَ ٱلطَّيْرِ فَصُرْهُنَّ إِلَيْكَ ثُمَّ ٱجْعَلْ عَلَىٰ كُلِّ جَبَلٍ مِّنْهُنَّ جُزْءًا ثُمَّ ٱدْعُهُنَّ يَأْتِينَكَ سَعْيًا ۚ ... ﴿٢٦٠﴾ ﴾

﴾And [remember] when Ibraaheem [Abraham] said, 'My Lord! Show me how You give life to the dead.' He [Allah] said: 'Do you not believe?' He [Ibraaheem

(Abraham)] said: 'Yes [I believe], but to be stronger in Faith.' He said: 'Take four birds, then cause them to incline towards you [then slaughter them, cut them into pieces], and then put a portion of them on every hill, and call them, they will come to you in haste'...﴾

(Qur'an 2: 260)

So Allah commanded him to slaughter those birds, then to cut them into pieces, and scatter them across a number of hills, then to call them. The scattered pieces came back together, and were as they had been before, then life came back to them and they flew up into the air. Glory be to Allah, how great He is...

3) The signs of Allah's Prophet Moosa (Moses) (عليه السلام)

Allah (سبحانه وتعالى) gave the Prophet Moosa nine clear signs:

﴿ وَلَقَدْ ءَاتَيْنَا مُوسَىٰ تِسْعَ ءَايَٰتٍ بَيِّنَٰتٍ ... ﴿١٠١﴾ ﴾

﴾And indeed We gave Moosa [Moses] nine clear signs...﴿ *(Qur'an 17: 101)*

1) The greatest of these signs was the stick which changed into a huge snake when he threw it onto the ground:

﴿ وَمَا تِلْكَ بِيَمِينِكَ يَٰمُوسَىٰ ﴿١٧﴾ قَالَ هِىَ عَصَاىَ أَتَوَكَّؤُا۟ عَلَيْهَا
وَأَهُشُّ بِهَا عَلَىٰ غَنَمِى وَلِىَ فِيهَا مَـَٔارِبُ أُخْرَىٰ ﴿١٨﴾ قَالَ أَلْقِهَا يَٰمُوسَىٰ ﴿١٩﴾
فَأَلْقَىٰهَا فَإِذَا هِىَ حَيَّةٌ تَسْعَىٰ ﴿٢٠﴾ قَالَ خُذْهَا وَلَا تَخَفْ سَنُعِيدُهَا
سِيرَتَهَا ٱلْأُولَىٰ ﴿٢١﴾ ﴾

﴾'And what is that in your right hand, O' Moosa [Moses]?' He said: 'This is my stick, whereon I lean, and wherewith I beat down branches for my sheep, and wherein I find other uses.' [Allah] said: 'Cast it down, O' Moosa [Moses]!' He cast it down, and behold! It was a snake, moving quickly. Allah said: 'Grasp it and fear not; We shall return it to its former state.'﴿

(Qur'an 20: 17-21)

This stick swallowed the dozens of ropes and sticks which the sorcerers of Pharaoh brought to compete with the Prophet Moosa:

﴿ قَالُوا۟ يَٰمُوسَىٰٓ إِمَّآ أَن تُلْقِىَ وَإِمَّآ أَن نَّكُونَ أَوَّلَ مَنْ أَلْقَىٰ ﴿٦٥﴾ قَالَ بَلْ أَلْقُوا۟ۖ
فَإِذَا حِبَالُهُمْ وَعِصِيُّهُمْ يُخَيَّلُ إِلَيْهِ مِن سِحْرِهِمْ أَنَّهَا تَسْعَىٰ ﴿٦٦﴾ فَأَوْجَسَ فِى
نَفْسِهِۦ خِيفَةً مُّوسَىٰ ﴿٦٧﴾ قُلْنَا لَا تَخَفْ إِنَّكَ أَنتَ ٱلْأَعْلَىٰ ﴿٦٨﴾ وَأَلْقِ مَا فِى
يَمِينِكَ تَلْقَفْ مَا صَنَعُوٓا۟ۖ إِنَّمَا صَنَعُوا۟ كَيْدُ سَٰحِرٍۖ وَلَا يُفْلِحُ ٱلسَّاحِرُ حَيْثُ أَتَىٰ
﴿٦٩﴾ ﴾

﴾They said: 'O' Moosa [Moses]! Either you throw first or we be the first to throw?' [Moosa (Moses)] said: 'Nay, throw you [first]!' Then behold! their ropes and their sticks, by their magic, appeared to him as though they moved fast. So Moosa [Moses] conceived fear in himself. We [Allah] said: 'Fear not! Surely, you will have the upper hand. And throw that which is in your right hand! It will swallow up that which they have made. That which they have made is only a magician's trick, and the magician will never be successful, to whatever amount [of skill] he may attain.'﴿

(Qur'an 20: 65-69)

When the sorcerers saw with their own eyes what the snake of Moosa did, they knew that this was not the action of a human being, rather it was the action of Allah, the Creator of man. They could not help but fall down before all the people, prostrating to Allah, the Lord of the Worlds:

﴿ فَأُلْقِىَ ٱلسَّحَرَةُ سُجَّدًا قَالُوٓا۟ ءَامَنَّا بِرَبِّ هَٰرُونَ وَمُوسَىٰ ﴿٧٠﴾ ﴾

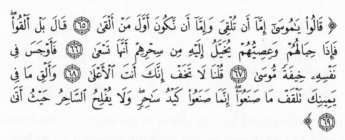

﴿So the magicians fell down prostrate. They said: 'We believe in the Lord of Haaroon [Aaron] and Moosa [Moses].'﴾ *(Qur'an 20: 70)*

2) Another of the signs with which Prophet Moosa (Moses) was sent was that which Allah (ﷻ) mentioned in the *aayah* (verse):

﴿ وَٱضْمُمْ يَدَكَ إِلَىٰ جَنَاحِكَ تَخْرُجْ بَيْضَآءَ مِنْ غَيْرِ سُوٓءٍ ءَايَةً أُخْرَىٰ ﴿٢٢﴾ ﴾

﴿And press your [right] hand to your [left] side: it will come forth white [and shining], without any disease as another sign.﴾ *(Qur'an 20: 22)*

He would put his hand into the sleeve of his garment, and it would be shining white like the moon, but with no disease, i.e., no leprosy or vitiligo alba (i.e., skin diseases which turn the skin white).

Allah (ﷻ) mentions seven signs in *Soorah al-A'raaf* the 7th chapter of the Qur'an, where He mentions that He inflicted upon them:

3) The years of drought and famine, caused by low water levels in the Nile and the withholding of rain from the land of Egypt.
4) Shortness of crops, whereby the land withheld its goodness, and what was produced was affected by stunted growth, etc.
5) The flood which inundated the fields and destroyed cities and villages.
6) The locusts which did not leave anything green or dry but they devoured it.
7) The lice, insects which caused physical harm to people.
8) The frogs which made their lives a misery because there were so many of them.
9) The blood which affected their food and drink.

﴿ وَلَقَدْ أَخَذْنَآ ءَالَ فِرْعَوْنَ بِٱلسِّنِينَ وَنَقْصٍ مِّنَ ٱلثَّمَرَٰتِ لَعَلَّهُمْ يَذَّكَّرُونَ ﴿١٣٠﴾ فَإِذَا جَآءَتْهُمُ ٱلْحَسَنَةُ قَالُوا۟ لَنَا هَٰذِهِۦ ۖ وَإِن تُصِبْهُمْ سَيِّئَةٌ

يَطَّيَّرُواْ بِمُوسَىٰ وَمَن مَّعَهُۥٓۗ أَلَآ إِنَّمَا طَٰٓئِرُهُمْ عِندَ ٱللَّهِ وَلَٰكِنَّ أَكْثَرَهُمْ لَا
يَعْلَمُونَ ﴿١٣١﴾ وَقَالُواْ مَهْمَا تَأْتِنَا بِهِۦ مِنْ ءَايَةٍ لِّتَسْحَرَنَا بِهَا فَمَا نَحْنُ لَكَ
بِمُؤْمِنِينَ ﴿١٣٢﴾ فَأَرْسَلْنَا عَلَيْهِمُ ٱلطُّوفَانَ وَٱلْجَرَادَ وَٱلْقُمَّلَ وَٱلضَّفَادِعَ وَٱلدَّمَ
ءَايَٰتٍ مُّفَصَّلَٰتٍ فَٱسْتَكْبَرُواْ وَكَانُواْ قَوْمًا مُّجْرِمِينَ ﴿١٣٣﴾ ﴾

﴿And indeed We punished the people of Fir'awn [Pharaoh] with years of drought and shortness of fruits [crops], that they might remember [take heed]. But whenever good came to them, they said: 'Ours is this.' And if evil afflicted them, they ascribed it to evil omens connected with Moosa [Moses] and those with him. Be informed! Verily, their evil omens are with Allah but most of them know not. They said [to Moosa (Moses)]: 'Whatever *Aayaat* [proofs, evidences, verses, lessons, signs, revelations, etc.] you may bring to us, to work therewith your sorcery on us, we shall never believe in you.' So We sent on them: the flood, the locusts, the lice, the frogs, and the blood [as a succession of] manifest signs, yet they remained arrogant, and they were of those people who were *Mujrimoon* [criminals, polytheists and sinners].﴾ *(Qur'an 7: 130-133)*

Other signs

These are the nine signs with which Prophet Moosa (Moses) (عليه السلام) was sent to Pharaoh. But there were many more miracles which Allah (سبحانه وتعالى) caused to happen at the hands of Moosa, such as when Moosa struck the sea with his stick and it parted, and when he struck the rock and twelve springs flowed forth from it, and when the manna and quails came down to the Children of Israel in the desert of Sinai, and other signs.

4) The miracles of Allah's Prophet 'Eesa (Jesus) (عليه السلام)

Among the miracles which Allah has told us about is that he ('Eesa) used to fashion something resembling a bird out of clay, then he would breathe into it and it would become a bird by the will and decree of Allah. He would touch the blind and he would be healed, by the will of Allah; he would touch the leper and Allah would take away his leprosy; he would pass by the dead and call to them, and Allah would bring them back to life. The Qur'an tells us this in the words in which Allah (سبحانه وتعالى) addresses 'Eesa (Jesus):

﴿ ... وَإِذْ تَخْلُقُ مِنَ ٱلطِّينِ كَهَيْـَٔةِ ٱلطَّيْرِ بِإِذْنِى فَتَنفُخُ فِيهَا فَتَكُونُ
طَيْرًۢا بِإِذْنِى ۖ وَتُبْرِئُ ٱلْأَكْمَهَ وَٱلْأَبْرَصَ بِإِذْنِى ۖ وَإِذْ تُخْرِجُ ٱلْمَوْتَىٰ بِإِذْنِى
... ﴿١١٠﴾ ﴾

﴾...And when you made out of the clay, a figure like that of a bird, by My Permission, and you breathed into it, and it became a bird by My Permission, and you healed those born blind, and the lepers by My Permission, and when you brought forth the dead by My Permission.﴿

(Qur'an 5: 110)

And among his signs is that table which Allah sent down from heaven, when the Disciples asked Prophet 'Eesa to bring it down, and it was as 'Eesa had asked for it, a festival for the first and the last of them.

﴿ إِذْ قَالَ ٱلْحَوَارِيُّونَ يَٰعِيسَى ٱبْنَ مَرْيَمَ هَلْ يَسْتَطِيعُ رَبُّكَ أَن يُنَزِّلَ
عَلَيْنَا مَآئِدَةً مِّنَ ٱلسَّمَآءِ ۖ قَالَ ٱتَّقُوا۟ ٱللَّهَ إِن كُنتُم مُّؤْمِنِينَ ﴿١١٢﴾ قَالُوا۟
نُرِيدُ أَن نَّأْكُلَ مِنْهَا وَتَطْمَئِنَّ قُلُوبُنَا وَنَعْلَمَ أَن قَدْ صَدَقْتَنَا وَنَكُونَ
عَلَيْهَا مِنَ ٱلشَّٰهِدِينَ ﴿١١٣﴾ قَالَ عِيسَى ٱبْنُ مَرْيَمَ ٱللَّهُمَّ رَبَّنَآ أَنزِلْ عَلَيْنَا مَآئِدَةً
مِّنَ ٱلسَّمَآءِ تَكُونُ لَنَا عِيدًا لِّأَوَّلِنَا وَءَاخِرِنَا وَءَايَةً مِّنكَ ۖ وَٱرْزُقْنَا وَأَنتَ خَيْرُ
ٱلرَّٰزِقِينَ ﴿١١٤﴾ قَالَ ٱللَّهُ إِنِّى مُنَزِّلُهَا عَلَيْكُمْ ۖ فَمَن يَكْفُرْ بَعْدُ مِنكُمْ فَإِنِّىٓ أُعَذِّبُهُۥ
عَذَابًا لَّآ أُعَذِّبُهُۥٓ أَحَدًا مِّنَ ٱلْعَٰلَمِينَ ﴿١١٥﴾ ﴾

﴾[Remember] when *Al-Ḥawaariyoon* [the disciples] said: 'O' 'Eesa [Jesus], son of Maryam [Mary]! Can your Lord send down to us a table spread [with food] from heaven?' 'Eesa [Jesus] said: 'Fear Allah, if you are indeed believers.' They said: 'We wish to eat thereof and to satisfy our hearts [to be stronger in Faith], and to know that you have indeed told us the truth and that we ourselves be its witnesses.' 'Eesa [Jesus], son of Maryam [Mary], said: 'O' Allah, our Lord! Send us from the heaven a table spread [with food] that there may be for us - for the first and the last of us - a festival and a sign from You; and provide us with sustenance, for You are the Best of sustainers.' Allah said, 'I am going to send it down unto you, but if any of you after that disbelieves, then I will punish him with a torment such as I have not inflicted on anyone among [all] the *'Aalameen* [mankind and jinn].'﴿ *(Qur'an 5: 112-115)*

5) Signs of the Seal of the Prophets and Final Messenger (ﷺ)

Allah caused dazzling miracles and clear signs to happen at the hands of our Prophet Muhammad (ﷺ). When the seeker of truth examines them, they will show him that this is a testimony from Allah bearing witness to the truth of His Messenger (ﷺ). Some of the scholars listed them, and they amounted to some thousand miracles. Books have been written about them, and the scholars of *Tawḥeed*, *tafseer*, hadith and history have all discussed and explained them.

The greatest sign

The greatest of the signs which Allah gave to our Messenger (ﷺ), indeed the greatest sign of all the Messengers, is the Holy Qur'an, the clear Book. It is a sign which addresses both the heart and the mind, a sign which will abide until the Day of Judgement, which cannot be changed or altered.

﴿... وَإِنَّهُۥ لَكِتَٰبٌ عَزِيزٌ ﴿٤١﴾ لَّا يَأْتِيهِ ٱلْبَٰطِلُ مِنۢ بَيْنِ يَدَيْهِ وَلَا مِنْ خَلْفِهِۦ ۖ تَنزِيلٌ مِّنْ حَكِيمٍ حَمِيدٍ ﴿٤٢﴾﴾

﴿...And verily, it is an honourable well-fortified respected Book [because it is Allah's Speech, and He has protected it from corruption]. Falsehood cannot come to it from before it or behind it, [it is] sent down by the All-Wise, Worthy of all praise [Allah].﴾ *(Qur'an 41: 41-42)*

Allah challenged the most eloquent of the Arabs with this Book. Eloquence was the area in which the Arabs excelled. The Arabs were hostile towards the call of Islam and the Messenger of Islam, and they could have destroyed the call of Islam if their most eloquent speakers had managed to produce something to rival this Book, but they were unable to do so:

﴿ وَإِن كُنتُمْ فِى رَيْبٍ مِّمَّا نَزَّلْنَا عَلَىٰ عَبْدِنَا فَأْتُوا۟ بِسُورَةٍ مِّن مِّثْلِهِۦ وَٱدْعُوا۟ شُهَدَآءَكُم مِّن دُونِ ٱللَّهِ إِن كُنتُمْ صَٰدِقِينَ ﴿٢٣﴾ فَإِن لَّمْ تَفْعَلُوا۟ وَلَن تَفْعَلُوا۟ فَٱتَّقُوا۟ ٱلنَّارَ ٱلَّتِى وَقُودُهَا ٱلنَّاسُ وَٱلْحِجَارَةُ ۖ أُعِدَّتْ لِلْكَٰفِرِينَ ﴿٢٤﴾﴾

﴿And if you [Arab pagans, Jews, and Christians] are in doubt concerning that which We have sent down [i.e. the Qur'an] to Our slave [Muhammad], then produce a *Soorah* [chapter] of the like thereof and call your witnesses [supporters and helpers] besides Allah, if you are truthful. But if you do it not, and you can never do it, then fear the Fire [Hell] whose fuel is men and stones, prepared for the disbeliever.﴾ *(Qur'an 2: 23-24)*

A unique kind of miracle

Allah (ﷻ) willed that the miracle of the last Prophet, Muhammad (ﷺ) should be of a kind that was different from the miracles of the other Messengers. Allah could have sent down a physical miracle that would have dazzled those who saw it:

﴿ إِن نَّشَأْ نُنَزِّلْ عَلَيْهِم مِّنَ ٱلسَّمَآءِ ءَايَةً فَظَلَّتْ أَعْنَـٰقُهُمْ لَهَا خَـٰضِعِينَ ﴿٤﴾ ﴾

﴾If We will, We could send down to them from the heaven a sign, to which they would bend their necks in humility.﴿ *(Qur'an 26: 4)*

If Allah had willed, He could have sent down from heaven an overwhelming sign which they could not have disputed and they would have had no choice but to believe, and they would have had to express their submission to it in a physical manner: ﴾...to which they would bend their necks in humility﴿ *(Qur'an 26: 4)*, as if this posture would have become permanent. But Allah willed that the miracle of this final message should be a sign, mighty, overwhelming and non-vanquishing, so He made its sign the Qur'an, a complete way of life, a miracle in every aspect.

It is miraculous in its semantic construction, its artistic order and its literary style, consistent in its quality and level; it does not vary and its quality does not change, as is the case with the work of human beings, where the work of a single individual may be of a higher or lower standard, stronger or weaker. But the semantic quality of this Qur'an remains consistent, in one style, on one level, unchanging. This indicates that it comes from a source which is not subject to change.

It is miraculous in terms of its intellectual ideas and in the harmony and complementary nature of its parts. There is nothing coincidental and nothing of a haphazard nature. All its instructions and laws come together in a harmonious and complementary fashion, encompassing all of human life, offering fulfilment and motivation without any of them going against human nature or falling short in guiding it. All of them are tied to one focal point, in such harmony that no human experience could produce such a thing. There has to have been some unlimited knowledge, not subject to the constraints of time and space, that produced such comprehensive guidance and organized it in such a manner.

It is miraculous in the ease with which it penetrates hearts and souls, turning their locks and opening their doors in such a moving and effective manner, how it approaches problems in an amazing and simple way, and guides and controls (people) in the gentlest way, without any complexities, contortions or contradictions.

Allah, the All-Gloriouis, All-Powerful, willed that this Qur'an should be the miracle of this message. He did not will that an overwhelming material sign should be sent down, to which people would bend their necks in humility which would force them to submit. That is because this final message is a message which is open to all the nations and to all generations. It is not a message which is restricted to the people of one time or one place. So it is appropriate that its miracles should likewise be open to all, near and far, to every nation and every generation. In the case of overwhelming miracles, it is only those who see them who "bend their necks"; after that they simply become stories that are told, not something real to be witnessed. But the Qur'an, more than thirteen centuries later, is still an open book and a clearly-defined path, from which the people of this age take that which will direct their lives - if they decide to take it as their guide - and will fulfil all their needs, and ultimately lead them to a better world, a loftier horizon, and a greater destiny. And those who come after us will find things that we did not find, because it gives every seeker that which will fulfil his needs, without that detracting from it in the slightest; rather it is constantly regenerated.[7]

The Night Journey and Ascent into heaven (*Israa'* and *Mi'raaj*)

Another of the clear signs and extraordinary miracles was when Allah took His Prophet by night from *Al-Masjid al-Ḥaraam* (in Makkah) to *Al-Masjid al-Aqṣaa* (in Jerusalem), where Allah brought the Prophets together with him and he led them in prayer as their Imam:

﴿ سُبْحَٰنَ ٱلَّذِىٓ أَسْرَىٰ بِعَبْدِهِۦ لَيْلًا مِّنَ ٱلْمَسْجِدِ ٱلْحَرَامِ إِلَى ٱلْمَسْجِدِ
ٱلْأَقْصَا ٱلَّذِى بَٰرَكْنَا حَوْلَهُۥ لِنُرِيَهُۥ مِنْ ءَايَٰتِنَآ ... ﴿١﴾ ﴾

﴿Glorified [and Exalted] be He [Allah] [above all that (evil) they associate with Him] Who took His slave [Muhammad] for a journey by night from *Al-Masjid al-Ḥaraam* [at Makkah] to *Al-Masjid al-Aqṣaa* [in Jerusalem], the neighbourhood whereof We have blessed, in order that We might show him [Muhammad] of Our *Aayaat* [proofs, evidences, lessons, signs, etc.]...﴾ *(Qur'an 17: 1)*

Thence he was taken up to the highest heavens, where he saw some of the greatest signs of his Lord. He saw the Archangel Jibreel (Gabriel) (عليه السلام) in the real form with which Allah had created him. He saw *Sidrat al-Muntahaa* (the Lote-Tree of the utmost boundary), he passed beyond the seven heavens, and the Most Merciful spoke with him and drew him nigh.

﴿ أَفَتُمَٰرُونَهُۥ عَلَىٰ مَا يَرَىٰ ﴿١٢﴾ وَلَقَدْ رَءَاهُ نَزْلَةً أُخْرَىٰ ﴿١٣﴾ عِندَ سِدْرَةِ ٱلْمُنتَهَىٰ
﴿١٤﴾ عِندَهَا جَنَّةُ ٱلْمَأْوَىٰٓ ﴿١٥﴾ إِذْ يَغْشَى ٱلسِّدْرَةَ مَا يَغْشَىٰ ﴿١٦﴾ مَا زَاغَ ٱلْبَصَرُ
وَمَا طَغَىٰ ﴿١٧﴾ لَقَدْ رَأَىٰ مِنْ ءَايَٰتِ رَبِّهِ ٱلْكُبْرَىٰٓ ﴿١٨﴾ ﴾

---

[7] See *Fi Ẓilaal al-Qur'an*, 19/2584.

﴾Will you then dispute with him [Muhammad] about what he saw [during the *Mi'raaj*: (Ascent of the Prophet to the seven heavens)]. And indeed he [Muhammad] saw him [Jibreel (Gabriel)] at a second descent [i.e. another time]. Near *Sidrat-ul-Muntahaa* [a lote tree of the utmost boundary over the seventh heaven beyond which none can pass]. Near it is the Paradise of Abode. When that covered the lote tree which did cover it! The sight [of Prophet Muhammad] turned not aside [right or left], nor it transgressed beyond the limit [ordained for it]. Indeed he [Muhammad] did see of the Greatest Signs, of his Lord [Allah].﴿ *(Qur'an 53: 12-18)*

Quraysh thought that the claim of the Messenger of Allah (ﷺ) was a lie, because it used to take the caravans weeks to go to *Bayt al-Maqdis* (Jerusalem) and return; how could a man claim to have gone there and come back in less than a night? This was something amazing. Indeed it was amazing, but our amazement subsides when we realize that the One Who took him on that night journey was Allah, and Allah is Able to do all things.

The splitting of the moon

Another of the miracles of the Prophet (ﷺ) was the splitting of the moon. The people of Makkah asked the Messenger (ﷺ) for a sign, so the moon was split in two, until they could see (a place called) Al-Ḥarraa' between the two halves. At the time when the moon was split it was full. Allah (ﷻ) recorded this sign in His Book, where He said:

﴿ ٱقْتَرَبَتِ ٱلسَّاعَةُ وَٱنشَقَّ ٱلْقَمَرُ ① وَإِن يَرَوْا۟ ءَايَةً يُعْرِضُوا۟ وَيَقُولُوا۟ سِحْرٌ مُّسْتَمِرٌّ ② ﴾

﴾The Hour has drawn near, and the moon has been cleft asunder [the people of Makkah requested Prophet

> Muhammad to show them a miracle, so he showed them the splitting of the moon]. And if they see a sign, they turn away, and say: 'This is continuous magic.'﴿
>
> *(Qur'an 54: 1-2)*

Ibn Katheer narrated that the Muslims were unanimously agreed that this sign took place, and that the *aḥaadeeth* which mention the splitting of the moon are *mutawaatir*, with so many isnads that this has to be certain.[8]

This miracle was seen by people throughout the Arabian Peninsula. The people of Makkah did not believe it and they said, "Muhammad has bewitched us." Then they had second thoughts and said, "Wait and listen to what the travelers tell you, for Muhammad cannot bewitch all the people." The following day, they asked those who had come to them from outside Makkah, and they told them that they had seen it too.

People also saw the splitting of the moon from beyond the Arabian Peninsula. Ibn Katheer said: "Its splitting was seen in many parts of the world. It is said that this is recorded in some parts of India. A building was built that night, and dated as the night when the moon split."[9]

It is said that the splitting of the moon is not something impossible, for science witnessed the splitting of the comet Procus into two parts in 1889 CE, and the comet Bila split into two parts in 1846 CE. The astronomer Spencer Jones discussed the splitting of comets and meteors in his book *Worlds Without End*.[10]

---

8 *Al-Bidaayah wan-Nihaayah*, 3/118.

9 Ibid, 3/120.

10 Ibid, 130.

In response, to this statement it is said: "The difference between the splitting of the moon and the splitting of these two comets is that they (the comets) were not put back together after they split, but the moon was put back together. This is the difference which is to be expected between a natural astronomical phenomenon and an astronomical miracle which occurred at the hands of a Messenger, because a miracle is of limited duration and ceases when its purpose has been fulfilled; if it had continued it would simply have been a natural phenomenon and would no longer have been something miraculous."[11]

He (ﷺ) caused food to increase

This happened to the Prophet (ﷺ) more than once. For example, Anas (رضي الله عنه) narrated:

> "Abu Ṭalḥah said to Umm Sulaym, 'I heard the voice of the Messenger of Allah (ﷺ) sounding weak, and I knew that he was hungry. Do you have anything?' She said, 'Yes.' She brought out some loaves made from barley. Then she took out a cloth of hers, and rolled the bread up. Then she placed it under my arm, and wrapped the extra cloth around my head. Then she sent me to the Messenger of Allah (ﷺ) and I took the food to him. I found the Messenger of Allah (ﷺ) in the mosque, and the people were with him. I stood there and the Messenger of Allah (ﷺ) said to me, 'Did Abu Ṭalḥah send you?' I said, 'Yes.' He said, 'With food?' I said, 'Yes.' The Messenger of Allah (ﷺ) said to those who were with him, 'Get up.' Then he set out, and I set out ahead of them until I came to Abu Ṭalḥah and told him.

---

[11] Ibid, 131.

Abu Ṭalḥah said, 'O' Umm Sulaym, the Messenger of Allah (ﷺ) has brought the people, and we do not have enough to feed them.' She said, 'Allah and His Messenger know best.'

Abu Ṭalḥah went out to meet the Messenger of Allah (ﷺ), and the Messenger of Allah (ﷺ) came with Abu Ṭalḥah. The Messenger of Allah (ﷺ) said: 'Tell me, O' Umm Sulaym, what do you have?' She brought that bread. The Messenger of Allah (ﷺ) ordered that it should be cut into pieces. Umm Sulaym squeezed butter skin on top of it, then the Messenger of Allah (ﷺ) said what Allah willed that he should say. Then he said, 'Let ten of them come and eat.' So they came and ate until they had had enough, then they left. Then he said, 'Let (another ten) come and eat.' So they came and ate until they had had enough, then they left.. Then he said, 'Let (another ten) come and eat.' So they came and ate until they had had enough, then they left. Then he said, 'Let (another ten) come and eat.' So all the people ate and had enough, and there were seventy or eighty men." (This is narrated by both Bukhari and Muslim)[12]

The report of Jaabir ibn 'Abdullah

Another example narrated by both Bukhari and Muslim from Jaabir ibn 'Abdullah. He said:

"I came to my wife (on the day of Al-Khandaq) and said, 'Have you got anything? For I have seen the Prophet (ﷺ) very hungry.' She brought out a bag in which there was a *ṣaa'* of barley, and we had a black rooster, so I slaughtered it and ground the barley, and we put the meat

---

[12] *Mishkaat al-Maṣaabeeḥ*, 3/182.

in an earthenware pot. Then I came to the Prophet (ﷺ) and whispered to him, saying, 'O' Messenger of Allah, we have slaughtered a rooster of ours and ground a *saa'* of barley. Come and bring a few people with you.' The Prophet (ﷺ) announced in a loud voice, 'O' people of Al-Khandaq! Jaabir has made food, come on!'
The Messenger of Allah (ﷺ) said to Jaabir, 'Do not set down your earthenware pot or bake your bread until I come.' He came, and the dough was brought out to him. He spat in it and blessed it (prayed for blessing for it), then he went to our earthenware pot and spat in it and blessed it. Then he said, 'Call the baker woman so that she may help you to make the bread; scoop food from your pot but do not remove it from the fire. There were a thousand people, and I swore by Allah that they kept on eating until they had eaten their fill and turned away, and our pot was still bubbling, full of food as it had been in the beginning, and our dough was also as it had been at the beginning."[13]

He caused water to increase, it flowed from between his fingers

This happened often by the Messenger (ﷺ); we will mention a few examples. Both Bukhari and Muslim narrated from Jaabir ibn 'Abdullah stating:

> "The people became thirsty on the day of Al-Ḥudaybiyah. The Messenger of Allah (ﷺ) had in front of him a vessel from which he did *wuḍoo'*, then the people came to him and said, 'We do not have any water for *wuḍoo'* or to drink except for what is in your vessel.' So the Prophet (ﷺ) put his hand in the vessel and then

[13] *Mishkaat al-Maṣaabeeḥ*, 3/168.

water started to flow from between his fingers like springs. We drank it and we did *wuḍoo'*. Jaabir was asked, 'How many were you?' He said, 'If we had been one hundred thousand it would have sufficed us, but we were fifteen hundred.'"[14]

He (ﷺ) also increased the water of the well of Al-Ḥudaybiyah on the day of Al-Ḥudaybiyah. Bukhari narrated from Al-Baraa' ibn 'Aazib:

"We were fourteen hundred people with the Messenger of Allah (ﷺ) on the day of Al-Ḥudaybiyah. From the well Al-Ḥudaybiyah we drank and made it dry, i.e. did not leave a drop of water in it. The Messenger (ﷺ) heard about this, so he came to the well and sat at its edge, then he called for a vessel of water, did *wuḍoo'*, then rinsed his mouth; then he supplicated and poured the water into the well. He said, 'Leave it for a while.' Then they drank from it themselves and gave it to their animals, until they left that place."[15]

Bukhari narrated from 'Abdullah ibn Mas'ood that he said:

"We used to think that the signs were a blessing, but you think they are something frightening. We were with the Prophet (ﷺ) on a journey, and our water supply ran low. He (ﷺ) said, 'Bring me some water.' They brought a vessel in which there was a little water. He put his hand in the vessel then said, 'Come to the blessed, the pure, and the blessing is from Allah.' I saw the water welling up between the fingers of the Messenger of Allah (ﷺ), and we used to hear the *tasbeeḥ* (saying *Subḥaanallah*) of the food as he was eating.'"

---

[14] Ibid, 3/170.

[15] *Mishkaat al-Maṣaabeeḥ*, 3/170.

His enemies were prevented from harming him

Among the examples Allah answered the prayer of the Prophet (ﷺ) is that when he was migrating from Makkah to Madeenah,

> "Suraaqah ibn Maalik caught up with him. Suraaqah's horse sank to its belly in the ground and could not move. Suraaqah said, 'I see that you have prayed against me. Pray for me, and by Allah I will divert the search away from you.' So the Prophet (ﷺ) prayed for him, and he was saved. Thereafter whenever Suraaqah met anyone he told them, 'I have already looked in this direction, so don't bother to look.' Everyone he met, he turned him/them back." (Bukhari and Muslim)[16]

Again at the battle of Ḥunayn,

> "The Muslims were routed but the Messenger (ﷺ) and a few of the believers - those who had offered their oath of allegiance beneath the tree - stood firm. When the fighting grew intense, the Prophet (ﷺ) took some pebbles and threw them towards the faces of the *kuffaar* (the fighting disbelievers), then he said: 'They have been defeated by the Lord of Muhammad.'"

Al-'Abbaas, the narrator of the hadith, said: "By Allah, as soon as he threw the pebbles, I started to see that their force had been spent and they began to retreat." This is narrated by Muslim.[17]

According to a report narrated by Salamah ibn al-Akwa', recorded by Muslim:

---

[16] Ibid, 3/166.

[17] *Mishkaat al-Maṣaabeeḥ*, 3/172.

"We were with the Messenger of Allah (ﷺ) during the campaign of Ḥunayn, and the Muslim army fled, deserting the Messenger of Allah (ﷺ). When the enemy came near, the Messenger of Allah (ﷺ) got down from his mule, picked up a handful of dust from the ground, threw it into their (enemy) faces and said: 'May these faces be deformed!' There was no one among the enemy whose eyes were not filled with the dust from this handful, and they fled in retreat. Thus Allah defeated them, and the Messenger of Allah (ﷺ) distributed their booty among the Muslims."[18]

Another example narrated by Mulsim:

"When Abu Jahl swore by Al-Laat and Al-'Uzza that if he saw the Messenger (ﷺ) praying in the mosque where Quraysh used to gather, he would step on his neck or rub his face in the dust. When he saw the Messenger (ﷺ) prostrating, he wanted to do what he had sworn to do, but when he approached him, he was suddenly thrown onto his back, raising his arms as if to protect himself. He was asked, 'What is the matter with you?' He said, 'Between me and him there is a ditch of fire, and terror, and wings.'

The Messenger of Allah (ﷺ) said:

'Had he come near me, the angels would have torn him limb by limb.'"[19]

---

[18] Ibid.

[19] *Jaami' al-Uṣool*, 12/94.

Answers to his Prayers[20]

The mother of Abu Hurayrah was guided by the prayer of the Messenger (ﷺ)

It is narrated that Abu Hurayrah (رضي الله عنه) said:

> "I used to call my mother to Islam when she was a *mushrikah*. I called her one day, and she said something about the Messenger of Allah (ﷺ) that I did not like to hear. I came to the Messenger of Allah (ﷺ) weeping. I said, 'O' Messenger of Allah, pray to Allah to guide the mother of Abu Hurayrah.' He said, 'O' Allah, guide the mother of Abu Hurayrah.' I went out, feeling optimistic because of the prayer of the Prophet (ﷺ). When I reached my house, I found the door closed. I heard my mother's footsteps and she said, 'Stay where you are!' Then I heard the sound of water. She washed herself then got dressed and put on her *khimaar* (head covering). She then opened the door and said, 'O' Abu Hurayrah, I bear witness that there is no god but Allah and I bear witness that Muhammad is His slave and Messenger.' I went back to the Messenger of Allah, weeping with joy. He praised Allah and uttered very good words."[21]

Jareer became a horseman because of his prayer

Both Bukhari and Muslim narrated from Jareer ibn 'Abdullah who said: The Messenger of Allah (ﷺ) said to me,

> "Will you not get rid of Dhu'l-Khalaṣah[22] for me?' I

---

[20] *Mu'jizaat al-Muṣṭafa* by Khayr ad-Deen Waa'ili, Pp. 61.

[21] Muslim.

[22] This was the house of the false gods of Khath'am, which was known as the Ka'bah of Al-Yamaamah.

said, 'Of course.' I was not a strong horseman and I mentioned that to the Messenger of Allah (ﷺ). He struck me hard on the chest, so that I could see the mark left by his hand, and said, 'O' Allah, make him a strong horseman and make him one who guides and is guided.' I never fell off my horse after that. I set out with one hundred and fifty brave horsemen of Quraysh, and we burned it with fire and destroyed it.

It is further narrated by both Bukhari and Muslim that Anas (رضي الله عنه) said,

"The people were stricken with a year of famine during the time of the Messenger of Allah (ﷺ). Whilst the Prophet (ﷺ) was delivering sermon one Friday, a Bedouin stood up and said, 'O' Messenger of Allah, our wealth has been destroyed and our children are starving; pray to Allah for us. He raised his hands, and we could not see even the smallest cloud in the sky, but by the One in Whose hand is my soul, no sooner had he lowered his hands the clouds began to build like mountains, and hardly had he come down from the *minbar*, when I saw the rain dripping from his beard. It rained all that day, and the following day, and until the following Friday, when the same Bedouin or another stood up and said, 'O' Messenger of Allah, our buildings are destroyed and our property is drowned; pray to Allah for us.' So he raised his hands and said, 'O' Allah, (let it rain) around us and not on us.' No sooner did he point to the clouds in any direction, they withdrew, and Madeenah was surrounded by clouds but there were no clouds over it, and the valley of Qanaa flowed with water for a month, and nobody came from any direction but he spoke of the rain.

According to another report he said, 'O' Allah, (let it rain) around us and not on us; O' Allah (let it rain) on the hills and mountains and the valley bottoms and the groves of trees.' Then it stopped and we went out walking in the sun."

The hand of an arrogant person was affected by his prayer

Muslim narrated from Salamah ibn al-Akwa' that,

> "A man was eating in the presence of the Messenger of Allah, using his left hand. He said, 'Eat with your right hand.' The man said, 'I cannot.' The Prophet (ﷺ) said, 'May you never be able to.' Nothing was preventing him from doing so except his arrogance. Salamah said, he never raised it to his mouth again after that."

The blessing of the Messenger's prayer reached the camel of Jaabir

Both Bukhari and Muslim narrated from Jaabir who said:

> "I went out on a military campaign with the Messenger of Allah (ﷺ), and I was riding a camel used for carrying water. The camel was thus exhausted and could hardly walk. The Prophet (ﷺ) joined me and said, 'What is the matter with your camel?' I said, 'It is exhausted.' The Messenger of Allah (ﷺ) dropped behind, shouted at the camel and prayed for it, and from that point onwards the camel was always ahead of the others. He said to me, 'How do you find your camel?' I said, 'It is well, your blessing has reached it.' He said, 'Will you sell it to me for one *wiqiyah* (of gold)?' I sold it to him on the condition that I ride it back to Madeenah. When the Messenger of Allah (ﷺ) reached Madeenah, I brought

the camel to him the next morning and he gave me its price and then gave it back to me."

Healing the Sick [23]

He healed a person whose leg was broken

It is narrated that Al-Baraa' said: The Messenger of Allah (ﷺ) sent a group of people to Abu Raafi'.[24]

> " 'Abdullah ibn 'Ateek entered his house one night when he was sleeping and killed him. 'Abdullah ibn 'Ateek said: 'I thrust my sword into his stomach until it came out of his back, then I knew that I had killed him. I then came back. To open the doors I put my leg on the step. I stumbled and fell on a moonlit night, and broke my leg. I wrapped it with my turban and went to my companions, then I came to the Prophet (ﷺ) and told him (what had happened). He said, 'Stretch forth your leg.' So I stretched forth my leg and he wiped it with his hand, and it was as if nothing had happened to it.' "[25]

He (ﷺ) healed the eyes of 'Ali ibn Abi Ṭaalib (رضي الله عنه)

Both Bukhari and Muslim narrated from Sahl ibn Sa'd that on the day of Khaybar, the Messenger of Allah (ﷺ) said:

> "Tomorrow I will give this banner to a man at whose hands Allah will grant victory. He loves Allah and His Messenger, and Allah and His Messenger love him.' The

---

[23] *Mu'jizaat al-Muṣṭafa* by Khayr ad-Deen Waa'ili.

[24] Abu Raafi' was a Jew who was the bitterest enemy of the Messenger of Allah (ﷺ); he broke the treaty and attacked him in verse.

[25] Bukhari.

following morning, the people came to the Messenger of Allah, each of them hoping that he would be given the banner. He said, 'Where is 'Ali ibn Abi Ṭaalib?' They said, 'O' Messenger of Allah, he has something wrong with his eyes.' He said, 'Send for him.' He was brought to him, then the Messenger of Allah spat in his eyes, and he was healed and it appeared as if he had never suffered any pain. Then he gave him the banner, and 'Ali said, 'O' Messenger of Allah, shall I fight them until they are like us?' He said, 'Set out, and take it easy until you reach their territory, then call them to Islam and tell them what duties they have towards Allah. For by Allah, if Allah were to guide one man at your hands, that would be better for you than having red camels.'"

The shin of Salamah ibn al-Akwa'

Bukhari narrated that Yazeed ibn Abi 'Ubayd said:

"I saw the mark of a blow on the shin of Salamah ibn al-Akwa', and I said, 'O' Abu Muslim, what is this blow?' He said, 'A blow that I had on the day of Khaybar. The people said, Salamah has been wounded. I came to the Prophet (ﷺ) and he blew on it three times, and I never noticed it until now.'"

He expelled the jinn from one who was possessed

It is narrated that Ya'laa ibn Murrah ath-Thaqafi said:

"We were on a campaign with the Messenger of Allah, and we passed by a well. A woman brought a son of hers who was possessed by the jinn. The Prophet (ﷺ) took hold of his nose and said, 'Come out! I am Muhammad the Messenger of Allah!' Then we moved on, and when we came back to that place (the woman was there at the well). He (ﷺ) asked her about the boy. She said, 'By the One Who sent you with the truth, we have never seen anything wrong with him since.'"[26]

He told of unseen matters

Among the information of the unseen, he (ﷺ) spoke of Allah and His names, attributes and actions; he spoke of the angels and their attributes; he spoke of the world of the jinn, and of Paradise and Hell. He spoke of events which happened in the past, as he spoke of Adam, Nooḥ (Noah), Hood (Hud), Ṣaaliḥ, Ibraaheem (Abraham), Moosa (Moses), 'Eesa (Jesus) and other Prophets and Messengers, and what happened between them and their peoples. He spoke in detail of these matters, the like of which could not be produced by an un-lettered man who could neither read nor write, who did not mix with those who had studied history of the nations and knew about them. Moreover, he brought information which had not come to the knowledge of the world, information which the scholars of the People of the Book had concealed. He corrected a great deal of the information they had. All of this indicates that he brought this knowledge from the All-Knowing, All-Aware. In the words of the Qur'an:

﴿ تِلْكَ مِنْ أَنۢبَآءِ ٱلْغَيْبِ نُوحِيهَآ إِلَيْكَ ۖ مَا كُنتَ تَعْلَمُهَآ أَنتَ وَلَا قَوْمُكَ مِن قَبْلِ هَٰذَا ... ﴿٤٩﴾ ﴾

﴾This is of the news of the Unseen which We reveal unto you [O' Muhammad]; neither you nor your people knew it before this...﴿ *(Qur'an 11: 49)*

---

[26] *Sharḥ as-Sunnah*; narrated by Imam Aḥmad in his *Musnad* (4/172) with a *ṣaḥeeḥ* isnad; also in *Al-Mishkaat* (3/188), edited by our *shaykh* Muhammad Naaṣiruddeen al-Albaani.

The Qur'an refers to this knowledge in a number of places, such as what is said in the context of the story of Maryam (Mary):

﴿... وَمَا كُنتَ لَدَيْهِمْ إِذْ يُلْقُونَ أَقْلَٰمَهُمْ أَيُّهُمْ يَكْفُلُ مَرْيَمَ وَمَا كُنتَ لَدَيْهِمْ إِذْ يَخْتَصِمُونَ ﴿٤٤﴾﴾

﴿...You were not with them, when they cast lots with their pens as to which of them should be charged with the care of Maryam [Mary]; nor were you with them when they disputed.﴾ *(Qur'an 3: 44)*

Similarly in the context of the story of Moosa (Moses) the Qur'an informs:

﴿وَمَا كُنتَ بِجَانِبِ ٱلطُّورِ إِذْ نَادَيْنَا وَلَٰكِن رَّحْمَةً مِّن رَّبِّكَ لِتُنذِرَ قَوْمًا مَّآ أَتَىٰهُم مِّن نَّذِيرٍ مِّن قَبْلِكَ لَعَلَّهُمْ يَتَذَكَّرُونَ ﴿٤٦﴾﴾

﴿And you [O' Muhammad] were not at the side of the Ṭoor [Mount] when We did call [it is said that Allah called the followers of Muhammad, and they answered His Call, or that Allah called Moosa (Moses)]. But [you are sent] as a mercy from your Lord, to give warning to a people to whom no warner had come before you, in order that they may remember or receive admonition.﴾ *(Qur'an 28: 46)*

To cite further he told of unseen matters at the time when they were happening. Imam Bukhari recorded that,

"He spoke of the martyrdom of the three Muslim leaders at the battle of Mu'tah, and of Khaalid ibn al-Waleed's taking up the flag after they had died on the day on which the event took place.[27]

[27] *Mishkaat al-Maṣaabeeḥ*, 1/172.

When the Negus died, he told of his passing on the same day; the same happened when Chosroes died.

He also foretold unseen events which were yet to come. Some of them already happened at the forecasted time during his time and some happened after some time as he foretold and others will follow.

Another example is that he foretold the places where the leaders of the *kuffaar* (disbelievers) would fall in battle, before the battle of Badr began. Muslim narrated that Anas (ﷺ) said:

> "The Messenger of Allah (ﷺ) mobilized the people, then they set out until they stopped at Badr. The Messenger of Allah (ﷺ) said, 'Here is the place where So and so will fall,' and he put his hand on the ground here and there.' Then none of them passed the spot where the Messenger of Allah (ﷺ) had put his hand, (but the persons named by him fell)."[28]

Again he spoke of the unseen matters that were to happen after his death. For example, Abu Hurayrah (ﷺ) narrated that the Messenger of Allah (ﷺ) said,

> "When Chosroes dies, there will be no Chosroes after him, and when Caesar dies, there will be no Caesar after him. By the One in Whose hand is my soul, their wealth will be spent for the sake of Allah."

- This has been narrated by Bukhari, Muslim and Tirmidhi.[29] And it happened as the Prophet (ﷺ) had foretold.

The Messenger (ﷺ) often spoke of the events that were to happen in the future. Ḥudhayfah ibn al-Yamaan said:

---

[28] Ibid, 3/167.

[29] *Jaami' al-Uṣool*, 12/59.

"The Messenger of Allah (ﷺ) stood before us and he did not leave out anything that was to happen between that day and the onset of the Hour except he told us about it. Those who memorized it memorized it, and those who forgot it forgot it. These Companions of mine know it, but there may be some things that I have forgotten, but when I see it happen I remember, just as a man remembers the face of a man who has been away from him, and when he sees him he recognizes him."

- This hadith is narrated by Bukhari, Muslim and Abu Dawood.[30]

Similarly he spoke of the tribulations and signs of the Hour, etc, mentioned in the books of hadith.

The sorrow of the tree stump

In *Ṣaḥeeḥ al-Bukhari* and elsewhere it is narrated that the Messenger of Allah (ﷺ) used to deliver sermons leaning on a tree stump. When, after the construction of the pulpit, he started to use the minbar, the tree stump was filled with sorrow and its cry could be heard. He came to it and touched it. According to Bukhari's report,

"When the minbar was built, we heard a sound like the sound of a camel coming from the tree stump, until the Messenger of Allah (ﷺ) came down and placed his hand on it."[31]

The trees submitted to him, greeted him with *salaam* and spoke to him[32]

Muslim narrated from Jaabir that he said:

---

[30] Ibid, 12/63.

[31] *Jaami' al-Uṣool*, 12/68.

[32] *Mu'jizaat al-Muṣṭafa*, Pp. 84.

> "We went out on a campaign with the Messenger of Allah (ﷺ), and we stopped in a wide valley. The Messenger of Allah (ﷺ) went to relieve himself, but he did not see anything behind which to conceal himself, apart from two trees on the edge of the valley. The Messenger of Allah (ﷺ) went to one of them, took hold of one of its branches and said, 'Follow me by the will of Allah,' and it followed him like a camel led by its nose ring in the hand of its rider. Then he came to the other tree, took hold of one of its branches and said, 'Follow me by the will of Allah.' So it also followed him. Then he stood between the two trees and said, 'Come together and cover me by the will of Allah' and they joined together. I sat thinking to myself, then I saw the Messenger of Allah (ﷺ) coming towards me, and the two trees had separated and each of them was standing in its place."

It is narrated that Ya'laa ibn Murrah ath-Thaqafi said:

> "We went out on a campaign with the Messenger of Allah (ﷺ), and stopped to rest. The Prophet (ﷺ) fell asleep, and a tree came, plowing through the earth, and came close to him, then it went back to its place. When the Messenger of Allah (ﷺ) woke up, I told him about that and he said: 'That is a tree which asked its Lord for permission to greet the Messenger of Allah (ﷺ), and permission was granted to it.'"[33]

Daarimi narrated from Anas (رضي الله عنه) that he said:

[33] *Sharḥ as-Sunnah*; Also narrated by Aḥmad. Its isnad is *ḍa'eef* (weak) but there is a corroborating report in the hadith of Jaabir narrated by Ad-Daarimi, 1/10. The story is sound as our *Shaykh* Al-Albaani said in his commentary on *Al-Mishkaat*, 3/188.

"Jibreel (Gabriel) (عليه السلام) came to the Prophet (ﷺ) when he was sitting upset, stained with blood because of the persecution of the people of Makkah. He said, 'O' Messenger of Allah, would you like us to show a sign?' He said, 'Yes.' He looked at a tree that was behind him and said, 'Call it.' So he called it and it came and stood before him. Then he said, 'Tell it to go back.' So he told it to go back and it did so. The Messenger of Allah ﷺ said, '(That is) sufficient for me, (that is) sufficient for me.'"[34]

Imam Tirmidhi narrated from Ibn 'Abbaas that he said:

"A Bedouin came to the Messenger of Allah (ﷺ) and said, 'How can I know that you are a Prophet?' He said, 'If I call this bunch of dates from this palm-tree, it will bear witness that I am the Messenger of Allah.' So the Messenger of Allah (ﷺ) called it, and it came down from the palm-tree until it came to the Prophet (ﷺ). Then he said, 'Go back,' and it went back. Then the Bedouin entered Islam."[35]

Both Bukhari and Muslim narrated from Ḥaqq ibn 'Abdur-Raḥmaan that he said:

I heard my father say, I asked Masrooq, "How did the Prophet (ﷺ) know about the jinn on the night when they listened to him reciting Qur'an?" He said, "Your father - meaning 'Abdullah ibn Mas'ood - told me that he said, 'a tree told him about that.'"[36]

Daarimi narrated from Ibn 'Umar:

---

[34] Its isnad is *ṣaḥeeḥ* as mentioned in *Al-Mishkaat* 3/188.

[35] He (Tirmidhi) classed it as *ṣaḥeeḥ*.

[36] Bukhari and Muslim.

> "We were with the Prophet (ﷺ) on a journey. A Bedouin came and when he was near, the Messenger of Allah (ﷺ) said to him: 'Do you bear witness that there is no god except Allah alone, with no partner or associate, and that Muhammad is His slave and Messenger?' He said, 'Who bears witness to what you have said?' He said, 'This desert tree.' The Messenger of Allah (ﷺ) called it, and he was standing on the edge of the valley. The tree came, plowing through the earth, and stood before him, and bore witness three times that he was as he had said, then it went back to its place."[37]

The greeting of the rock

Muslim and Tirmidhi narrated from Jaabir ibn Samurah that the Messenger of Allah (ﷺ) said:

> "I know a rock in Makkah which used to greet me before my mission began. I still know which one it is."

The complaint of the camel

It is narrated that Ya'laa ibn Murrah ath-Thaqafi said:

> "Whilst we were on a journey with the Messenger of Allah (ﷺ), we passed by a camel which carried drinking water on its back. When the camel saw him, it started to make noise and it rested the front part of its neck on the ground. The Prophet (ﷺ) went and stood beside it and said, 'Where is the owner of this camel?' The man came to him, and he (the Prophet) said, 'Sell it to me.' He said, 'No, I will give it to you, O' Messenger of Allah, but it

---

[37] Its isnad is *ṣaḥeeḥ* as our *Shaykh*, Muhammad Naaṣiruddeen al-Albaani said, in his commentary on *Mishkaat al-Maṣaabeeḥ*, 3/189.

> belongs to a family who has no other source of livelihood.' He said, 'If that is the case (you do not have to give it to me), but it complained to me that it is being overworked and underfed, so treat it kindly.'"[38]

It is narrated that 'Abdullah ibn Ja'far said:

> "I rode behind the Messenger of Allah (ﷺ) one day, and he told me something which I was not to tell to anyone. The Messenger loved to hide himself behind something like a wall, a tree, a hill or a grove of palm trees. He entered a garden belonging to a man among the Anṣaar. When a camel saw the Prophet (ﷺ), it made a sound and its eyes overflowed with tears. The Prophet (ﷺ) came to it and patted its back between its hump and the bone behind its ears, then it calmed down. He said, 'Who is the owner of this camel?' Who does this camel belong to?' A young man from among the Anṣaar came and said, 'It is mine, O' Messenger of Allah.' He said, 'Do you not fear Allah with regard to this animal over whom Allah has given you power? It complained to me that you are starving it and exhausting it.'"[39]

---

[38] *Sharḥ as-Sunnah*, also by Aḥmad. Its isnad is weak but there is a corroborating report from the hadith of Jaabir, narrated by Daarimi (1/10). So the story is true as our *shaykh*, Al-Albaani, said in *Al-Mishkaat* 3/188.

[39] This hadith is narrated by Abu Dawood, Al-Ḥaakim, Aḥmad and Ibn 'Asaakir. This version is narrated by Ibn 'Asaakir. Its isnad is *ṣaḥeeḥ* according to the conditions of Muslim, who narrated it with this isnad without the story of the camel. *Al-Aḥaadeeth aṣ-Ṣaḥeeḥah* by our *shaykh*, Al-Albaani, 1/28.

Miracles of People other than the Prophets

The *karaamaat* of the *awliyaa'*

One of the basic principles of *Ahl as-Sunnah wal-Jamaa'ah* is to believe in the *karaamaat* (miracles)[40] of the *awliyaa'* (close friends of Allah - saints) and the extraordinary feats that Allah causes to happen at their hands, such as the knowledge that they have which is beyond the grasp of ordinary folk, and various kinds of power and influence.[41]

Some sects of Muslims denied the *karaamaat* of the *awliyaa'*. One such group was the *Mu'tazilah*, who based their claim on the idea that if it were possible for people other than the Prophets to perform extraordinary feats, then people would confuse the Prophets with the *awliyaa'*, and miracles would no longer be proof of the truth of a Prophet.[42]

This view of theirs is to be rejected, because some of the *karaamaat* of the *awliyaa'* (saints) are spoken of in the Qur'an and in the *ṣaḥeeḥ aḥaadeeth* (authentic hadiths); the reports reach the level of being *mutawaatir* and people have witnessed such events at all times and places.

The specious argument which they suggest can only apply to cases where a so-called *wali* (saint) performs a "miracle" and claims to be a prophet, but this does not happen. If he claims to be a prophet then he

---

[40] The scholars of *Tawḥeed* describe a *karaamah* (pl. *karaamaat*) as being an extraordinary feat which is not accompanied by claims of Prophethood and does not serve as the forerunner to any such claim, which happens at the hands of one who is manifestly righteous and who is a follower of a Prophet whose law he is obliged to follow, accompanied by sound belief and righteous deeds, whether he is aware of that *karaamah* or not. *Lawaami' al-Anwaar al-Bahiyah*, 2/393.

[41] *Majmoo' al-Fataawa Shaykh al-Islam*, 3/156.

[42] *Sharḥ al-'Aqeedah aṭ-Ṭaḥaawiyah*, Pp. 563.

is no longer a *wali* but a pretender to prophethood and a liar.[43] Imam Aḥmad denounced those who denied the *karaamaat* of the Prophets and did not believe in them, and he declared them to have gone astray.[44]

The wisdom behind *karaamaat* being given to the *awliyaa'*

Allah bestows extraordinary things upon some of His slaves in order to honour them for their righteousness and their strength of faith. That may also serve to fulfil some of their needs, such as the need for food and drink and safety. He may also bestow that upon them in order to support His religion, to make His word prevail and confirm the truth and repulse falsehood.[45]

For example, the Qur'an tells us about the case of Maryam (Mary), who used to have winter fruits in the summer and summer fruits in the winter:

﴿... كُلَّمَا دَخَلَ عَلَيْهَا زَكَرِيَّا ٱلْمِحْرَابَ وَجَدَ عِندَهَا رِزْقًا ۖ قَالَ يَٰمَرْيَمُ أَنَّىٰ لَكِ هَٰذَا ۖ قَالَتْ هُوَ مِنْ عِندِ ٱللَّهِ ۖ إِنَّ ٱللَّهَ يَرْزُقُ مَن يَشَآءُ بِغَيْرِ حِسَابٍ ۝٣٧﴾

> ﴿...Every time he [Zakariyya] entered *Al-Miḥraab* [a praying place or private room] to [visit] her, he found her supplied with sustenance. He said: 'O' Maryam [Mary]! From where have you got this?' She said, 'This is from Allah.' Verily, Allah provides sustenance to whom He wills, without limit.﴾ *(Qur'an 3: 37)*

---

[43] Ibid.

[44] *Lawaami' al-Anwaar al-Bahiyah*, 2/393.

[45] Many of the scholars of *kalaam* do not believe in miracles except in the case of the Prophets; they do not believe that anyone else could perform miracles. *Sharḥ aṭ-Ṭaḥaawiyah*, Pp. 158.

Another example is what happened to the people of the Cave, when Allah sealed their ears in the Cave for three hundred (solar) years, adding nine (for lunar years) *(Qur'an 18: 25)*, and Allah preserved their bodies during that lengthy period of time, as He tells us in *Soorah al-Kahf*, the 18th chapter of the Qur'an.

And there are also examples which happened to the Companions of the Messenger of Allah (ﷺ).

Lights in sticks

For example, Usayd ibn Ḥuḍayr and 'Abbaad ibn Bishr were speaking with the Prophet (ﷺ) about some issue with which they were concerned, until part of the night had passed, on a very dark night. Then they left the Messenger of Allah to go home. Each of them had a stick in his hand, and the stick of one of them shone so that they could walk in its light. Then when their ways parted, the stick of the other also shone, so that each of them walked in the light of his own stick, until he reached his family. This is narrated by Bukhari.[46]

Blessed food

Abu Bakr aṣ-Ṣiddeeq (رضي الله عنه) brought home three guests from among *Ahl aṣ-Ṣuffah*. The Messenger (ﷺ) had enjoined upon the Muslims to offer hospitality to these people. Abu Bakr left them in his house so that his family could take care of them, and he went to the Messenger of Allah (ﷺ). He came back late, and his wife said to him, "What kept you from your guests?" He said, "Did you not give them dinner?" She said, "They refused to eat until you came." He got angry and said, "By Allah I will never eat this food!" His wife swore

46 *Mishkaat al-Maṣaabeeḥ*, 3/197.

that she would never eat that food, and the guests swore that they would never eat that food. Then Abu Bakr said, "This is from the *Shayṭaan* (Satan)." Then he called for food, and he ate and they ate, and they did not lift any morsel to their mouths but what was left in the dish was more than what had been taken. He said to his wife, "O' sister of Bani Firaas, what is this?" She said, "My goodness! Now it is three times more than before." They ate and he sent some of it to the Prophet (ﷺ), and it was mentioned that he ate some of it. (Bukhari and Muslim)[47]

This event was an honour from Allah to Abu Bakr because of his virtue. And because he did not persist in his anger when he swore not to eat any of the food. So he annoyed the *Shayṭaan*, and Allah (ﷻ) honoured him for that.

Sufaynah and the lion

This Sufaynah was a freed slave of the Messenger of Allah (ﷺ), who had lost track of the Muslim army in the land of the Romans, or had been taken prisoner. He set out, fleeing and looking for the army, when he was faced with a lion. He said, "O' Abu al-Ḥaarith (the nickname of the lion), I am the freed slave of the Messenger of Allah (ﷺ), and this is what has happened to me." The lion started moving its tail and came to stand beside him. Every time he heard a sound he went to check it out, then he came back and walked beside him, until he reached the army. Then the lion went back.[48]

---

[47] *Mishkaat al-Maṣaabeeḥ*, 3/198.

[48] At-Tabreezi said in *Mishkaat al-Maṣaabeeḥ*, this is narrated in *Sharḥ as-Sunnah*. The editor said, a similar report has been narrated by Al-Ḥaakim, and he said, it is *ṣaḥeeḥ* according to the conditions of Muslim, and Dhahabi agreed with him, and it is as they said. (*Mishkaat al-Maṣaabeeḥ*, 3/199)

A shout in Madeenah echoes in Syria

'Umar ibn al-Khaṭṭaab (رضى) sent an army and appointed a man called Saariyah to lead them. Whilst 'Umar was preaching, he started to shout, "O' Saariyah, the mountain!" Then a messenger came from the army and said, "O' *Ameer al-Mu'mineen*, we met our enemy and they were defeating us, then we heard someone shouting, 'O' Saariyah, the mountain!' Then we protected our backs by putting the mountain behind us, and Allah defeated them."[49]

Some *karaamaat* of the *awliyaa'*

Ibn Taymiyah mentioned a number of these *karaamaat* apart from those which we have mentioned above. We will quote some examples here[50]:

When Khubayb ibn 'Adiy was a prisoner at the hands of the *mushrikeen* (polytheists) in Makkah, Allah (ﷻ), provided grapes for him to eat, when there were no grapes in Makkah.

When Umm Ayman set out to migrate to Madeenah (hijrah), she had no food or water with her. She almost died of thirst. When the time for breaking the fast came, as she was fasting, she heard a sound above her head and looked up. There she saw a bucket suspended in the air. She drank from it until her thirst was quenched, and she never felt thirsty again in her life.

Whenever Al-Baraa' ibn 'Aazib swore an oath beseeching Allah to do something, Allah would fulfil his oath. When the fighting became intense for the Muslims in jihad, they would say, "O' Baraa', swear

---

[49] At-Tabreezi said: This is narrated by Al-Bayhaqi in *Dalaa'il an-Nubuwwah*. The editor of *Al-Mishkaat* said, Ibn 'Asaakir narrated something similar with a *ḥasan* isnad.

[50] *Majmoo' al-Fataawa Shaykh al-Islam*, 11/276-281.

an oath beseeching your Lord." He would say, "O' Lord, I urge You, let us defeat them." Then the enemy would be defeated. On the day of Al-Qaadisiyyah, he said, "I beseech you, O' Lord, to grant us victory over them and let me be the first martyr." They defeated them, and Al-Baraa' was killed as a martyr.

Khaalid ibn al-Waleed besieged some stronghold, and they said, "We will not surrender until you drink poison." He drank it, and it did not harm him.

When Az-Zubayrah was persecuted for her Islam for the sake of Allah, she refused to follow any religion but Islam. She lost her sight, and the *mushrikeen* said, "Al-Laat and Al-'Uzza have taken away her sight." She said, "No, by Allah," then Allah restored her sight to her.

Al-Ḥasan al-Baṣri hid from Ḥajjaaj. The troops reached him six times and he prayed to Allah, and they did not see him. He prayed against one of the *Khawaarij* who would persecute him, and he fell dead. When Uways al-Qarni died, they found among his clothes shrouds which he did not have before, and they found a grave already dug for him, complete with *laḥd* (niche), in a rock, where they buried him after shrouding him in those garments.

Righteousness is the greatest *karaamah*

A *karaamah* is not proof that the one to whom it has been bestowed is better than anyone else. Allah may grant *karaamah* to one who is weak in faith, in order to strengthen his faith, and the one who has not been bestowed with such a thing may be more perfect in faith and a closer friend of Allah, and therefore in no need of that which is granted to others. Hence extraordinary things happened more among the *Taabi'een* than among the *Ṣaḥaabah*. We therefore should not preoccupy ourselves with seeking *karaamaat*, or feel upset if they are not bestowed to us. Abu 'Ali al-Jawzjaani spoke the truth when he said: "Be a seeker of righteousness, not a seeker of *karaamah*, for your soul is naturally inclined to seek *karaamah*, but your Lord demands of you righteousness." Some of those who understood what he was saying said: "This is a major principle concerning this matter, and a subtle idea which many seekers of truth fail to comprehend."[51]

Miracles and devilish exploits[52]

Many people go astray because they think that everyone who performs extraordinary feats is one of the righteous friends of Allah (*awliyaa'*). Some people fly through the air and walk on water, and so on, but they are the most evil of Allah's creation. They may even claim to be prophets, such as Al-Ḥaarith ad-Dimashqi, who emerged in Syria at the time of 'Abdul Malik ibn Marwaan, and claimed to be a prophet. He performed many extraordinary feats. They would tie his legs with ropes and he would free himself; he would be struck with weapons and that would not harm him; if he touched a marble slab it would start reciting *tasbeeḥ* (to say "*Subḥaanallah*"). He would show the people images of men and horses in the air, and would say that these were the angels. But these and similar feats were the work of the devils. Hence if some righteous people are present at these devilish events, and they mention Allah and recite *Aayat al-Kursiy* and other passages of the Qur'an, this will put a stop to these devilish feats. When the Muslims seized the liar Al-Ḥaarith ad-Dimashqi to kill him, one of them stabbed him with a spear and it did not penetrate. 'Abdul Malik said to him, "You did not pronounce the name of Allah." So he pronounced the name of Allah, then he stabbed him and killed him.[53]

---

[51] *Majmoo' al-Fataawa Shaykh al-Islam*, 11/320.

[52] For more information on this topic, see our book *'Aalam al-Jinn wa ash-Shayaaṭeen* (The World of the Jinn and the Devils).

[53] *Majmoo' al-Fataawa Shaykh al-Islam*, 11/284-285.

The *Dajjaal* (Pseudo-Christ) will perform extraordinary feats which will dazzle those who see them, but at the same time he will claim to be divine.

Thus extraordinary feats (miraculous deeds) from a person are not a sign that he is a close friend of Allah (a *wali* or saint). *Karamaat* come about because of faith, piety and steadfastness in obeying Allah (ﷻ). If the extraordinary event comes about because of *kufr, shirk*, falsehood, wrongdoing and immorality, then it is a devilish feat, not *karaamah* from the Most Merciful.

2 - THE PREVIOUS NATIONS WERE TOLD ABOUT THE COMING OF THE PROPHET (ﷺ)

Allah (ﷻ) says:

﴿ أَوَلَمْ يَكُن لَّهُمْ ءَايَةً أَن يَعْلَمَهُۥ عُلَمَـٰٓؤُا۟ بَنِىٓ إِسْرَٰٓءِيلَ ﴿١٩٧﴾ ﴾

﴿Is it not a sign to them that the learned scholars of the Children of Israel knew it [as true]?﴾

(Qur'an 26: 197)

This *aayah* (verse) states that among the clear signs that pointed to the veracity of the Messenger Muhammad (ﷺ) and the truth of the Message that he brought was the fact that the Children of Israel knew that. This fact was recorded and preserved, written in their books which were in circulation among them, as Allah (ﷻ) says:

﴿ وَإِنَّهُۥ لَفِى زُبُرِ ٱلْأَوَّلِينَ ﴿١٩٦﴾ ﴾

﴿And verily, it [the Qur'an, and its revelation to Prophet Muhammad] is [announced] in the Scriptures [i.e. the *Tawraat* (Torah) and the *Injeel* (Gospel)] of former people.﴾ *(Qur'an 26: 196)*

The Qur'an tells us that the earlier Prophets foretold the coming of our Prophet Muhammad (ﷺ)

The Qur'an which has come down to us from our Lord, the All-Knowing, All-Aware, tells us that mention of Muhammad and his nation is to be found in the previous divinely-revealed Books, and that the previous Prophets gave glad tidings of his coming. A number of *mufassireen* (exegetes) interpreted the *aayah* (verse):

﴿ وَإِذْ أَخَذَ ٱللَّهُ مِيثَٰقَ ٱلنَّبِيِّـۧنَ لَمَآ ءَاتَيْتُكُم مِّن كِتَٰبٍ وَحِكْمَةٍ ثُمَّ جَآءَكُمْ رَسُولٌ مُّصَدِّقٌ لِّمَا مَعَكُمْ لَتُؤْمِنُنَّ بِهِۦ وَلَتَنصُرُنَّهُۥ قَالَ ءَأَقْرَرْتُمْ وَأَخَذْتُمْ عَلَىٰ ذَٰلِكُمْ إِصْرِى قَالُوٓا۟ أَقْرَرْنَا قَالَ فَٱشْهَدُوا۟ وَأَنَا۠ مَعَكُم مِّنَ ٱلشَّٰهِدِينَ ﴿٨١﴾ ﴾

﴾And [remember] when Allah took the Covenant of the Prophets, saying: 'Take whatever I gave you from the Book and *Ḥikmah* [understanding of the Laws of Allah], and afterwards there will come to you a Messenger [Muhammad] confirming what is with you; you must, then, believe in him and help him.' Allah said: 'Do you agree [to it] and will you take up My Covenant [which I conclude with you]?' They said: 'We agree.' He said: 'Then bear witness; and I am with you among the witnesses [for this].'﴿ *(Qur'an 3: 81)*

- as meaning that Allah took the promise and covenant from every Prophet that if Muhammad (ﷺ) was sent during his lifetime, he would believe in him and abandon his own laws in order to follow Muhammad's laws. Hence we learn that he was known to each of the earlier Prophets.

The supplication of Prophet Ibraaheem (Abraham) (عليه السلام)

It is narrated from Al-'Arbaaḍ ibn Saariyah that the Messenger of Allah (ﷺ) said:

> "I was recorded with Allah as the Seal of the Prophets, when Adam was still clay. I shall inform you of the beginning of my affair: the supplication of (Prophet) Ibraaheem (Abraham), the glad tidings of (Prophet) 'Eesa (Jesus) and the vision of my mother which she saw when she gave birth to me. And there went out for her a light which illuminated the palaces of Syria."

- This has been narrated in *Sharḥ as-Sunnah*.[54]

Allah tells us that when the Close Friend of the Most Merciful, Prophet Ibraaheem, and his son Ismaa'eel were building the Ka'bah and praying, part of that supplication was that which is narrated to us in the 2nd chapter of the Qur'an - *Soorah al-Baqarah*:

﴿ وَإِذْ يَرْفَعُ إِبْرَٰهِـۧمُ ٱلْقَوَاعِدَ مِنَ ٱلْبَيْتِ وَإِسْمَـٰعِيلُ رَبَّنَا تَقَبَّلْ مِنَّآ ۖ إِنَّكَ
أَنتَ ٱلسَّمِيعُ ٱلْعَلِيمُ ﴿١٢٧﴾ رَبَّنَا وَٱجْعَلْنَا مُسْلِمَيْنِ لَكَ وَمِن ذُرِّيَّتِنَآ أُمَّةً
مُّسْلِمَةً لَّكَ وَأَرِنَا مَنَاسِكَنَا وَتُبْ عَلَيْنَآ ۖ إِنَّكَ أَنتَ ٱلتَّوَّابُ ٱلرَّحِيمُ ﴿١٢٨﴾ رَبَّنَا
وَٱبْعَثْ فِيهِمْ رَسُولًا مِّنْهُمْ يَتْلُوا۟ عَلَيْهِمْ ءَايَـٰتِكَ وَيُعَلِّمُهُمُ ٱلْكِتَـٰبَ
وَٱلْحِكْمَةَ وَيُزَكِّيهِمْ ۚ إِنَّكَ أَنتَ ٱلْعَزِيزُ ٱلْحَكِيمُ ﴿١٢٩﴾ ﴾

﴾And [remember] when Ibraaheem [Abraham] and [his son] Ismaa'eel [Ishmael] were raising the foundations of the House [the Ka'bah at Makkah], [saying], 'Our Lord! Accept [this service] from us. Verily, You are the All-Hearer, the All-Knower. Our Lord! And make us submissive unto You and of our offspring a nation

---

[54] *Mishkaat al-Maṣaabeeḥ* by At-Tabreezi, 3/127. *Shaykh* Naaṣiruddeen al-Albaani said: A *ṣaḥeeḥ* hadith.

> submissive unto You, and show us our *Manaasik* [all the ceremonies of pilgrimage - Ḥajj and 'Umrah], and accept our repentance. Truly, You are the One Who accepts repentance, the Most Merciful. Our Lord! Send amongst them a Messenger of their own [and indeed Allah answered their invocation by sending Muhammad], who shall recite unto them Your Verses and instruct them in the Book [this Qur'an] and *Al-Ḥikmah* [full knowledge of the Islamic laws and jurisprudence or wisdom or Prophethood], and purify them. Verily, You are the All-Mighty, the All-Wise.'﴿
>
> *(Qur'an 2: 127-129)*

Allah answered the prayer of His Close Friend Ibraaheem and his son the Prophet of Allah Ismaa'eel. Muhammad (ﷺ) was the outcome of that answer. The *Tawraat* (Torah) which is extant today - despite the fact that it has been distorted - still contains something of those glad tidings. We see in it that Allah answered Ibraaheem's prayer for Ismaa'eel. In the Bible, in the Book of Genesis, it says:

"And as for Ishmael, I have heard you: I will surely bless him; I will make him fruitful and will greatly increase his numbers. He will be the father of twelve rulers, and I will make him into a great nation." (Genesis 17:20 - NIV)

In the Samaritan Torah this verse is very similar. The literal translation of the Hebrew text is: "And as for Ishmael, I have heard you: I will surely bless him; I will increase his numbers by means of *ma'ad ma'ad*."[55] Ibn al-Qayyim mentioned that in some ancient copies of the Torah the text was as quoted here.

---

[55] *Nubuwwat Muhammad min ash-Shakk ilal-Yaqeen*, Pp. 250; *Muhammad Nabi al-Islam*, Pp. 3.

This points to the coming of our Prophet Muhammad (ﷺ) in several ways:

a) The nation that is great in the sight of Allah must be a Muslim nation, and this nation did not exist among the descendents of Ismaa'eel until after the Messenger had been sent and the Muslims spread east and west.

b) The Hebrew text "*ma'ad ma'ad*" is a clear reference to the name of the Messenger (ﷺ). The translators rendered it as "very very" or "much much", but the correct translation is Muhammad, because in Hebrew it is pronounced as *me'od me'od*, and the Hebrew pronunciation is close to the Arabic.

c) It says that twelve rulers will be born, and this is in accordance with the statement of the Messenger (ﷺ) that this ummah would be ruled by twelve *Khulafa* (Caliphs), all of them from Quraysh.

Prophet Moosa (Moses) foretold the coming of the Prophet (ﷺ)

Definitive news came to the Children of Israel long ago of the unlettered Prophet, via the Prophet of Allah Moosa (Moses). He brought them the certain news of his mission, his attributes, the nature of his message and the characteristics of his nation. He would be an unlettered Prophet and he would enjoin his ummah to do good and forbid them to do evil. He would permit them all that was good and forbid them all that was evil. He would relieve those among the Children of Israel of the burdens and fetters that Allah knew would be imposed upon them because of their sin. The followers of this Prophet would fear their Lord, pay their zakah and believe in the signs of Allah. The certain news came to them that those who believed in this unlettered Prophet, venerated him, respected him, supported him, helped him and followed the light which had come down with him, would be those who would be successful. Allah, the

All-Glorious, All-Powerful says:

﴿ ... عَذَابِىٓ أُصِيبُ بِهِۦ مَنْ أَشَآءُ ۖ وَرَحْمَتِى وَسِعَتْ كُلَّ شَىْءٍ ۚ
فَسَأَكْتُبُهَا لِلَّذِينَ يَتَّقُونَ وَيُؤْتُونَ ٱلزَّكَوٰةَ وَٱلَّذِينَ هُم بِـَٔايَٰتِنَا يُؤْمِنُونَ
﴿١٥٦﴾ ٱلَّذِينَ يَتَّبِعُونَ ٱلرَّسُولَ ٱلنَّبِىَّ ٱلْأُمِّىَّ ٱلَّذِى يَجِدُونَهُۥ مَكْتُوبًا
عِندَهُمْ فِى ٱلتَّوْرَىٰةِ وَٱلْإِنجِيلِ يَأْمُرُهُم بِٱلْمَعْرُوفِ وَيَنْهَىٰهُمْ عَنِ
ٱلْمُنكَرِ وَيُحِلُّ لَهُمُ ٱلطَّيِّبَٰتِ وَيُحَرِّمُ عَلَيْهِمُ ٱلْخَبَٰٓئِثَ وَيَضَعُ
عَنْهُمْ إِصْرَهُمْ وَٱلْأَغْلَٰلَ ٱلَّتِى كَانَتْ عَلَيْهِمْ ۚ فَٱلَّذِينَ ءَامَنُوا۟ بِهِۦ
وَعَزَّرُوهُ وَنَصَرُوهُ وَٱتَّبَعُوا۟ ٱلنُّورَ ٱلَّذِىٓ أُنزِلَ مَعَهُۥٓ ۙ أُو۟لَٰٓئِكَ هُمُ
ٱلْمُفْلِحُونَ ﴿١٥٧﴾ ﴾

﴾...[As to] My punishment I afflict therewith whom I will and My Mercy embraces all things. That [Mercy] I shall ordain for those who are the *Muttaqoon* [the pious], and give Zakah; and those who believe in Our *Aayaat* [proofs, evidences, verses, lessons, signs and revelations, etc.]; Those who follow the Messenger, the Prophet who can neither read nor write [i.e. Muhammad] whom they find written with them in the *Tawraat* [Torah] and the *Injeel* [Gospel] - he commands them for *Al-Ma'roof* [i.e. Islamic Monotheism and all that Islam has ordained]; and forbids them from *Al-Munkar* [i.e. disbelief, polytheism of all kinds, and all that Islam has forbidden]; he allows them as lawful *Aṭ-Ṭayyibaat* [i.e. all good and lawful as regards things, deeds, beliefs, persons and foods], and prohibits them as unlawful *Al-Khaba'ith* [i.e. all evil and unlawful as regard to things, deeds, beliefs, persons and foods], he releases them from their heavy burdens [of Allah's Covenant with the children of Israel], and from the fetters [bindings] that were upon them. So those who believe in him [Muhammad], honour him, help him, and follow the light [the Qur'an] which has been sent down with him, it is they who will be successful.﴿

(Qur'an 7: 156-157)

Other traces of this foretelling in the Bible

There are some traces of this foretelling left in the Bible. In the Book of Deuteronomy God says to (Prophet) Moses:

"I will raise up for them (i.e., for the Children of Israel) a prophet like you from among their brothers; I will put my words in his mouth, and he will tell them everything I command him. If anyone does not listen to my words that the prophet speaks in my name, I myself will call him to account." (Deuteronomy 18:18-19 - NIV)

The fact that this refers to our Messenger (ﷺ) is quite clear, because he is from among the children of Ismaa'eel, who are the brothers of the Children of Israel. Their grandfather was Isḥaaq (Isaac), and Ismaa'eel (Ishmael) and Isḥaaq were brothers. Muhammad (ﷺ) is from among the Arabs and is from the best family among them. The phrase "like you" means one who brings a law like Moosa. Muhammad (ﷺ) is the one in whose mouth Allah put His words, for he was unlettered and did not read from the scriptures, but Allah revealed to him His words, and he memorized them and recited them. He was the Messenger who was sent to all of mankind, and the Children of Israel are required to follow him and to give up their laws and follow his laws. Whoever does not do that, Allah (ﷻ) will punish him:

"If anyone does not listen to my words that the prophet speaks in my name, I myself will call him to account." (Deuteronomy 18:19 - NIV)

What this tells us is that this is a remnant of the great glad tidings which Allah revealed to Prophet Moosa (Moses) and of which the Qur'an tells us, is the fact that this was narrated in a particular context, where Moosa chose seventy men from among his people to meet Allah, and they were seized with the violent earthquake. That was because they had demanded to see Allah. So Moosa (Moses) prayed to his Lord and beseeched Him, then Allah brought them back to life after they had died. Allah said after Moosa had beseeched and prayed: ﴿...[As to] My punishment I afflict therewith whom I will and My Mercy embraces all things. That [Mercy] I shall ordain for those who are the *Muttaqoon* [the pious]...﴾ *(Qur'an 7: 157).*

If you look at the Bible, at the Book of Exodus, you will find that these glad tidings [of the coming of Muhammad (ﷺ)] were revealed to Prophet Moosa (Moses) after he had gone to meet Allah. The Bible speaks of something similar to the earthquake:

"When the people saw the thunder and lightening and heard the trumpet and saw the mountain in smoke, they trembled with fear. They stayed at a distance..." (Exodus 20:18 - NIV).

'Eesa (Jesus) foretold the coming of the Prophet (ﷺ)

Allah tells us that Prophet 'Eesa (Jesus) (عليه السلام) foretold the coming of our Messenger Muhammad (ﷺ):

﴿ وَإِذْ قَالَ عِيسَى ٱبْنُ مَرْيَمَ يَٰبَنِىٓ إِسْرَٰٓءِيلَ إِنِّى رَسُولُ ٱللَّهِ إِلَيْكُم مُّصَدِّقًا لِّمَا بَيْنَ
يَدَىَّ مِنَ ٱلتَّوْرَىٰةِ وَمُبَشِّرًۢا بِرَسُولٍ يَأْتِى مِنۢ بَعْدِى ٱسْمُهُۥٓ أَحْمَدُ ۖ فَلَمَّا جَآءَهُم بِٱلْبَيِّنَٰتِ قَالُوا۟
هَٰذَا سِحْرٌ مُّبِينٌ ﴿٦﴾ ﴾

﴿And [remember] when 'Eesa [Jesus], son of Maryam [Mary], said: 'O' Children of Israel! I am the Messenger of Allah unto you, confirming the *Tawraat* [(Torah) which came] before me, and giving glad tidings of a Messenger to come after me, whose name shall be Aḥmad. But when he [Aḥmad, i.e. Muhammad] came to them with clear proofs, they said: 'This is plain magic.'﴾

(Qur'an 37: 6)

Aḥmad is one of the names of our Prophet Muhammad (ﷺ), as was proven in *Ṣaḥeeḥ al-Bukhari*, where it is narrated that Jubayr ibn Muṭ'im said: I heard the Messenger of Allah (ﷺ) say,

> "I have (several) names. I am Muhammad; I am Aḥmad; I am *Al-Maaḥi* by means of whom Allah eliminates *kufr*; I am *Al-Ḥaashir* at whose feet (i.e., behind whom) the people will be gathered (on the Day of Resurrection); and I am *Al-'Aaqib* (i.e. the one who succeeds the other prophets in bringing about good)."

- Muslim also narrated something similar.[56]

Two likenesses of the *Tawraat* and *Injeel*

Allah (سبحانه وتعالى) cited two likenesses of the *Tawraat* and *Injeel* for our Messenger Muhammad (ﷺ) and his Companions:

﴿ مُّحَمَّدٌ رَّسُولُ ٱللَّهِ ۚ وَٱلَّذِينَ مَعَهُۥٓ أَشِدَّآءُ عَلَى ٱلْكُفَّارِ رُحَمَآءُ بَيْنَهُمْ ۖ تَرَىٰهُمْ رُكَّعًا
سُجَّدًا يَبْتَغُونَ فَضْلًا مِّنَ ٱللَّهِ وَرِضْوَٰنًا ۖ سِيمَاهُمْ فِى وُجُوهِهِم مِّنْ أَثَرِ
ٱلسُّجُودِ ۚ ذَٰلِكَ مَثَلُهُمْ فِى ٱلتَّوْرَىٰةِ ۚ وَمَثَلُهُمْ فِى ٱلْإِنجِيلِ كَزَرْعٍ أَخْرَجَ شَطْـَٔهُۥ
فَـَٔازَرَهُۥ فَٱسْتَغْلَظَ فَٱسْتَوَىٰ عَلَىٰ سُوقِهِۦ يُعْجِبُ ٱلزُّرَّاعَ لِيَغِيظَ بِهِمُ ٱلْكُفَّارَ ۗ
وَعَدَ ٱللَّهُ ٱلَّذِينَ ءَامَنُوا۟ وَعَمِلُوا۟ ٱلصَّٰلِحَٰتِ مِنْهُم مَّغْفِرَةً وَأَجْرًا عَظِيمًۢا ﴿٢٩﴾ ﴾

﴾Muhammad is the Messenger of Allah. And those who are with him are severe against disbelievers, and merciful among themselves. You see them bowing and falling down prostrate [in prayer], seeking Bounty from Allah and [His] Good Pleasure. The mark of them [i.e. of their Faith] is on their faces [foreheads] from the traces of prostration [during prayers]. This is their description in the *Tawraat* [Torah]. But their description in the *Injeel*

---

[56] *Tafseer Ibn Katheer*, 6/646.

> [Gospel] is like a [sown] seed which sends forth its shoot, then makes it strong, and becomes thick and it stands straight on its stem, delighting the sowers, that He may enrage the disbelievers with them. Allah has promised those among them who believe [i.e. all those who follow Islamic Monotheism, the religion of Prophet Muhammad till the Day of Resurrection] and do righteous good deeds, forgiveness and a mighty reward [i.e. Paradise].﴾ *(Qur'an 48: 29)*

Foretelling in the Old Testament

The Old Testament which is in circulation nowadays has been distorted and altered. This is indicated by the contradictions which we find concerning many issues. There are three versions of the Old Testament: Hebrew, Greek and Samaritan. Each of these peoples claims that their version is the correct one. There are clear differences between the editions and translations of the Bible. This distortion led to many of the foretellings being lost or obscured. Nevertheless, traces are left of many of these foretellings, and they are not hidden to one who ponders the matter and compares them to the life of the Messenger of Allah (ﷺ), keeping away from the influence of whims and desires.

The Messenger (ﷺ) is mentioned by name in the Bible

Some of these glad tidings clearly mention the name of Muhammad (ﷺ). Some Muslim scholars discovered these texts, but the ongoing distortion of this book led to the subsequent elimination of these texts. An example of that is what is mentioned in the Book of *'Isaiah*[57]: "I have made you praiseworthy (Muhammad), O' Muhammad, the one who is held in high esteem by the Lord, your

---

[57] *Al-Jawaab aṣ-Ṣaḥeeḥ*, 3/326.

name existed from eternity." The statement that the name of Muhammad existed from eternity is in accordance with the words of the Messenger (ﷺ):

"I was a Prophet even when Adam was still clay."[58]

In the Hebrew Bible it says in the third chapter of the book of *Habakkuk*:[59] "The earth was filled with the praise of Aḥmad, and his right hand held sway over the nations."

In the edition published in London in 1848 CE, and the other published in Beirut in 1884 CE and in the ancient scripts, it is stated even more clearly:

"The heavens are illuminated with the glory of Muhammad and the earth is filled with his praise... your voice is in the rivers and in the seas, O' Muhammad come nigh, the mountains saw you and are filled with awe."

Places and events connected with the Messenger (ﷺ) are mentioned

In some places the location where his mission began is mentioned. In chapter thirty-three of the Book of Deuteronomy it says:

"The Lord came from Sinai and dawned over them from Seir; he shone forth from Mount Paran." (Deuteronomy 33:2 - NIV)

Sinai is the place where Allah spoke to Prophet Moosa (Moses); Saa'eer (Seir) is the place where Allah sent Revelation to Prophet 'Eesa; and Faraan (Paran) means the mountain of Makkah, where Allah sent Revelation to Muhammad (ﷺ). The fact that Mount Paran refers to Makkah is indicated by the texts of the Bible. Allah

---

[58] *Muhammad Nabi al-Islam*, Pp. 18.

[59] *Al-Jawaab aṣ-Ṣaḥeeḥ*, 3/313.

mentioned these holy places together in the *aayah*:

﴿ وَٱلتِّينِ وَٱلزَّيْتُونِ ۝١ وَطُورِ سِينِينَ ۝٢ وَهَٰذَا ٱلْبَلَدِ ٱلْأَمِينِ ۝٣ ﴾

﴿By the fig, and the olive. By Mount Sinai. By this city of security [Makkah].﴾ *(Qur'an 95: 1-3)*

The Bible mentions the place where revelation would come down to Muhammad (ﷺ). In the Book of Isaiah it says:

"Revelation from the direction of the land of the Arabs in rugged terrain." (Isaiah 21)

And the beginning of Revelation in the land of the Arabs came in the rugged terrain of the cave of Ḥiraa'.

This passage also mentions the *hijrah* of the Messenger (ﷺ) and refers to the place to which he would migrate:

"Bring water for the thirsty; you who live in Tema, bring food for the fugitives. They flee from the sword, from the drawn sword, from the bent bow and from the heat of battle." (Isaiah 21:14-15 - NIV)

Teemaa' (Tema) lies on the outskirts of Madeenah, and if you examine the text you will clearly see that it is speaking of the *Hijrah* (migration) of the Messenger (ﷺ). The concluding text says:

"This is what the Lord says to me: 'Within one year, as a servant bound by contract would count it, all the pomp of Kedar will come to an end. The survivors of the bowmen, the warriors of Kedar, will be few.' The Lord, the God of Israel, has spoken." (Isaiah 21:16-17 - NIV)

This text speaks of the battle of Badr, for it came one year, as a servant bound by contract would count it, after the Hijrah. All the pomp of Kedar came to an end, for Kedar (in Arabic, Qeedaar) was one of the children of Ismaa'eel, and his descendents were the people of Makkah, and the bowmen of Kedar were few after the battle of Badr.

The Bible refers to one of the features of the place to which the Messenger (ﷺ) migrated

Some Biblical texts refer to the place to which the Messenger (ﷺ) would migrate. In the Book of Isaiah it says:

"Let the desert and its towns raise their voices; let the settlements where Kedar lives rejoice. Let the people of Sela sing for joy; let them shout from the mountaintops. Let them give glory to the Lord and proclaim his praise..." (Isaiah 42:11-12 NIV)

Kedar was one of the sons of Ismaa'eel, as is stated in Genesis 25:13.

Saali' (Sela) is the mountain of Sala' in Madeenah.

The shouting and proclaiming mentioned here is the *adhaan* (call for prayer) which still echoes five times a day, that magnification and praise on the 'Eids and at all times during the day and the night, was called out by the pure mouths of the people of Madeenah beside the mountain of Sala'.

The Bible refers to things that happened at the hands of the Prophet (ﷺ)

The texts mention the spread of his call and some of the things that happened to the Messenger (ﷺ). In the third chapter of the Book of Habakkuk it says:

"God came from Teman, the Holy One from Mount Paran, Sela. His glory covered the heavens and his praise filled the earth. His splendour was like the sunrise; rays flashed from his hand, where his power was hidden. Plague went before him; pestilence followed his steps. He stood, and shook the earth; he looked, and made the nations tremble. The ancient mountains crumbled and the age-old hills collapsed." (Habakkuk 3:3-6 - NIV)

This is a foretelling of the great victory which the Messenger (ﷺ) and his followers attained, and of how his call would spread throughout the earth. The ancient mountains - meaning the powerful nations of ancient glory - would crumble and the age-old hills - meaning the lesser nations - would collapse. All of that came to pass. This also refers to two other matters which will be understood by those who have knowledge of the Prophet's biography: rays like light from his hand and plague going before him and pestilence following his steps.

The rays and light which shone from his hand

The text says, "His splendour was like the sunrise; rays flashed from his hand, where his power was hidden." Then it says: "He stood, and shook the earth; he looked, and made the nations tremble." It seems to me that this is speaking of a specific incident. This is what happened to the Prophet (ﷺ), when the *Ṣaḥaabah* were unable to break up a rock whilst they were digging the trench. The Messenger (ﷺ) came and struck it a mighty blow, and one-third of it came away and there came from it a light. His Companions said, "*Allaahu Akbar!*" Then he struck it a second and a third time. The Messenger (ﷺ) said that by the first light he saw the palaces of Syria, by the second light he saw the palaces of Persia and by the third light he saw the gates of Ṣan'aa'.

Nasaa'i and Aḥmad narrated with a *ḥasan* isnad that Al-Baraa' ibn 'Aazib said:

> "The Messenger of Allah (ﷺ) commanded us to dig the ditch. In one part of the ditch we were faced with a rock in which none of our pick-axes were able to make a dent. We complained about that to the Prophet (ﷺ). He came and took the pick-axe, then he said, '*Bismillaah*,' and stuck the rock. One third of it came away. Then he said, '*Allaahu Akbar*, I have been given the keys of Syria. By

> Allah, I can see its red palaces right now.' Then he struck it a second time and the second third came away; he said, '*Allaahu Akbar*, I have been given the keys of Persia. By Allah I can see the white palace of Al-Madaa'in.' Then he struck it a third time, and said, '*Bismillaah.*' Then he broke up the rest of the rock, and said, '*Allaahu Akbar.* I have been given the keys of the Yemen. By Allah I can see the gates of Ṣan'aa' from where I am right now.'"[60]

According to a report by Ṭabaraani:

> "He struck the rock and lightning blazed forth from it. He said '*Allaahu Akbar!* as did the Muslims... [The Prophet (ﷺ) said:] 'The first flash of lightning illuminated the palaces of Syria, and Jibreel told me that my ummah would prevail over them...'"[61]

Look again at the text that we quoted above: "His splendour was like the sunrise; rays flashed from his hand, where his power was hidden. He stood, and shook the earth..."

Then think about the *aḥaadeeth* that we have quoted here. Is this not the event which fulfils this prophecy?

Plague went before him; pestilence followed his steps

This prophecy says: "Plague went before him; pestilence followed his steps." This - by Allah - is a clear prophecy that is not open to any other interpretation. Before the Messenger (ﷺ) came to it, Madeenah was known for the fever. According to a hadith narrated by Ibn 'Abbaas,

---

[60] *Fatḥ al-Baari*, 7/397.

[61] Ibid.

> "When the Messenger (ﷺ) and his Companions came to Makkah to perform 'Umrah - the 'Umrah which is known as *'Umrat al-Qaḍaa'* (the fulfilled pilgrimage) - the *mushrikeen* said: "There has come to you a group which has been weakened by the fever of Yathrib."

- This has been narrated by Bukhari.[62]

This fever affected the Companions of the Messenger (ﷺ) when they first came to Madeenah, and the Messenger of Allah (ﷺ) prayed to his Lord to take away the fever.

It is narrated that 'Aa'ishah (may Allah be pleased with her) said: "When the Messenger of Allah (ﷺ) came to Madeenah, Abu Bakr (رضي الله عنه) and Bilaal (رضي الله عنه) became ill. I met them and said, 'O' my father, how do you feel? O' Bilaal, how do you feel?' When Abu Bakr fell ill he would recite a couplet:

"Every man wakes up among his family,
but death is closer than his shoelace."

When the sickness would leave Bilaal (رضي الله عنه), he would recite the couplets:

"I wonder whether I will spend night
In the valley (of Makkah) with *idhkhir* and *jaleel* (kinds of grass) around me?
Will I one day drink the water of Mijannah?
Will I be able to see (the hills of) Shaamah and Ṭafeel?"

Bukhari narrated from the mother of the believers, 'Aa'ishah, who said:

> "I came to the Messenger of Allah (ﷺ) and told him, and he said, 'O' Allah, make Madeenah as dear to us as

---

62 *Fatḥ al-Baari*, 3/469.

> Makkah, or more so, and make it healthy. Bless its weights and measures for us, and take its fever away to Al-Juḥfah.'"[63]

At the end of *Kitaab al-Ḥajj* Bukhari added: "Then Bilaal said: 'O' Allah, curse 'Utbah ibn Rabee'ah, Shaybah ibn Rabee'ah and Umayyah ibn Khalaf, as they have expelled us to the land of pestilence.'"[64]

Yathrib was infected with fever, and hardly anyone could enter it without being afflicted

Allah (ﷻ) answered His Messenger's prayer, and took the fever away from it, and made it healthy. And He prevented the plague from entering Madeenah. According to the hadith narrated by Aḥmad in his *Musnad* from Abu 'Usayb, the freed slave of the Messenger of Allah (ﷺ): The Messenger of Allah (ﷺ) said:

> "Jibreel (Gabriel) (عليه السلام) came to me with the fever and the plague. I kept the fever in Madeenah and sent the plague to Syria."[65]

Perhaps the fever was kept in Madeenah at the beginning, then it was sent to Al-Juḥfah, or perhaps what is meant is that it was kept in the region where Madeenah is, because Al-Juḥfah is close to Madeenah. Whatever the case, the prophecy came to pass as foretold in the Bible.

General prophecies

In some cases, the prophecies are general and mention the attributes of the Messenger (ﷺ) and the Revelation that Allah would send to

---

[63] *Fatḥ al-Baari*, 7/262.

[64] Ibid, 7/263.

[65] *Musnad* by Aḥmad, 5/81.

him, and news of his ummah, and the help that would come down to him and how the angels would support them, and some of the things that Allah would bestow upon His Messenger, such as his ascent to heaven (*Al-Mi'raaj*) and so on. An example of that is the prophecy of Daniel.

Daniel[66] said, warning the Jews and describing to them the ummah of Muhammad (ﷺ):

"God will cause them to prevail over you; He will send among them a Prophet and reveal to them a Book. Your necks will be under their control, and they will subdue you and humiliate you with the truth. The men of Kedar will emerge among the nations, accompanied by angels on white horses. They will encompass you and your end will be the Fire. We seek refuge with God from the Fire."

Kedar was the son of Ismaa'eel (Ishmael). They spread throughout the land and seized control of Syria, Arabia, Egypt and 'Iraq. Many reports state that the angels used to come down on white horses, as they came down on the day of Badr and the day of Al-Aḥzaab. Daniel said, clearly stating the name of Muhammad (ﷺ): "Many arrows will be shot from your bows, and arrows will be drenched with blood by your command, O' Muhammad."

Daniel also said: "I asked God and beseeched Him to show me what would happen to the Children of Israel and whether He would forgive them and restore to them the kingdom and send Prophets among them, or would that be given to others? The angel appeared to me in the form of a young man with a handsome face, and said, 'Peace be upon you, O' Daniel. God says: 'The Children of Israel have angered Me and rebelled against Me. They have worshipped other gods instead of Me. They have gone from knowledge to ignorance, from

---

66 *Al-Jawaab aṣ-Ṣaḥeeḥ*, 3/331, 4/3.

truth to falsehood. So I sent Nebuchadnezzar (Bakht Naṣr) against them, and he killed their men and enslaved their women and children, destroyed their places of worship and burned their books. Those who came after him did likewise to them. I am displeased with them and I will not help them when they face adversity. They will remain subject to My wrath until I send the Messiah (Jesus), son of the virgin, and I will conclude the matter with curses and wrath. They will remain cursed and humiliated, until I send the Prophet from among the children of Ishmael, of whom I sent glad tidings to Hagar, when I sent my angels to her with glad tidings. I will send revelation to that Prophet, and teach him the names. I will adorn him with piety and make his way the way of kindness and piety. I will make his speech true and his nature loyal and fair and wise. I will bestow upon him a Book which will confirm the Books that came before him, abrogating some of that which they contain. I will bring him to Me on a journey by night, and bring him up from one heaven to another, ascending until I bring him close to Me and greet him with peace, and bestow revelation upon him. Then I will send him back to My slaves with joy and happiness, taking care of that which is entrusted to him, learning by heart that which I tell him. He will call people to worship Me alone with gentle speech and beautiful preaching, with no harshness or yelling in the marketplaces. He will be kind to his friends and merciful towards his enemies, calling his people to worship Me and Me alone telling them what he has seen of My signs. But they will reject him and persecute him."

Ibn Taymiyah said: "Then Daniel mentioned the story of the Messenger of Allah (ﷺ) as he heard it from the angel, ending with the Trumpet blast and the end of this world."

He then said: "This prophecy is still extant among the Jews and Christians. They read it but they say that this person has not yet appeared."

Prophecies from the Gospel

In the Gospel of Matthew it says:

"And if you are willing to accept it, he is the Elijah who was to come. He who has ears, let him hear." (Matthew 11:14-15 - NIV)

The Messenger (ﷺ) told us that there was no Prophet between him and 'Eesa (Jesus). So the "Elijah" of whom 'Eesa spoke has to be Muhammad (ﷺ). From the context it seems that the "Elijah" whom the Jews loved is equal to Muhammad.

In the Gospel of John it says:

"If you love me, you will obey what I command. And I will ask the Father, and he will give you another Counsellor to be with you forever." (John 14:15-16 - NIV)

In other languages, it says, "And he will give you paracletos to be with you forever." The literal meaning of the Greek word paracletos is Aḥmad, which is one of the names of the Messenger (ﷺ).[67]

In the Gospel of John it says: "When the Counsellor comes, whom I send to you from the Father, the Spirit of truth who goes out from the Father, he will testify about me." (John 15:26 - NIV)

"He will testify about me" because the Prophet Muhammad (ﷺ) bore witness that the Messiah (Jesus) was a Prophet and a Messenger. The spirit of truth is a metaphor for the Messenger Muhammad (ﷺ). The meaning indicated in this modern translation is not precise, because the original Greek - the language from which these Gospels were translated - says paracletos. In the Arabic translation published in 1821, 1831 and 1844 CE in London, it says "*faraqleeṭ*," which is closest to the Greek word referred to.[68] But the translation of this

[67] *Muhammad Nabi al-Islam*, Pp. 36.

[68] Ibid.

word in modern translations as *al-mu'azzi* (counselor) is the kind of distortion for which Allah (ﷻ) condemned the People of the Book. In the words of the Qur'an:

﴿ ... يُحَرِّفُونَ ٱلْكَلِمَ عَن مَّوَاضِعِهِۦ ... ﴿٤٦﴾ ﴾

﴾...Some who displace words from [their] right places ...﴿
(Qur'an 4: 46)

It should also be noted that there is a missing sentence before the sentence mentioned in verse 26 of this chapter of the Bible, which is omitted in modern translations but which is clearly stated in older editions of the Gospel. This sentence says: "If the *munahmana* whom God sent comes to you." The literal meaning of *munahmana* in Syriac is Muhammad.[69]

Other prophecies from the Gospels[70]

In the twenty-first chapter of the Gospel of Matthew it says:

"Jesus said to them, 'Have you never read in the Scriptures: 'The stone the builders rejected has become the capstone (or cornerstone); the Lord has done this and it is marvelous in our eyes'? Therefore I tell you that the kingdom of God will be taken away from you and given to a people who will produce its fruit. He who falls on this stone will be broken to pieces, but he on whom it falls will be crushed.'" (Matthew 21:42-44 - NIV)

This stone is our Prophet Muhammad (ﷺ). Both Bukhari and Muslim narrated from Abu Hurayrah and Jaabir ibn 'Abdullah that the Messenger of Allah (ﷺ) said:

---

69 op.cit., Pp. 39. *Shaykh al-Islam* Ibn Taymiyah quoted all the reports in which Prophet 'Eesa (Jesus) foretold the coming of the Prophet (ﷺ) and highlighted the evidence contained therein. See *Al-Jawaab aṣ-Ṣaḥeeḥ*, 4/6.

70 *Nubuwwat Muhammad min ash-Shakk ilal-Yaqeen*, Pp. 297.

> "The likeness of me and the Prophets who came before me is that of a man who built a house and made it beautiful, apart from the place of one brick in the corner. The people started walking around it and admiring it, saying, 'Why did you not put this brick here?' I am that brick and I am the Seal of the Prophets."

Ibn al-Qayyim[71] said: "Think about what the Messiah (Jesus) said in another prophecy: 'The stone the builders left (delayed?) has become the capstone (or cornerstone).' How this is in accordance with the words of the Prophet (ﷺ):

> 'The likeness of me and the Prophets who came before me is that of a man who built a house and made it beautiful, apart from the place of one brick in the corner. The people started walking around it and admiring it, saying, 'Why did you not put this brick here?' I am that brick.'

Think about what the Messiah (Jesus) said in this prophecy: "and it is marvelous in our eyes," and "the kingdom of God will be taken away from you and given to a people..." This is in accordance with the words of Allah:

﴿ وَلَقَدْ كَتَبْنَا فِي ٱلزَّبُورِ مِنۢ بَعْدِ ٱلذِّكْرِ أَنَّ ٱلْأَرْضَ يَرِثُهَا عِبَادِيَ ٱلصَّٰلِحُونَ ﴿١٠٥﴾ ﴾

> ﴿And indeed We have written in *Az-Zaboor* [i.e. all the revealed Holy Books the *Tawraat* (Torah), the *Injeel* (Gospel), the Psalms, the Qur'an] after [We have already written in] *Al-Lawḥ al-Maḥfooz* [the Book that is in the heaven with Allah] that My righteous slaves shall inherit the land.﴾ *(Qur'an 21: 105)*

---

[71] *Hidaayah al-Ḥayaaraa*, 381-382.

And:

﴿ وَعَدَ ٱللَّهُ ٱلَّذِينَ ءَامَنُوا۟ مِنكُمْ وَعَمِلُوا۟ ٱلصَّـٰلِحَـٰتِ لَيَسْتَخْلِفَنَّهُم فِى ٱلْأَرْضِ ... ﴿٥٥﴾ ﴾

﴾Allah has promised those among you who believe and do righteous good deeds, that He will certainly grant them succession to [the present rulers] in the land...﴿ *(Qur'an 24: 55).*"

A similar text appears in the eighth chapter of the Book of Matthew:

"I say to you that many will come from the east and the west, and will take their places at the feast with Abraham, Isaac and Jacob in the kingdom of heaven. But the subjects of the kingdom will be thrown outside, into the darkness, where there will be weeping and gnashing of teeth." (Matthew 8:11 - NIV)

This prophecy refers to the victory of the ummah of Islam, which comes from the east and the west, and which will earn the pleasure of Allah along with those whom Allah has blessed, namely the Prophets, the *ṣiddeeqoon* (those followers of the Prophets who were first and foremost to believe in them), the martyrs and the righteous - and how excellent these companions are! *(Qur'an 4: 69)*

It says in *Al-Faariq*:

"O' Christians, if you are fair-minded you will accept that those who come from the east and from the west are the ummah of Muhammad. You were present there and you were addressed when the Messiah, peace be upon him, spoke of a people who would come in the future and excluded you when he said, 'But the people of Divine'..."[72]

Another passage occurs in the fourth chapter of the Gospel of John:

---

[72] *Al-Faariq*, 54.

"Believe me, woman, a time is coming when you will worship [God] neither on this mountain nor in Jerusalem." (John 4:20-24 - NIV)

This text points to the emergence of a new religion, whose center would move from Jerusalem, and it indicates that the direction of worship would shift from *Bayt al-Maqdis* (Jerusalem) to the Ka'bah, the direction of worship of the followers of the new religion. This is confirmed in the *aayah* (verse) in which Allah (ﷻ) says:

﴿ قَدْ نَرَىٰ تَقَلُّبَ وَجْهِكَ فِي ٱلسَّمَآءِ ۖ فَلَنُوَلِّيَنَّكَ قِبْلَةً تَرْضَىٰهَا ۚ فَوَلِّ
وَجْهَكَ شَطْرَ ٱلْمَسْجِدِ ٱلْحَرَامِ ۚ وَحَيْثُ مَا كُنتُمْ فَوَلُّوا۟ وُجُوهَكُمْ شَطْرَهُۥ ۗ
وَإِنَّ ٱلَّذِينَ أُوتُوا۟ ٱلْكِتَٰبَ لَيَعْلَمُونَ أَنَّهُ ٱلْحَقُّ مِن رَّبِّهِمْ ۗ وَمَا ٱللَّهُ بِغَٰفِلٍ عَمَّا
يَعْمَلُونَ ﴿١٤٤﴾ ﴾

﴿Verily, We have seen the turning of your [Muhammad's] face towards the heaven. Surely, We shall turn you to a *Qiblah* [prayer direction] that shall please you, so turn your face in the direction of *Al-Masjid al-Ḥaraam* [at Makkah]. And wheresoever you people are, turn your faces [in prayer] in that direction. Certainly, the people who were given the Scripture [i.e. Jews and the Christians] know well that, that [your turning towards the direction of the Ka'bah at Makkah in prayers] is the truth from their Lord. And Allah is not unaware of what they do.﴾ *(Qur'an 2: 144)*

In the beginning the Muslims used to face *Bayt al-Maqdis* (Jerusalem) when they prayed, then this *aayah* was revealed, commanding them to turn towards the sacred House of Allah in Makkah.

From the Gospel of Luke

The author of *Al-Injeel waṣ-Ṣaleeb*[73] tells us that it says in the Gospel of Luke:

"Glory to God in the highest, and on earth Islam and to mankind Aḥmad." (Luke 2:14)

But the translators of the Gospel rendered it as follows:

"Glory to God in the highest, and on earth peace to men on whom his favour rests." (Luke 2:14 - NIV)

The author of this book thinks that the correct translation is that which he mentioned.

The author states that there are two words mentioned in the original language of which no one knows what the exact meaning is. So these two words were not translated as they should have been in the old translation from Syriac.

These two words are: *Eiriny*, which they translated as peace, and *eudokia*, which they translated as favour (KJV good will).

The first of these two words, *eiriny*, has been translated as peace (*salaam*), but the author believes that the correct translation is Islam. On page 40 he says: "It is well known that the word Islam covers a very broad range of meanings which includes the meanings of words such as peace, reconciliation, cessation of fighting, security, tranquility, and it includes another meaning which is greater, more general, more comprehensive and stronger in meaning. The words of the angels, "and on earth peace", cannot mean general reconciliation and cessation of fighting, because everything that exists, especially living beings, and especially humankind that lives on this small

[73] *Nubuwwat Muhammad min ash-Shakk ilal-Yaqeen*, Pp. 300.

planet Earth is subject to natural and social laws which dictate that there will be events and disasters such as disputes and wars and confrontations... It is impossible for people to live on earth in reconciliation and for fighting to cease."

Then he quotes the words of the Messiah (Jesus):

"Do not suppose that I have come to bring peace to the earth. I did not come to bring peace but a sword." (Matthew 10:34 - NIV)

"I have come to bring fire on the earth, and how I wish it were already kindled!...Do you think I came to bring peace on earth? No, I tell you, but division." (Luke 12:49, 51 - NIV)

So the translation does not fit with the words and mission of the Messiah. The correct meaning, therefore, is "and on earth Islam".

He also thinks that *eudokia* means Aḥmad and not happiness or good will, as it is translated by the bishops. That is because the Greeks do not say *eudokia* for good will, rather they say *euthelyma.*

He states that the word *doxazo* has the meaning of praise, longing, desire, love and expressing one's thoughts. Hence the adjective derived from this word, *doxa*, means praise, praised, praiseworthy, precious, desired, wanted and glorious.

He quotes many examples of that in Greek. And he says that they translated the word *mahamadaytu* in Isaiah 64:11 (we treasured) as *endoxa heimon*, and they translated the adjectives derived from it - praiseworthy, illustrious, glorious, praised, modest, victorious - as *endoxos.*

Thus, he concluded that the correct translation of what Luke mentioned is Ahmad or Muhammad, not happiness or good will. So the correct translation of the angels' words is:

"Glory to God in the highest, and on earth Islam and to mankind Ahmad."[74]

Prophecies in the Gospel of Barnabas

This Gospel is filled with clear prophecies of the Chosen Messenger. For example, it says:

"God said, Be patient O' Muhammad..."

"His blessed name is Muhammad..."

"O' God, send us Your Messenger, O' Muhammad, come quickly to save the world."

A view of the Gospel of Barnabas

No doubt this Gospel is one of the Gospels which were known in ancient times. It is mentioned in books from the second and third centuries CE, but it is not mentioned thereafter, until a copy of it was discovered at the beginning of the eighteenth century. This copy is still in the "Palace Library" in Vienna.

When this book was published, it caused a great stir - at that time - in Europe, among the academic and religious societies. The Arabic translation of this book has been published twice, the second edition produced by *Daar al-Qalam* in Kuwait.

I have read this book and examined it carefully, and I noticed something to which I discovered no one else has drawn attention. Even though this book is authentic to some extent, it has undoubtedly been tampered with by Muslim hands, who have inserted in it things that do not belong to it. What made me reach this conclusion is not the comments in Arabic which are to be found in the margins of the

[74] See *Al-Injeel waṣ-Ṣaleeb* by Al-Abb 'Abdul-Aḥad Dawood, 34-53.

original copy in Vienna, rather it is the exaggerated terms in which the Gospel describes the Messenger (ﷺ). We believe that the Gospel foretells the coming of the Messenger (ﷺ), but we believe that it is extremely unlikely that there would be widespread among the People of the Book the myths which became widespread among the Muslims after the coming of the Messenger (ﷺ) and which were attributed to him. In this Gospel we read that Allah gave His Messenger Muhammad (ﷺ) all things, that He created all things for his sake, that He created him before all things. In one passage it narrates that the Messenger (ﷺ) says, "O' Lord, I remember that when You created me, You wanted to create the universe, Paradise, the angels and mankind out of love for me, so that they might glorify You through me. And I am Your slave."

Elsewhere it says, "Be patient, O' Muhammad. For your sake I want to create Paradise and the universe, and a great number of people whom I will give to you..."

And: "This is the one for whose sake Allah created all things."

And: "Hence before all other things, Allah created His Messenger."

These words are undoubtedly incorrect, and they contradict the truth which we know. Allah created mankind, the angels and the jinn to worship Him:

﴿ وَمَا خَلَقْتُ ٱلْجِنَّ وَٱلْإِنسَ إِلَّا لِيَعْبُدُونِ ﴿٥٦﴾ ﴾

> ﴿And I [Allah] created not the jinn and mankind except that they should worship Me [Alone].﴾
>
> *(Qur'an 51: 56)*

The first thing to be created was the Pen, as it says in the hadith: "The first thing that Allah created was the Pen." These exaggerated opinions became widespread among the Muslims, who put them in the form of *aḥaadeeth* which they attributed to the Messenger (ﷺ).

Among these *ḍa'eef* (weak) and *mawḍoo'* (fabricated) *aḥaadeeth* are the following:

"Were it not for you, I would not have created the stars." (*Silsilat al-Aḥaadeeth aḍ-Ḍa'eefah wal-Mawḍoo'ah*, hadith no. 282)

"I was a Prophet when Adam was still between the water and the clay." (hadith no. 302, 303)

"I was the first of the Prophets to be created and the last to be sent." (*Al-Fawaa'id al-Majmoo'ah* by Shawkaani, Pp. 326)

"I have created the world and its inhabitants so that they might know how dear you are to Me and how great your status is before Me. Were it not for you, O' Muhammad, I would not have created this world." (*Tanzeeh ash-Sharee'ah al-Marfoo'ah 'an al-Aḥaadeeth aḍ-Ḍa'eefah wal-Mawḍoo'ah*, Pp. 325)

"Allah created me from His light and He created Abu Bakr from my light." (Ibid., Pp. 337)

If you compare these weak and fabricated *aḥaadeeth* with what is narrated in the Gospel of Barnabas, you will realize that the one who inserted these descriptions into it was of the same type as the one whose mind was infested with these kind of false *aḥaadeeth*.

There are also other things which are falsely attributed to the Messenger (ﷺ), which go against the truth that we know. For example, it says, "Hell will tremble because of the presence of the Messenger, peace be upon him, and the Fire will cease to cause suffering for the duration of the Messenger of Allah's stay to see Hell." This goes against the clear statement of the Qur'an:

﴿ لَا يُفَتَّرُ عَنْهُمْ وَهُمْ فِيهِ مُبْلِسُونَ ﴿٧٥﴾ ﴾

﴿[The torment] will not be lightened for them, and they will be plunged into destruction with deep regrets, sorrows and in despair therein.﴿ *(Qur'an 43: 75)*

This book also describes 'Eesa (Jesus) as saying: "I am not fit to untie the shoe laces of the Messenger of Allah." Such a comment does not befit one of the Messengers of strong will. [cf. Qur'an 46:35]

Moreover, this book describes the Messenger (ﷺ) in terms which imply disrespect. For example, it says that he will be like a crazy man, and it says that on the Day of Resurrection Allah will take away his memory.

Prophecies in other world scriptures

Mawlana 'Abdul-Ḥaqq Qadyaarti wrote a book in English entitled *Mohammed in World Scriptures*, in which he was able to compare and contrast the texts, based on his knowledge of Farsi (Persian), Hindi, Hebrew, Arabic and some European languages. He did not limit himself to the Torah and Gospel; he broadened his study to include the books of Persia, India and ancient Babylon. He was successful in some of his discoveries, and his work matches the best of similar studies on the same topic.

Mawlana 'Abdul-Ḥaqq states that the name of the Arab Messenger, Aḥmad, appears in its Arabic form in the *Samavida*, one of the books of the Brahmins. It is narrated in the sixth and eighth chapters of the second part, where it says that, "Ahmad received the law from his Lord and it is filled with wisdom, and light is derived from it as light is derived from the sun..." The author believes that the Prophet Muhammad is mentioned in many places in the books of the Brahmins, described in a manner that refers to much praise and a far-reaching reputation. Among the descriptive names that he is given is *Sushrava* which is mentioned in the book *Atharpha vida*. He also examined the books of *Zaraadasht* (*Zoroaster/Zarathustra*)which are widely known as the books of the Magians (Zoroastrians). In the book of *Zend Avesta* he found a prophecy foretelling a Messenger who is described as a mercy to the worlds (*soeshyant*), who would be confronted by an enemy who is called, in ancient Persian, *Angra Mainyu* or the Father of Flame (Abu Lahab). He would call people to one God, to Whom there is none co-equal or comparable; He has no beginning and no end, no equal, no peer, no partner, no father, no mother, no wife, no child, no son, no dwelling, no body, no form, no colour, no scent.

These are some of the attributes with which Allah is described in Islam: the One, the Self-Sufficient Master, Who begets not nor was He begotten, to Whom there is none co-equal or comparable, Who has no wife and no child.

In addition to that he quotes prophecies from the books of the *Zaraadasht* (Zoroaster) which speak of the call to truth which will be brought by the promised Prophet. In these prophecies there is mention of the Arabian desert. He has translated some of them into English without altering anything: "When the nation of *Zaraadasht* (Zoroaster) neglects its religion, it will become weakened and there will emerge a man in the land of the Arabs whose followers will conquer Persia and subjugate the arrogant Persians. After having worshipped fire in their temples, they will turn their faces towards the Ka'bah of Ibraaheem (Abraham) which will be cleansed of idols. On that day they, the followers of the Prophet who is a mercy to the worlds, will become the masters of Persia, Midyan, Ṭoos and Balkh, which are places that are sacred to the *Zaraadashtis* (Zoroastrians) and the neighbouring people. Their Prophet will be eloquent and will speak of miracles."[75]

---

[75] *Mohammed in World Scriptures*, Pp. 47, quoting from *Maṭla' an-Noor* by Prof. 'Abbaas Maḥmood al-'Aqqaad, 14-17.

These prophecies were widely known before the Prophet came

These prophecies were widely known before the Prophet (ﷺ) came. The People of the Book did not conceal them at that time, rather they propagated them and claimed that they would follow him when he came. The Muslims have preserved some of these prophecies for us. The Anṣaar of Madeenah have transmitted some of the things that the Jews said about these prophecies before the coming of the Prophet. Some of the People of the Book recognized the Messenger (ﷺ) when he was a child, and some of the People of the Book benefited from these prophecies and became believers.

Description of our Messenger (ﷺ) in the Torah

Bukhari narrated from 'Aṭaa' ibn Yasaar that he said: "I met 'Abdullah ibn 'Amr ibn al-'Aaṣ, and said, 'Tell me about the description of the Messenger of Allah in the *Tawraat*.' He said, 'Certainly, by Allah, he is described in some of the same terms as he is described in the Qur'an: ﴿O' Prophet [Muhammad]! Verily, We have sent you as witness, and a bearer of glad tidings, and a warner.﴾ *(Qur'an 33: 45)*; a guide for the unlettered; you are My slave and Messenger. I have named you *Al-Mutawakkil* (the one who puts his trust in Allah), without being harsh or rough, not shouting in the market-place, and not repelling evil with evil, rather overlooking and forgiving. Allah will not take his soul until He has set right the crooked way of the people through him so that they may say, there is no god but Allah. Through him, He will open blind eyes, deaf ears and heedless minds.'"[76]

Daarimi narrated something similar from 'Aṭaa' ibn Salaam[77] and from Ka'b, who was one of the scholars of the Jews who believed in

[76] Bukhari. *Mishkaat al-Maṣaabeeḥ*, 3/125.

[77] *Mishkaat al-Maṣaabeeḥ*, 3/125.

the Prophet (ﷺ). Ka'b said, "We find written in the Tawraat: Muhammad is the Messenger of Allah, My Chosen slave. He is not harsh or rough, and he does not shout in the market-places. He does not repay evil with evil, rather he overlooks and forgives. His place of birth will be Makkah and his place of migration will be Ṭeebah (Madeenah). And his dominion will reach Syria. His ummah will be those who give praise, they will praise Allah in good times and bad, praising Allah in every place, glorifying Him in the high places. They will pay attention to the movements of the sun and will pray when the time for prayer comes. They will wear garments that reach their calves and they will wash their limbs (before prayer). Their proclaimer will proclaim in the open. Their rank in fighting and in prayer will be the same, and they will make an indistinct sound at night like the humming of bees."[78] At-Tabreezi said: this is the version narrated in *Al-Maṣaabeeḥ*; a slightly amended version is narrated by Daarimi.

Where is this prophecy in the Torah?

This prophecy is not to be found in the Torah that is extant nowadays among the Jews and Christians. If what we mean by Torah is that which is specifically known as Torah, then this prophecy is one the things that have been concealed by the Jews; they may be among the things that are hidden by them and are known only to their rabbis.[79]

---

[78] Ibid, 3/129.

[79] It seems to us that until the time of the Messenger (ﷺ) there existed copies of the *Tawraat* and *Injeel* that had not been distorted, because Allah says:

﴾Let the people of the *Injeel* [Gospel] judge by what Allah has revealed therein.﴿ *(Qur'an 4: 47)*

﴾But how do they come to you for decision while they have the *Tawraat* [Torah], in which is the [plain] Decision of Allah.﴿ *(Qur'an 5: 43)*

﴾O' people of the Scripture [Jews and Christians]! You have nothing [as regards guidance] till you act according to the *Tawraat* [Torah], the *Injeel* [Gospel], and =

But the word *Tawraat* (Torah) may refer to something other than the *Tawraat* of Prophet Moosa (Moses). It may refer to any book that was revealed from Allah, just as the word Qur'an may apply to any book which has been revealed from Allah, as in the hadith, "The 'Qur'an' was made easy for Prophet Dawood (David); between saddling his beast and mounting it he could recite the 'Qur'an'." What is referred to is his 'Qur'an' i.e., the *Zaboor* (Psalms or Scripture of Dawood).

In some prophecies concerning this ummah it says that, "Their Gospel (*Injeel*) is in their hearts" - i.e., the Qur'an is described as a "Gospel". On this basis, we may say that, this prophecy existed in the Book of Isaiah, where it said:

"My servant with whom I am pleased; I send down to him My revelation. He will cause My justice to prevail among the nations and will enjoin the commandments upon them. He will not laugh, his voice will not be heard in the market places. He will open blind eyes and deaf ears, and he will revive empty hearts. What I will give to him I will not give to anyone else. He will praise God very much; he will come from the farthest reaches of the earth. The earth and its

---

= what has [now] been sent down to you from your Lord [the Qur'an].﴾ *(Qur'an 5: 68)*

There were many distorted copies and some copies which had not been distorted, but the Jews used to conceal them. Perhaps some of these copies are still extant nowadays, concealed by some of the Jewish and Christian scholars. The author of *Muhammad Nabi al-Islam* (Pp. 46) says, quoting from the British *Economist* magazine that the first task required of the candidate for the position of Curia, i.e., the Central Administration of the Catholic church, is to swear a sacred vow to conceal everything that he comes to know or see, especially information concerning the treasures of the church and its income, in addition to the artistic treasures owned by the Vatican which are regarded as being among the most precious treasures in the world. Undoubtedly the phrase "artistic treasures" includes the huge Vatican library with its store of books on Christian religion which, if they were made available for free academic research, would shed much light on the early, dark centuries of Christian history of which little is known.

inhabitants will rejoice; they will proclaim the oneness of God from every high place and they will glorify Him on every hill. He will never be weak or defeated, and he will not be influenced by whims and desires. He will not humiliate the righteous who are weak; rather he will support the believers of truth. He will be the support of the humble. He is the light of God which will never be extinguished and the mark of his authority will be on his shoulders."[80]

The story of Ibn al-Haybaan

One of the stories that the books of Sunnah have narrated to us from the Jewish scholars before Islam tells us that a Jew called Ibn al-Haybaan, came to Madeenah and settled among the Jews of Bani Qurayẓah, two years before Islam. The narrator of the story said: "We have never seen a man who does not pray the five daily prayers was better than him. He settled amongst us and whenever we were faced with a drought we would say to him, 'Go out, 'O Ibn al-Haybaan, and pray for rain for us.' He would say, 'No by Allah, not until you give charity before we go out.' We would ask him, 'How much?' He would say, 'A *ṣaa'* of dates' or 'Two *madd* of barley.' We would give that, then he would go out to the fields and pray for rain for us. By Allah, he would hardly leave that place when clouds would come and rain would fall. This happened more than once, more than two or three times.

Then he lay on his deathbed, and when he realized that he was dying, he said, 'O' Jews, what do you think brought me here from a land of plenty to a land of poverty and hunger?' We said, 'Allah knows best.'

He said, 'I only came to this land expecting and hoping to see the emergence of a Prophet whose time has come. This is the land to which he will emigrate. I had hoped that Allah would send him so I

---

[80] *Al-Jawaab aṣ-Ṣaḥeeḥ* by Ibn Taymiyah, 3/281.

could follow him. His time is near so do not let anyone beat you to following him, O' Jews, for he will be sent with the shedding of blood and capturing of women and children of those who oppose him. Nothing should prevent you (from following him). Some of the Jewish youth of Bani Qurayẓah benefitted from the advice of Ibn al-Haybaan, namely Tha'labah ibn Sa'yah, Usayd ibn Sa'yah and Asad ibn 'Ubayd. When the Messenger (ﷺ) besieged Bani Qurayẓah, these young men said, 'O' Bani Qurayẓah, by Allah, he is the Prophet about whom Ibn al-Haybaan told you.' They said, 'No he isn't.' They said, 'Yes he is, he has the attributes (of that Prophet).' Then they went out and embraced Islam, thus saving their blood, wealth and property."[81]

When what they knew came to them, they disbelieved in it

Abu Na'eem narrated in *Dalaa'il an-Nubuwwah* with his isnad that Muhammad ibn Salamah said: "There was only one Jew among Bani 'Abd al-Ashhal. His name was Yoosha'. I heard him saying - when I was a young boy wearing only a lower garment - 'The time is approaching when a Prophet will be sent from the direction of that house,' and he pointed towards the House of Allah (the Ka'bah). 'Whoever lives to meet him, let him believe in him.' Then the Messenger of Allah was sent and we became Muslim whilst he (that Jew) was among us, but he did not become Muslim out of envy and hatred.'"[82]

'Abdullah ibn Salaam benefited from his knowledge

'Abdullah ibn Salaam was the leader of the Jews and the most knowledgeable of them, the son of the leader of the Jews and the

[81] *Al-Bidaayah wan-Nihaayah,* 1/310.

[82] Ibid, 2/309.

most knowledgeable of them. He said: "When I heard about the Messenger of Allah and I learned about his attributes, his name, his appearance and his time, which we were waiting for, I was in Quba', and I was keeping quiet about him. When the Messenger of Allah (ﷺ) came to Madeenah, he stopped at Quba', among Bani 'Amr ibn 'Awf. A man came and told us of his arrival. I was at the top of a date-palm tree of mine, working on it, and my maternal aunt Khaalidah bint al-Ḥaarith was beneath me. When I heard the news that the Prophet (ﷺ) had come, I said, *'Allaahu Akbar!'* When she heard me say *'Allaahu Akbar!'*, my aunt said, 'If you heard of Moosa ibn 'Imraan [Prophet Moosa (Moses)] you would not have said more.' I said to her, 'O' aunt, by Allah he is the brother of Moosa ibn 'Imraan, and he has been sent with the same religion and the same message.' She said, 'O' son of my brother, is this the one who we have been told will be sent with the approach of the Hour?' I said, 'Yes.' She said, 'Then this is the one.'"[83]

Bukhari narrated the story of how 'Abdullah ibn Salaam came to the Messenger (ﷺ) and embraced Islam, and how he asked the Messenger (ﷺ) to send for the Jews and ask them about him before they found out that he had become Muslim. When they came, the Messenger (ﷺ) said,

> "O' Jews, woe to you! Fear Allah, for by Allah, besides Whom there is no other god, you know that I am indeed the Messenger of Allah and that I have come to you with the truth, so become Muslim.' They said, 'We do not know that.' He said, 'What kind of man is 'Abdullah ibn Salaam among you?' They said, 'He is our leader and the son of our leader, the most knowledgeable among us and the son of the most knowledgeable among us.' He

[83] Ibn Isḥaaq, *As-Seerah* (*Al-Bidaayah*, 3/211).

> said, 'What do you think, if he became a Muslim?' They said, 'Impossible! He would never become a Muslim.' He said, 'O' Ibn Salaam, come out to them.' So he came out and said, 'O' Jews, fear Allah besides Whom there is no other god, for you know that he is the Messenger of Allah and that he has come with the truth.' They said, 'You are lying.' So the Messenger of Allah (ﷺ) asked them to leave."[84]

The testimony of a Jew boy

Anas ibn Maalik (رضي الله عنه) narrated that there was a Jewish boy who used to serve the Prophet (ﷺ). He fell sick and the Messenger of Allah (ﷺ) came to visit him, and found his father sitting by his head, reading the *Tawraat* (Torah). The Messenger of Allah (ﷺ) said,

> "O' Jew, I abjure you by Allah Who revealed the *Tawraat* to Moosa, do you find any description of me and any reference to my coming in the *Tawraat*?" He said, "No." The child said, "On the contrary, by Allah, O' Messenger of Allah, we find reference to your description and your coming in the *Tawraat*. I bear witness that there is no god except Allah and that you are the Messenger of Allah."

- This is narrated by Bayhaqi with a *ṣaḥeeḥ* isnad.[85]

The insight of a monk

One of the monks recognized the Messenger when he was still young, when he traveled on business with his paternal uncle Abu Ṭaalib to Syria. Abu Moosa narrated that Abu Ṭaalib went to Syria,

---

[84] *Al-Bidaayah* 3/211.

[85] *Al-Jawaab aṣ-Ṣaḥeeḥ*, 3/287.

and the Prophet (ﷺ) went with him, along with some of the elders of Quraysh. When they came near where the monk was, they dismounted and loosened their saddles. The monk came out to meet them. They had passed that way before and he had never come out to meet them. So they loosened their saddles, and the monk started to go about among them, until he came and took the hand of the Messenger of Allah (ﷺ) and said, "This is the leader of the worlds, this is the Messenger of the Lord of the Worlds. Allah will send him as a mercy to the worlds."

The elders of Quraysh said to him, "How do you know?" He said, "When you came over the hill not a tree or a stone failed to bow in prostration, and they prostrate themselves only before a Prophet. I recognize him by the seal of prophecy, like an apple, below the end of his shoulder-blade." He then went and prepared food for them, and when he brought it to them the Prophet (ﷺ) was looking after the camels, so he told them to send for him. He came with a cloud above him shading him and when he came to the people he found they had gone before him into the shade of a tree. Then when he sat down the shade of the tree inclined over him, and the monk said, "Look how the shade of the tree has inclined over him."[86]

The Jewish scholars knew when the Prophet (ﷺ) would emerge

When the time of the emergence of the Chosen Prophet (ﷺ) drew nigh, the People of the Book knew of that from the signs that they knew. Abu Zar'ah narrated with a *ṣaḥeeḥ* isnad from Usaamah ibn Zayd from his father Zayd ibn Ḥaarithah that the Messenger (ﷺ) met

[86] This hadith is narrated by Tirmidhi who said, it is a *ḥasan ghareeb* hadith. See *Mishkaat al-Maṣaabeeḥ*, 3/187. *Shaykh* Naaṣiruddeen al-Albaani said in his commentary on the hadith in *Al-Mishkaat*: Its men are *thiqaat* and the hadith is *ṣaḥeeḥ* as I have explained in an article published in *Majallah at-Tamaddun al-Islami*.

Zayd ibn 'Amr ibn Nufayl before his mission. "Among the things that Zayd told the Messenger (ﷺ) was that he had travelled in search of the true religion, the religion of *Tawḥeed*, and a monk in Syria had told him, 'You are asking about a religion of which we know no one who worships Allah according to this religion except a *shaykh* in Arabia.'

He said: 'So I went out, and came to him (i.e., the *shaykh* in Arabia), and I told him why I had come out to him.' He said, 'Everyone you see is following misguidance. Who do you belong to?' I said, 'I am from the people of the House of Allah, the people of thorns and desert trees.' He said, 'There has emerged in your land a Prophet, or he will emerge, for his star has appeared. So go back and believe in him, and follow him.' So I went back but I have not seen anything yet."[87]

Zayd was speaking to this Messenger (ﷺ), before he was sent. He did not know that the one who was speaking to him was the Messenger whose star had already appeared. Zayd died several years before the Prophet's mission began.

We have mentioned above the story of Ibn al-Haybaan, who left Syria and went to Madeenah. When he was dying he told the Jews: "The only thing that brought me here was the expectation of a Prophet whose time has come, and this is the land to which he will migrate."

In Bukhari it is narrated that Heraclius used to observe the stars. He looked and said that the king of the circumcised has appeared.

3 - A GLIMPSE AT THE PROPHETS

If you want to probe a person deeply and find out how truthful and honest he is, then you have to look at the contours of his face, examine what he does and says, and follow his movements. Those

[87] *Al-Jawaab aṣ-Ṣaḥeeḥ*, 3/285.

concerning whom you cannot have certain knowledge are those whom you meet only briefly, or those who try to conceal their true nature, making a pretence in their words and deeds so that they do not show what they are really like.

The Prophets and Messengers used to mix with their peoples, sitting with them, dealing with them and interacting with them in various matters. Thus the people had the opportunity to study and examine them closely. Before his mission began, Quraysh used to call the Messenger of Allah (ﷺ) *Al-Ameen* (the trustworthy), because of his truthfulness and sincerity. When, at the beginning of the call, the Messenger (ﷺ) asked them,

> "If I were to tell you that beyond this valley there is an army which intends to attack you, would you believe me?" They said, "We have never known you to tell a lie." (Bukhari)

The Qur'an also tells us to use this kind of reasoning:

﴿ قُل لَّوْ شَآءَ ٱللَّهُ مَا تَلَوْتُهُۥ عَلَيْكُمْ وَلَآ أَدْرَىٰكُم بِهِۦ ۖ فَقَدْ لَبِثْتُ فِيكُمْ عُمُرًا مِّن قَبْلِهِۦٓ ۚ أَفَلَا تَعْقِلُونَ ﴿١٦﴾ ﴾

> ﴿Say [O' Muhammad]: 'If Allah had so willed, I should not have recited it to you nor would He have made it known to you. Verily, I have stayed amongst you a lifetime before this. Have you then no sense?'﴾
>
> *(Qur'an 10: 16)*

He told them, I stayed among you for a long time before I told you that I am a Prophet. How did I live among you? How truthful was I towards you? Would I refrain from telling lies about people and lie about the Lord of mankind (have you then no sense)? Why don't you use your brains and let them guide you to the truth?

A precious metal speaks for itself; a good fruit is known from its colour, shape, smell and taste; the light of a bright lamp guides one to it.

﴿... يَكَادُ زَيْتُهَا يُضِيٓءُ وَلَوْ لَمْ تَمْسَسْهُ نَارٌ نُّورٌ عَلَىٰ نُورٍ يَهْدِى ٱللَّهُ لِنُورِهِۦ مَن يَشَآءُ ... ﴿٣٥﴾﴾

﴾...Whose oil would almost glow forth [of itself], though no fire touched it. Light upon Light! Allah guides to His Light whom He wills...﴿ *(Qur'an 24: 35)*

Some people did not need any proof or evidence to show them that the Messenger (ﷺ) spoke the truth, because his personality, life and biography formed the greatest evidence. One of these people was Abu Bakr aṣ-Ṣiddeeq (رضي الله عنه). When the Messenger (ﷺ) called him, he did not hesitate. 'Abdullah ibn Salaam looked at the face of the Messenger (ﷺ) once, and it was enough to tell him that this was the face of one who spoke the truth, not the face of a liar. The Messenger (ﷺ) came to Madeenah and 'Abdullah ibn Salaam, the scholar of the Jews, came out with the people and looked at the face of the Messenger (ﷺ). He said: "When I saw his face, I knew that this was not the face of a liar."[88]

Khadeejah (may Allah be pleased with her) knew the Messenger as a husband and was closely acquainted with him before he became a Prophet and a Messenger. She did not hesitate to reassure him that Allah would never forsake him and that no harm would come to him. That is because the way in which Allah deals with people such as the Messenger (ﷺ) is, to honour them. Hence, when he came to her and told her that he feared for himself - after the Revelation had come upon him suddenly in the Cave of Ḥiraa' - she said to him, "Never!

---

[88] Aḥmad: *Musnad*; Tirmidhi: *Sunan*. He said (it is) a *ṣaḥeeḥ* hadith; Ibn Maajah: *Sunan*. (*Al-Bidaayah wan-Nihaayah*, 3/210)

By Allah, Allah will never disgrace you. You keep good relations with your kith and kin, help the poor and the destitute, serve your guests generously and assist the calamity-afflicted ones."[89]

Heraclius and Abu Sufyaan

Heraclius, the king of the Romans, used his brain to find out about the Messengers and their attributes. Thus, he reached the conclusion that Muhammad was sent from his Lord, but he did not believe for fear of losing his kingdom.

The Messenger (ﷺ) sent letters to the kings of the earth, calling them to Islam. Heraclius, the king of the Romans, was one of those to whom a letter was sent. When the letter of the Messenger (ﷺ) was sent to him, he sent for the Arabs who were there. Abu Sufyaan had gone to Syria with a group of Quraysh to engage in trade, so he (Heraclius) asked him about the Prophet (ﷺ). He questioned Abu Sufyaan, and ordered the others to tell him if he was lying. Their silence meant that they agreed with what he said.

Following is the account of the conversation between them, as narrated by Abu Sufyaan:

The first question he (Heraclius) asked me about him was:
'What is his family status amongst you?'
'I replied, 'He (the Prophet) belongs to a good (noble) family amongst us."
He asked, 'Has anybody amongst you ever made the same claim (i.e. to be a Prophet) before him?'
I replied, 'No.'
He asked, 'Was anybody amongst his ancestors a king?'
I replied, 'No.'

---

[89] *Ṣaḥeeḥ al-Bukhari* (*Fatḥ al-Baari*, 1/22).

He asked, 'Do the nobles or the poor follow him?'
I replied, 'It is the poor who follow him.'
He asked, 'Are his followers increasing or decreasing (day by day)?'
I replied, 'They are increasing.'
He asked, 'Does anybody amongst them become displeased and renounce the religion afterwards?'
I replied, 'No.'
He asked, 'Have you ever accused him of telling lies before his claim (to be a Prophet)?'
I replied, 'No.'
He asked, 'Does he break his promises?'
I replied, 'No. We are in a state of truce with him but we do not know what he will do in it.' I could not find an opportunity to say anything against him except that.
He asked, 'Have you ever fought him?'
I replied, 'Yes.'
He asked, 'What was the outcome of the battles?'
I replied, 'It alternated. Sometimes he was victorious and sometimes we were.'
Heraclius said, 'What does he order you to do?'
I said, 'He tells us to worship Allah alone and not to worship anything along with Him, and to renounce all that our ancestors had said. He orders us to pray, to speak the truth, to be chaste and to keep good relations with our kith and kin.'"

Heraclius said to the translator: "Tell him: 'I asked you about his family and your reply was that he belonged to a very noble family. All the Messengers come from noble families amongst their respective peoples. I asked you whether anybody else amongst you had made such a claim, and you said no. If you had said yes, I would have thought that this man was copying the previous man. Then I asked you whether any of his ancestors was a king, and you said no. If you had said yes, I would have thought that this man wanted to take back his ancestral kingdom.

I further asked whether he was ever accused of telling lies before he said what he said, and you said no. So I wondered how a person who does not tell a lie about others could ever tell a lie about Allah. I then asked you whether the rich people followed him or the poor. You said that it is the poor who follow him, and they were the followers of all the Messengers. Then I asked you whether his followers were increasing or decreasing. You replied that they were increasing, and in fact this is the way of true faith, till it is complete in all respects. I further asked you whether there was anybody who, after embracing his religion, became displeased and discarded his religion. You said no, and this is (the sign of) true faith, when its delight enters the hearts and mixes with them completely. I asked you whether he had ever betrayed anyone, and you said no. Likewise the Messengers never betray anyone. Then I asked you what he ordered you to do. You replied that he ordered you to worship Allah alone and not to worship any thing along with Him; he forbade you to worship idols and ordered you to pray, to speak the truth and to be chaste. If what you have said is true, he will very soon occupy this place beneath my feet. I knew (from the Scriptures) that he was going to appear but I did not know that he would be from amongst you. If I knew that I could meet with him, I would immediately go to meet him and if I were with him, I would certainly wash his feet.'"[90]

Their abstinence from the luxuries of this world

Another sign of the truthfulness of the Messengers, which can be seen from reading their biographies, is that they were the most ascetic of people in their abstinence from the conveniences and transient luxuries of this world and its false splendour. They did not ask for any

---

[90] Bukhari in his *Ṣaḥeeḥ, Kitaab Baad' al-Waḥy*. See *Fatḥ al-Baari*, 1/31.

reward or money from the people whom they called. They did good things for them but did not expect any reward or thanks. The first of the Messengers said to his people:

﴿ وَيَٰقَوۡمِ لَآ أَسۡـَٔلُكُمۡ عَلَيۡهِ مَالًاۖ إِنۡ أَجۡرِيَ إِلَّا عَلَى ٱللَّهِۚ ... ﴿٢٩﴾ ﴾

﴾And O' my people! I ask of you no wealth for it, my reward is from none but Allah...﴿ *(Qur'an 11: 29)*

And Allah commanded the last of the Messengers to say likewise:

﴿ قُلۡ مَآ أَسۡـَٔلُكُمۡ عَلَيۡهِ مِنۡ أَجۡرٍ إِلَّا مَن شَآءَ أَن يَتَّخِذَ إِلَىٰ رَبِّهِۦ سَبِيلًا ﴿٥٧﴾ ﴾

﴾Say: 'No reward do I ask of you for this [that which I have brought from my Lord and its preaching], save that whosoever wills, may take a Path to his Lord.'﴿ *(Qur'an 25: 57)*

In *Soorah ash-Shu'araa'*, the 26th chapter of the Qur'an, Allah (ﷻ) tells us part of the story of the Prophets Nooḥ (Noah), Hood (Hud), Ṣaaliḥ, Looṭ (Lot) and Shu'ayb (may Allah's peace be upon them all), each of whom said to his people:

﴿ وَمَآ أَسۡـَٔلُكُمۡ عَلَيۡهِ مِنۡ أَجۡرٍۖ إِنۡ أَجۡرِيَ إِلَّا عَلَىٰ رَبِّ ٱلۡعَٰلَمِينَ ﴿١٠٩﴾ ﴾

﴾No reward do I ask of you for it [my Message of Islamic Monotheism]; my reward is only from the Lord of the *'Aalameen* [mankind, jinn and all that exists].﴿ *(Qur'an 26: 109 etc.)*

4 - THE CALL OF THE MESSENGERS

Examining the call of the Messengers gives abundant evidence which shows us the extent of their sincerity. The Messengers brought an integrated system for the reform of mankind and of human society. A religion such as this, whose Messengers said that it comes from

Allah, should be of the utmost perfection, free from faults and shortcomings, not incompatible with human nature or the laws of the universe. The Qur'an instructs us to follow this line of reasoning, as Allah (ﷻ) says:

﴿... وَلَوْ كَانَ مِنْ عِندِ غَيْرِ ٱللَّهِ لَوَجَدُوا۟ فِيهِ ٱخْتِلَـٰفًا كَثِيرًا ۝٨٢﴾

﴿...Had it [the Qur'an] been from other than Allah, they would surely, have found therein many a contradiction.﴾ *(Qur'an 4: 82)*

The fact that it is an integrated unit, parts of it confirming other parts, with no contradictions or differences, is a clear indication of the truthfulness of the one who brought it.

Examining the objectives, virtues and values advocated by the Messengers is one of the greatest indications of their truthfulness. Allah (ﷻ) says:

﴿إِنَّ هَـٰذَا ٱلْقُرْءَانَ يَهْدِى لِلَّتِى هِىَ أَقْوَمُ ... ۝٩﴾

﴿Verily, this Qur'an guides to that which is most just and right...﴾ *(Qur'an 17: 9)*

The scholars have written books explaining the perfect and comprehensive nature of this religion and the wisdom of its laws, and describing the basic principles which make this religion a solid structure. People keep examining it but they cannot find any faults or shortcomings.

Allah, the All-Glorious, All-Wise has privileged mankind by giving them the faculty of reason, and He has instilled in them the ability to recognize evil as evil and good as good. But His mercy dictates that He should not punish his creatures for neglecting to do good and for doing evil, so long as no proof has been established against them by sending the Messengers.

A Bedouin was asked, how did you know that Muhammad is the Messenger of Allah? He said, he never enjoins something and reason wishes that he had forbidden it, and he never forbids something and reason wishes that he had enjoined it.[91]

The way of thinking exercised by this Bedouin was excellent. For the Messenger brought from Allah knowledge and laws which, when the fair-minded person ponders the matter, he will realize that they cannot be merely human opinions or ideas.

The call of our Prophet Muhammad (ﷺ)

Anyone who examines the call of our Prophet Muhammad (ﷺ) will be extremely arrogant if he does not appreciate it and believe in it, for our Prophet (ﷺ) brought this Qur'an, the like of which mankind and the jinn were unable to produce. It includes reports of the past and the future, and different kinds of knowledge which make the fair-minded person submit to Allah and Praise Him.

This Book and this knowledge came to us at the hands of an unlettered man, who never held a pen and never read anything written by the scholars and scribes who came before him.

﴿ وَمَا كُنتَ تَتْلُوا۟ مِن قَبْلِهِۦ مِن كِتَٰبٍ وَلَا تَخُطُّهُۥ بِيَمِينِكَ ۖ إِذًا لَّٱرْتَابَ ٱلْمُبْطِلُونَ ﴿٤٨﴾ ﴾

﴾Neither did you [O' Muhammad] read any book before it [this Qur'an], nor did you write any book [whatsoever] with your right hand. In that case, indeed, the followers of falsehood might have doubted.﴿ *(Qur'an 29: 48)*

It is no ordinary matter for an unlettered man to become overnight the teacher of mankind, conveying knowledge to the people, evaluating

---

[91] *Miftaaḥ Daar as-Sa'aadah*, 2/6-7.

the knowledge of those who came before and explaining the distortions and changes that have occurred therein.

This evidence was in the minds of the people of Makkah, who knew Muhammad (ﷺ) before he brought them what he brought them. They knew that he was unlettered, therefore all they could do was to deny and reject the truth after they came to know it.

﴿ ... فَإِنَّهُمْ لَا يُكَذِّبُونَكَ وَلَٰكِنَّ ٱلظَّٰلِمِينَ بِـَٔايَٰتِ ٱللَّهِ يَجْحَدُونَ ﴿٣٣﴾ ﴾

﴿..It is not you that they deny, but it is the Verses [the Qur'an] of Allah that the *Zaalimoon* [polytheists and wrongdoers] deny.﴾ *(Qur'an 6: 33)*

Their folly reached such an extent that they claimed that the one who gave this knowledge to Muhammad (ﷺ) was a Roman blacksmith who was in Makkah. This is a ridiculous lie:

﴿ ... لِّسَانُ ٱلَّذِى يُلْحِدُونَ إِلَيْهِ أَعْجَمِىٌّ وَهَٰذَا لِسَانٌ عَرَبِىٌّ
مُّبِينٌ ﴿١٠٣﴾ ﴾

﴿...The tongue of the man they refer to is foreign, while this [the Qur'an] is a clear Arabic tongue.﴾

(Qur'an 16: 103)

5 - THE HELP AND SUPPORT GIVEN BY ALLAH TO HIS MESSENGERS

Another indication of the truthfulness of the Prophets and Messengers is the fact that Allah supported them and protected them. It is impossible that someone would tell lies about Allah and claim falsely to have been sent by Him, and Allah would help him and support him, and send angels to make him steadfast and guard him. If an earthly king did that, if someone claimed falsely that he had been sent from him and the king came to know of it, he would pursue him, and if he caught him he would punish him severely. So how can it be appropriate for the Creator of the universe, the All-Knowing, Most Wise, to see and hear a man telling lies about Him and claiming to be His Messenger, permitting and prohibiting things in His name, issuing laws, fighting enemies, claiming to do that by the will and command of Allah and with His approval, and Allah will help him, support him, and not subject him to His punishment and wrath? This could never be. If such a thing did happen, if a rebellious liar did do such a thing and became strong and prevailed, that would not last for long. Allah would inevitably show him up and expose him, and send against him one who would defeat him and make him a lesson for others, as Allah did with Musaylimah, Sajaaḥ and Al-Aswad al-'Ansi.[92] Allah (ﷻ) also refers to this kind of evidence in the *aayah*:

﴿ ... إِنَّ ٱلَّذِينَ يَفْتَرُونَ عَلَى ٱللَّهِ ٱلْكَذِبَ لَا يُفْلِحُونَ ﴿١١٦﴾ ﴾

﴿...Verily, those who invent lies against Allah will never prosper.﴾ *(Qur'an 16: 116)*

He ruled that they would not succeed, as He (ﷻ) says:

﴿ وَلَوْ تَقَوَّلَ عَلَيْنَا بَعْضَ ٱلْأَقَاوِيلِ ﴿٤٤﴾ لَأَخَذْنَا مِنْهُ بِٱلْيَمِينِ ﴿٤٥﴾ ثُمَّ لَقَطَعْنَا مِنْهُ ٱلْوَتِينَ ﴿٤٦﴾ ﴾

﴿And if he [Muhammad] had forged a false saying concerning Us [Allah], We surely would have seized him by his right hand [or with power and might], and then We certainly would have cut off his life artery [aorta].﴾ *(Qur'an 69: 44-46)*

What this means is that if the Messenger (ﷺ) had fabricated any lies against Allah that Allah had not said, then Allah would have

---

92 *Sharḥ al-'Aqeedah aṭ-Ṭaḥaawiyah*, Pp. 165-167. Ibn al-Qayyim said something similar in his book *Hidaayat al-Ḥayaara*. See *Al-Jaami'*, Pp. 562.

destroyed him.

This evidence had a great influence on people. When the Arabs saw how victorious Islam was, they believed and entered the religion of Allah in crowds:

﴿ إِذَا جَآءَ نَصۡرُ ٱللَّهِ وَٱلۡفَتۡحُ ۝١ وَرَأَيۡتَ ٱلنَّاسَ يَدۡخُلُونَ فِي دِينِ ٱللَّهِ أَفۡوَاجٗا ۝٢ ﴾

﴿When there comes the Help of Allah [to you, O' Muhammad against your enemies] and the Conquest [of Makkah]. And you see that the people enter Allah's religion [Islam] in crowds.﴾ *(Qur'an 110: 1-2)*

A specious argument

The response to what some of those who disbelieve in the Message of Muhammad (ﷺ) say, about the victories of Pharaoh, Nimrod, Genghis Khan and other *kaafir* rulers ancient and modern, is quite clear. None of these kings claimed to be a prophet, and none of them claimed that Allah commanded him to call mankind to worship and obey Him; whoever obeys Him will enter Paradise and whoever disobeys Him will enter Hell. This is unlike one who claims that Allah has sent him, then Allah helps and supports him, and supports his followers and causes them ultimately to prevail. Such a one cannot be anything but a truthful Messenger, for if he were a liar, Allah would inevitably wreak vengeance upon him and destroy him. There is a lesson to be learned in the cases of Musaylimah, Al-Aswad al-'Ansi and Sajaaḥ, and the *Dajjaal* (Pseudo Christ), who will fabricate lies against Allah and will claim to be divine, but Allah will expose him and show his true nature to those who have insight. He will be a one-eyed man, between whose eyes is written "*kaafir*", but those who are not blessed with the light of faith will be confused concerning him.

CHAPTER EIGHT

THE VIRTUE OF THE PROPHETS AND THEIR VARYING STATUS

THE SUPERIORITY OF THE PROPHETS OVER OTHERS

Allah created His creation and He has differentiated between them:

﴿ وَرَبُّكَ يَخْلُقُ مَا يَشَآءُ وَيَخْتَارُ ... ﴿٦٨﴾ ﴾

﴾And your Lord creates whatsoever He wills and chooses...﴿ *(Qur'an 28: 68)*

From His earth, He (ﷻ) chose Makkah, and made it the location of His Ancient House; whoever enters it will be safe. He filled men's hearts with love towards it and enjoined upon mankind pilgrimage to it (Ḥajj), for those who have the means to do so. He forbade hunting within its precincts and forbade cutting down its trees. He made the desire to commit evil therein deserving of a painful punishment:

﴿ ... وَمَن يُرِدْ فِيهِ بِإِلْحَادٍ بِظُلْمٍ نُّذِقْهُ مِنْ عَذَابٍ أَلِيمٍ ﴿٢٥﴾ ﴾

﴾...And whoever inclines to evil actions therein or to do wrong [i.e. practise polytheism and leave Islamic Monotheism], him We shall cause to taste from a painful torment.﴿ *(Qur'an 22: 25)*

Among the months, He chose Ramaḍaan; among the nights, He chose *Laylat al-Qadr*; among the days He chose the Day of *'Arafah*; among the days of the week, He chose Friday. Allah differentiated among the angels and chose from among them the angels who bore His Message to His Messengers and Prophets. From among the sons of Adam, Allah chose the Prophets, so the Prophets are the best of mankind, and the best of the Prophets are the Messengers:

﴿ ٱللَّهُ يَصْطَفِي مِنَ ٱلْمَلَـٰٓئِكَةِ رُسُلًا وَمِنَ ٱلنَّاسِ ۚ إِنَّ ٱللَّهَ سَمِيعٌۢ بَصِيرٌ ﴿٧٥﴾ ﴾

﴾Allah chooses Messengers from angels and from men. Verily, Allah is All-Hearer, All-Seer.﴿ *(Qur'an 22: 75)*

The ummah is unanimously agreed that the Prophets are superior[1] to others, to the believers of truth (*Aṣ-Ṣiddeeqeen*), the martyrs and the righteous. The differentiation between them is indicated by the *aayah* (verse):

﴿ وَتِلْكَ حُجَّتُنَآ ءَاتَيْنَـٰهَآ إِبْرَٰهِيمَ عَلَىٰ قَوْمِهِۦ ۚ نَرْفَعُ دَرَجَـٰتٍ مَّن نَّشَآءُ ۗ إِنَّ رَبَّكَ حَكِيمٌ عَلِيمٌ ﴿٨٣﴾ وَوَهَبْنَا لَهُۥٓ إِسْحَـٰقَ وَيَعْقُوبَ ۚ كُلًّا هَدَيْنَا ۚ وَنُوحًا هَدَيْنَا مِن قَبْلُ ۖ وَمِن ذُرِّيَّتِهِۦ دَاوُۥدَ وَسُلَيْمَـٰنَ وَأَيُّوبَ وَيُوسُفَ وَمُوسَىٰ وَهَـٰرُونَ ۚ وَكَذَٰلِكَ نَجْزِى ٱلْمُحْسِنِينَ ﴿٨٤﴾ وَزَكَرِيَّا وَيَحْيَىٰ وَعِيسَىٰ وَإِلْيَاسَ ۖ كُلٌّ مِّنَ ٱلصَّـٰلِحِينَ ﴿٨٥﴾ وَإِسْمَـٰعِيلَ وَٱلْيَسَعَ وَيُونُسَ وَلُوطًا ۚ وَكُلًّا فَضَّلْنَا عَلَى ٱلْعَـٰلَمِينَ ﴿٨٦﴾ ﴾

﴾And that was Our Proof which We gave Ibraaheem [Abraham] against his people. We raise whom We will in degrees. Certainly your Lord is All-Wise, All-Knowing. And We bestowed upon him Isḥaaq [Isaac] and Ya'qoob [Jacob], each of them We guided, and before him, We guided Nooḥ [Noah], and among his progeny Dawood [David], Sulaymaan [Solomon], Ayyoob [Job], Yoosuf [Joseph], Moosa [Moses], and Haaroon [Aaron]. Thus do We reward *Al-Muḥsinoon* [the good-doers]. And Zakariyya [Zachariya], and Yahyaa [John] and 'Eesa [Jesus] and Ilyaas [Elias], each one of them was of the righteous. And Ismaa'eel [Ishmael] and Al-Yasaa' [Elisha], and Yoonus [Jonah] and Looṭ [Lot], and each

[1] *Majmoo' al-Fataawa Shaykh al-Islam*, 11/321.

one of them We preferred above the *'Aalameen* [mankind and jinn (of their times)].﴿

(Qur'an 6: 83-86)

The Messenger (ﷺ) told us,

> "After the Prophets and Messengers, the sun has never risen or set on anyone better than Abu Bakr."

From this hadith it may be understood that the Prophets and Messengers are the best of mankind, and that the best man after them is Abu Bakr aṣ-Ṣiddeeq (رضي الله عنه).

In a similar hadith, the Messenger (ﷺ) says of Abu Bakr and 'Umar (may Allah be pleased with them),

> "They are the leaders of the middle-aged men of Paradise, among the first and the last, apart from the Prophets and Messengers."

Allah (سبحانه وتعالى) divided His blessed slaves whom He has blessed into four categories, as He said:

﴿ وَمَن يُطِعِ ٱللَّهَ وَٱلرَّسُولَ فَأُو۟لَـٰٓئِكَ مَعَ ٱلَّذِينَ أَنْعَمَ ٱللَّهُ عَلَيْهِم مِّنَ ٱلنَّبِيِّـۧنَ
وَٱلصِّدِّيقِينَ وَٱلشُّهَدَآءِ وَٱلصَّـٰلِحِينَ ۚ وَحَسُنَ أُو۟لَـٰٓئِكَ رَفِيقًا ﴿٦٩﴾ ﴾

﴾And whoso obey Allah and the Messenger [Muhammad], then they will be in the company of those on whom Allah has bestowed His Grace, of the Prophets, the *Ṣiddeeqoon* [those followers of the Prophets who were first and foremost to believe in them, like Abu Bakr aṣ-Ṣiddeeq], the martyrs, and the righteous. And how excellent these companions are!﴿

(Qur'an 4: 69)

The first and highest of these categories is the Prophets, followed by the *Ṣiddeeqeen*, then the martyrs, then the righteous.

There is no room for coincidence

Some may think that there is room for coincidence here, and that among the Prophets are those who were given Prophethood when they did not deserve it. Allah forbid! Rather Allah, the All-Knowing, Most Wise, All-Aware looked into the essence of His slaves and their hearts, and He chose from among them, selecting those who were superior and more perfect. Allah (ﷻ) spoke the truth when He said:

﴿...ٱللَّهُ أَعۡلَمُ حَيۡثُ يَجۡعَلُ رِسَالَتَهُۥ... ﴿١٢٤﴾﴾

﴿...Allah knows best with whom to place His Message...﴾
(Qur'an 6: 124)

The wisdom and knowledge of Allah dictated that Prophethood and Messengership should only be given to those who were prepared (by Allah) for it and able to bear it.[2] If you think about the lives of the Prophets and Messengers of Allah, you will see that they were the most righteous of mankind at heart, the deepest in knowledge, the

[2] Those who follow the guidance of the Qur'an and Sunnah believe that the Messengers are the best and most perfect of creation, chosen by the All-Knowing, All-Aware (Allah) to be His ambassadors to His creatures. We should differentiate between the virtues and characteristics that Allah has created in them and that which He has revealed to them. They could not have had any knowledge of that which He revealed to them, and their intelligence and cleverness had nothing to do with it. Hence Allah said to His Messenger: ﴿And thus We have sent to you [O' Muhammad] *Rooḥ* [a revelation, and a mercy] of Our Command. You knew not what is the Book, nor what is Faith.﴾ *(Qur'an 42: 52)*

This refutes that type of people who claim to venerate the Messenger (ﷺ) and describe him as brilliant, but then they ascribe all of that to his brilliance, even the knowledge that came to him. This is a devious trick by means of which they aim to deny the revelation and attribute this divine knowledge to the brilliance of Muhammad (ﷺ). In refuting them, we do not go to the other extreme, of denying the attributes and virtues of the Messenger; rather we refute the false aspects of their idea and affirm the true aspects of it, that Muhammad was not only brilliant, but he was also the Messenger of the Lord of the Worlds.

most alert and intelligent, the most patient and forbearing, the kindest in nature... So it is no wonder that Allah chose them to be entrusted with His revelation, the ones to establish His religion. For they represent the pinnacle which no one else can hope to reach.

The belief that the Imams are superior to the Prophets

Some groups which call themselves Muslims have disagreed with this issue on which the ummah is unanimously agreed. Among these groups are the Imami Ithna' 'Asha'ri Shi'ah. One of their prominent contemporary scholars[3] says on this topic: "Among the essential beliefs of our school of thought is that our Imams occupy a position which no angel who is close to Allah and no Prophet who was sent has ever reached."[4] He also said: "It is narrated from them (i.e., the Imams) that 'we have a level of closeness to Allah which no angel who is close to Allah and no Prophet who was sent has ever reached; Faaṭimah az-Zahraa' also attained this level.'"[5]

---

[3] This is Khomeini who led the revolution in Iran.

[4] *Al-Ḥukoomah al-Islamiyah* by Khomeini, Pp. 52.

[5] Ibid. Khomeini exaggerated greatly concerning the Imams and raised them above the human level to a divine level. He says in his book *Al-Ḥukoomah al-Islamiyah*, Pp. 52: "The Imam occupies a position of praise and glory, a lofty degree, and universal dominion to which all the atoms of the universe submit." I do not understand what he means by this universal dominion to which all the atoms of the universe submit, unless it is that which Allah attributes to Himself in the *aayah* (verse): ﴿Verily, His command, when He intends a thing, is only that He says to it, "Be!" and it is.﴾ *(Qur'an 36: 82)*

He (Khomeini) also says in the same book, "Before this universe (came into being), the Imaams were lights which Allah placed near His Throne, and He gave them a level of closeness which is known to no one except Allah." Think about how he describes them as having existed before this universe came into being, and that they existed as light, close to the Throne. All of this is extreme exaggeration which goes against what is clearly stated in the Qur'an and Sunnah.

After preparing this book, before it was sent to print, we heard on the news and read in the papers of something said by Khomeini which is no less serious than =

Al-Aloosi (may Allah have mercy on him) said in *Mukhtasar at-Tuḥfah* (Pp. 100), discussing what the Shi'ah say concerning this

---

= the words we have quoted from his book, he said on the occasion of the birthday of the Absent Mahdi, who the *Shi'ah* claim has been hidden for more than one thousand years, but who they claim is still alive and will return once more to fill the earth with justice after it was filled with injustice and oppression.

In this speech he claimed that all of the Prophets and Messengers, including Muhammad (ﷺ), did not succeed in reforming mankind and implementing justice, and that the one who would succeed in doing that would be the awaited Mahdi, the only person in the world who will achieve that.

In his speech published in the Kuwaiti newspaper *Al-Ra'iy al-'Aam* on 30/6/1980, he said: "All the Prophets came to lay the foundation for justice throughout the world, but they did not succeed. Even Prophet Muhammad (ﷺ), the Seal of the Prophets, who came to reform mankind and implement justice, did not succeed in doing so in his lifetime. The person who will succeed in doing that, who will lay the foundations of justice in all parts of the world and will correct deviations is the awaited Mahdi."

No, by Allah, this is not true and it is not right. No one succeeded in implementing justice as Muhammad (ﷺ) did. No one who comes after him will achieve what the Chosen Prophet (ﷺ) achieved. Khomeini reinforced this idea further when he said: "There is no one on earth other than the Mahdi who will implement justice in the true sense." And he said: "Imam al-Mahdi (peace be upon him) will strive to spread justice throughout the world and he will succeed where the Prophets and *awliya'* failed because of the obstacles which lay in their path..." Hence Khomeini thought that the birthday of the Mahdi was the greatest 'Eid of the Muslims: "The 'Eid of the Mahdi is the greatest festival for all of mankind." This means that it is greater than *'Eid al-Fiṭr* and *'Eid al-Aḍha*. He even gave it precedence over the birthday of the Prophet (ﷺ) in one sense: "This festival, which is a great festival for the Muslims, is to be considered as greater than the birthday of the Prophet (ﷺ) in one regard. His 'Eid is an 'Eid for all of mankind, because he will guide all of mankind." He concluded his speech by giving him precedence over all others: "I cannot call him a leader because he is greater and higher than that. I cannot call him the first man because there is no one after him. He has no second in command, so I cannot describe him in any words other than the promised, awaited Mahdi." We do not find these words strange after what we have read in *Al-Ḥukoomah al-Islamiyah*. *Laa ḥawla wa laa quwwata illa Billaah* (There is no strength and no power except with Allah).

matter: "The *Imamiyah* are unanimously agreed that the Imam is of a higher status than the Messengers of strong will (cf. Qur'an 46: 35) and the Prophets, but he is not of a higher status than the Seal of the Prophets (ﷺ). But with regard to the other Messengers of strong will, some of them refrained from comment, such as Ibn al-Muṭahhar al-Ḥilli and others, and some of them believed that he is equal to them. This goes against what narrated from the Imams. Al-Kullayni narrated from Hishaam al-Aḥwal from Zayd ibn 'Ali that the Prophets are of a higher status than the Imams, and that whoever says otherwise has gone astray. Ibn Baabawayh narrated from *Aṣ-Ṣaadiq* that the Prophets are more beloved to Allah than 'Ali."

Al-Aloosi (may Allah have mercy on him) refuted their views by quoting texts from the Qur'an, by debating in a reasonable manner, by demonstrating the weakness of the texts on which they rely by proving their narrators to be weak (*ḍa'eef*), and by showing that these reports contradict other texts which are to be found in their books. This is clear refutation for those who want to know the truth, and it may be referred to for more information.

These views which give the Imams precedence over the Prophets are repeated often in the books of the *Shi'ah*. 'Ali Moosa al-Bahbahaani mentioned in his book *Miṣbaaḥ al-Hidaayah fi Ithbaat al-Wilaayah*[6] (Pp. 61-62) that the position of Imam is superior to that of Prophet.

Hence they judged as a *kaafir* anyone who denies the Imamate of their Imams or of one of them. Ibn Baabawayh al-Qummi, whom they call *Aṣ-Ṣadooq*, said:

"Our belief concerning one who denies the Imamate of the *Ameer al-Mu'mineen* 'Ali ibn Abi Ṭaalib (رضي الله عنه) and the Imams who came after

---

[6] We have taken these quotations, with mention of their sources, from *Kitaab al-Imaamah* by Dr. 'Ali Aḥmad as-Saaloos, Pp. 19.

him is that he is like one who denies the Prophethood of all the Prophets. Our belief concerning one who affirms *Ameer al-Mu'mineen* ('Ali) but denies even one of the Imams who came after him is that he is like one who affirms all the Prophets but denies the Prophethood of our Prophet Muhammad." (*Risaalah fil-I'tiqaadaat*, Pp. 103)

Al-Mufeed said: "The *Imamiyah* are agreed that whoever denies the Imamate of one of the Imams and denies the obligation of obeying them that Allah has enjoined, is a misguided *kaafir* who deserves to abide in Hell forever." (*Baḥaar al-Anwaar* by Al-Majlisi, 23/390) Al-Majlisi quoted the words of Al-Mufeed to support his own view.

Some of them think that denying the Imams is worse than denying the Prophets. Al-Ḥilli, who is known among the *Ja'fariyah* as *Al-'Allaamah* (great scholar) said: "Imamate is a comprehensive blessing whereas Prophethood is a restricted blessing. It is possible for there to be an era in which there is no living Prophet, unlike the Imam. Denying the comprehensive blessing is worse than denying the restricted blessing." (*Kitaab al-Alfayn fi Imamat Ameer al-Mu'mineen* by Al-Ḥasan ibn Yoosuf al-Muṭahhar al-Ḥilli, 1/3). One of their scholars commented on this by saying, "What he said is good." And he added: "This is what *Aṣ-Ṣadooq* was referring to when he said that the one who denies the Imamate is the worst of the three. It is narrated that he said, the *Naaṣibi* is worse than a Jew. He was asked, 'How is that, O' son of the Messenger of Allah?' He said, 'Because the Jew denies the blessing of Prophethood which is restricted, but the *Naaṣibi* denies the blessing of Imamate which is comprehensive.'" (See footnote on Pp. 43 of *An-Naafi' Yawm al-Ḥashr* by Jamaaluddeen Miqdaad ibn 'Abdullah as-Sayoori)

The Seal of the *Awliyaa'* and the Seal of the Prophets[7]

Some of the *Ṣufis* claim that *wilaayah* (position of *wali*, "sainthood") is of a higher status than Prophethood. They claim that the Seal of the *Awliyaa'* is superior to the Seal of the Prophets. Among those who made this false claim was Al-Ḥakeem at-Tirmidhi and Ibn 'Arabi who believed in *Waḥdat al-Wujood*. They lied in what they said, for it is not narrated in the Book of Allah or in the Sunnah of His Messenger (ﷺ) that there is any seal of the *awliyaa'*, neither is it narrated that he is of a higher status than other *awliyaa'*, let alone being the best of them. None of those who have deep knowledge and are fit to be followed as leaders and taken as examples spoke of this matter.

Their error began when they looked and found that Muhammad (ﷺ) was the Seal of the Messengers and the best of the Messengers. They said that he is the best of them because he is the last of them. This was a mistake, because precedence is not based on being first or last. Prophet Ibraaheem (Abraham) came first but he was of a higher status than Moosa (Moses); Ibraaheem and Moosa came first but they are of a higher status than Prophet 'Eesa (Jesus). It is narrated in a *ṣaḥeeḥ* report from the Messenger (ﷺ) that the best among this ummah are his *Ṣaḥaabah* (the Companions) who were with him, and that even if a Muslim were to spend the equivalent of Mount Uḥud in gold (in charity), he would not reach their level, or even come halfway. Again it is narrated that he (ﷺ) said:

> "The best of generations are my generation, then those who follow them, then those who follow them."

---

[7] Concerning this issue see: *Lawaami' al-Anwaar al-Bahiyah*, 2/300; *Majmoo' al-Fataawa Shaykh al-Islam*, 2/222, 11/221.

In the field of knowledge, those who come first may become more prominent than those who come later. An example of this is Seebawayh in the field of grammar. It may be that in some fields which rely on accumulation of knowledge those who come later may supercede those who came before them. But in the field of Prophethood and Messengership, it is a different matter. Prophethood and its knowledge are a divine gift which cannot be attained through hard work and striving. This issue opens the doors to evil and makes everyone who thinks highly of himself and everyone who wants to do harm to this ummah claim that he is the seal of the *awliyaa'*, and that he gets his knowledge from Allah without any intermediary. This is serious misguidance. No one among this ummah has the right to claim that he is of a higher status than one of the Prophets, and no one has the right to claim that it is acceptable to worship Allah in a manner that goes against the way of the Messenger (ﷺ).

Precedence of some Prophets and Messengers over others

Allah (سبحانه وتعالى) tells us that He has given some of the Prophets precedence over others, as He says:

﴿ ... وَلَقَدْ فَضَّلْنَا بَعْضَ ٱلنَّبِيِّـۧنَ عَلَىٰ بَعْضٍۢ ۖ وَءَاتَيْنَا دَاوُۥدَ زَبُورًا ﴿٥٥﴾ ﴾

> ﴿...And indeed, We have preferred some of the Prophets above others, and to Dawood [David] We gave the *Zaboor* [Psalms].﴾ *(Qur'an 17: 55)*

The ummah is unanimous that the Messengers are superior to the Prophets, and that there are distinctions among the Messengers, as Allah (سبحانه وتعالى) says:

﴿ ۞ تِلْكَ ٱلرُّسُلُ فَضَّلْنَا بَعْضَهُمْ عَلَىٰ بَعْضٍۢ ۘ مِّنْهُم مَّن كَلَّمَ ٱللَّهُ ۖ وَرَفَعَ
بَعْضَهُمْ دَرَجَـٰتٍۢ ۚ وَءَاتَيْنَا عِيسَى ٱبْنَ مَرْيَمَ ٱلْبَيِّنَـٰتِ وَأَيَّدْنَـٰهُ بِرُوحِ
ٱلْقُدُسِ ۗ ... ﴿٢٥٣﴾ ﴾

﴾Those Messengers! We preferred some of them to others; to some of them Allah spoke [directly]; others He raised to degrees [of honour]; and to 'Eesa [Jesus], the son of Maryam [Mary], We gave clear proofs and evidences, and supported him with *Rooḥ-ul-Qudus* [Jibreel (Gabriel)]...﴿ *(Qur'an 2: 253)*

The Messengers of strong will are the highest in status of the Messengers

The highest in status of the Messengers and Prophets are five: Muhammad (ﷺ), Nooḥ, Ibraaheem, Moosa and 'Eesa. These are the Messengers of strong will:

﴿ فَٱصۡبِرۡ كَمَا صَبَرَ أُوْلُواْ ٱلۡعَزۡمِ مِنَ ٱلرُّسُلِ ... ﴿٣٥﴾ ﴾

﴾Therefore be patient [O' Muhammad] as did the Messengers of strong will...﴿ *(Qur'an 46: 35)*

Allah (ﷻ) mentions them in many places in His Book:

﴿ ۞ شَرَعَ لَكُم مِّنَ ٱلدِّينِ مَا وَصَّىٰ بِهِۦ نُوحٗا وَٱلَّذِيٓ أَوۡحَيۡنَآ إِلَيۡكَ وَمَا وَصَّيۡنَا بِهِۦٓ إِبۡرَٰهِيمَ وَمُوسَىٰ وَعِيسَىٰٓۖ أَنۡ أَقِيمُواْ ٱلدِّينَ وَلَا تَتَفَرَّقُواْ فِيهِۚ ... ﴿١٣﴾ ﴾

﴾He [Allah] has ordained for you the same religion [Islamic Monotheism] which He ordained for Nooḥ [Noah], and that which We have revealed to you [O' Muhammad], and that which We ordained for Ibraaheem [Abraham], Moosa [Moses] and 'Eesa [Jesus] saying you should establish religion [i.e. to do what it orders you to do practically] and make no divisions in it [religion] [i.e. various sects in religion]...﴿
(Qur'an 42: 13)

﴿ وَإِذْ أَخَذْنَا مِنَ ٱلنَّبِيِّـۧنَ مِيثَـٰقَهُمْ وَمِنكَ وَمِن نُّوحٍ وَإِبْرَٰهِيمَ وَمُوسَىٰ وَعِيسَى ٱبْنِ مَرْيَمَ ... ﴿٧﴾ ﴾

﴿And [remember] when We took from the Prophets their covenant, and from you [O' Muhammad], and from Nooḥ [Noah], Ibraaheem [Abraham], Moosa [Moses], and 'Eesa [Jesus] son of Maryam [Mary]...﴾ *(Qur'an 33: 7)*

How are the Prophets and Messengers distinguished from one another?[8]

Anyone who ponders the two *aayaat* (verses) which mention the differentiation of the Prophets and Messengers will find that Allah has given to those whom He has made superior something that He did

---

[8] The Prophets and Messengers vary in status as we have explained here, for Allah has differentiated between them. Some people attribute things to the Prophets and Messengers, thinking that they are venerating them thereby, but they go beyond the limits of truth and fairness. For example, many Muslims pray to the Messenger (ﷺ), saying "O' the first one whom Allah created, O' light of the Throne of Allah." All such kinds of words are misguided, including praying to and calling upon the Messenger. It is only Allah, and none other, Who should be called upon.

Another sense in which such words are misguided is the claim that the Messenger (ﷺ) was created from light, and that he was the first thing that Allah created. There is no proof for these claims apart from false *aḥaadeeth* whose isnads are not *ṣaḥeeḥ*. The first thing that Allah created was the Pen which wrote the decrees of all things. The Messenger (ﷺ) was created from the same thing as the rest of mankind, but the fact that he was created from the same thing as the rest of mankind and he was created towards the end of time does not undermine his position, because created beings are not differentiated solely on the basis of that from which they were created. A believer may be created from a *kaafir*, or a *kaafir* from a believer, as the son of Nooḥ (Noah) was created from him, and Ibraaheem (Abraham) was created from Aazar. Allah created Adam from mud, and when He formed him and breathed into him of the soul that He had created, He made the angels prostrate to him and gave him precedence over them by teaching him the names of all things, and by creating him with His own hand.

not give to others, or by raising them in status above others, or by their striving harder to worship Allah and call people to Him, or they carried out the commands of Allah in the proper manner.

Allah (ﷻ), favoured Prophet Dawood (عليه السلام) by giving him the *Zaboor*:

﴿ ... وَءَاتَيْنَا دَاوُۥدَ زَبُورًا ﴿٥٥﴾ ﴾

﴾...And to Dawood [David] We gave the *Zaboor* [Psalms].﴿ *(Qur'an 17: 55)*

Allah gave Prophet Moosa (عليه السلام) the *Tawraat*:

﴿ وَإِذْ ءَاتَيْنَا مُوسَى ٱلْكِتَٰبَ وَٱلْفُرْقَانَ لَعَلَّكُمْ تَهْتَدُونَ ﴿٥٣﴾ ﴾

﴾And [remember] when We gave Moosa [Moses] the Scripture [the *Tawraat* (Torah)] and the criterion [of right and wrong] so that you may be guided aright.﴿ *(Qur'an 2: 53)*

﴿ إِنَّآ أَنزَلْنَا ٱلتَّوْرَىٰةَ فِيهَا هُدًى وَنُورٌ ... ﴿٤٤﴾ ﴾

﴾Verily, We did send down the *Tawraat* [Torah] [to Moosa (Moses)], therein was guidance and light...﴿ *(Qur'an 5: 44)*

And He gave Prophet 'Eesa (عليه السلام) the *Injeel*:

﴿ وَقَفَّيْنَا عَلَىٰٓ ءَاثَٰرِهِم بِعِيسَى ٱبْنِ مَرْيَمَ مُصَدِّقًا لِّمَا بَيْنَ يَدَيْهِ مِنَ ٱلتَّوْرَىٰةِ
وَءَاتَيْنَٰهُ ٱلْإِنجِيلَ فِيهِ هُدًى وَنُورٌ ... ﴿٤٦﴾ ﴾

﴾And in their footsteps, We sent 'Eesa [Jesus], son of Maryam [Mary], confirming the *Tawraat* [Torah] that had come before him, and We gave him the *Injeel* [Gospel], in which was guidance and light...﴿ *(Qur'an 5: 46)*

Allah singled out Adam to be the "father of mankind". Allah created him with His hand, and breathed into him of the soul that He had created, and He commanded the angels to prostrate to him.

He favoured Prophet Nooḥ (Noah) (ﷺ) by making him the first of the Messengers to the people of the earth, and Allah called him a thankful slave.

He favoured Prophet Ibraaheem (ﷺ) by choosing him as a close friend (*Khaleel*):

﴿... وَاتَّخَذَ اللَّهُ إِبْرَاهِيمَ خَلِيلًا ﴿١٢٥﴾﴾

﴾And Allah did take Ibraaheem [Abraham] as a *Khaleel* [an intimate friend]...﴿ *(Qur'an 4: 125)*

And He made him a leader for mankind:

﴿... قَالَ إِنِّي جَاعِلُكَ لِلنَّاسِ إِمَامًا ... ﴿١٢٤﴾﴾

﴾...He [Allah] said [to him], 'Verily, I am going to make you an Imam [a leader] for mankind [to follow you].'...﴿ *(Qur'an 2: 124)*

Allah favoured Prophet Moosa (ﷺ) by sending him as His Messenger and by speaking with him:

﴿قَالَ يَٰمُوسَىٰٓ إِنِّي ٱصْطَفَيْتُكَ عَلَى ٱلنَّاسِ بِرِسَٰلَٰتِي وَبِكَلَٰمِي ... ﴿١٤٤﴾﴾

﴾[Allah] said: 'O' Moosa [Moses] I have chosen you above men by My Messages, and by My speaking [to you]...'﴿ *(Qur'an 7: 144)*

And He chose him for Himself:

﴿وَٱصْطَنَعْتُكَ لِنَفْسِي ﴿٤١﴾﴾

﴾And I have chosen you for Myself.﴿ *(Qur'an 20: 41)*

He favoured Prophet 'Eesa by making him a Messenger of Allah, and His Word which he bestowed upon Maryam and a spirit created by Him, and he spoke to people from the cradle:

﴿... إِنَّمَا ٱلْمَسِيحُ عِيسَى ٱبْنُ مَرْيَمَ رَسُولُ ٱللَّهِ وَكَلِمَتُهُۥٓ أَلْقَىٰهَآ إِلَىٰ مَرْيَمَ وَرُوحٌ مِّنْهُ ... ﴿١٧١﴾﴾

﴿...The Messiah 'Eesa [Jesus], son of Maryam [Mary], was [no more than] a Messenger of Allah and His Word, ['Be!' - and he was] which He bestowed on Maryam [Mary] and a spirit [*Rooḥ*] created by Him...﴾

(Qur'an 4: 171)

The Prophets may also be differentiated in other ways. A Prophet may be simply a Prophet, or he may be a Prophet-king, or he may be a slave-Messenger. A Prophet who is disbelieved and not followed or obeyed, is a Prophet but he is not a king. The one who is believed, followed and obeyed, if he enjoins only that which Allah commands him, is a slave-Prophet but is not a king. If he commands what he wants of things that are permitted to him, then he is a Prophet-King, as Allah said to Prophet Sulaymaan (عليه السلام):

﴿هَٰذَا عَطَآؤُنَا فَٱمْنُنْ أَوْ أَمْسِكْ بِغَيْرِ حِسَابٍ ﴿٣٩﴾﴾

﴿This is Our Gift, so spend you or withhold, no account will be asked of you.﴾ *(Qur'an 38: 39)*

The Prophet-king is in contrast to the slave-Messenger, as it was said to the Prophet (ﷺ), "Choose whether you want to be a slave-Messenger, or a Prophet-king." The slave-Messenger is more perfect than the Prophet-king, as was the position of our Prophet Muhammad (ﷺ), who was a slave-Messenger who was supported, obeyed and followed. Thus he will have a reward equal to that of those who followed him. Mankind benefitted because of him; they will be granted mercy because of him and he will be granted mercy because of them. He did not choose to be a king, lest that undermine his share in the Hereafter, because it implies enjoyment of leadership and wealth.

The slave-Messenger is better in the sight of Allah than the Prophet-king. Hence the position of the Prophets Nooḥ (Noah), Ibraaheem (Abraham), Moosa (Moses) and 'Eesa ibn Maryam (Jesus) is higher before Allah than the position of the Prophets Dawood (David), Sulaymaan (Solomon) and Yoosuf (Joseph).[9]

The virtue of the Final Messenger Muhammad (ﷺ)

When Allah (ﷻ) will resurrect the first and the last on the Day of Resurrection, our Messenger (ﷺ) will be the leader of the children of Adam, carrying the banner of praise. On that Day the Prophets and Messengers will be beneath his banner. The Messenger (ﷺ) said:

> "I will be the leader of the children of Adam on the Day of Resurrection, and I am not boasting. In my hand there will be a banner of praise, and I am not boasting. There will be no Prophet that Day, Adam or anyone else, but he will be beneath my banner. I will be the first one to intercede and the first one to be called upon to intercede, and I am not boasting." - This is narrated by Aḥmad, Tirmidhi and Ibn Maajah.[10]

When the people's distress on that Day becomes too intense, the people will ask the great Messengers to intercede with Allah to pass judgement among His slaves. The Messengers will try to avoid that, each of them telling them to go to someone else, until, when they come to Prophet 'Eesa (Jesus), he will say: "Go to Muhammad, the slave whose past and future sins were forgiven by Allah."

---

[9] *Majmoo' al-Fataawa Shaykh al-Islam.*

[10] *Ṣaḥeeḥ al-Jaami' aṣ-Ṣagheer*, 2/21.

This will be his status on that great Day. This is only because of the favours that Allah bestowed upon him, his great characteristics, noble attitude, striving for the sake of Allah and doing as He commands. Allah has blessed him with virtues in his own self, in his call and in his ummah. For example, He took him as a close friend as He did with Prophet Ibraaheem (Abraham). According to a hadith narrated by Muslim in his *Ṣaḥeeḥ* and by Abu 'Awaanah,

> "Allah has taken me as a close friend as He took Ibraaheem as a close friend."[11]

He gave him the Noble Qur'an, the like of which was given to no other Prophet or Messenger:

﴿ وَلَقَدْ ءَاتَيْنَٰكَ سَبْعًا مِّنَ ٱلْمَثَانِى وَٱلْقُرْءَانَ ٱلْعَظِيمَ ﴿٨٧﴾ ﴾

> ﴾And indeed, We have bestowed upon you seven of *Al-Mathaani* [seven repeatedly-recited Verses], [i.e. *Soorah al-Faatiḥah*) and the Grand Qur'an.﴿ *(Qur'an 15: 87)*

Allah singled him out to receive six things that were not given to any Prophet before him. According to the hadith,

> "I have been favoured over the Prophets with six things: I have been given concise speech; I have been supported with fear (from me, cast in the hearts of my enemies); the spoils of war have been made permissible to me; the earth has been made a means of purification and a place of worship for me; I have been sent to all of mankind; and I am the last of the Prophets."

- This is narrated by Muslim and Tirmidhi.[12]

---

[11] *Taḥqeeq aṭ-Ṭaḥaawiyah*. See *Sharḥ aṭ-Ṭaḥaawiyah*, Pp. 175.

[12] *Ṣaḥeeḥ al-Jaami'*, 2/21.

The Messenger (ﷺ) narrated that Allah favoured him over others with six things.

1) He was given concise speech, which means that he was able to include profound meanings in brief words.

2) Being supported with fear means that Allah cast into the hearts of his enemies fear of His Messenger and the followers of His Messenger (ﷺ).

3) The spoils of war were made permissible to him; before that the spoils of war gained by the Messengers and their followers would be gathered, then fire would come down from heaven and burn them.

4) The earth has been made a place of worship and a means of purification for him and his followers. Wherever a man of this ummah is when the time for prayer comes, he can do *wuḍoo'*, and if he cannot find water then he can do *tayammum*, then he may pray in a mosque, or in a house, or in the open desert.

5) He was sent to all of mankind, Arabs and non-Arabs, (regardless of race or ethnicity)[13], those who were alive at the time of his mission and those who came after him, until the Hour begins:

---

[13] Nehru claimed in his book *Glimpses of World History* that Muhammad was sent to the Arabs only. This claim was also made by some Christian groups in the past and now. *Shaykh al-Islam* Ibn Taymiyah wrote his book *Al-Jawaab aṣ-Ṣaḥeeḥ* to refute the specious arguments of a Christian. One of the specious arguments which Ibn Taymiyah refuted at length was the claim of this Christian that Muhammad was sent to the Arabs and not to other nations. It is sufficient in order to refute this lie to point out their contradictions to them. For if they agree that he was a Prophet who was sent, this implies that they should believe what he said, and he said that he was sent to all of mankind. If they believe that he was a Prophet who was sent, but they disbelieved in him and said, "You were sent to the Arabs only," they clearly contradicted themselves and it is obvious that they are trying to justify their disbelief in him.

﴿ قُلْ يَٰٓأَيُّهَا ٱلنَّاسُ إِنِّى رَسُولُ ٱللَّهِ إِلَيْكُمْ جَمِيعًا ... ﴿١٥٨﴾ ﴾

﴿Say [O' Muhammad]: 'O' mankind! Verily, I am sent to you all as the Messenger of Allah...'﴾ *(Qur'an 7: 158)*

And he (ﷺ) was sent to the jinn just as he was sent to mankind. After listening to the Qur'an and believing in the truth that had been revealed, a group of the jinn went back to call their people to faith:

﴿ يَٰقَوْمَنَآ أَجِيبُوا۟ دَاعِىَ ٱللَّهِ وَءَامِنُوا۟ بِهِۦ يَغْفِرْ لَكُم مِّن ذُنُوبِكُمْ وَيُجِرْكُم مِّنْ عَذَابٍ أَلِيمٍ ﴿٣١﴾ وَمَن لَّا يُجِبْ دَاعِىَ ٱللَّهِ فَلَيْسَ بِمُعْجِزٍ فِى ٱلْأَرْضِ وَلَيْسَ لَهُۥ مِن دُونِهِۦٓ أَوْلِيَآءُ ۚ أُو۟لَٰٓئِكَ فِى ضَلَٰلٍ مُّبِينٍ ﴿٣٢﴾ ﴾

﴿O' our people! Respond [with obedience] to Allah's Caller [i.e. Allah's Messenger Muhammad], and believe in him [i.e. believe in that which Muhammad has brought from Allah and follow him]. He [Allah] will forgive you of your sins, and will save you from a painful torment [i.e. Hell-fire]. And whosoever does not respond to Allah's Caller, he cannot escape on earth, and there will be no *Awliyaa'* [lords, helpers, supporters, protectors] for him besides Allah [from Allah's punishment]. Those are in manifest error.﴾ *(Qur'an 46: 31-32)*

6) The sixth blessings is that he is the Seal of the Prophets, after whom there will be no Prophet:

﴿ ... وَلَٰكِن رَّسُولَ ٱللَّهِ وَخَاتَمَ ٱلنَّبِيِّـۧنَ ... ﴿٤٠﴾ ﴾

﴿...But he is the Messenger of Allah and the last [end] of the Prophets...﴾ *(Qur'an 33: 40)*

If our Messenger (ﷺ) is the final Prophet then he is also the final Messenger, because every Messenger is a Prophet.

What his being the last of the Prophets and Messengers means is that no Messenger will be sent after him to change his laws[14] or to annul any part of his religion. When Prophet 'Eesa (Jesus) descends at the end of time, which is a matter of truth confirmed by the Prophet (ﷺ), that he (Jesus) will not come down to rule by the law of the *Tawraat* and *Injeel*, rather he will rule according to the Qur'an; he will break the cross and kill the pigs, and will call people to prayer.

The texts which forbid making a distinction between the Prophets

There are *aḥaadeeth* which forbid the Muslims from favouring some of the Prophets over others. For example, Abu Sa'eed al-Khudri narrated that the Messenger (ﷺ) said:

> "Do not say that some of the Prophets are better than others."[15]

---

[14] After the time of the Messenger (ﷺ) there appeared a number of false prophets, such as Musaylimah, Al-Aswad al-'Ansi and Sajaaḥ. Other false prophets still appear from time to time. In the nineteenth century there appeared 'Ali Muhammad ash-Shirazi (b. 1819 CE) who was known as *Al-Baab*, and whose followers were known as *Al-Baabiyah*. He claimed to be a prophet sometimes, and to be divine sometimes. He was followed by his student known as Baha'ullah, whose followers are known as *Al-Bahaa'iyah* (Baha'is). Another of these pretenders was Mirza Ghulam Aḥmad al-Qadiyaani, whose followers are spread throughout India, Germany, England and America, where they have "mosques" which they use to mislead the Muslims. They are called *Al-Qadiyaaniyah* (Qadianis), after the name of the birth place of Mirza Ghulam Aḥmad in Punjab, India, they call themselves *Aḥmadiyah* (Ahmadis), after the last part of the name Mirza Ghulam Aḥmad. The purpose is also to mislead the slaves of Allah.
The last of these pretenders was a man who appeared in Sudan, claiming to be a prophet. Allah has exposed all of those who make such claims and has shown them for what they really are. ﴾Say: 'Verily, those who invent a lie against Allah will never be successful.'﴿ *(Qur'an 10: 69)*

[15] Bukhari and Muslim. *Mishkaat al-Maṣaabeeḥ*, 3/114.

It is narrated that Abu Hurayrah (ﷺ) stated: The Messenger of Allah (ﷺ) said:

> "Do not favour some of the Prophets over others"[16]
> - i.e., do not say that So and so is better than So and so.

These *aḥaadeeth* do not contradict the Qur'anic texts which indicate that Allah has preferred some of the Prophets and Messengers over others. The prohibition mentioned in the *aḥaadeeth* should be interpreted as meaning that it is not permitted to make a distinction between them if that is based on tribalism or the desire to undermine the status of some of them, or if that making a distinction will lead to dispute or tribulation (*fitnah*).[17] This is indicated by the background to the hadith. In *Ṣaḥeeḥ al-Bukhari* and elsewhere it is narrated from Abu Hurayrah (ﷺ) that:

> "A Muslim man debated with a Jew insulting each other. The Muslim said, 'By the One Who chose Muhammad (ﷺ) over the worlds' - when he was swearing an oath. The Jew said, 'By the One Who chose Moosa over the worlds.' The Muslim raised his hand at that point and slapped the Jew. The Jew went to the Prophet (ﷺ) and told him what had happened between him and the Muslim man. He [the Prophet (ﷺ)] said, 'Do not prefer me over Moosa, for the people will swoon (on the Day of Resurrection), and I will be the first one to wake up, and I will see Moosa holding on to the side of the Throne. I know not whether he was one of those who swooned and woke up before me, or whether he was one of those exempted by Allah.'"[18]

---

[16] Bukhari quoted by *Mishkaat al-Maṣaabeeḥ*, 3/114.

[17] *Sharḥ aṭ-Ṭaḥaawiyah*, Pp. 170.

[18] Bukhari: *Kitaab al-Anbiyaa', Baab Wafaat Moosa*. See *Fatḥ al-Baari*, 6/441.

According to a report narrated by Bukhari,

> "Do not favour me over the (other) Prophets."

According to another report,

> "Do not make a distinction between the Prophets."

Ibn Ḥajar said concerning this matter: "The scholars said concerning the prohibition on making distinction between the Prophets is that this refers to someone who speaks on the basis of his own opinion, not one who speaks on the basis of evidence (*daleel*); or it refers to one who speaks in such a manner as to undermine the position of the one who is of a lower status, or to lead to arguments and disputes; or it may mean, do not favour one Prophet over another in all aspects in such a way that you do not leave anything good to be said of the one who is of a lower status.."[19]

Further it is narrated that one of the scholars said: "The reports which were narrated forbidding or favouring (some of the Prophets over others) have to do with disputing with the People of the Book and favouring some of the Prophets over others on the basis of personal preference, because if such debates occur between two people who follow different religions, there is no guarantee that one of them will not end up looking down on the other, and this may lead to *kufr*. But if that distinction is based on comparing characteristics and virtues to see which of them is of a higher status, then this is not included in the prohibition."[20]

---

[19] *Fatḥ al-Baari*, 6/446.

[20] Ibid. For more information, see *Tafseer Ibn Katheer* and *Tafseer al-Qurṭubi*, commentary on *Soorah al-Baqarah* (Qur'an 2: 253).

PART TWO

THE DIVINELY-REVEALED MESSAGES

CHAPTER ONE
BELIEF IN THE MESSAGES

THE OBLIGATION OF BELIEVING IN THE MESSAGES

One of the basic principles of faith is to believe with strong conviction in the Messages which Allah revealed to His slaves via His Messengers and Prophets, and to believe that they conveyed them to mankind. Allah (ﷻ) said to Prophet Moosa (Moses) (ﷺ):

﴿ ... يَٰمُوسَىٰٓ إِنِّى ٱصْطَفَيْتُكَ عَلَى ٱلنَّاسِ بِرِسَٰلَٰتِى وَبِكَلَٰمِى ... ﴿١٤٤﴾ ﴾

﴾...O' Moosa [Moses] I have chosen you above men by My Messages, and by My speaking [to you]...﴿ *(Qur'an 7: 144)*

Allah praised His Messengers who conveyed His message and were not deterred by those who objected to that:

﴿ ٱلَّذِينَ يُبَلِّغُونَ رِسَٰلَٰتِ ٱللَّهِ وَيَخْشَوْنَهُۥ وَلَا يَخْشَوْنَ أَحَدًا إِلَّا ٱللَّهَ ... ﴿٣٩﴾ ﴾

﴾Those who convey the Message of Allah and fear Him, and fear none save Allah...﴿ *(Qur'an 33: 39)*

The nations were destroyed because of their disbelief in the Messages of Allah. Look at the attitude of Prophet Ṣaaliḥ after his people were destroyed:

﴿ فَتَوَلَّىٰ عَنْهُمْ وَقَالَ يَٰقَوْمِ لَقَدْ أَبْلَغْتُكُمْ رِسَالَةَ رَبِّى وَنَصَحْتُ لَكُمْ وَلَٰكِن لَّا تُحِبُّونَ ٱلنَّٰصِحِينَ ﴿٧٩﴾ ﴾

﴾Then he [Ṣaaliḥ (Saleh)] turned from them, and said: 'O' my people! I have indeed conveyed to you the Message of my Lord, and have given you good advice but you like not good advisers.'》 *(Qur'an 7: 79)*

And the attitude of Prophet Shu'ayb after his people were destroyed:

﴿ فَتَوَلَّىٰ عَنْهُمْ وَقَالَ يَٰقَوْمِ لَقَدْ أَبْلَغْتُكُمْ رِسَٰلَٰتِ رَبِّي وَنَصَحْتُ لَكُمْ فَكَيْفَ ءَاسَىٰ عَلَىٰ قَوْمٍ كَٰفِرِينَ ﴿٩٣﴾ ﴾

《Then he [Shu'ayb] turned from them and said: 'O' my people! I have indeed conveyed my Lord's Messages unto you and I have given you good advice. Then how can I sorrow for the disbelieving people's [destruction].'》 *(Qur'an 7: 93)*

Belief in all the Messages

What Allah (ﷻ) revealed to His Messengers may have been revealed from heaven in writing, like the *Tawraat* (Torah) which was sent down to Prophet Moosa (Moses). Allah says:

﴿ وَكَتَبْنَا لَهُۥ فِي ٱلْأَلْوَاحِ مِن كُلِّ شَيْءٍ مَّوْعِظَةً وَتَفْصِيلًا لِّكُلِّ شَيْءٍ فَخُذْهَا بِقُوَّةٍ وَأْمُرْ قَوْمَكَ يَأْخُذُوا۟ بِأَحْسَنِهَا ... ﴿١٤٥﴾ ﴾

《And We wrote for him on the Tablets the lesson to be drawn from all things and the explanation for all things [and said]: 'Hold unto these with firmness, and enjoin your people to take the better therein...'》*(Qur'an 7: 145)*

Or it might have been a written Book (in the Heaven), but it was sent down verbally in recited form, like the Qur'an:

﴿ وَقُرْءَانًا فَرَقْنَٰهُ لِتَقْرَأَهُۥ عَلَى ٱلنَّاسِ عَلَىٰ مُكْثٍ وَنَزَّلْنَٰهُ تَنزِيلًا ﴿١٠٦﴾ ﴾

《And [it is] a Qur'an which We have divided [into parts], in order that you might recite it to men at intervals. And We have revealed it by stages [in 23 years].》 *(Qur'an 17: 106)*

That which was revealed from heaven may have been compiled in a book like the Scripture of Ibraaheem (Abraham) and the Books which were revealed to Moosa, Dawood, 'Eesa and Muhammad, may the blessings and peace of Allah be upon them all. Or it may have been revelation which was given to the Messenger or Prophet, but not in the form of a book, like the revelation which came down to Ismaa'eel, Isḥaaq, Ya'qoob and the Asbaaṭ, and the *Waḥy* which came to our Prophet (ﷺ) other than the Qur'an.

We are obliged to believe in all the Revelation sent down by the Almighty:

﴿ قُولُوٓاْ ءَامَنَّا بِٱللَّهِ وَمَآ أُنزِلَ إِلَيۡنَا وَمَآ أُنزِلَ إِلَىٰٓ إِبۡرَٰهِـۧمَ وَإِسۡمَٰعِيلَ وَإِسۡحَٰقَ وَيَعۡقُوبَ وَٱلۡأَسۡبَاطِ وَمَآ أُوتِيَ مُوسَىٰ وَعِيسَىٰ وَمَآ أُوتِيَ ٱلنَّبِيُّونَ مِن رَّبِّهِمۡ لَا نُفَرِّقُ بَيۡنَ أَحَدٖ مِّنۡهُمۡ وَنَحۡنُ لَهُۥ مُسۡلِمُونَ ١٣٦ ﴾

﴿Say [O' Muslims]: 'We believe in Allah and that which has been sent down to us and that which has been sent down to Ibraaheem [Abraham], Ismaa'eel [Ishmael], Isḥaaq [Isaac], Ya'qoob [Jacob], and to *Al-Asbaaṭ* [the offspring of the twelve sons of Ya'qoob (Jacob)], and that which has been given to Moosa [Moses] and 'Eesa [Jesus], and that which has been given to the Prophets from their Lord. We make no distinction between any of them, and to Him we have submitted [in Islam].﴾

(Qur'an 2: 136)

Allah said to His Messenger:

﴿ ... وَقُلۡ ءَامَنتُ بِمَآ أَنزَلَ ٱللَّهُ مِن كِتَٰبٖۖ وَأُمِرۡتُ لِأَعۡدِلَ بَيۡنَكُمُۖ ... ١٥ ﴾

﴿... Say: 'I believe in whatsoever Allah has sent down of the Book [all the holy Books, this Qur'an and the Books of the old from the *Tawraat* (Torah), or the *Injeel* (Gospel) or the Pages of Ibraaheem (Abraham)] and I am commanded to do justice among you...﴿

(Qur'an 42: 15)

And He said to the believers:

﴿ يَٰٓأَيُّهَا ٱلَّذِينَ ءَامَنُوٓا۟ ءَامِنُوا۟ بِٱللَّهِ وَرَسُولِهِۦ وَٱلْكِتَٰبِ ٱلَّذِى نَزَّلَ عَلَىٰ
رَسُولِهِۦ وَٱلْكِتَٰبِ ٱلَّذِىٓ أَنزَلَ مِن قَبْلُ ... ﴿١٣٦﴾ ﴾

﴾O' you who believe! Believe in Allah, and His Messenger [Muhammad], and the Book [the Qur'an] which He has sent down to His Messenger, and the Scripture which He sent down to those before [him]...﴿

(Qur'an 4: 136)

Whatever Allah has told us about in detail - such as the Books which He has mentioned, namely the *Ṣuḥuf* of Ibraaheem, the *Tawraat* of Moosa, the *Zaboor* of Dawood, the *Injeel* of 'Eesa, and the Qur'an revealed to Muhammad (ﷺ), Allah's speaking to Moosa, the revelation that Allah sent to Ṣaaliḥ, Hood and Shu'ayb, the *Waḥy* which Allah sent to His Messenger Muhammad (ﷺ) other than the Qur'an, which is included in the books of Sunnah - we believe in that according to the details which Allah has told us of. We believe that there are other Books and that there are other Revelations which Allah has not told us about.

How should we believe in the Messages?

We believe in what was said in the previous divinely-revealed Messages, and this means that ruling according to it was obligatory upon the nations to whom the Books were sent. We believe that the divinely-revealed Books confirm one another and do not disprove one another. The *Injeel* confirms the *Tawraat* (Torah). Allah (ﷻ) says concerning the *Injeel*:

﴿... وَءَاتَيْنَٰهُ ٱلْإِنجِيلَ فِيهِ هُدًى وَنُورٌ وَمُصَدِّقًا لِّمَا بَيْنَ يَدَيْهِ مِنَ ٱلتَّوْرَىٰةِ ... ﴿٤٦﴾﴾

﴿...And We gave him the *Injeel* [Gospel], in which was guidance and light and confirmation of the *Tawraat* [Torah] that had come before it...﴾ *(Qur'an 5: 46)*

Whoever denies anything that Allah has revealed is a *kaafir*:

﴿... وَمَن يَكْفُرْ بِٱللَّهِ وَمَلَٰٓئِكَتِهِۦ وَكُتُبِهِۦ وَرُسُلِهِۦ وَٱلْيَوْمِ ٱلْءَاخِرِ فَقَدْ ضَلَّ ضَلَٰلًۢا بَعِيدًا ﴿١٣٦﴾﴾

﴿...And whosoever disbelieves in Allah, His Angels, His Books, His Messengers, and the Last Day, then indeed he has strayed far away.﴾ *(Qur'an 4: 136)*

And Allah (ﷻ) says:

﴿إِنَّ ٱلَّذِينَ كَذَّبُوا۟ بِـَٔايَٰتِنَا وَٱسْتَكْبَرُوا۟ عَنْهَا لَا تُفَتَّحُ لَهُمْ أَبْوَٰبُ ٱلسَّمَآءِ وَلَا يَدْخُلُونَ ٱلْجَنَّةَ حَتَّىٰ يَلِجَ ٱلْجَمَلُ فِى سَمِّ ٱلْخِيَاطِ ... ﴿٤٠﴾﴾

﴿Verily, those who belie Our *Aayaat* [proofs, evidences, verses, lessons, signs, revelations, etc.] and treat them with arrogance, for them the gates of heaven will not be opened, and they will not enter Paradise until the camel goes through the eye of the needle [which is impossible]...﴾ *(Qur'an 7: 40)*

We believe that each subsequent law abrogated the law that came before it, in whole or in part. Allah (ﷻ) permitted Adam to marry his daughters to his sons, then this was abrogated. One of the things that were permitted to Ya'qoob was that a man could be married to two sisters at one time, and Ya'qoob did this, then it was abrogated. The *Injeel* permitted some things which had been forbidden in the *Tawraat*:

﴿ وَمُصَدِّقًا لِّمَا بَيْنَ يَدَىَّ مِنَ ٱلتَّوْرَىٰةِ وَلِأُحِلَّ لَكُم بَعْضَ ٱلَّذِى حُرِّمَ عَلَيْكُمْ ... ﴾ (٥٠)

﴾And I have come confirming that which was before me of the *Tawraat* [Torah], and to make lawful to you part of what was forbidden to you...﴿ *(Qur'an 3: 50)*

The Qur'an abrogated much of what was written in the *Tawraat* and *Injeel*:

﴿ ٱلَّذِينَ يَتَّبِعُونَ ٱلرَّسُولَ ٱلنَّبِىَّ ٱلْأُمِّىَّ ٱلَّذِى يَجِدُونَهُۥ مَكْتُوبًا عِندَهُمْ فِى ٱلتَّوْرَىٰةِ وَٱلْإِنجِيلِ يَأْمُرُهُم بِٱلْمَعْرُوفِ وَيَنْهَىٰهُمْ عَنِ ٱلْمُنكَرِ وَيُحِلُّ لَهُمُ ٱلطَّيِّبَـٰتِ وَيُحَرِّمُ عَلَيْهِمُ ٱلْخَبَـٰٓئِثَ وَيَضَعُ عَنْهُمْ إِصْرَهُمْ وَٱلْأَغْلَـٰلَ ٱلَّتِى كَانَتْ عَلَيْهِمْ ... ﴾ (١٥٧)

﴾Those who follow the Messenger, the Prophet who can neither read nor write [i.e. Muhammad] whom they find written with them in the *Tawraat* [Torah] and the *Injeel* [Gospel] - he commands them for *Al-Ma'roof* [i.e. Islamic Monotheism and all that Islam has ordained]; and forbids them from *Al-Munkar* [i.e. disbelief, polytheism of all kinds, and all that Islam has forbidden]; he allows them as lawful *Aṭ-Ṭayyibaat* [i.e. all good and lawful as regards things, deeds, beliefs, persons and foods], and prohibits them as unlawful *Al-Khaba'ith* [i.e. all evil and unlawful as regards things, deeds, beliefs, persons and foods], he releases them from their heavy burdens [of Allah's Covenant with the children of Israel], and from the fetters [bindings] that were upon them...﴿ *(Qur'an 7: 157)*

It is not sufficient only to believe in the Qur'an

We should believe in the previous divinely-revealed books, but simply believing is not sufficient in the case of the Qur'an. We must follow it as well when we believe it and obey its commands and heed to its prohibitions:

﴿ الٓمٓصٓ ﴿١﴾ كِتَٰبٌ أُنزِلَ إِلَيۡكَ فَلَا يَكُن فِي صَدۡرِكَ حَرَجٞ مِّنۡهُ لِتُنذِرَ بِهِۦ وَذِكۡرَىٰ لِلۡمُؤۡمِنِينَ ﴿٢﴾ ٱتَّبِعُواْ مَآ أُنزِلَ إِلَيۡكُم مِّن رَّبِّكُمۡ وَلَا تَتَّبِعُواْ مِن دُونِهِۦٓ أَوۡلِيَآءَۗ قَلِيلٗا مَّا تَذَكَّرُونَ ﴿٣﴾ ﴾

> ﴾*Alif-Laam-Meem-Saad*. [These letters are one of the miracles of the Qur'an and none but Allah (Alone) knows their meanings.] [This is the] Book [the Qur'an] sent down unto you [O' Muhammad], so let not your breast be narrow therefrom, that you warn thereby; and a reminder unto the believers. [Say (O' Muhammad) to these idolaters (pagan Arabs) of your folk:] Follow what has been sent down unto you from your Lord [the Qur'an and Prophet Muhammad's Sunnah], and follow not any *Awliya'* [protectors and helpers who order you to associate partners in worship with Allah], besides Him [Allah]. Little do you remember!﴿ *(Qur'an 7: 1-3)*

The Qur'an is the only divinely-revealed Book by means of which we may reach Allah after the coming of the Messenger (ﷺ). The Messenger (ﷺ) said, addressing his Companions,

> "Rejoice, for this Qur'an is in the hand of Allah, and its edge is in your hands, so adhere firmly to it, for you will never be destroyed and will never go astray after this."

- This is narrated by Ṭabaraani in *Al-Kabeer.*[1]

The Qur'an gives protection against going astray and against doom for the one who adheres to it. The Messenger (ﷺ) often urged the ummah to adhere to this Book. In one of his sermons he said:

---

[1] A *ṣaḥeeḥ* hadith; *Ṣaḥeeḥ al-Jaami'*, 1/66.

> "O' people, I am only a human being, and soon the messenger of my Lord will come and I will respond. I am leaving among you two things, the first of which is the Book of Allah, in which there is guidance and light. Whoever adheres to it and follows it will be guided, and whoever turns away from it will go astray. So follow the Book of Allah and cling to it. And the members of my household, I remind you of Allah with regard to the members of my household, I remind you of Allah with regard to the members of my household." This is narrated by Muslim and Aḥmad.[2]

The trials that the Muslim faces and with which the ummah is beset can only be gotten rid of by adhering to this Book. How beautiful the following description of the Book of Allah is: "The Book of Allah, in which there is news of those who came before you, news of what will happen after you are gone, rulings concerning matters between you. It is the distinguisher and is not jesting. If any overweening person abandons it Allah will break him, and if anyone seeks guidance elsewhere Allah will lead him astray. It is the strong rope of Allah, it is the wise reminder, it is the straight path, it is that by which the desires do not swerve nor the tongues become confused, and the learned cannot grasp it completely. It does not become worn out by repetition and its wonders do not come to an end. Whoever speaks in accordance with it speaks the truth, whoever acts in accordance with it will be rewarded, whoever judges according to it will be just, and whoever calls people towards it calls them to the straight path."[3]

---

[2] *Ṣaḥeeḥ al-Jaami'*, 1/426.

[3] This hadith is narrated by Tirmidhi and others. *Shaykh* Naaṣir said concerning it (*Sharḥ aṭ-Ṭaḥaawiyah*, Pp. 68): This is a hadith whose meaning is very good, but its isnad is *ḍa'eef* (weak). It includes Al-Ḥaarith al-A'war, who is *layyin*, and indeed some of the Imams accused him of lying. Perhaps the original version of this hadith was *mawqoof* 'Ala 'Ali and Al-Ḥaarith made a mistake by attributing it to the Prophet (ﷺ).

CHAPTER TWO
COMPARISON BETWEEN THE MESSAGES

1 - THEIR SOURCE AND THE PURPOSE BEHIND THEIR REVELATION

The divinely-revealed books all came from one source:

﴿ الٓمٓ ۝١ ٱللَّهُ لَآ إِلَٰهَ إِلَّا هُوَ ٱلْحَىُّ ٱلْقَيُّومُ ۝٢ نَزَّلَ عَلَيْكَ ٱلْكِتَٰبَ بِٱلْحَقِّ مُصَدِّقًا لِّمَا بَيْنَ يَدَيْهِ وَأَنزَلَ ٱلتَّوْرَىٰةَ وَٱلْإِنجِيلَ ۝٣ مِن قَبْلُ هُدًى لِّلنَّاسِ وَأَنزَلَ ٱلْفُرْقَانَ ... ۝٤ ﴾

﴿*Alif-Lam-Meem*. [These letters are one of the miracles of the Qur'an, and none but Allah (Alone) knows their meanings.] Allah! *Laa ilaaha illa Huwa* [none has the right to be worshipped but He], *Al-Ḥayyul-Qayyoom* [the Ever Living, the One Who sustains and protects all that exists]. It is He Who has sent down the Book [the Qur'an] to you [Muhammad] with truth, confirming what came before it. And He sent down the *Tawraat* [Torah] and the *Injeel* [Gospel], aforetime, as a guidance to mankind. And He sent down the criterion [of judgement between right and wrong (this Qur'an)]...﴾

(Qur'an 3: 1-4)

The divinely-revealed books were all revealed for one purpose and with one aim. They were revealed to show the way for mankind to live on this earth, to lead them by means of teachings, directions and guidance. They were revealed to be a spirit and light to revive and illuminate their souls, and to remove their darkness and the darkness of life.

The Qur'an tells in one place the purpose for which Allah sent down the *Tawraat*, *Injeel* and Qur'an, which are the greatest of the Books which were sent down from Allah:

﴿ إِنَّآ أَنزَلۡنَا ٱلتَّوۡرَىٰةَ فِيهَا هُدٗى وَنُورٞۚ يَحۡكُمُ بِهَا ٱلنَّبِيُّونَ ٱلَّذِينَ
أَسۡلَمُواْ لِلَّذِينَ هَادُواْ وَٱلرَّبَّٰنِيُّونَ وَٱلۡأَحۡبَارُ بِمَا ٱسۡتُحۡفِظُواْ مِن كِتَٰبِ
ٱللَّهِ وَكَانُواْ عَلَيۡهِ شُهَدَآءَۚ فَلَا تَخۡشَوُاْ ٱلنَّاسَ وَٱخۡشَوۡنِ وَلَا
تَشۡتَرُواْ بِـَٔايَٰتِي ثَمَنٗا قَلِيلٗاۚ وَمَن لَّمۡ يَحۡكُم بِمَآ أَنزَلَ ٱللَّهُ فَأُوْلَٰٓئِكَ هُمُ
ٱلۡكَٰفِرُونَ (٤٤) وَكَتَبۡنَا عَلَيۡهِمۡ فِيهَآ أَنَّ ٱلنَّفۡسَ بِٱلنَّفۡسِ وَٱلۡعَيۡنَ
بِٱلۡعَيۡنِ وَٱلۡأَنفَ بِٱلۡأَنفِ وَٱلۡأُذُنَ بِٱلۡأُذُنِ وَٱلسِّنَّ بِٱلسِّنِّ وَٱلۡجُرُوحَ
قِصَاصٞۚ فَمَن تَصَدَّقَ بِهِۦ فَهُوَ كَفَّارَةٞ لَّهُۥۚ وَمَن لَّمۡ يَحۡكُم بِمَآ
أَنزَلَ ٱللَّهُ فَأُوْلَٰٓئِكَ هُمُ ٱلظَّٰلِمُونَ (٤٥) وَقَفَّيۡنَا عَلَىٰٓ ءَاثَٰرِهِم بِعِيسَى ٱبۡنِ مَرۡيَمَ
مُصَدِّقٗا لِّمَا بَيۡنَ يَدَيۡهِ مِنَ ٱلتَّوۡرَىٰةِۖ وَءَاتَيۡنَٰهُ ٱلۡإِنجِيلَ فِيهِ هُدٗى وَنُورٞ وَمُصَدِّقٗا
لِّمَا بَيۡنَ يَدَيۡهِ مِنَ ٱلتَّوۡرَىٰةِ وَهُدٗى وَمَوۡعِظَةٗ لِّلۡمُتَّقِينَ (٤٦) وَلۡيَحۡكُمۡ أَهۡلُ
ٱلۡإِنجِيلِ بِمَآ أَنزَلَ ٱللَّهُ فِيهِۚ وَمَن لَّمۡ يَحۡكُم بِمَآ أَنزَلَ ٱللَّهُ فَأُوْلَٰٓئِكَ هُمُ
ٱلۡفَٰسِقُونَ (٤٧) وَأَنزَلۡنَآ إِلَيۡكَ ٱلۡكِتَٰبَ بِٱلۡحَقِّ مُصَدِّقٗا لِّمَا بَيۡنَ يَدَيۡهِ مِنَ
ٱلۡكِتَٰبِ وَمُهَيۡمِنًا عَلَيۡهِۖ فَٱحۡكُم بَيۡنَهُم بِمَآ أَنزَلَ ٱللَّهُۖ وَلَا تَتَّبِعۡ
أَهۡوَآءَهُمۡ عَمَّا جَآءَكَ مِنَ ٱلۡحَقِّۚ لِكُلّٖ جَعَلۡنَا مِنكُمۡ شِرۡعَةٗ وَمِنۡهَاجٗاۚ وَلَوۡ
شَآءَ ٱللَّهُ لَجَعَلَكُمۡ أُمَّةٗ وَٰحِدَةٗ وَلَٰكِن لِّيَبۡلُوَكُمۡ فِي مَآ ءَاتَىٰكُمۡۖ فَٱسۡتَبِقُواْ
ٱلۡخَيۡرَٰتِۚ إِلَى ٱللَّهِ مَرۡجِعُكُمۡ جَمِيعٗا فَيُنَبِّئُكُم بِمَا كُنتُمۡ فِيهِ تَخۡتَلِفُونَ
(٤٨) وَأَنِ ٱحۡكُم بَيۡنَهُم بِمَآ أَنزَلَ ٱللَّهُ وَلَا تَتَّبِعۡ أَهۡوَآءَهُمۡ وَٱحۡذَرۡهُمۡ أَن
يَفۡتِنُوكَ عَنۢ بَعۡضِ مَآ أَنزَلَ ٱللَّهُ إِلَيۡكَۖ فَإِن تَوَلَّوۡاْ فَٱعۡلَمۡ أَنَّمَا يُرِيدُ ٱللَّهُ أَن
يُصِيبَهُم بِبَعۡضِ ذُنُوبِهِمۡۗ وَإِنَّ كَثِيرٗا مِّنَ ٱلنَّاسِ لَفَٰسِقُونَ (٤٩) أَفَحُكۡمَ ٱلۡجَٰهِلِيَّةِ
يَبۡغُونَۚ وَمَنۡ أَحۡسَنُ مِنَ ٱللَّهِ حُكۡمٗا لِّقَوۡمٖ يُوقِنُونَ (٥٠) ﴾

﴿Verily, We did send down the *Tawraat* [Torah] [to Moosa (Moses)], therein was guidance and light, by which the Prophets, who submitted themselves to Allah's Will, judged for the Jews. And the rabbis and the priests [too judged for the Jews by the *Tawraat* (Torah) after those Prophets], for to them was entrusted the protection of Allah's Book, and they were witnesses thereto. Therefore fear not men but fear Me [O' Jews] and sell not My Verses for a miserable price. And whosoever does not judge by what Allah has revealed, such are the *Kaafiroon* [i.e. disbelievers - of a lesser degree as they do not act on Allah's Laws]. And We ordained therein for them: Life for life, eye for eye, nose for nose, ear for ear, tooth for tooth, and wounds equal for equal. But if anyone remits the retaliation by way of charity, it shall be for him an expiation. And whosoever does not judge by that which Allah has revealed, such are the *Ẓaalimoon* [polytheists and wrongdoers - of a lesser degree]. And in their footsteps, We sent 'Eesa [Jesus], son of Maryam [Mary], confirming the *Tawraat* [Torah] that had come before him, and We gave him the *Injeel* [Gospel], in which was guidance and light and confirmation of the *Tawraat* [Torah] that had come before it, a guidance and an admonition for *Al-Muttaqoon* [the pious]. Let the people of the *Injeel* [Gospel] judge by what Allah has revealed therein. And whosoever does not judge by what Allah has revealed [then] such [people] are the *Faasiqoon* [the rebellious i.e. disobedient (of a lesser degree)] to Allah. And We have sent down to you [O' Muhammad] the Book [this Qur'an] in truth, confirming the Scripture that came before it and *Muhaymin* [trustworthy in highness and a witness] over it [old Scriptures]. So judge among them by what Allah has revealed, and follow not their vain desires, diverging away from the truth that has come to you. To each among you, We have prescribed a law and a clear way. If Allah had willed, He would have made you one nation, but that [He] may test you in what He has given you; so compete in good deeds. The return of you [all] is to Allah; then He will inform you about that in which you used to differ. And so judge [you O' Muhammad] among them by what Allah has revealed and follow not their vain desires, but beware of them lest they turn you [O' Muhammad] far away from some of that which Allah has sent down to you. And if they turn away, then know that Allah's Will is to punish them for some sins of theirs. And truly, most of men are *Faasiqoon* [rebellious and disobedient to Allah]. Do they then seek the judgement of [the days of] Ignorance? And who is better in judgement than Allah for a people who have firm Faith.﴾ *(Qur'an 5: 44-50)*

Sayyid Quṭb (may Allah have mercy on him) said concerning the *tafseer* of these *aayaat*:[1] "Every revelation came from Allah to be a way of life, a way of life to be put into practice. Religion came to be in a position of leadership, organizing, directing and protecting human life. Religion did not come to be mere beliefs in the heart or mere rituals to be performed in the temple or place of worship. Beliefs and rituals - even though they are essential to human life and are important in disciplining the human soul - are not enough on their own to lead, organize, direct and protect human life, unless they form the basis of a system and law which is to be applied in a practical sense to people's lives and implemented by the law and the authorities, and people are taken to task for breaking the laws and are punished when necessary.

Human life cannot be sound unless it receives beliefs, rituals, and laws from one source which has power over people's hearts and

[1] *Fi Ẓilaal al-Qur'an*, Pp. 895.

minds, as well as over their actions and behaviour, which rewards or punishes people according to His laws in this world and rewards or punishes them according to His Reckoning in the Hereafter.

If there is more than one source (of guidance and teachings), when authority is divided and authority is given to Allah only with regard to hearts and minds, whilst authority is given to someone other than Him with regard to systems and laws, when authority is given to Allah with regard only to reward and punishment in the Hereafter whilst authority is given to someone other than Him with regard to punishments in this world, then the human soul is fragmented and split between two different authorities, between two different directions, between two different systems. Then human life becomes corrupt in the manner indicated in various places in the Qur'an:

﴿ لَوْ كَانَ فِيهِمَآ ءَالِهَةٌ إِلَّا ٱللَّهُ لَفَسَدَتَا ... ﴿٢٢﴾ ﴾

> ﴾Had there been therein [in the heavens and the earth] *aalihah* [gods] besides Allah, then verily, both would have been ruined...﴿ *(Qur'an 21: 22)*

﴿ وَلَوِ ٱتَّبَعَ ٱلْحَقُّ أَهْوَآءَهُمْ لَفَسَدَتِ ٱلسَّمَٰوَٰتُ وَٱلْأَرْضُ وَمَن فِيهِنَّ ... ﴿٧١﴾ ﴾

> ﴾And if the truth had been in accordance with their desires, verily, the heavens and the earth, and whosoever is therein would have been corrupted!...﴿ *(Qur'an 23: 71)*

﴿ ثُمَّ جَعَلْنَٰكَ عَلَىٰ شَرِيعَةٍ مِّنَ ٱلْأَمْرِ فَٱتَّبِعْهَا وَلَا تَتَّبِعْ أَهْوَآءَ ٱلَّذِينَ لَا يَعْلَمُونَ ﴿١٨﴾ ﴾

> ﴾Then We have put you [O' Muhammad] on a [plain] way of [Our] commandment [like the one which We commanded Our Messengers before you (i.e. legal ways and laws of the Islamic Monotheism)]. So follow you

that [Islamic Monotheism and its laws], and follow not the desires of those who know not.﴿ *(Qur'an 45: 18)*

For this reason every revelation came from Allah to be a way of life, whether this revelation came to a town or a nation, or to all of mankind throughout all generations. It brought particular laws to deal with the realities of life, as well as the belief which creates the proper concept of life and the rituals of worship which connect people's hearts to Allah... These three aspects form the basic principles of every revelation that came from Allah because human life cannot be right or proper unless the religion of Allah is the way of life.

In the Qur'an there is a great deal of evidence to show that the early revelations, which came to some town or tribe, contained all three elements in a form that was suited to the stage through which that town or tribe was passing. This *aayah* (verse) explains the fact that these elements were present in the three major religions, namely Judaism, Christianity and Islam.

The *aayah* which we are discussing starts by mentioning the *Tawraat*:

﴿ إِنَّآ أَنزَلْنَا ٱلتَّوْرَىٰةَ فِيهَا هُدًى وَنُورٌ ... ﴿٤٤﴾ ﴾

﴾Verily, We did send down the *Tawraat* [Torah] [to Moosa (Moses)], therein was guidance and light...﴿
(Qur'an 5: 44)

The *Tawraat* - as it was revealed by Allah - is the Book of Allah which came to guide the Children of Israel and to light their way to Allah throughout life. It came bearing the message of *Tawḥeed* and various rituals of worship, and the law:

﴿ ... يَحْكُمُ بِهَا ٱلنَّبِيُّونَ ٱلَّذِينَ أَسْلَمُوا۟ لِلَّذِينَ هَادُوا۟ وَٱلرَّبَّـٰنِيُّونَ وَٱلْأَحْبَارُ بِمَا ٱسْتُحْفِظُوا۟ مِن كِتَـٰبِ ٱللَّهِ وَكَانُوا۟ عَلَيْهِ شُهَدَآءَ ... ﴿٤٤﴾ ﴾

﴾...By which the Prophets, who submitted themselves to Allah's Will, judged for the Jews. And the rabbis and the priests [too judged for the Jews by the *Tawraat* (Torah) after those Prophets], for to them was entrusted the protection of Allah's Book, and they were witnesses thereto...﴿ *(Qur'an 5: 44)*

Allah (ﷻ) sent down the *Tawraat* not only to be a guide and a light for hearts in the area of belief and acts of worship, but also to be a guide and a light through its laws which were to be put into practice in real life according to the way of Allah, and to protect this life within the framework of this system. The Prophets who submitted themselves to Allah were to judge according to it, for they made no claims for themselves, rather it was all for Allah. They had no say, no authority and no claim to any divine attributes. This is Islam in the true sense of the word, by which the Prophets led the Jews. This was their own law which was revealed to them to be applied to their circumstances and according to which their rabbis - who were their judges and scholars - were to judge them. They were entrusted with preserving the Book of Allah, and to be witnesses thereto, and to bear witness to it in themselves by shaping their private lives in accordance with its teachings, just as they were entrusted to bear witness to it among their people by implementing its laws among them..."

Without the divinely-revealed Message, mankind becomes divided and lost, unable to agree upon a way:

﴿ كَانَ ٱلنَّاسُ أُمَّةً وَٰحِدَةً فَبَعَثَ ٱللَّهُ ٱلنَّبِيِّـۧنَ مُبَشِّرِينَ وَمُنذِرِينَ وَأَنزَلَ مَعَهُمُ ٱلْكِتَٰبَ بِٱلْحَقِّ لِيَحْكُمَ بَيْنَ ٱلنَّاسِ فِيمَا ٱخْتَلَفُوا۟ فِيهِ ... ﴿٢١٣﴾ ﴾

﴾Mankind were one community and Allah sent Prophets with glad tidings and warnings, and with them He sent down the Scripture in truth to judge between people in matters wherein they differed...﴿ *(Qur'an 2: 213)*

2 - THE GENERAL MESSAGE AND THE SPECIFIC MESSAGE

The previous Divinely-revealed Messages were sent to specific peoples, but the final Message which was revealed to the Seal of the Prophets and Messengers was a general Message for all of mankind. This implies that this Message should be distinct from other Messages in a manner that makes it suitable for all times and places. Allah (ﷻ) has made it so; He revealed to His Messenger (ﷺ) just before he died:

﴿ ... ٱلْيَوْمَ أَكْمَلْتُ لَكُمْ دِينَكُمْ وَأَتْمَمْتُ عَلَيْكُمْ نِعْمَتِى وَرَضِيتُ لَكُمُ ٱلْإِسْلَٰمَ دِينًا ... ﴿٣﴾ ﴾

> ﴾...This day, I have perfected your religion for you, completed My Favour upon you, and have chosen for you Islam as your religion...﴿ *(Qur'an 5: 3)*

Sayyid Quṭb (may Allah have mercy on him) explained this meaning in his commentary on this verse. He said: "The believer stands before the perfection of this religion, looking at the caravan of faith, the Messages and the Messengers, from the dawn of humanity, from the first of the Messengers - Adam (ﷺ) - to this final Message, the Message of the unlettered Prophet to all of mankind. What does he see? He sees this ongoing caravan, the caravan of guidance and light. He sees the signposts all along the road, but he finds that each Messenger - except the Seal of the Prophets - was sent only to his own people; and he sees that each Message - before the final Message - came at a certain time, a specific Message for a specific group in a specific environment. So all these Messages were tailored to their circumstances and suited to deal with those circumstances. All of them called people to One God - which is *Tawḥeed* - and all of them called people to submit themselves solely to this One God - which is Islam. But each of them had a law to be implemented in real life that was suited to that group, that environment, that time and those circumstances.

Until, when Allah willed to conclude His Message to mankind, He sent to all of mankind a Messenger, the Seal of the Prophets, with a Message for mankind, not for a group or a people in a specific environment, at a specific time, in specific circumstances... a message for mankind that transcends circumstances, environment and time, because it is addressed to human nature which does not alter or change.

﴿ ... فِطْرَتَ ٱللَّهِ ٱلَّتِى فَطَرَ ٱلنَّاسَ عَلَيْهَا ۚ لَا تَبْدِيلَ لِخَلْقِ ٱللَّهِ ۚ ذَٰلِكَ ٱلدِّينُ ٱلْقَيِّمُ ... ﴿٣٠﴾ ﴾

﴾...Allah's *Fiṭrah* [i.e. Allah's Islamic Monotheism] with which He has created mankind. No change let there be in *Khalq-illaah* [i.e. the religion of Allah - Islamic Monotheism], that is the straight religion...﴿

(Qur'an 30: 30)

In this Message, He sent a detailed law which deals with all aspects of human life and activity, setting out holistic principles and general rules with regard to matters which develop and alter according to time and place, and detailed rulings and laws with regard to matters which do not develop and alter according to time and place. Thus shari'ah, with its holistic principles and detailed rulings includes all the rules, directions, laws and systems that human life needs, from the time this Message was revealed until the end of time, in order to continue, grow, develop and renew itself around this idea and within this framework."[2]

This meaning - the perfect and comprehensive nature of the Message - is referred to in more than one place in the Qur'an, for example:

---

[2] *Fi Ẓilaal al-Qur'an*, 6/482.

﴿ ... وَنَزَّلْنَا عَلَيْكَ ٱلْكِتَـٰبَ تِبْيَـٰنًا لِّكُلِّ شَىْءٍ ... ﴿٨٩﴾ ﴾

﴾...And We have sent down to you the Book [the Qur'an] as an exposition of everything...﴿ *(Qur'an 16: 89)*

﴿ ... مَّا فَرَّطْنَا فِى ٱلْكِتَـٰبِ مِن شَىْءٍ ... ﴿٣٨﴾ ﴾

﴾...We have neglected nothing in the Book...﴿ *(Qur'an 6: 38)*

The final law incorporated the beauties of the former Messages, and surpassed them in perfection and glory. Al-Ḥasan al-Baṣri said: "Allah revealed one hundred and four Books, all the knowledge of which was gathered in four: the *Tawraat*, the *Injeel*, the *Zaboor* and *Al-Furqaan* (the Qur'an). Then the knowledge of the three was gathered in the Qur'an."[3]

3 - PRESERVATION OF THE MESSAGES

Because the previous messages were connected to a particular time, they were not eternal and would not abide. So Allah (ﷻ) did not guarantee to preserve them. The task of preserving them was entrusted to the scholars of the nation to which they were sent. So the preservation of the *Tawraat* (Torah) was entrusted to the rabbis and priests:

﴿ ... وَٱلرَّبَّـٰنِيُّونَ وَٱلْأَحْبَارُ بِمَا ٱسْتُحْفِظُوا۟ مِن كِتَـٰبِ ٱللَّهِ وَكَانُوا۟ عَلَيْهِ شُهَدَآءَ ... ﴿٤٤﴾ ﴾

﴾...And the rabbis and the priests [too judged for the Jews by the *Tawraat* (Torah) after those Prophets], for to them was entrusted the protection of Allah's Book, and they were witnesses thereto.﴿ *(Qur'an 5: 44)*

---

[3] *Al-Ikleel* by As-Suyooṭi (*Aḍwaa' al-Bayaan*, 3/336).

But the rabbis and priests were unable to preserve their Books. Some of them betrayed the trust by changing, altering and distorting them. It is sufficient for you to look at the Torah to see the alterations and changes in it, not only with regard to minor issues but also with regard to basic matters. They attributed to Allah things which make one's flesh crawl, and they attributed to the Messengers things which even the riffraff would hate to have attributed to them.[4]

But in the case of the final Message, He Himself guaranteed to preserve it, and He did not entrust that task to human beings. Allah (ﷻ) said:

﴿ إِنَّا نَحْنُ نَزَّلْنَا ٱلذِّكْرَ وَإِنَّا لَهُۥ لَحَٰفِظُونَ ۝٩ ﴾

> ﴿Verily, We, it is We Who have sent down the *Dhikr* [i.e. the Qur'an] and surely, We will guard it [from corruption].﴾ *(Qur'an 15: 9)*

---

[4] We have described some of the fabrications which the Jews made against Allah in the first part of this series, and we have described some of their fabrications against the Messengers in Part One [of this book], The Messengers. Here I will give one example of the distortions of the Jews, one which makes the Torah contradict itself. The original text of the Torah is, "Take your only son, whom you love, and sacrifice him." This son was Ismaa'eel (Ishmael), but the Jews could not bear to see this honour being given to Ismaa'eel and his descendents, the Arabs, so they inserted the word "Isaac" into the text, so as to attribute this honour to themselves. So the text in the distorted Torah which they have in their possession today says, "Take your son, your only son Isaac, whom you love... [and] sacrifice him." (Genesis 22:2 NIV). But the one who altered this text did not notice that it contradicts other texts in the Torah. For it was narrated in the Torah that Ishmael was born when Abraham was eighty-six years old (see Genesis 16), therefore Ishmael was the only son. With regard to Isaac, the Torah says that when he was born, "Abraham was a hundred years old when his son Isaac was born to him." (Genesis 21:5) Do you not see how Allah exposes their trickery and plots, and shows their distortions and alterations? I mentioned some of this tampering in the chapter on the evidence of the truth of the Messengers.

If you look at this world nowadays, east and west, you will find huge numbers of people who have memorized the Qur'an by heart,[5] such that even if a heretic, Jew or Crusader wanted to change a single letter of it, a young boy, a housewife or an old woman who cannot see her way would be able to correct him and point out where he had gone wrong or fabricated something, let alone the scholars who have committed it to memory, understood its meanings and are filled with knowledge of it.

Look at the history of this Book, and how much care and attention was devoted to its compilation, commentary, grammar, stories, news and rulings.

None of this could have happened, were it not for that divine protection. This Book will remain until Allah decrees that this universe should come to an end and be destroyed.

4 - SIMILARITIES AND DIFFERENCES BETWEEN THE DIVINELY-REVEALED MESSAGES

The One Religion

The Messages which were brought by the Prophets were all revealed from Allah, the All-Knowing, Most Wise, All-Aware. Hence they represent one way to be followed by earlier and later generations alike. When examining the call of the Messengers which is referred to in the Qur'an, we find that the religion to which all the Messengers called people is one and the same, namely Islam:

﴿ إِنَّ ٱلدِّينَ عِندَ ٱللَّهِ ٱلْإِسْلَٰمُ ... ﴿١٩﴾ ﴾

---

[5] One of the reasons why it has been preserved is that Allah has made the Qur'an easy to recite and to memorize: ﴿And We have indeed made the Qur'an easy to understand and remember; then is there any that will remember [or receive admonition]?﴾ *(Qur'an 54: 22)*

﴿Truly, the religion with Allah is Islam...﴾ *(Qur'an 3: 19)*

Islam in the language of the Qur'an, is not the name of a particular religion, rather it is the name of the common religion which was preached by all the Prophets. Prophet Nooḥ (Noah) (ﷺ) said to his people:

﴿ ... وَأُمِرْتُ أَنْ أَكُونَ مِنَ ٱلْمُسْلِمِينَ ﴿٧٢﴾ ﴾

﴿...And I have been commanded to be of the Muslims [i.e. those who submit to Allah's Will].﴾ *(Qur'an 10: 72)*

Islam is the religion which Allah enjoined upon the father of the Prophets, Prophet Ibraaheem (Abraham) (ﷺ):

﴿ إِذْ قَالَ لَهُۥ رَبُّهُۥٓ أَسْلِمْ ۖ قَالَ أَسْلَمْتُ لِرَبِّ ٱلْعَٰلَمِينَ ﴿١٣١﴾ ﴾

﴿When his Lord said to him, 'Submit [i.e. be a Muslim]!' He said, 'I have submitted myself [as a Muslim] to the Lord of the *'Aalameen* [mankind, jinn and all that exists].'﴾ *(Qur'an 2: 131)*

Both Prophet Ibraaheem and Ya'qoob advised their children, saying,

﴿ ... فَلَا تَمُوتُنَّ إِلَّا وَأَنتُم مُّسْلِمُونَ ﴿١٣٢﴾ ﴾

﴿...Then die not except in the Faith of Islam [as Muslims - Islamic Monotheism].﴾ *(Qur'an 2: 132)*

The sons of Prophet Ya'qoob (ﷺ) responded to their father:

﴿ ... نَعْبُدُ إِلَٰهَكَ وَإِلَٰهَ ءَابَآئِكَ إِبْرَٰهِـۧمَ وَإِسْمَٰعِيلَ وَإِسْحَٰقَ إِلَٰهًا وَٰحِدًا
وَنَحْنُ لَهُۥ مُسْلِمُونَ ﴿١٣٣﴾ ﴾

﴿...We shall worship your *Ilaah* [God - Allah] the *Ilah* [God] of your fathers, Ibraaheem [Abraham], Ismaa'eel [Ishmael], Isḥaaq [Isaac], One *Ilah* [God], and to Him we submit [in Islam].﴾ *(Qur'an 2: 133)*

Prophet Moosa (Moses) (ﷺ) said to his people:

﴿ ... يَٰقَوۡمِ إِن كُنتُمۡ ءَامَنتُم بِٱللَّهِ فَعَلَيۡهِ تَوَكَّلُوٓاْ إِن كُنتُم مُّسۡلِمِينَ ٨٤ ﴾

﴾...O' my people! If you have believed in Allah, then put your trust in Him if you are Muslims [those who submit to Allah's Will].﴿ *(Qur'an 10: 84)*

The Disciples said to Prophet 'Eesa (Jesus) (ﷺ):

﴿ ... ءَامَنَّا بِٱللَّهِ وَٱشۡهَدۡ بِأَنَّا مُسۡلِمُونَ ٥٢ ﴾

﴾...We believe in Allah, and bear witness that we are Muslims [i.e. we submit to Allah].﴿ *(Qur'an 3: 52)*

When a group of the People of the Book heard the Qur'an,

﴿ ... قَالُوٓاْ ءَامَنَّا بِهِۦٓ إِنَّهُ ٱلۡحَقُّ مِن رَّبِّنَآ إِنَّا كُنَّا مِن قَبۡلِهِۦ مُسۡلِمِينَ ٥٣ ﴾

﴾...They say: 'We believe in it. Verily, it is the truth from our Lord. Indeed even before it we have been from those who submit themselves to Allah in Islam as Muslims.'﴿ *(Qur'an 28: 53)*

Islam was the common word which was spoken by all the Prophets and their followers from the most ancient of times until the time of the Prophet Muhammad (ﷺ).

How to determine Islam

Islam means obedience, surrender and submission to Allah, by doing that which He commands and abstaining from that which He forbids. Hence, Islam at the time of Prophet Nooḥ (Noah) meant following that which Nooḥ brought. Islam at the time of Prophet Moosa (Moses) meant following the Law of Moosa. Islam at the time of Prophet 'Eesa (Jesus) meant following the *Injeel*. And Islam at the time of Muhammad (ﷺ) meant following the Noble Messenger (ﷺ).

The essence of the Messengers' call

The essence of the call of the Messengers and the Divinely-revealed messages is the call to worship Allah alone, with no partner or associate, and forsaking anything that is worshipped besides Him. The Qur'an discussed this topic and confirmed it in numerous places. Sometimes it mentions the call of the Messengers: so Prophet Nooḥ (Noah) (ﷺ) said to his people:

﴿... يَٰقَوۡمِ ٱعۡبُدُواْ ٱللَّهَ مَا لَكُم مِّنۡ إِلَٰهٍ غَيۡرُهُۥٓ ... ﴿٥٩﴾﴾

﴿...O' my people! Worship Allah! You have no other *Ilah* [God] but Him...﴾ *(Qur'an 7: 59)*

And Prophet Ibraaheem said to his people:

﴿... ٱعۡبُدُواْ ٱللَّهَ وَٱتَّقُوهُۖ ذَٰلِكُمۡ خَيۡرٞ لَّكُمۡ إِن كُنتُمۡ تَعۡلَمُونَ ﴿١٦﴾﴾

﴿...Worship Allah [Alone], and fear Him: that is better for you if you did but know.﴾ *(Qur'an 29: 16)*

And Prophet Hood said to his people:

﴿... يَٰقَوۡمِ ٱعۡبُدُواْ ٱللَّهَ مَا لَكُم مِّنۡ إِلَٰهٍ غَيۡرُهُۥٓ ... ﴿٦٥﴾﴾

﴿...O' my people! Worship Allah! You have no other *Ilah* [God] but Him...﴾ *(Qur'an 7: 65)*

and Prophet Ṣaaliḥ said to his people:

﴿... يَٰقَوۡمِ ٱعۡبُدُواْ ٱللَّهَ مَا لَكُم مِّنۡ إِلَٰهٍ غَيۡرُهُۥۖ ... ﴿٧٣﴾﴾

﴿...O' my people! Worship Allah! You have no other *Ilah* [God] but Him...﴾ *(Qur'an 7: 73)*

Sometimes the Qur'an tells us that Allah sent all the Messengers with one mission:

﴿ وَمَآ أَرْسَلْنَا مِن قَبْلِكَ مِن رَّسُولٍ إِلَّا نُوحِىٓ إِلَيْهِ أَنَّهُۥ لَآ إِلَٰهَ إِلَّآ أَنَا۠ فَٱعْبُدُونِ ﴿٢٥﴾ ﴾

﴾And We did not send any Messenger before you [O' Muhammad] but We revealed to him [saying]: *'Laa ilaaha illa Ana* [none has the right to be worshipped but I (Allah)], so worship Me [Alone and none else].'﴿ *(Qur'an 21: 25)*

Sometimes it narrates the stories of the Prophets and the Messengers, all following the same path, and describes them as being one nation with one God:

﴿ إِنَّ هَٰذِهِۦٓ أُمَّتُكُمْ أُمَّةً وَٰحِدَةً وَأَنَا۠ رَبُّكُمْ فَٱعْبُدُونِ ﴿٩٢﴾ ﴾

﴾Truly, this, your Ummah [Shari'ah or religion (Islamic Monotheism)] is one religion, and I am your Lord, therefore worship Me [Alone].﴿ *(Qur'an 21: 92)*

Sometimes it describes responding to Allah and becoming truly enslaved to Him as being the true religion and describes those who reject that to have judged themselves to be misguided fools:

﴿ وَمَن يَرْغَبُ عَن مِّلَّةِ إِبْرَٰهِۦمَ إِلَّا مَن سَفِهَ نَفْسَهُۥ ... ﴿١٣٠﴾ ﴾

﴾And who turns away from the religion of Ibraaheem [Abraham] [i.e. Islamic Monotheism] except him who befools himself?...﴿ *(Qur'an 2: 130)*

And the religion of Prophet Ibraaheem is defined as:

﴿ إِنِّى وَجَّهْتُ وَجْهِىَ لِلَّذِى فَطَرَ ٱلسَّمَٰوَٰتِ وَٱلْأَرْضَ حَنِيفًا ۖ وَمَآ أَنَا۠ مِنَ ٱلْمُشْرِكِينَ ﴿٧٩﴾ ﴾

﴾Verily, I have turned my face towards Him Who has created the heavens and the earth *Ḥaneefa* [Islamic

Monotheism, i.e. worshipping none but Allah Alone], and I am not of *Al-Mushrikoon.*﴿ *(Qur'an 6: 79)*

Sometimes it explains that this was the advice that the Messengers and Prophets gave to those who came after them:

﴿ أَمْ كُنتُمْ شُهَدَآءَ إِذْ حَضَرَ يَعْقُوبَ ٱلْمَوْتُ إِذْ قَالَ لِبَنِيهِ مَا تَعْبُدُونَ مِنۢ بَعْدِى قَالُوا۟ نَعْبُدُ إِلَٰهَكَ وَإِلَٰهَ ءَابَآئِكَ إِبْرَٰهِـۧمَ وَإِسْمَٰعِيلَ وَإِسْحَٰقَ إِلَٰهًا وَٰحِدًا ... ﴿١٣٣﴾ ﴾

﴾Or were you witnesses when death approached Ya'qoob [Jacob]? When he said unto his sons, 'What will you worship after me?' They said, 'We shall worship your *Ilah* [God - Allah] the *Ilah* [God] of your fathers, Ibraaheem [Abraham], Ismaa'eel [Ishmael], Isḥaaq [Isaac], One *Ilah* [God]...'﴿[6]

(Qur'an 2: 133)

And sometimes it states that the religion brought by the great Messengers is one:

---

[6] It is narrated in the Sunnah that Prophet Nooḥ (Noah) advised his son in similar terms. It is narrated that 'Abdullah ibn 'Amr said: the Messenger of Allah (ﷺ) said: "The Prophet of Allah Nooḥ (عليه السلام), when death was approaching, said to his son: 'I am advising you, I will enjoin upon you two things and forbid you to do two things. I enjoin upon you *'Laa ilaaha ill-Allah'*, for if the seven heavens and the seven earths were to be placed in one pan (of a balance) and *'Laa ilaaha ill-Allah'* were to be placed in the other pan, they would be outweighed by *'Laa ilaaha ill-Allah'*. If the seven heavens and the seven earths were a closed circle, it would be broken by *'Laa ilaaha ill-Allah'*. [And I enjoin upon you] *'Subḥaan Allah wa bi ḥamdihi'* (glory and praise be to Allah), for this is the prayer of all things, and by it creation receives its provision. And I forbid you to engage in *shirk* and arrogance.'" This is narrated by Bukhari: *Al-Adab al-Mufrad*, Pp. 548; Aḥmad: 2/169, 170, 225; Al-Bayhaqi: *Al-Asma'*, 79 (Indian edn.). See *Silsilat al-Aḥaadeeth aṣ-Ṣaḥeeḥah*, hadith no. 134.

﴿ شَرَعَ لَكُم مِّنَ ٱلدِّينِ مَا وَصَّىٰ بِهِۦ نُوحًا وَٱلَّذِىٓ أَوْحَيْنَآ إِلَيْكَ وَمَا وَصَّيْنَا بِهِۦٓ إِبْرَٰهِيمَ وَمُوسَىٰ وَعِيسَىٰٓ أَنْ أَقِيمُوا۟ ٱلدِّينَ وَلَا تَتَفَرَّقُوا۟ فِيهِ ... ﴿١٣﴾ ﴾

﴿He [Allah] has ordained for you the same religion [Islamic Monotheism] which He ordained for Nooḥ [Noah], and that which We have revealed to you [O' Muhammad], and that which We ordained for Ibraaheem [Abraham], Moosa [Moses and 'Eesa [Jesus] saying you should establish religion [i.e. to do what it orders you to do practically] and make no divisions in it [religion] [i.e. various sects in religion]...﴾ *(Qur'an 42: 13)*

The previous Messages describe the reasons which oblige us to worship Allah

The previous Messages did not only propagate the worship of Allah (ﷻ) Alone, they also explained the reasons which make this call the truth which no one can deny, by listing the Divine characteristics and speaking of the blessings of Allah which He has bestowed upon His slaves, and by directing man's sight and mind to look into the realms of the heavens and the earth. So Prophet Nooḥ said to his people:

﴿ مَّا لَكُمْ لَا تَرْجُونَ لِلَّهِ وَقَارًا ﴿١٣﴾ وَقَدْ خَلَقَكُمْ أَطْوَارًا ﴿١٤﴾ أَلَمْ تَرَوْا۟ كَيْفَ خَلَقَ ٱللَّهُ سَبْعَ سَمَٰوَٰتٍ طِبَاقًا ﴿١٥﴾ وَجَعَلَ ٱلْقَمَرَ فِيهِنَّ نُورًا وَجَعَلَ ٱلشَّمْسَ سِرَاجًا ﴿١٦﴾ وَٱللَّهُ أَنۢبَتَكُم مِّنَ ٱلْأَرْضِ نَبَاتًا ﴿١٧﴾ ثُمَّ يُعِيدُكُمْ فِيهَا وَيُخْرِجُكُمْ إِخْرَاجًا ﴿١٨﴾ وَٱللَّهُ جَعَلَ لَكُمُ ٱلْأَرْضَ بِسَاطًا ﴿١٩﴾ لِّتَسْلُكُوا۟ مِنْهَا سُبُلًا فِجَاجًا ﴿٢٠﴾ ﴾

﴿What is the matter with you, that [you fear not Allah (His punishment), and] you hope not for reward [from Allah or you believe not in His Oneness]. While He has created you in [different] stages. See you not how Allah has created the seven heavens one above another? And has made the moon a light therein, and made the sun a lamp? And Allah has brought you forth from the [dust of] earth? Afterwards He will return you into it [the earth], and bring you forth [again on the Day of Resurrection)? And Allah has made for you the earth a wide expanse. That you may go about therein in broad roads.﴾ *(Qur'an 71: 13-20)*

This message was repeated in the scriptures of Prophets Ibraaheem and Moosa, as the Qur'an tells us:

﴿وَأَنَّ إِلَىٰ رَبِّكَ ٱلْمُنتَهَىٰ ﴿٤٢﴾ وَأَنَّهُۥ هُوَ أَضْحَكَ وَأَبْكَىٰ ﴿٤٣﴾ وَأَنَّهُۥ هُوَ
أَمَاتَ وَأَحْيَا ﴿٤٤﴾ وَأَنَّهُۥ خَلَقَ ٱلزَّوْجَيْنِ ٱلذَّكَرَ وَٱلْأُنثَىٰ ﴿٤٥﴾ مِن نُّطْفَةٍ إِذَا تُمْنَىٰ
﴿٤٦﴾ وَأَنَّ عَلَيْهِ ٱلنَّشْأَةَ ٱلْأُخْرَىٰ ﴿٤٧﴾ وَأَنَّهُۥ هُوَ أَغْنَىٰ وَأَقْنَىٰ ﴿٤٨﴾ وَأَنَّهُۥ هُوَ رَبُّ
ٱلشِّعْرَىٰ ﴿٤٩﴾ وَأَنَّهُۥٓ أَهْلَكَ عَادًا ٱلْأُولَىٰ ﴿٥٠﴾ وَثَمُودَا۟ فَمَآ أَبْقَىٰ ﴿٥١﴾ وَقَوْمَ نُوحٍ
مِّن قَبْلُ ۖ إِنَّهُمْ كَانُوا۟ هُمْ أَظْلَمَ وَأَطْغَىٰ ﴿٥٢﴾﴾

﴿And that to your Lord [Allah] is the End [Return of everything]. And that it is He [Allah] Who makes [whom He wills] laugh, and makes [whom He wills] weep. And that it is He [Allah] Who causes death and gives life. And that He [Allah] creates the pairs, male and female, From *Nutfah* [drops of semen male and female discharges] when it is emitted. And that upon Him [Allah] is another bringing forth [Resurrection]. And that it is He [Allah] Who gives much or a little [of wealth and contentment]. And that He [Allah] is the Lord of Sirius [the star which the pagan Arabs used to worship]. And that it is He [Allah] Who destroyed the former 'Aad [people], and Thamood [people]. He spared none of them. And the people of Nooḥ [Noah] aforetime. Verily, they were more unjust and more rebellious and transgressing [in disobeying Allah and His Messenger Nooḥ [Noah].﴾ *(Qur'an 53: 42-52)*

ETERNAL PRINCIPLES

Matters of belief

The call to worship Allah (ﷻ) alone is not the only matter on which the messages are agreed. There are many points which they have in common, for example the matters of belief which include one concept and one basis for all the Messengers and their followers. The first of the Messengers, Nooḥ (Noah) (ﷺ), reminded his people of the Resurrection, as he said to them:

﴿ وَٱللَّهُ أَنۢبَتَكُم مِّنَ ٱلْأَرْضِ نَبَاتًا ﴿١٧﴾ ثُمَّ يُعِيدُكُمْ فِيهَا وَيُخْرِجُكُمْ إِخْرَاجًا ﴿١٨﴾ ﴾

﴿And Allah has brought you forth from the [dust of] earth? Afterwards He will return you into it [the earth], and bring you forth [again on the Day of Resurrection]?﴾ *(Qur'an 71: 17-18)*

He told them about the angels and the jinn, hence the *kuffaar* among his people said:

﴿ ... مَا هَٰذَآ إِلَّا بَشَرٌ مِّثْلُكُمْ يُرِيدُ أَن يَتَفَضَّلَ عَلَيْكُمْ وَلَوْ شَآءَ ٱللَّهُ لَأَنزَلَ مَلَٰٓئِكَةً مَّا سَمِعْنَا بِهَٰذَا فِىٓ ءَابَآئِنَا ٱلْأَوَّلِينَ ﴿٢٤﴾ إِنْ هُوَ إِلَّا رَجُلٌۢ بِهِۦ جِنَّةٌ ... ﴿٢٥﴾ ﴾

﴿...He is no more than a human being like you, he seeks to make himself superior to you. Had Allah willed, He surely, could have sent down angels. Never did we hear such a thing among our fathers of old. He is only a man in whom is madness...﴾ *(Qur'an 23: 24-25)*

Belief in the Last Day was clearly a part of the faith of Prophet Ibraaheem (Abraham):

﴿... رَبِّ ٱجْعَلْ هَٰذَا بَلَدًا ءَامِنًا وَٱرْزُقْ أَهْلَهُۥ مِنَ ٱلثَّمَرَٰتِ مَنْ ءَامَنَ مِنْهُم بِٱللَّهِ
وَٱلْيَوْمِ ٱلْءَاخِرِ ۖ قَالَ وَمَن كَفَرَ فَأُمَتِّعُهُۥ قَلِيلًا ثُمَّ أَضْطَرُّهُۥٓ إِلَىٰ عَذَابِ ٱلنَّارِ ۖ وَبِئْسَ
ٱلْمَصِيرُ ﴿١٢٦﴾﴾

﴾...'My Lord, make this city [Makkah] a place of security and provide its people with fruits, such of them as believe in Allah and the Last Day.' He [Allah] answered: 'As for him who disbelieves, I shall leave him in contentment for a while, then I shall compel him to the torment of the Fire, and worst indeed is that destination.'﴿ *(Qur'an 2: 126)*

It is more clear in the call of Prophet Moosa (Moses), hence we see that when the sorcerers fell down in prostration, they said to Pharaoh:

﴿إِنَّآ ءَامَنَّا بِرَبِّنَا لِيَغْفِرَ لَنَا خَطَٰيَٰنَا وَمَآ أَكْرَهْتَنَا عَلَيْهِ مِنَ ٱلسِّحْرِ ۗ وَٱللَّهُ خَيْرٌ
وَأَبْقَىٰٓ ﴿٧٣﴾ إِنَّهُۥ مَن يَأْتِ رَبَّهُۥ مُجْرِمًا فَإِنَّ لَهُۥ جَهَنَّمَ لَا يَمُوتُ فِيهَا وَلَا يَحْيَىٰ
﴿٧٤﴾ وَمَن يَأْتِهِۦ مُؤْمِنًا قَدْ عَمِلَ ٱلصَّٰلِحَٰتِ فَأُو۟لَٰٓئِكَ لَهُمُ ٱلدَّرَجَٰتُ ٱلْعُلَىٰ
﴿٧٥﴾ جَنَّٰتُ عَدْنٍ تَجْرِى مِن تَحْتِهَا ٱلْأَنْهَٰرُ خَٰلِدِينَ فِيهَا ۚ وَذَٰلِكَ جَزَآءُ مَن تَزَكَّىٰ
﴿٧٦﴾﴾

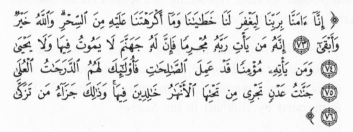

﴾Verily, we have believed in our Lord, that He may forgive us our faults, and the magic to which you did compel us. And Allah is better as regards reward in comparison to your [Fir'awn's (Pharaoh)] reward, and more lasting [as regards punishment in comparison to your punishment]. Verily, whoever comes to his Lord as a *Mujrim* [criminal, polytheist, sinner, disbeliever in the Oneness of Allah and His Messengers], then surely, for him is Hell, wherein he will neither die nor live. But whoever comes to Him [Allah] as a believer [in the Oneness of Allah], and has done righteous good deeds, for such are the high ranks [in the Hereafter], 'Adn [Eden] Paradise [everlasting Gardens], under which rivers flow, wherein they will abide forever: such is the reward of those who purify themselves [by abstaining from all kinds of sins and evil deeds which Allah has forbidden and by doing all that Allah has ordained].﴾ *(Qur'an 20: 73-76)*

In the scripture of Prophets Ibraaheem and Moosa it says:

﴿ بَلْ تُؤْثِرُونَ ٱلْحَيَوٰةَ ٱلدُّنْيَا ﴿١٦﴾ وَٱلْـَٔاخِرَةُ خَيْرٌ وَأَبْقَىٰٓ ﴿١٧﴾ ﴾

﴿Nay, you prefer the life of this world, although the Hereafter is better and more lasting.﴾ *(Qur'an 87: 16-17)*

All the Messengers and Prophets warned their nations about the *Dajjaal* (Pseudo Christ). According to a *ṣaḥeeḥ* hadith narrated from 'Umar (رضي الله عنه), the Prophet (ﷺ) said:

"Allah did not send any Prophet but he warned his nation about the *Dajjaal*. Nooḥ and the Prophets who came after him warned (their nations) about him." - This is narrated by Bukhari in his *Ṣaḥeeḥ*.[7]

General principles

The divinely revealed books affirmed the general principles which mankind must believe in at all times, such as the principle of reward and punishment, which states that man will be called to account for his deeds, and he will be punished for his sins but he will not be brought to task for the sins of others; and he will be rewarded for his efforts, but not for the efforts of others:

---

[7] *Ṣaḥeeḥ al-Jaami'*, 5/133; see also *Fatḥ al-Baari*, 6/370.

﴿ أَمْ لَمْ يُنَبَّأْ بِمَا فِي صُحُفِ مُوسَىٰ ﴿٣٦﴾ وَإِبْرَٰهِيمَ ٱلَّذِى وَفَّىٰٓ ﴿٣٧﴾ أَلَّا تَزِرُ
وَازِرَةٌ وِزْرَ أُخْرَىٰ ﴿٣٨﴾ وَأَن لَّيْسَ لِلْإِنسَٰنِ إِلَّا مَا سَعَىٰ ﴿٣٩﴾ وَأَنَّ سَعْيَهُۥ
سَوْفَ يُرَىٰ ﴿٤٠﴾ ثُمَّ يُجْزَىٰهُ ٱلْجَزَآءَ ٱلْأَوْفَىٰ ﴿٤١﴾ ﴾

﴾Or is he not informed with what is in the Pages [Scripture] of Moosa [Moses], and of Ibraaheem [Abraham] who fulfilled [or conveyed] all that [Allah ordered him to do or convey]: That no burdened person [with sins] shall bear the burden [sins] of another. And that man can have nothing but what he does [good or bad]. And that his deeds will be seen. Then he will be recompensed with a full and the best recompense.﴿ *(Qur'an 53: 36-41)*

So true success can only be achieved by purifying oneself in the manner prescribed by Allah and by becoming totally enslaved to Him, and by giving precedence to the ultimate over the immediate:

﴿ قَدْ أَفْلَحَ مَن تَزَكَّىٰ ﴿١٤﴾ وَذَكَرَ ٱسْمَ رَبِّهِۦ فَصَلَّىٰ ﴿١٥﴾ بَلْ تُؤْثِرُونَ ٱلْحَيَوٰةَ
ٱلدُّنْيَا ﴿١٦﴾ وَٱلْءَاخِرَةُ خَيْرٌ وَأَبْقَىٰٓ ﴿١٧﴾ إِنَّ هَٰذَا لَفِى ٱلصُّحُفِ ٱلْأُولَىٰ ﴿١٨﴾
صُحُفِ إِبْرَٰهِيمَ وَمُوسَىٰ ﴿١٩﴾ ﴾

﴾Indeed whosoever purifies himself [by avoiding polytheism and accepting Islamic Monotheism] shall achieve success, and remembers [glorifies] the Name of his Lord [worships none but Allah], and prays [five compulsory prayers and *Nawaafil* - additional prayers]. Nay, you prefer the life of this world, although the Hereafter is better and more lasting. Verily, this is in the former Scriptures - The Scriptures of Ibraaheem [Abraham] and Moosa [Moses].﴿ *(Qur'an 87: 14-19)*

And those who will deserve to inherit the land are the righteous:

﴿ وَلَقَدْ كَتَبْنَا فِي ٱلزَّبُورِ مِنۢ بَعْدِ ٱلذِّكْرِ أَنَّ ٱلْأَرْضَ يَرِثُهَا عِبَادِيَ ٱلصَّٰلِحُونَ ﴿١٠٥﴾ ﴾

﴾And indeed We have written in *Az-Zaboor* [i.e. all the revealed Holy Books the *Tawraat* (Torah), the *Injeel* (Gospel), the Psalms, the Qur'an] after [We have already written in] *Al-Lawḥ al-Maḥfooẓ* [the Book that is in the heaven with Allah] that My righteous slaves shall inherit the land [i.e. the land of Paradise].﴿ *(Qur'an 21: 105)*

Abu Dharr (رضي الله عنه) asked the Messenger (ﷺ) about what was contained in the scripture of Ibraaheem and the scripture of Moosa. According to the hadith narrated by Ibn Ḥibbaan and Al-Ḥaakim from Abu Dharr, he said: "I said, 'O' Messenger of Allah, what was the scripture of Ibraaheem?' He said,

'It was all proverbs and metaphors: O' ruler who has full authority and who has been tested and deceived, I did not appoint you to accumulate worldly goods but I sent you to respond on My behalf to the call of the oppressed, for I do not reject that call even if it comes from a *kaafir*.
The wise man, if he is in full control of his mental faculties, should find time for certain things: a time for conversing with his Lord, a time for taking stock of himself, a time for pondering the creation of Allah, and a time for meeting his needs for food and drink.
The wise man should not travel except for three reasons: to prepare himself for the Hereafter, to seek provision, or for purposes of pleasure that is not forbidden.
The wise man should be aware of the times in which he lives; he should look after himself; he should restrain his tongue. Whoever counts his words as part of his deeds will speak little, except in matters that are of his concern.'

I said, 'O' Messenger of Allah, what was the scripture of Moosa?' He said,

> 'It was all exhortations (lessons): I find it strange that one who is certain of death would rejoice. I find it strange that one who is certain of Hell would laugh. I find it strange that one who believes in *qadar* (divine decree) would exhaust himself. I find it strange that one who sees this world and its uncertainties would feel safe and be content with it. I find it strange that one who is certain of the Reckoning tomorrow would not strive.'"

The Qur'an tells us that all the Messengers bore the scales of justice and fairness:

﴿ لَقَدْ أَرْسَلْنَا رُسُلَنَا بِٱلْبَيِّنَٰتِ وَأَنزَلْنَا مَعَهُمُ ٱلْكِتَٰبَ وَٱلْمِيزَانَ لِيَقُومَ ٱلنَّاسُ بِٱلْقِسْطِ ... ﴿٢٥﴾ ﴾

> ﴾Indeed We have sent Our Messengers with clear proofs, and revealed with them the Scripture and the Balance [justice] that mankind may keep up justice...﴿
>
> *(Qur'an 57: 25)*

They were commanded to earn their living from permissible sources:

﴿ يَٰٓأَيُّهَا ٱلرُّسُلُ كُلُوا۟ مِنَ ٱلطَّيِّبَٰتِ وَٱعْمَلُوا۟ صَٰلِحًا ... ﴿٥١﴾ ﴾

> ﴾O' [you] Messengers! Eat of the *Ṭayyibaat* [all kinds of *Ḥalaal* (lawful) foods which Allah has made lawful (meat of slaughtered eatable animals, milk products, fats, vegetables, fruits)] and do righteous deeds...﴿
>
> *(Qur'an 23: 51)*

Many of the acts of worship that we do were known to the earlier Messengers and their followers:

﴿ ... وَأَوْحَيْنَآ إِلَيْهِمْ فِعْلَ ٱلْخَيْرَٰتِ وَإِقَامَ ٱلصَّلَوٰةِ وَإِيتَآءَ ٱلزَّكَوٰةِ ... ﴿٧٣﴾ ﴾

﴿...And We revealed to them the doing of good deeds, performing Ṣalaah [Iqaamat-aṣ-Ṣalaah], and the giving of Zakah...﴾   *(Qur'an 21: 73)*

Prophet Ismaa'eel (عَلَيْهِ السَّلَام),

﴿ وَكَانَ يَأْمُرُ أَهْلَهُ بِٱلصَّلَوٰةِ وَٱلزَّكَوٰةِ ... ﴿٥٥﴾ ﴾

﴿...Used to enjoin on his family and his people Aṣ-Ṣalaah [the prayers] and the Zakah...﴾*(Qur'an 19: 55)*

Allah (سبحانه وتعالى) said to Moosa (عَلَيْهِ السَّلَام):

﴿ ... فَٱعْبُدْنِي وَأَقِمِ ٱلصَّلَوٰةَ لِذِكْرِىٓ ﴿١٤﴾ ﴾

﴿...So worship Me, and perform Aṣ-Ṣalaah [Iqaamat-aṣ-Ṣalaah] for My remembrance.﴾   *(Qur'an 20: 14)*

Prophet 'Eesa (Jesus) (عَلَيْهِ السَّلَام) said:

﴿ ... وَأَوْصَٰنِي بِٱلصَّلَوٰةِ وَٱلزَّكَوٰةِ مَا دُمْتُ حَيًّا ﴿٣١﴾ ﴾

﴿...And has enjoined on me Ṣalaah [prayer], and Zakah, as long as I live.﴾   *(Qur'an 19: 31)*

Fasting was enjoined upon those who came before us as it is enjoined upon us:

﴿ يَٰٓأَيُّهَا ٱلَّذِينَ ءَامَنُوا۟ كُتِبَ عَلَيْكُمُ ٱلصِّيَامُ كَمَا كُتِبَ عَلَى ٱلَّذِينَ مِن قَبْلِكُمْ لَعَلَّكُمْ تَتَّقُونَ ﴿١٨٣﴾ ﴾

﴿O' you who believe! Observing Aṣ-Ṣawm [the fasting] is prescribed for you as it was prescribed for those before you, that you may become Al-Muttaqoon [the pious].﴾   *(Qur'an 2: 183)*

Ḥajj was enjoined by Prophet Ibraaheem (ﷺ). After he had built the Ka'bah, Allah (ﷻ) commanded him to call people to Ḥajj:

﴿ وَأَذِّن فِي ٱلنَّاسِ بِٱلۡحَجِّ يَأۡتُوكَ رِجَالٗا ... ﴿٢٧﴾ ﴾

﴾And proclaim to mankind the Ḥajj [pilgrimage]. They will come to you on foot...﴿[8] *(Qur'an 22: 27)*

Each nation had its rituals and acts of worship:

﴿ وَلِكُلِّ أُمَّةٖ جَعَلۡنَا مَنسَكٗا لِّيَذۡكُرُواْ ٱسۡمَ ٱللَّهِ عَلَىٰ مَا رَزَقَهُم مِّنۢ بَهِيمَةِ ٱلۡأَنۡعَٰمِۗ ... ﴿٣٤﴾ ﴾

﴾And for every nation We have appointed religious ceremonies, that they may mention the Name of Allah over the beast of cattle that He has given them for food...﴿ *(Qur'an 22: 34)*

﴿ لِّكُلِّ أُمَّةٖ جَعَلۡنَا مَنسَكًا هُمۡ نَاسِكُوهُۖ ... ﴿٦٧﴾ ﴾

﴾For every nation We have ordained religious ceremonies [e.g. slaughtering of the cattle during the three days of stay at Mina (Makkah) during the Ḥajj (pilgrimage)] which they must follow...﴿ *(Qur'an 22: 67)*

---

[8] After that, the Pilgrimage to the Ancient House was part of the guidance of the Prophets. Prophet Moosa and Yoonus performed the Pilgrimage to the House. In Muslim it is narrated that Ibn 'Abbaas said: "We went out on a campaign with the Messenger (ﷺ) between Makkah and Madeenah, and we passed by a wadi. He said, 'What wadi is this?' They said, 'Wadi al-Azraq.' He said, 'It is as if I am looking at Moosa,' and he said something about his colour and hair, '... putting his fingers in his ears, praying to Allah and reciting the *Talbiyah*, passing through this valley.' Then we travelled on until we came to a mountain pass, and he said, 'What mountain pass is this?' They said, 'Hirsh or Lift.' He said 'It is as if I am looking at Yoonus atop a red camel, wearing a woolen cloak, the reins of his camel woven of palm tree fibres, passing through this valley reciting the *Talbiyah*.'" (See *Mishkaat al-Maṣaabeeḥ*, 3/116)

Another of the matters which the messages had in common is that they explained what is evil and false and called upon people to fight it and eradicate it, whether that was the worship of idols, doing mischief on the earth, deviating from the natural state of man as the people of Prophet Looṭ (Lot) (ﷺ) did, or committing aggression against people by means of banditry or cheating in weights and measures.

Differences between the laws

Although the religion brought by the Messengers was one, namely Islam, the laws of the Prophets differed from one another. The law of Prophet 'Eesa (Jesus) differed from that of Prophet Moosa (Moses) in some respects, and the law of the last Prophet Muhammad (ﷺ) differed from the laws of Moosa and 'Eesa. Allah (ﷻ) says:

﴿ ... لِكُلٍّ جَعَلْنَا مِنكُمْ شِرْعَةً وَمِنْهَاجًا ... ﴾ (٤٨)

﴿...To each among you, We have prescribed a law and a clear way...﴾ *(Qur'an 5: 48)*

This does not mean that the laws were completely different from one another. The one who examines the laws will see that they are agreed on basic matters. We have mentioned above the texts which state that Allah prescribed prayer, zakah and Ḥajj to the previous nations, and taking food from *ḥalaal* sources, and so on. The differences between them had to do with the details of these rulings.

The number of prayers, their conditions and essential parts, the amount to be paid in zakah, the places where rituals were to be performed, etc., differed from one law to another. Allah may have permitted something in one law for a reason, then forbidden it in another law for a reason.

We will give three examples of that:

1) Fasting. The one who was fasting used to break his fast at sunset, then it was permitted for him to eat, drink and have intercourse until just before dawn so long as he did not sleep. If he slept before dawn, then all of that would be forbidden to him until the sun set on the second day. But Allah made it easier for this ummah and permitted those things to them from sunset until just before dawn, regardless of whether they slept or not.

Allah (ﷻ) says:

﴿ أُحِلَّ لَكُمْ لَيْلَةَ ٱلصِّيَامِ ٱلرَّفَثُ إِلَىٰ نِسَآئِكُمْ ۚ هُنَّ لِبَاسٌ لَّكُمْ وَأَنتُمْ لِبَاسٌ لَّهُنَّ ۗ عَلِمَ ٱللَّهُ أَنَّكُمْ كُنتُمْ تَخْتَانُونَ أَنفُسَكُمْ فَتَابَ عَلَيْكُمْ وَعَفَا عَنكُمْ ۖ فَٱلْـَٔـٰنَ بَـٰشِرُوهُنَّ وَٱبْتَغُوا۟ مَا كَتَبَ ٱللَّهُ لَكُمْ ۚ وَكُلُوا۟ وَٱشْرَبُوا۟ حَتَّىٰ يَتَبَيَّنَ لَكُمُ ٱلْخَيْطُ ٱلْأَبْيَضُ مِنَ ٱلْخَيْطِ ٱلْأَسْوَدِ مِنَ ٱلْفَجْرِ ۖ ثُمَّ أَتِمُّوا۟ ٱلصِّيَامَ إِلَى ٱلَّيْلِ ۚ ... ﴿١٨٧﴾ ﴾

﴿It is made lawful for you to have sexual relations with your wives on the night of *As-Ṣawm* [the fasts]. They are *Libaas* [i.e. body-cover, or screen, or *Sakan* (i.e. you enjoy the pleasure of living with them)] for you and you are the same for them. Allah knows that you used to deceive yourselves, so He turned to you [accepted your repentance] and forgave you. So now have sexual relations with them and seek that which Allah has ordained for you [offspring], and eat and drink until the white thread [light] of dawn appears to you distinct from the black thread [darkness of night], then complete your *Ṣawm* [fast] till the nightfall...﴾ *(Qur'an 2: 187)*

2) Covering the *'awrah* (private parts) when bathing was not obligatory for the Children of Israel. According to the hadith narrated by Bukhari and Muslim,

"The Children of Israel used to bathe naked, looking at one another, but Moosa used to bathe alone."[9]

3) Forbidden matters. One of the things that Allah permitted to Adam (ﷺ) was to marry his daughters to his sons, then Allah forbade that afterwards. Taking a woman as a concubine in addition to one's wife was permitted according to the law of the Prophet Ibraaheem (Abraham) (ﷺ), as Ibraaheem did that in the case of Ḥajar, whom he took as a concubine in addition to his wife Saarah, but Allah forbade that to the Children of Israel in the *Tawraat*. It was permitted to be married to two sisters at the same time, as was done by Prophet Ya'qoob (Jacob) (ﷺ), then it was forbidden to them in the *Tawraat*. And Ya'qoob forbade himself the meat and milk of camels.[10] The reason for that, as reported in the hadith, was that,

> "Israa'eel (Ya'qoob) became very sick and his illness lasted for a long time. He vowed to Allah that if Allah healed him from his sickness, he would give up the food and drink that he liked best. The food which he liked best was camel meat, and the drink that he liked best was camel's milk."[11]

What Israa'eel forbade himself, Allah also forbade to the Children of Israel, and it was forbidden in the *Tawraat*:

﴿ كُلُّ ٱلطَّعَامِ كَانَ حِلًّا لِّبَنِىٓ إِسْرَٰٓءِيلَ إِلَّا مَا حَرَّمَ إِسْرَٰٓءِيلُ عَلَىٰ نَفْسِهِۦ مِن قَبْلِ أَن تُنَزَّلَ ٱلتَّوْرَىٰةُ ... ﴿٩٣﴾ ﴾

﴿All food was lawful to the Children of Israel, except what Israel made unlawful for himself before the *Tawraat* [Torah] was revealed...﴾ *(Qur'an 3: 93)*

---

[9] *Ṣaḥeeḥ al-Jaami' aṣ-Ṣagheer*, 4/160.

[10] *Tafseer Ibn Katheer*, 2/73.

[11] Aḥmad: *Musnad*; *Tafseer Ibn Katheer*, 2/71.

Other things that Allah forbade to the Jews are mentioned in *Soorah al-An'aam* the 6th chapter of the Qur'an:

﴿ وَعَلَى ٱلَّذِينَ هَادُوا۟ حَرَّمْنَا كُلَّ ذِى ظُفُرٍ ۖ وَمِنَ ٱلْبَقَرِ
وَٱلْغَنَمِ حَرَّمْنَا عَلَيْهِمْ شُحُومَهُمَآ إِلَّا مَا حَمَلَتْ ظُهُورُهُمَآ أَوِ ٱلْحَوَايَآ
أَوْ مَا ٱخْتَلَطَ بِعَظْمٍ ۚ ذَٰلِكَ جَزَيْنَٰهُم بِبَغْيِهِمْ ۖ وَإِنَّا لَصَٰدِقُونَ ﴿١٤٦﴾ ﴾

﴾And unto those who are Jews, We forbade every [animal] with undivided hoof, and We forbade them the fat of the ox and the sheep except what adheres to their backs or their entrails, or is mixed up with a bone. Thus We recompensed them for their rebellion [committing crimes like murdering the Prophets and eating of Riba]. And verily, We are Truthful.﴿ *(Qur'an 6: 146)*

Allah forbade to them every animal which has claws, unless the foot is cloven, as in the case of camels, sheep; birds such as ostriches, geese and ducks were also permitted. He forbade them the fat of cattle and sheep, apart from the fat which adheres to their backs and entrails, or is mixed with the bones.

This prohibition was not because the things which were forbidden were dirty or bad, but because their father Ya'qoob had committed himself to observing some prohibitions and had committed his children to them also. And some of the prohibitions were because of the wrongdoing of the Children of Israel: ﴾...Thus We recompensed them for their rebellion...﴿ *(Qur'an 6: 146)* And Allah (ﷻ) said:

﴿ فَبِظُلْمٍ مِّنَ ٱلَّذِينَ هَادُوا۟ حَرَّمْنَا عَلَيْهِمْ طَيِّبَٰتٍ أُحِلَّتْ لَهُمْ وَبِصَدِّهِمْ عَن
سَبِيلِ ٱللَّهِ كَثِيرًا ﴿١٦٠﴾ ﴾

﴾For the wrongdoing of the Jews, We made unlawful for them certain good foods which had been lawful for them - and for their hindering many from Allah's Way.﴿ *(Qur'an 4: 160)*

Then came Prophet 'Eesa (Jesus) (ﷺ) and permitted to the Children of Israel some of that which had been forbidden to them:

﴿... وَلِأُحِلَّ لَكُم بَعْضَ ٱلَّذِى حُرِّمَ عَلَيْكُمْ ... ﴿٥٠﴾﴾

﴿...And to make lawful to you part of what was forbidden to you...﴾ *(Qur'an 3: 50)*

And the final Law came to establish the principle of permitting that which is good and forbidding that which is bad or evil.

The Prophets are half-brothers

The Messenger (ﷺ) coined a likeness to describe the fact that all the Messengers followed one religion whilst their laws differed. He said:

"The Prophets are half-brothers born from different mothers; their mothers are different, but their religion is one."[12]

Ibn Ḥajar said: "The Prophets are brothers from different mothers. 'Different mothers (*al-'allaat*)' means co-wives, and the children of co-wives are brothers through their father, but their mothers are different. What the hadith means is that the basis of their religion is one and the same, namely *Tawḥeed*, even though the lesser details of their laws differed."[13]

5 - HOW LONG OR SHORT THEIR BOOKS WERE, AND WHEN THEY WERE REVEALED

The Noble Qur'an is the longest and most comprehensive of the Divinely-revealed books. According to a hadith:

---

[12] Bukhari, Muslim, Aḥmad and Abu Dawood. *Ṣaḥeeḥ al-Jaami'*, 2/14.

[13] *Fatḥ al-Baari*, 6/489.

> "In place of the *Tawraat* (Torah) I have been given the seven long *soorahs* (chapters); in place of the *Zaboor* (Psalm) I have been given the *soorahs* of one hundred *aayahs* (verses); in place of the *Injeel* (Gospel) I have been given the seven repeatedly-recited verses (*Al-Faatiḥah*), and in addition I have been given the *mufaṣṣal soorahs* (from *Soorah Qaf* until the end of the Qur'an)."

This is narrated by Ṭabaraani in *Al-Kabeer.*[14]

The Divinely-revealed Books which are known to us were all revealed in the month of Ramaḍaan. It says in the hadith:

> "The *Ṣuḥuf* of Ibraaheem were revealed on the first night of Ramaḍaan. The *Tawraat* was revealed on the sixth of Ramaḍaan. The *Injeel* was revealed on the thirteenth of Ramaḍaan. The *Zaboor* was revealed on the eighteenth of Ramaḍaan. And the Qur'an was revealed on the twenty-fourth of Ramaḍaan."

- This is narrated by Ṭabaraani.[15]

The attitude of the final Message towards the previous Messages

Allah (ﷻ) explains this in His Book, where He says:

﴿ وَأَنزَلْنَآ إِلَيْكَ ٱلْكِتَٰبَ بِٱلْحَقِّ مُصَدِّقًا لِّمَا بَيْنَ يَدَيْهِ مِنَ ٱلْكِتَٰبِ وَمُهَيْمِنًا عَلَيْهِ ... ﴿٤٨﴾ ﴾

> ﴾And We have sent down to you [O' Muhammad] the Book [this Qur'an] in truth, confirming the Scripture

---

[14] *Ṣaḥeeḥ al-Jaami' aṣ-Ṣagheer*, 1/350. The editor said, its isnad is *ṣaḥeeḥ*.

[15] *Ṣaḥeeḥ al-Jaami' aṣ-Ṣagheer*, 2/28. *Shaykh* Naaṣiruddeen al-Albaani said, its isnad is *ḥasan*.

that came before it and *Muhaymin* [trustworthy in highness and a witness] over it [old Scriptures]...》 *(Qur'an 5: 48)*

The Qur'an confirms the Scripture that came before it in several ways:

1) The previous divinely-revealed Books mentioned and praised this Qur'an, and said that Allah would reveal it to His slave and Messenger Muhammad (ﷺ). It was revealed in the manner described in this previous Books as a confirmation of those Books, and this increased the faith of those among the bearers of the previous Books who had insight, who submitted to the command of Allah and followed the laws of Allah, and believed in the Messengers of Allah, as Allah (ﷻ) said:

﴿... إِنَّ ٱلَّذِينَ أُوتُوا۟ ٱلْعِلْمَ مِن قَبْلِهِۦٓ إِذَا يُتْلَىٰ عَلَيْهِمْ يَخِرُّونَ لِلْأَذْقَانِ سُجَّدًا
(١٠٧) وَيَقُولُونَ سُبْحَٰنَ رَبِّنَآ إِن كَانَ وَعْدُ رَبِّنَا لَمَفْعُولًا (١٠٨)﴾

《...Verily, those who were given knowledge before it [the Jews and the Christians like 'Abdullah ibn Salaam and Salmaan al-Farisi], when it is recited to them, fall down on their faces in humble prostration. And they say: 'Glory be to our Lord! Truly, the Promise of our Lord must be fulfilled.'》 *(Qur'an 17: 107-108)*

- meaning that whatever Allah promised in His previous Books and on the lips of His Messengers, saying that He would reveal the Qur'an and send Muhammad, must be fulfilled, i.e., it would inevitably come to pass.[16]

2) The Qur'an brought things which confirmed the previous divinely-revealed Books by mentioning some things which were similar.

---

[16] *Tafseer Ibn Katheer*, 2/586.

﴿ وَمَا جَعَلْنَآ أَصْحَٰبَ ٱلنَّارِ إِلَّا مَلَٰٓئِكَةً ۙ وَمَا جَعَلْنَا عِدَّتَهُمْ إِلَّا فِتْنَةً لِّلَّذِينَ كَفَرُوا۟
لِيَسْتَيْقِنَ ٱلَّذِينَ أُوتُوا۟ ٱلْكِتَٰبَ وَيَزْدَادَ ٱلَّذِينَ ءَامَنُوٓا۟ إِيمَٰنًا ۙ ... ﴿٣١﴾ ﴾

﴿And We have set none but angels as guardians of the Fire. And We have fixed their number [19] only as a trial for the disbelievers, in order that the people of the Scripture [Jews and Christians] may arrive at a certainty [that this Qur'an is the truth as it agrees with their Books regarding the number (19) which is written in the *Tawraat* (Torah) and the *Injeel* (Gospel)] and that the believers may increase in Faith...﴾ *(Qur'an 74: 31)*

The certainty referred to is because those who were given the Scripture knew that from their Books.

3) The Qur'an speaks of the revelation of the previous Books and says that they came from Allah; it enjoins us to believe in them as stated above.

In Arabic, the word *Muhaymin* means one who is in charge of something.[17] It is one of the names of Allah, meaning that Allah is in-charge of the affairs of His creation, disposing of their affairs, managing them and taking care of them.

The Qur'an takes care of the previous divinely-revealed Books by commanding us to believe in them, explaining the truth contained in them and denying the distortions and alterations that have been perpetrated on them. It is the controller or regulator of those Books because it is the final divine Message which must be followed, consulted and referred to for judgement. Everything in the previous Books that goes against it is either a distortion and alteration, or has been abrogated.

---

17 *Lisaan al-'Arab*, 3/833, under the heading *Hamana.*

Ibn Katheer (may Allah have mercy on him) said, after quoting the view of the salaf on the meanings of the word *muhaymin*: “These views are all close in meaning, for the name *Muhaymin* includes all of that. *Muhaymin* means guardian, witness, judge of the Books that came before it. Allah has made this great Book which He has revealed the last of His Books and the greatest and most perfect. He compiled in it the best features of those which came before, and added many aspects of perfection that were not present in any other Book. So He made it a witness, a guardian and the judge of them all.”[18]

This implies that this Book should be the first and last reference point for learning about the religion which Allah wants, and that it is not permissible for us to judge the Qur’an by the previous divinely-revealed Books, as the misguided Christians and Jews do.

﴿ ... وَإِنَّهُۥ لَكِتَٰبٌ عَزِيزٌ ﴿٤١﴾ لَّا يَأْتِيهِ ٱلْبَٰطِلُ مِنۢ بَيْنِ يَدَيْهِ وَلَا مِنْ خَلْفِهِۦ ۖ تَنزِيلٌ مِّنْ حَكِيمٍ حَمِيدٍ ﴿٤٢﴾ ﴾

﴾...And verily, it is an honourable well-fortified respected Book [because it is Allah’s Speech, and He has protected it from corruption]. Falsehood cannot come to it from before it or behind it, [it is] sent down by the All-Wise, Worthy of all praise [Allah].﴿ *(Qur’an 41: 41-42)*

The final law is in no need of any other law

The final Divine Law has no need to refer to the laws which came before, or to the laws which came after it, unlike the law of the Messiah, who referred his followers to the *Tawraat* in most cases. The Messiah came to complete the *Tawraat*, hence the Christians needed the messages of the Prophets who came before the Messiah, such as the *Tawraat* and *Zaboor* (Psalm). The nations before us

[18] *Tafseer Ibn Katheer*, 2/587.

needed the *muḥaddathoon* (those who were inspired), unlike the ummah of Muhammad (ﷺ), for Allah has made them independent of any such need, so they are in no need of any other Prophet or *muḥaddath*.[19]

THE GENEOLOGICAL CHART OF THE PROPHETS is on page no. 359. The names of the Messengers and Prophets are given below in both Arabic transliteration and English.

Aadam — Adam
Idrees — Enoch
Nooḥ — Noah
Hood — Hud
Ṣaaliḥ — Saleh
Ibraheem — Abraham
Looṭ — Lot
Ismaa'eel — Ishmael
Isḥaaq — Isaac
Shu'ayb — Shuayb (Some identify him with Jethro)
Ya'qoob — Jacob
Ayyoob — Job
Yusuf — Joseph
Yunus — Jonah
Dawood — David
Sulaymaan — Solomon
Moosa — Moses
Haroon — Aaron
Zakariyah — Zachariya
Yaḥyaa — John
Ilyaas — Elias
Yasaa' — Elisha
'Eesa ibn Maryam — Jesus, son of Mary
Muḥammad — Muhammad (may Allah's peace be upon them all)

---

[19] *Majmoo' al-Fataawa Shaykh al-Islam*, 11/224.

SYMBOLS' DIRECTORY

(سبحانه وتعالى) : *Subḥaanahu wa Ta'aala* - "The Exalted."

(صلى الله عليه وسلم) : *Ṣalla-Allahu 'Alayhi wa Sallam* -
"Blessings and Peace be upon him."

(عليه السلام) : *'Alayhis-Salaam* - "May Peace be upon him."

(رضي الله عنه) : *Raḍi-Allahu 'Anhu* - "May Allah be pleased with him."

GLOSSARY

Aa'immah	آئمة	: Sing. Imam; Leaders, Most reputed scholars of Islam
Al-'Aalameen	العالمين	: Sing. *'Aalam*; Worlds, Mankind, Jinn and all that exists
Aayah	آية	: Pl. *Aayaat*; Verse, Sign, Proof
Adhaan	اذان	: Call for the prayer
Aḥaadeeth	احاديث	: Sing. hadith; Prophet's sayings.
Ahl al-Kalaam	اهل الكلام	: Islamic philosophers, the Scholastics, scholars of Divinity
Al-'Aaqib	العاقب	: A name of the Prophet, i.e. the successor
Al-Amaanah	الأمانة	: The trust or moral responsibility or honesty and all the duties which Allah has ordained
Al-Ameen	الأمين	: Lit. Trustworthy; A name and the title of the last Prophet
Al-'Arab al-'Aaribah	العرب العاربة	: The original Arabs
Al-Asbaaṭ	الأسباط	: Sing. *sabṭ*; The twelve sons of Prophet Ya'qoob (Jacob)
Al-Ḥaashir	الحاشر	: Lit. the gatherer; A name of the last Prophet
Al-Ḥikmah	الحكمة	: Lit. Wisdom; Legal ways, orders, acts of worship, understanding of

			the law of Allah. It also means the Sunnah
Al-Khabaa'ith	الخبائث	:	All evil and unlawful as regard to things, deeds, beliefs, persons and foods, also female jinn
Al-Lawḥ al-Maḥfooẓ	اللوح المحفوظ	:	The Preserved Tablet, the book that is in the Heaven with Allah where everything is written
Al-Ma'roof	المعروف	:	Lit. well-known; Every good deed, Islamic monotheism and all that Islam has ordained, reasonable, commonly acceptable
Al-Mathaani	المثاني	:	Lit. Repeatedly; *Saba' al-Mathaani*: the seven repeated verses i.e. *Soorat al-Faatiḥah*, the first chapter of the Qur'an
Al-Miḥraab	المحراب	:	A nitche, a praying place or a private room for seclusion.
Al-Munkar	المنكر	:	Lit. Denounced; Unacceptable, disapproved, foul, immoral evil deeds; disbelief, polytheism, every deed that is bad, abominable, objectionable
Al-Mutawakkil	المتوكل	:	He who puts his trust in Allah
Ameer al-Mu'mineen	امير المؤمنين	:	A Caliph. The Commander of the believers, the title of a Caliph
'Aqeedah	عقيدة	:	Creed, Basic tenets of faith, Dogma
Al-Arab al-Musta'ribah	العرب المستعربة	:	Arabized Arabs

'Arafah	عرفة	:	The ninth day of the month of *Dhul-Ḥijjah*, a place near Makkah where the pilgrims stay as the basic part of the Ḥajj rituals
Arwaaḥ	أرواح	:	Sing. *Rooḥ*; Spirits, souls
'Aṣr	عصر	:	Afternoon, Afternoon prayer, Time
Awliyaa'	أولياء	:	Sing. *Wali*; Close friends of Allah, Saints, Supporters, Guardians
Aayat al-Kursi	آية الكرسي	:	The verse of the Throne. Qur'anic verse no. 255 of *Soorat al-Baqarah.* (the second chapter)
Bayt al-Maqdis	بيت المقدس	:	The famous mosque in Jerusalem regarded as the third sacred mosque in the Islamic world; the first and second being *Al-Masjid al-Ḥaraam* at Makkah and the mosque of the Prophet at Madeenah, respectively
Dajjaal	دجال	:	Pseudo - Christ; the false claimants of prophethood, a Pseudo-Messiah
Fitnah	فتنة	:	Trials, afflictions, persecution, confusion in the religion, conflicts and strives among the Muslims
Fuqahaa'	فقهاء	:	Sing. *Faqeeh*; Scholars of Islamic jurisprudence (*Fiqh*)
Ḥajj	حج	:	Fifth pillar of Islam, Pilgrimage to Makkah in the month of *Dhul-Ḥijja*. It is obligatory once in lifetime for every Muslim who can afford it
Ḥalaal	حلال	:	Permitted by Allah, legal in Islamic shari'ah

Ḥaraam	حرام	:	Forbidden by Allah, Illegal in Islamic shari'ah
Ḥawaariyoon	حواريون	:	Sing. *Ḥawaari*; The disciples of Prophet 'Eesa (Jesus), who belie in him and his Message
Hijrah	هجرة	:	Lit. Migration; migration for the sake of Islam, primarily the migration of the last Prophet and Companions from Makkah to Madeenah
Ḥoor	حور	:	Houris, Fair females in the Heav
Iblees	ابليس	:	A name for Satan in the Qur'an
Ilah	اله	:	Deity, god
Israa'	اسراء	:	Night journey, referring to the miraculous Night Journey of the la Prophet
Jamaa'ah	جماعه	:	Community
Khaleefah	خليفة	:	Vicegerent, Deputy, also Tempor Head of the Muslim community
Khimaar	خمار	:	Head covering
Khuṭbah	خطبة	:	Speech, Sermon
Khawaarij	خوارج	:	Lit. Secessionists; A group who fought with 'Ali against Mu'aawiyah, then rebelled agains 'Ali. Known as Khawaarij/ Kharijites (secessionists) because they seceded from the main strear of the Muslims. They consider th sinners as disbelievers

Kufr	كفر	:	Disbelieving
Laghw	لغو	:	Dirty, false, evil, vain talk
Laḥd	لحد	:	An oblong excavation in the side of the grave to place the body in it
Laylat al-Qadr	ليلة القدر	:	The Night of Decree. The Night of Power, one of the odd-numbered nights of the last ten days of Ramaḍaan. The Qur'an describes it as "Better than a thousand months" *(Qur'an 97: 3)*
Manaasik	مناسك	:	The rituals of Ḥajj and 'Umrah, i.e. *Iḥraam, Ṭawaaf, Sa'i,* staying at *'Arafaat* and others.
Marfoo'	مرفوع	:	A hadith with a *sanad* reaching to the Prophet
Mawdoo'	موضوع	:	A term in the hadith discipline; Concocted, Fabricated
Minbar	منبر	:	Pulpit, the steps on which the Imam stands to deliver the *Khuṭbah* at Friday prayer
Mufassireen	مفسرين	:	Sing. *Mufassir*; Qur'anic exegete, a scholar who comments and/or explains the meanings of the Qur'an
Muḥsinoon	محسنون	:	Sing. *Muḥsin*; The good doers, persons reaching the stage of *Iḥsaan* (excellence)
Mu'jizaat	معجزات	:	Sing. *Mu'jizah*; Miracles
Mujrimoon	مجرمون	:	Sing. *Mujrim* - a culprit;

			Disbelievers, Polytheists, Sinners
Munḥamannaa	منحمنّا	:	Prophet Muhammad's name in the original *Injeel* (Gospel)
Mushrikeen	مشركين	:	Sing. *Mushrik*; The Polytheists
Mutawaatir	متواتر	:	Lit. Continuous; A term in hadith discipline meaning a hadith reported by various chains of narrators
Mu'tazilah	معتزلة	:	Lit. Withdrawers; Waaṣil ibn 'Aṭaa is regarded as the founder of the heretical group heavily influenced by Greek philosophy. They negate Attributes of Allah. They think a *Faasiq* is neither a believer nor a disbeliever but would be in the Hell-fire forever, they call themselves *Ahl al-'Adl wa at-Tawḥeed*
Muttaqoon	متقون	:	Sing. *Muttaqi*; The Pious
Nabi	نبي	:	Prophet
Nifaas	نفاس	:	Bleeding following child birth, impurity.
Qiblah	قبله	:	Direction of Ka'bah in Makkah to which all Muslims turn their faces in prayer
Hadith Qudsi	حديث قدسي	:	A hadith in which the last Prophet transmits Allah's own words, other than the Qur'an
Rasool	رسول	:	Messenger

Rooḥ al-Qudus	روح القدس	:	Holy Spirit, a title of the archangel Gabriel
Ṣaḥaabah	صحابه	:	Sing. *Ṣaḥaabi*; The Companions of the last Prophet
Salaam	سلام	:	Greeting with peace
S̃hari'ah	شريعة	:	Islamic law
Shayṭaan	شيطان	:	Devil (Satan)
Shirk	شرك	:	Polytheism
Ṣiddeeqah	صدِّيقة	:	The truthful lady, the title of the mother of the believer's 'Aa'isha
Ṣiddeeqeen	صدِّيقين	:	Sing. *Ṣiddeeq*; Those followers of the Prophets who were first and foremost to believe in them (like Abu Bakr, Khadeejah, etc.)
Sidrat al-Muntaha	سدرة المنتهى	:	A lotus-tree of the utmost boundary over the seven heavens beyond which none can pass. A *Nabk* tree over the seventh heaven near the Paradise (the lotus tree of the utmost boundary)
Soorah	سورة	:	Chapter of the Qur'an
Taabi'een	تابعين	:	Sing. *Taabi'ee*. Lit. Follower; A member of the generation of Muslims after the *Ṣaḥaabah*. A Muslim who met or saw a *Ṣaḥaabi* is described as *At-Taabi'ee*, the Successors
Taaghoot	طاغوت	:	All false deities, all non-Islamic laws/customs etc.

Ṭalḥa	طلحة	:	Banana trees, name of a great Companion of the Prophet
Tasbeeḥ	تسبيح	:	Saying - *Subḥaan Allah*
Tawḥeed	توحيد	:	Islamic Monotheism
Tayammum	تيمم	:	Performing dry *Ṭahaara* using sa or stone or earth when water is n available or when it is harmful. This is performed instead of ablution (*wuḍoo'*) and *Ghusl* (in case of *Janaba* ie., ritual impurit
Ṭaiyibaat	طيبات	:	All kinds of lawful things, good things
'Uboodiyah	عبودية	:	Servant-hood, service, obedience with humility and love
Ummah	امة	:	Nation, Community
Waḥy	وحي	:	Revelation
Wuḍoo'	وضوء	:	Ritual ablution before prayer
Ẓaalimoon	ظالمون	:	Sing. *Ẓaalim*; The oppresser, the tyrant; Polytheists, wrongders an disbelievers in the oneness of All
Zaqqoom	زقوم	:	A plant growing in Hell whose bitterness and offensive face is matchless
Ẓulm	ظلم	:	Oppression, Wrongdoing, worshipping others besides Allal

REFERENCES

Al-Islam fi 'Aṣr al-'Ilm: Muhammad Aḥmad al-Ghamravi, *Daar al-Kutub al-Ḥadeethah*, Cairo.

Aḍwaa' al-Bayaan: Muhammad al-Ameen ash-Shinqiṭi, Al-Madani Est., Cairo, 1st printing.

A'alaam an-Nubuwwah: Al-Mawardi, *Maktabah al-Kulliyaat al-Azhariyah*, Cairo.

Al-Imaamah 'ind al-Jamhoor: Dr. 'Ali Aḥmad as-Saaloos, *Maktabah Ibn Taymiyah*, Kuwait.

Injeel Barnabas, *Daar al-Qalam*, Kuwait.

Al-Bidaayah wan-Nihaayah: Ibn Katheer, *Maktabah al-M'aarif*, Beirut, 2nd printing.

Baṣaa'er Dhawit-Tamiyeez: Fayruzabaadi, *Lajnat Iḥiya' at-Turaath al-Islami*, Cairo.

Tafseer Ibn Katheer, *Daar al-Andalus*, Beirut.

Tafseer Aaloosi, *Al-Matba'ah al-Muneeriyah*.

Tafseer al-Qurṭubi, *Daar al-Kutub al-'Arabiyah,* Beirut.

At-Tawraat as-Saamriyah, *Daar al-Anṣaar*, Cairo.

Jaami' al-Uṣool, Ibn al-Atheer, *As-Sunnat al-Muḥammadiyah*, Cairo, 1st printing.

Al-Jawaab aṣ-Ṣaḥeeḥ liman Badala Deen al-Maseeḥ: Ibn Taymiyah, Al-Madani Est., Cairo.

Al-Ḥukoomah al-Islamiyah: Al-Khumayni, *Al-Ḥarakah al-Islamiyah fi Iran*, *Maṭb'aat al-Khaleej*, Kuwait.

Ḥayaat Muḥammad: Muhammad Ḥusayn Haykal, *Daar al-M'aarif*, Cairo.

Zaad al-Maseer: Ibn al-Jawzi, *Al-Maktab al-Islami*, Beirut.

Zaad al-M'aad: Ibn al-Qayyim, *Al-Matb'ah al-Miṣriyah wa Maktabaha*, Cairo.

Az-Zahr an-Naḍar fi Naba' al-Khaḍar: Ibn Ḥajar, *Al-Maṭba'ah al-Muneeriyah*.

Silsilat al-Aḥaadeeth aṣ-Ṣaḥeeḥah: *Shaykh* Muhammad Naṣiruddeen al-Albani, *Al-Maktab al-Islami*, 1st edition.

Sharḥ al-'Aqeedah aṭ-Ṭaḥaawiyah: Muhammad ibn Abi al 'Izz al-Ḥanafi, *Al-Maktab al-Islami*, Beirut, 4th printing.

Ṣaḥeeḥ al-Bukhari, text from *Fatḥ al-Baari*, *As-Salafiyah*, Cairo.

Ṣaḥeeḥ al-Jaami' aṣ-Ṣagheer, *Shaykh* Naṣiruddeen al-Albani, *Al-Maktab al-Islami*, Beirut, Ist edition.

Ṣaḥeeḥ Muslim bi Sharḥ an-Nawami, *Al-Maṭba'ah al-Miṣriyah*, Cairo.

Ṣaḥeeḥ Muslim: Matn an-Nawawi 'Ala Muslim.

'Aalam al-Jinn wash-Shayaaṭeen: 'Umar Sulaymaan al-Ashqar, *Maktabat al-Falaḥ*, Kuwait.

'Aalam al-Mala'aikah al- Abraar: 'Umar Sulaymaan al-Ashqar, *Maktaba al-Falaḥ*, Kuwait.

'Aqaa'id al-Imaamiyah: Muhammad Raẓa, *Daar al-Ghadeer*, Beirut.

'Aqaa'id al-Imaamiyah al-Ithna 'Asha'riyah: Ibrahim al-Moosavi az-Zinjani, *Al-'Aalami lil Maṭboo'aat*, Beirut.

Al-'Aqeedah al-Islamiyah: 'Abdur-Raḥmaan Ḥabankah, Damascus, 1st edition.

Al-'Aqeedah fillaah: 'Umar Salaymaan al-Ashqar, *Maktabat al-Falaḥ*, Kuwait.

Fatḥ al-Baari, Sharḥ Ṣaḥeeḥ al-Bukhari: Ibn Ḥajar al-'Asqallani, *As-Salafiyah*.

Fi Ẓilaal al-Qur'an: Sayyid Quṭb, *Daar ash-Shurooq*.

Lisaan al-'Arab: Ibn Manẓoor Ed. by Yusuf Khayyaṭ and Nadeem Mar'ashli, *Daar Lisan al'Arab*, Beirut, 1st edition.

Lawami' al-Anwaar al-Bahiyah: Safaarini, Qaṭar.

Majmoo' al-Fataawa Shaykh al-Islam: Compiled by Ibn Qaasim, Riyadh, 1st publication.

Majmoo'at ar-Rasaa'il al-Muneeriyah, *Ṭab'ah Muṣawwarah*, Beirut.

Muhammad Nabi al-Islam.

Mukhtaṣar at-Tuḥfah al-Ithna 'Ashariyah: Maḥmood Shukri al-Aaloosi, *Al-Maṭba'ah as-Salafiyah*, Cairo, 1378 H.

Mukhtasar Ṣaḥeeḥ Muslim: *Al-Maktab al-Islami*, Beirut.

Musnad Imam Aḥmad: *Taṣweer al-Maktab al-Islami*, Beirut.

Mishkaat al-Maṣaabeeḥ: Tabreezi, *Al-Maktab al-Islami*, Damascus, 1st edition.

Al-Misbaah al-Muneer: Fuyoomi, *Daar al-Ma'arif*, Cairo.

Mu'jizaat al-Muṣṭafa: Khayruddeen Waa'ily, *Al-Khafiqeen Library and Est.*, Damascus.

Miftaah Daar as-S'aadah: Ibn al-Qayyim, *Ṣubayaḥ*, Cairo.

Al-Milal wan-Niḥal: Shahrastaani, *Daar al M'aarif*, Beirut.

Nubuwwat Muhammad Min ash-Shakk ila al-Yaqeen; Dr. Faaḍil as-Saamraee, *Maṭba'at al-Quds*, Baghdad.

Naẓaraat fin Nubuwwah: Ṣalaḥuddeen Majeed, *Maktabat al-Qu*

Nayl al-Awṭaar: Shawkani, *Ḥalabi*, Cairo, 2nd printing.

Hidaayat al-Ḥayari: Ibn al-Qayyim (part of the collection) *Al-Jaam* *al-Fareed*, *Daar al-Iftaa'*, Riyadh.

INDEX OF THE QUR'AN

23 - *Al-Mu'minoon*	**44**/30; **34**/102; **71**/303; **24-25**/318; **51**/323.
24 - *An-Noor*	**55**/75, 238; **51**/87; **39**/165; **35**/257.
25 - *Al-Furqaan*	**55**/80; **7**/100, 103; **21**/103; **22**/105; **1**/126; **70**/161; **57**/261.
26 - *Ash-Shu'ara*	**105**/47; **123**/47; **141**/47; **160**/48; **108**/72; **79-81**/108; **23-29**/124; **106-108**/171; **153-154**/175; **155**/176; **4**/185; **197**/216; **196**/216; **109**/261.
27 - *An-Naml*	**35**/30; **45**/175.
28 - *Al-Qaṣaṣ*	**7**/92, 130; **27-28**/113; **26**/120; **15-16**/156; **16**/162; **46**/202; **68**/267; **78**/269; **75**/286; **62**/290; **65-66**/291; **53**/312.
29 - *Al-'Ankaboot*	**45**/70; **48**/263; **16**/313.
30 - *Ar-Room*	**30**/307.
33 - *Al-Aḥzaab*	**39**/69, 291; **72**/99; **69**/117; **21**/159; **7**/278; **40**/285.
35 - *Faaṭir*	**24**/18,36; **32**/132.
37 - *Aṣ-Ṣaaffaat*	**102-105**/93; **6**/223.
38 - *Ṣaad*	**26**/86; **24-25**/156; **24**/162; **39**/281.
39 - *Az-Zumar*	**30**/108.
40 - *Ghaafir/Al-Mu'min*	**78**/37; **50**/85.
41 - *Fuṣṣilat*	**13**/76; **41-42**/184, 334.
42 - *Ash-Shoora*	**52**/57, 79, 166; **51**/92, 95; **13**/276, 316; **15**/293.
43 - *Az-Zukhruf*	**31-32**/90; **75**/244.
44 - *Ad-Dukhaan*	**37**/43.
45 - *Al-Jaathiyah*	**18**/304.

INDEX OF HADITH

Muslim	*Kitaab al-Faḍaa'il*	4275	121
		4221	123
		4379	140
		4222	207
		4362	430
	Kitaab Faḍaa'il aṣ-Ṣaḥaaba	4546	196
	Kitaab al-Jannah waṣ-Ṣifaat...	5113	103
	Kitaab al-Birr waṣ-Ṣilah...	4712	109
	Kitaab Ṣifat al-Qiyamah...	5005	195
	Kitaab al-Ashribah	3766	198
	Kitaab al-Fitan wa....	5147	204
	Kitaab az-Zuhd wa ar-Raqaai'q	5328	205
	Kitaab Masajid wa....	812	283
Tirmidhi	*Kitaab al-Amthaal*	2787	73
	Kitab az-Zuhd	2322	111
	Kitaab Tafseer al-Qur'an	3002	145
		3073	282
	Kitaab al-Fitan	2142	203
	Kitaab al-Manaaqib	3561	205
		3597	269
Aḥmad	*Musnad al-Anṣaar*	20566	37
		24998	109
	Musnad al-Mukaththareen	7964	42
		13555	101
		9099	148
		11955	211
	Musnad al-'Ashrah wa....	27	136

Note: The above given reference nos. of hadith are from the CD programme "Hadith Encyclopedia" by Harf Information Technology.

TRANSLITERATION CHART

أ	a
آ . ى	aa
ب	b
ت	t
ة	h or t (when followed by another Arabic word)
ث	th
ج	j
ح	ḥ
خ	kh
د	d
ذ	dh
ر	r
ز	z
س	s
ش	sh
ص	ṣ
ض	ḍ
ط	ṭ

ظ	ẓ
ع	‘
غ	gh
ف	f
ق	q
ك	k
ل	l
م	m
ن	n
هـ - ه - ـه	h
و	w
و (as vowel)	oo
ي	y
ي (as vowel)	ee
ء	’ (Omitted in initial position)

َ	Fatḥah	a
ِ	Kasra	i
ُ	Ḍammah	u
ّ	Shaddah	Double letter
ْ	Sukoon	Absence of vowel